HOMELAND SECURITY
OPERATIONAL ANALYSIS CENTER

Practical Terrorism Prevention

Reexamining U.S. National Approaches
to Addressing the Threat of Ideologically
Motivated Violence

BRIAN A. JACKSON, ASHLEY L. RHOADES, JORDAN R. REIMER, NATASHA LANDER,
KATHERINE COSTELLO, SINA BEAGHLEY

Published in 2019

Preface

As part of an overall reexamination of terrorism prevention (superseding the programs and activities previously known as countering violent extremism [CVE]) policy, the U.S. Department of Homeland Security (DHS) asked the Homeland Security Operational Analysis Center (HSOAC) to examine the state of knowledge regarding terrorism prevention organization, coordination, programming, and policy. HSOAC was tasked to examine past CVE and current terrorism prevention efforts by DHS and its interagency partners, and explore options for this policy area going forward.

The purpose of this report is to present the results of the study, synthesizing information from the published literature, international case studies, and material provided by DHS and other partners. We also include insights from interviews with researchers; current and former federal personnel; members of technology firms and nongovernmental organizations (NGOs); and practitioners at the state and local levels in government, academia, the private sector, and nongovernmental sectors supporting case studies of metropolitan areas in different parts of the country. The report presents a framework to consider different facets of terrorism prevention policy, issues with measurement and assessment, analysis of past CVE and current terrorism prevention funding in the United States and internationally, and assessments of current efforts and future options for each component of terrorism prevention. These findings should be of interest to policymakers at the federal, state, and local levels; members of organizations with interests in terrorism prevention activities; civil rights and civil liberties organizations; and the broader public.

This research was sponsored by the Office of Policy, DHS, and conducted within the Strategy, Policy, and Operations Program of the HSOAC federally funded research and development center (FFRDC).

Comments or questions about this report should be addressed to the project leaders, Brian A. Jackson and Sina Beaghley, at bjackson@rand.org and beaghley@rand.org, respectively.

About the Homeland Security Operational Analysis Center

The Homeland Security Act of 2002 (Section 305 of Public Law 107-296, as codified at 6 U.S.C. § 185), authorizes the Secretary of Homeland Security, acting through the Under Secretary for Science and Technology, to establish one or more FFRDCs to provide independent analysis of homeland security issues. The RAND Corporation operates HSOAC as an FFRDC for DHS under contract HSHQDC-16-D-00007.

The HSOAC FFRDC provides the government with independent and objective analyses and advice in core areas important to the Department in support of policy development, decisionmaking, alternative approaches, and new ideas on issues of significance. The HSOAC FFRDC also works with and supports other federal, state, local, tribal, and public- and private-sector organizations that make up the homeland security enterprise. The HSOAC FFRDC's research is undertaken by mutual consent with DHS and is organized as a set of discrete tasks. This report presents the results of research and analysis conducted under Task Order HSHQDC-17-J-00532, titled "Terrorism Prevention Study and Threat Prevention and Security Policy Support."

The results presented in this report do not necessarily reflect official DHS opinion or policy.

For more information on HSOAC, see www.rand.org/hsoac.

For more information on this publication, visit www.rand.org/t/RR2647.

Contents

Figures

Tables

Study Highlights

The U.S. Department of Homeland Security (DHS) Office of Policy asked the Homeland Security Operational Analysis Center (HSOAC) to examine the current state of terrorism prevention (superseding the programs and activities previously known as countering violent extremism, or CVE) in the United States and to develop policy options for this area.

What the HSOAC Study Found

The study found major gaps in national terrorism prevention efforts. Shortfalls came not only from limited programmatic focus and resource investment, but also as a result of sustained opposition that tried to constrain or halt such efforts. There have been some successes, including in community education, public-private partnerships, and development of local capacity to intervene with individuals at risk of radicalizing to violence. However, interviewees had concerns about whether these efforts could be sustained. The study found that the most effective path for the federal government is to enable state, local, nongovernmental, and private organizations' terrorism prevention efforts through funding and other support. There was strong consensus across all interviews that such efforts have to be locally designed, managed, driven, and implemented in a way that is acceptable to the communities they are intended to protect. Most interviewees also emphasized that terrorism prevention must include the threat of ideological violence from all sources and must do so not just in words but also in programming and investments.

What the Study Recommends

The study identified a robust menu of actions to support effective and practical federal policies and intervention options. A key role is to provide credible information, including sharing of best practices and tools, to organizations seeking to implement terrorism prevention efforts. Another priority is federal support of local initiatives via such options as grant funding, public-private partnerships, or helping communities identify programs to adopt. Programmatic support could allow putting federal field staff in place nationally to facilitate local efforts, as well as to support the development of human capital with terrorism prevention knowledge and skills, both inside and outside government. Increasing capabilities in the federal corrections system are needed to support recidivism reduction. The federal government also could play a key role in data gathering and analysis by providing situational awareness into public views and concerns and national intervention capacity, as well as by supporting research to improve measurement and evaluation capabilities, program sustainability, and risk assessment.

Summary

Terrorism prevention (superseding the programs and activities previously known as countering violent extremism [CVE]) is one component of the nation's broader response to the risk of terrorism and extremist or ideologically motivated violence. Terrorism prevention efforts complement criminal justice and enforcement-focused counterterrorism (CT) efforts, focusing on both preventing the emergence of threats to reduce the need for CT action inside the United States and managing individuals who have been convicted of terrorism-related offenses after their release. CVE programs have been a component of many nations' strategies to reduce the threat of terrorist attack from individuals who have traveled to conflict zones to fight or who have mobilized to support terrorist groups or carry out violence at home. The United States began to focus on radicalization and mobilization to violence shortly after the September 11, 2001, attacks (9/11), but significant U.S. activity related to CVE began after the attack at Fort Hood in 2009 and the attempted bombing in Times Square in 2010.

Terrorism prevention policies and programs are aimed at reducing the risk of terrorism in ways *other than* investigating and incarcerating the individuals suspected of planning or directly supporting violence. The tools for doing so span the entire life cycle of terrorism, from preventing recruitment by terrorist groups to limiting the influence of terrorist messaging to intervening with individuals who are at risk of radicalization to violence. Such tools also include programs to preclude recidivism for those incarcerated for terrorist-related crimes.

CVE efforts have been controversial, and that controversy persists with respect to terrorism prevention activities. Serious concerns persist regarding CVE and terrorism prevention efforts' potential to impinge on constitutionally protected rights because these efforts often focus on activities that occur before any crime has been committed. Because there are no unambiguous early indicators of future violent behavior, the performance of risk assessment tools and methods to distinguish individuals who *appear to be threats* from those who *actually do pose a threat* is limited, meaning that individuals to whom terrorism prevention efforts are intended to respond might not commit any future violence, even if no action is taken. Distinguishing activities supporting violence from those in pursuit of humanitarian or other goals (e.g., charitable contributions) also is not always straightforward. Past CVE efforts have been criticized for focusing disproportionately on Muslim communities—creating both stigma and prejudice—given national trends in ideologically motivated violence and terrorism. Critics have accused the government of using these programs as veiled surveillance to support enforcement action, in large part by encouraging community members to spy on one another.[1] These arguments, combined with reactions to aggressive counterterrorism investigation and enforcement in some communities, have significantly damaged trust in government, and particularly in federal CVE efforts and, by extension, terrorism prevention efforts going forward.

Others have argued that, whatever their intent, past CVE efforts have had limited scope and effect. Indeed, federal investment in programs and initiatives has been modest, mostly coming from reprogramming existing funds rather than a true national CVE initiative. The shift to terrorism prevention also has not been associated with an increase in federal funding to date. This led some critics of the national effort to cast it as "more talk than action," or—more charitably—as still in the pilot or experimental stages.

Designing effective terrorism prevention efforts while addressing the concerns they raise is complicated by the fact that many different entities and organizations have roles in this space. CVE in the United States has previously been an interagency effort, with four federal security-focused agencies—the U.S. Department of Homeland Security (DHS), U.S. Department of Justice (DOJ), Federal Bureau of Investigation (FBI), and National Counterterrorism Center (NCTC)—playing the most central roles, and with varied levels of involvement from other agencies.

Although much of the concern about these activities focuses on the role of government organizations—particularly law enforcement, from the FBI to local police—nongovernmental organizations (NGOs) have played important roles in the past and likely will have to do so in the future for national terrorism prevention efforts to succeed. Engagement efforts frequently rely on organizations from affected communities to be successful, and intervention requires access to capabilities for mental health services, employment assistance, and other capacities maintained by nonprofit and service organizations. Some NGO efforts have been connected to government (e.g., through multidisciplinary teams including government social services providers, police, or other agencies), while others have been designed to be explicitly separate from government (and law enforcement in particular), meaning that concerns about the effect of terrorism prevention efforts on threat and on individual rights can vary dramatically from program to program.

---

[1]   American Civil Liberties Union (ACLU), "ACLU Briefing Paper: What Is Wrong with the Government's 'Countering Violent Extremism' Programs," undated(a).

Framing of This Study

DHS's Office of Policy asked the Homeland Security Operational Analysis Center (HSOAC) to carry out a research effort to examine the state of knowledge regarding terrorism prevention organization, coordination, programming, and policy in support of DHS planning and strategy development efforts. As part of this effort, HSOAC examined past CVE efforts by DHS and its interagency partners, and explored options for terrorism prevention policy going forward. The scope of the effort included examining the current DHS and interagency posture, particularly structure, personnel, resources, and programs; whether current efforts are commensurate with the terrorist threat; what approaches have been shown to be effective for terrorism prevention and how success can be measured; and what federal organizational or programmatic changes should be considered going forward.

Researchers drew on published literature on CVE; reviewed material on current terrorism prevention efforts and programs; held interviews with current and former members of federal organizations with knowledge in CVE and terrorism prevention; had discussions with other researchers who had studied the topics; and held interviews with members of the technology industry and associated nonprofits related to online extremism concerns. The research team also carried out field visits with state, local, and nongovernmental organizations in five U.S. cities supporting case studies of CVE efforts and perceived needs in metropolitan areas in different parts of the country;[2] did case studies of seven countries' CVE efforts;[3] and examined available, open-source and unclassified threat information.[4]

Most of the representatives of organizations we spoke to at the local level ran programs that were not specific to terrorism, but rather were applicable to intervening with individuals at risk of committing violence more broadly. In total, the project involved approximately 100 discussions with about 175 individuals. In this effort, our focus was explicitly *on policies and programs within the United States* and our primary goal was to identify options for DHS policies, activities, and interagency coordination to support national terrorism prevention policy. However, we touched on U.S. CVE and terrorism prevention efforts abroad from the perspective of understanding coordination and

---

[2] The cities were Boston, Massachusetts; Denver, Colorado; Houston, Texas; Los Angeles, California; and Minneapolis–St. Paul, Minnesota.

[3] The countries were Australia, Belgium, Canada, Denmark, France, Germany, and the United Kingdom.

[4] A note on terminology: During the period of this study, the federal government was in the process of transitioning from using the term *CVE* (used in the period soon after 9/11 and ending in January 2017) to *terrorism prevention*. Other nations still use CVE terminology to describe their programming. To inform our analysis of prospective terrorism prevention policy, however, we draw on the experience of other nations; of federal, state, and local entities involved in CVE; and on literature analysis published before 2017. In this report, we have sought to use the appropriate term when referring to other nations' policies and programming and to distinguish U.S. efforts before and after the transition.

potential synergy between streams of activity. Our focus was also explicitly *federal*: Although discussions during our field visits explored the nature of available local programing, the primary goal was to identify lessons relevant to shaping federal policy.

The complexity and controversy inherent in both past CVE and future terrorism prevention efforts means that policy in this area will spark a spirited debate about appropriate programs, no matter what path is chosen. The debate will focus on questions related to the nature of appropriate programs, which agencies should and should not participate, how information is collected and shared, and the balance between the intended benefits of such programs and their unintended consequences. This research was designed to contribute to that process, learning from past efforts to address ideologically motivated violence and other societal challenges, and exploring possible paths forward to *effective* but, potentially more importantly, *practical* federal—and, by extension, national—terrorism prevention efforts.

Assessing Current Terrorism Prevention Policies and Capabilities

In the framing of this study, DHS defined four terrorism prevention lines of effort:

- promoting education and community awareness
- countering terrorist recruitment and propaganda
- providing early warning of individuals who have radicalized and responding to cases of radicalization to violence
- keeping suspects and individuals convicted of terrorism-related offenses from returning to violence.

These lines of effort focus on different stages of the process, from individuals becoming radicalized (at which point they may or may not pose a threat, since many who hold radical ideas channel them toward ends other than violence) to desistance from violence by individuals who are convicted of and incarcerated for terrorism-related offenses. Across the different lines of effort, the goal is to reduce the incidence of violence inspired by ideology, extremist causes, and other related sources and to expand the range of options to respond to that risk. By building options beyond traditional criminal justice tools of arrest, prosecution, and incarceration and involving organizations and capabilities outside government, terrorism prevention programs seek to enable action before individuals break the law and pose a risk to themselves and others.

Although DHS's four lines of effort specified at the initiation of this study—promoting education and community awareness, countering terrorist recruitment and propaganda, providing early warning of individuals who have radicalized and responding to cases of radicalization, and keeping individuals convicted of offenses from returning to violence—provided an initial breakdown of the different components of terrorism prevention programming, we mapped those lines of effort to a simple process model of radicalization for the purposes of this study.

The process of radicalization and mobilization to violence for individuals has been the focus of considerable research attention and policy debate for many years. Early attempts to understand the process posited well-defined steps and a progression of individuals from their starting point through adoption of extremist views and increasing levels of commitment culminating in violence. Different models have focused on different contributors to or risk factors of radicalization, ranging from the ideological to the individual, and have ascribed varied relative weights to different factors. Models have also disagreed on how deterministic or predictable the radicalization of an individual is, and therefore whether concepts like "an individual on the path to violence" have any objective meaning. More-recent studies of radicalization paint a more complex and diverse picture, noting the potential influence of many factors simultaneously, even for individuals nominally radicalized by the same ideological cause. Timelines can differ considerably. Even the role of ideology and extremism is complicated: A person can be an extremist without being violent (which is not only legal but constitutionally protected in the United States), and can be violent in the name of a cause without being particularly fervent regarding—or without correctly understanding—the tenets of the cause itself. Studies by the FBI have gone even further, pointing out that even when individuals are *making threats*, it is not necessarily definitive: "[M]any persons who make threats do not pose a threat."

Given our current understanding of radicalization processes—and the near certainty of great diversity across individuals and among different causes and ideologies that might inspire violence—we chose to use a very basic model to anchor our work. We thus divided the people involved in radicalization processes into three relevant populations (see Figure S.1):

- vulnerable population—i.e., all the people who might radicalize to violence
- individuals who are radical of thought but may or may not become violent
- individuals actually involved in attempted attacks (denoted by the red starburst in the figure).

The three populations are connected by two processes:

- radicalization to extremism (which, again, may or may not mean a greater chance of the individual becoming violent)
- mobilization to violence.

Given the level of threat in the United States, each successive population is much smaller than the population preceding it, with only a small percentage of any vulnerable population radicalizing and only a percentage of that population escalating to violence. This basic model is not specific to any given ideology or population.

Figure S.1
Radicalization and Terrorism Prevention Framework, with DHS's Terrorism Prevention Lines of Effort

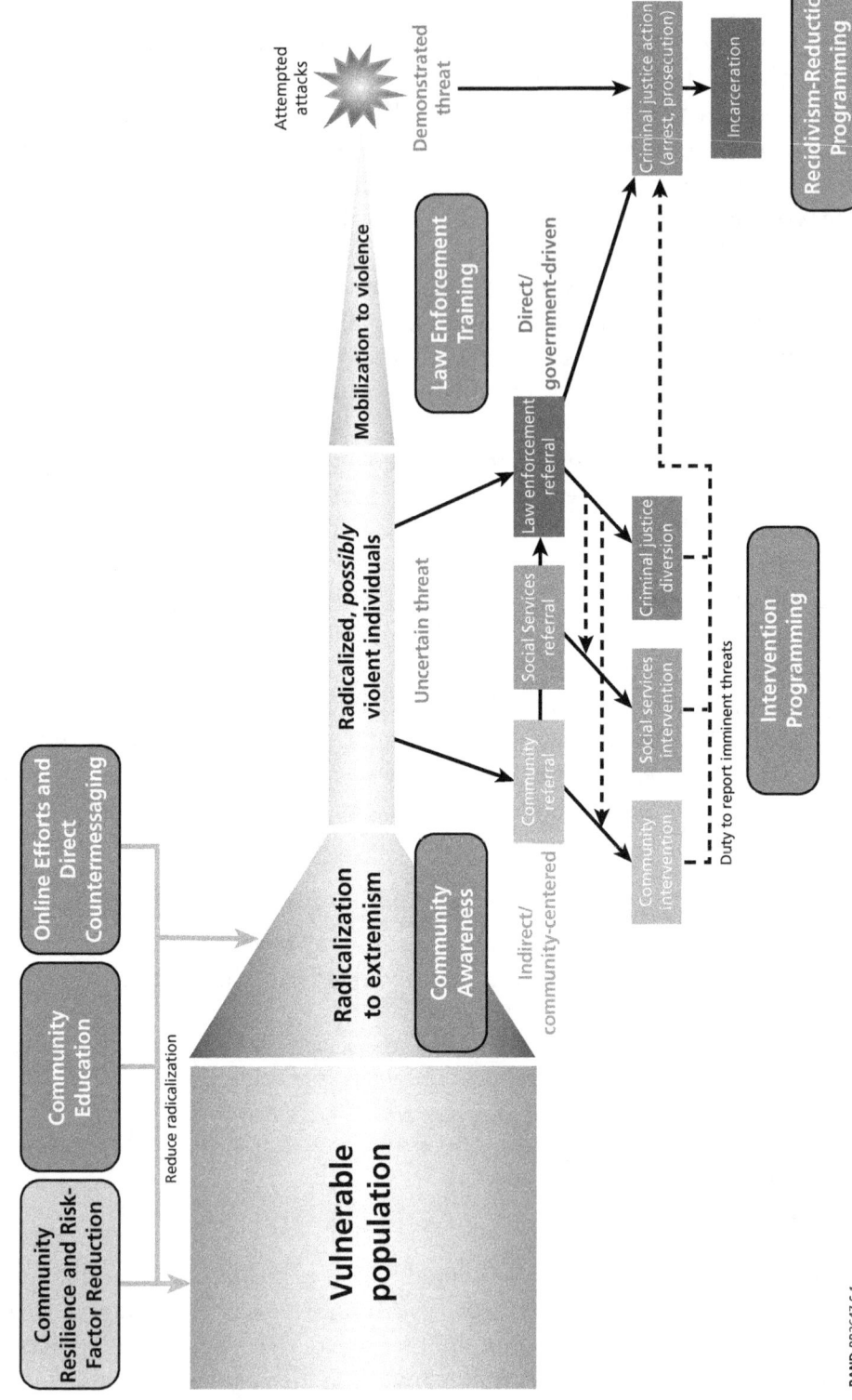

RAND *RR2647-S.1*

Because different points of the process involve distinct terrorism prevention activities, we divided the process into three phases: *early*, which focuses more broadly on vulnerable populations either to increase resistance to radicalization or reduce factors like extremist messages in the environment; *middle*, which focuses on individuals at risk of carrying out violence; and *late*, which addresses efforts aimed at individuals who have broken the law and are already involved in the criminal justice system.

Figure S.1 maps the lines of effort and their intended effects, including reducing radicalization through community education or direct countermessaging; recognizing and serving at-risk individuals through community awareness, law enforcement training, and intervention programs; and reducing recidivism by delivering services to individuals after their release from the corrections system. As illustrated in the portion of the figure focusing on intervention, efforts can involve entities from the community, social services sectors inside and outside government, other government entities, and law enforcement. The involvement of different types of organizations—from purely community to purely law enforcement—defines a range from indirect and community-centered options for terrorism prevention to direct and government-driven ones, given the involvement of criminal justice agencies. Depending on the circumstances in a local area, community, social service, or criminal justice terrorism prevention options may be entirely separate from one another (including in situations where multiple parallel and separate efforts coexist because of damaged trust between individuals, NGOs, government, and law enforcement agencies), independent efforts may collaborate, or the area may be served by one integrated, multidisciplinary program.

Our analysis of published literature and interviews with individuals involved in past CVE and current terrorism prevention efforts at the federal and local levels revealed a limited national capability for terrorism prevention activities. We used each of the main terrorism prevention components and corresponding lines of effort laid out in Figure S.1 as an organizing structure to identify central issues in the following five categories of terrorism prevention efforts:

- **Online countermessaging.** Efforts to respond to extremist messaging aimed inside the United States were viewed by interviewees as quite limited. However, multiple interviewees argued that increasing government investment in this activity could be very problematic, given concerns about infringement of constitutionally protected rights and freedoms. Limited effort inside the country stands in stark contrast to more-robust U.S. efforts internationally, where there is a deeper pool of resources and willingness to experiment with new initiatives.

    Private-sector and NGO efforts aimed at online messaging are more prevalent, including platform providers' actions to remove extremist content and NGOs responding and challenging that content when it appears. Although some campaigns have demonstrated substantial reach, evidence is limited that those who engage with countermessaging content online have a reduced risk of involvement in extremist violence. Furthermore, displacement of extremist content to smaller technology platforms that are harder to monitor and with less capability and capacity to respond is a concern. Public-private partnerships (like the Peer2Peer program) are viewed as success stories and a less risky way for the government to be involved in such efforts.

- **Community education, engagement, resilience, and risk-factor reduction.** Federal and other entities have devoted significant effort to community education and engagement in the course of past CVE efforts and these policies remain central to ongoing terrorism prevention initiatives. Our interviewees saw both value and unmet demand for these activities. Such efforts seek to "immunize" communities against extremist messages and build relationships and trust to support other types of programs. Staff reductions at DHS have constrained these efforts, leading to unmet demand for products like the Community Awareness Briefing (CAB) and Community Resilience Exercises (CREXs), which are delivered by DHS, NCTC, and other partners. One issue raised about both federal and nonfederal engagement and outreach efforts was the risk of stigmatizing communities—creating the impression that all members of a specific community are potential terrorists—when that is not the intention.

  The extent to which broad resilience and risk factor–reduction efforts fall within DHS's terrorism prevention lines of effort is an open question. Such broad programs—which focus on education, employment, strengthening families, or societal functioning—were very popular with interviewees, in part because they were not viewed as stigmatizing and could help to address multiple societal issues simultaneously. According to interviewees, many of these efforts were difficult to fund, and such funding should not have to be linked to security-focused efforts like terrorism prevention, but should instead come from nonsecurity agencies, like the U.S. Department of Health and Human Services, which have been reticent to participate robustly in CVE efforts because of resourcing and other concerns.

- **Referral promotion.** A specific component of education and training efforts in past CVE initiatives was focused on recognizing warning signs that an individual may be at risk of perpetrating ideologically motivated violence. The goal in doing so is for members of the public, professionals like teachers or medical providers, law enforcement, and others to recognize signs of concern that make it possible to intervene. This awareness-building has been included in both DHS's and others' education efforts, but, based on the data available to our study, it was difficult to assess the likelihood that an at-risk individual would be identified and referred for assistance in any specific geographic area.

  Uniform mechanisms for referrals for intervention also are not available, although ongoing DHS grants do fund local organizations in the early stages of building such capabilities. Although referral mechanisms do exist in some areas, they are largely in service-provision systems that are not specific to terrorism.

Options in this facet of terrorism prevention are relatively limited: Federal efforts to promote referrals are unlikely to be as fruitful as those led by local and community elements, given that some important communities have limited trust in the federal government and security-focused agencies.

- **Intervention.** If programs are not available to *help* at-risk individuals, whether those individuals are *identified* and *referred* to anyone becomes largely immaterial. Necessary programming includes different types of counseling, social services, and other tools to address potential violence risk. Again, because of damaged trust in the federal government and concerns about government action regarding individuals who have not committed a crime, intervention must be managed predominantly at the local level. Although the consensus across our interviewees was that intervention capacity is quite limited nationally, pockets of capacity are in place in some of the cities visited during the study.

  Generally, intervention capabilities have been built into existing programs for individuals or youth at risk of perpetrating violence for other reasons (e.g., mental health concerns, school violence). Interviewees viewed this approach as a pragmatic path, since the low incidence rate of terrorism in any area makes it impractical to build and maintain dedicated programs. The successes that do exist in building capability—in programs that respect both the individual needs of the people referred to them and the safety of the community—are viewed as fragile, driven in large part by the controversy surrounding CVE and terrorism prevention efforts and the limited funding to support such programs. Furthermore, the absence of more-robust intervention capacity reinforces perceptions of entities critical of past CVE and current terrorism prevention efforts that referring at-risk individuals is more likely to lead to prosecution than counseling.

- **Recidivism reduction.** Our interviewees argued that current recidivism-focused programming is not sufficient to meet the national need. Previous strategies to respond to terrorism—including prosecution on such charges as material support—resulted in intermediate-length sentences for the individuals involved, and significant numbers of terrorism-convicted offenders are approaching release from prison. Programming is being developed and piloted to address their needs and help support their desistance from violence, but those efforts are in their early stages.

Measuring the effectiveness of terrorism prevention policies and programs is difficult and metrics are lacking. Across all of these areas, analyses of the literature and our interviewees described shortfalls in the ability to measure the effects of terrorism prevention policies to demonstrate their effectiveness. However, lessons from other efforts to address violence and related social problems have demonstrated the effectiveness of programs that can be applied to terrorism prevention.

As suggested earlier, one of the critiques of past U.S. CVE and current terrorism prevention efforts is that comparatively small amounts of money have been devoted to it compared with either counterterrorism as a whole or efforts to manage other safety and health risks. Although the exact amount spent on terrorism prevention per year governmentwide is difficult to determine with precision, it is clear that the total is small (in the tens of millions of dollars). Terrorism prevention spending is dwarfed by the amounts spent by the U.S. government on law enforcement and other direct counterterrorism efforts. Comparisons to other Western democracies (adjusted by factors like relative threat level or population) show U.S. spending at the bottom of credible ranges. Other yardsticks—such as the costs involved in responding to individual terrorism cases through arrest, prosecution, and incarceration, or the costs incurred in the aftermath of even small terrorist attacks—suggest that more-significant expenditures on terrorism prevention can be justified.

Finally, there is work to be done to better integrate federal activities into a truly whole-of-government approach to terrorism prevention. During the latter phases of U.S. CVE efforts, interagency efforts were coordinated via the CVE Task Force, which provided a venue for decisionmaking and coordination of program efforts. Although most individuals who were involved praised the Task Force and its accomplishments, critical needs were also identified, including bringing nonsecurity agencies more substantially into terrorism prevention efforts, addressing interagency incentive issues that create barriers to innovation and effectiveness, and better serving state and local stakeholders.

Federal Options to Strengthen Terrorism Prevention Capabilities

Policymakers will face numerous challenges as they attempt to design effective terrorism prevention programs. First, despite attention to terrorism as a threat, ideologically motivated violence is a low-base-rate problem in any specific city or area compared with issues like crime, drugs, and gangs. Terrorism prevention policies must therefore be approached with practicality in mind. One consequence of this reality is the argument that, where possible, either terrorism prevention should be integrated into existing programs for responding to individuals at risk of committing violence more broadly or that terrorism prevention programs should be implemented so that they can serve the needs of broader populations (e.g., school violence) in addition to terrorism. As a result, while programming needs to be responsive to the specific ideologies that are inspiring violent action, programs that are highly ideologically specific may be difficult to sustain.[5] Second, identifying potential rare threats carries the inherent

---

[5]   Interviewees emphasized that programs focusing on individual communities or ideologies risk stigmatizing populations and undermining the ability of terrorism prevention efforts to reduce terrorism risk. As a result, where programs that are specific to individual communities or ideologies are supported, government investments

risk of false positives—i.e., people being viewed as potential threats who are not—so programs must be designed with the goal of minimizing both the costs to them and the chance of their being stigmatized as a result of their "participation" in a terrorism prevention program. Third, controversy and intense suspicion of federal involvement in some communities have handicapped efforts from the outset and scared away key potential partners, which made it difficult to build out CVE capability in the past. This remains a challenge for terrorism prevention both now and in the future. These concerns have made some organizations reticent to accept federal grant dollars connected to the topic.

Given these challenges, what is the right strategy for the federal government and for DHS in particular? The answer to that question varied somewhat across different facets of terrorism prevention, but the most effective path discussed was for the federal government to support state, local, NGO, and private actors rather than to build capabilities itself. There was strong consensus across interviewees at all levels that terrorism prevention efforts have to be locally designed, managed, and driven. Not unexpectedly, there was near consensus on the need for the federal government to find ways to fund those local efforts—although the controversy means that there is work to be done to determine the best ways to do so. Interviewees emphasized that the federal government must approach terrorism prevention with patience. This is not a policy area where there is a short-term "silver bullet" policy solution, and it will take time to build consensus around acceptable and workable local approaches, but local success will translate to national success.

There was relatively strong consensus that reinvestment in federal field staff—personnel located around the country who have a stake in their areas and the expertise to perform key terrorism prevention roles and facilitate local initiatives—would be beneficial. Having someone aware of the federal picture who is locally based can help to build relationships, strengthen trust, and act as an on-the-ground facilitator of local terrorism prevention efforts. This was viewed as an option that could deliver immediate results and help to build for the longer term. We found stark differences between cities with a dynamic, supported, and engaged federal staff—where relationships were stronger and programs were more robust—and cities where such staff were absent.

There also was consensus among interviewees that a major part of what was required to broaden viable federal action for terrorism prevention was in how the topic is framed from the federal level, and whether local areas have the flexibility to reframe it in ways that are appropriate for their circumstances. We heard different variations of the message that "words matter" over and over again. But it is not just how the policy area is described: "So one of the lessons from [this city] is that how you scope this really

---

as a portfolio should be balanced across ideological sources of violence, based on objective data on relative threat and prevalence.

matters. [But] it's not just how you scope this in words."[6] Most interviewees illustrated this point by citing the view that, since the initiation of CVE at the federal level, although it has been said that all forms of extremism were covered, the main focus was on jihadist violence and, as a result, on Muslim communities. The vast majority of our interviewees emphasized (echoing some recent statements by DHS leadership) that terrorism prevention must be inclusive of the threat of ideological violence from *all* sources—from ISIS to white supremacists to environmentally inspired violence—and must do so not only in statements, but also in programming and investment.[7]

It is not clear that the federal government should take the further step argued by some interviewees at the local level and treat terrorism prevention as one component of general violence reduction and eliminate efforts specifically "branded" as focusing on terrorism. Increasing the involvement of nonsecurity agencies in terrorism prevention could yield some of the benefits of that proposal while maintaining terrorism prevention as a distinct program area. However, at the local level, it is clear that many organizations are already "mainstreaming terrorism prevention" into more-general initiatives that respond to individuals at risk of violent behavior irrespective of how the federal government defines the problem, reflecting both what is practical for them and what is effective for their communities.

The federal options fall into four main categories of activity and focus on enabling terrorism prevention initiatives from the bottom up and supporting the development of a national approach to this issue. We discuss the different types of policy options across the phases of terrorism prevention and summarize the specific options identified in this report in Table S.1.[8] These options represent a menu that policymakers can draw from to build out the federal policy and program portfolio for terrorism prevention.

The timing of this study (with the changeover in administrations) presents an opportunity to look at what had been done before and explore paths forward. When the research team integrated available information on both national and local CVE and terrorism prevention initiatives, the picture that emerged was one of an effort still at an early stage. Some federally supported initiatives were viewed as showing real promise. There are examples of local initiatives that are taking on the challenge of addressing violence risk in individuals who have not yet committed a crime, includ-

---

[6]   Interview with a federal representative in one of the studied U.S. cities, 2018.

[7]   The organization's name transliterates from Arabic as al-Dawlah al-Islamiyah fi al-'Iraq wa al-Sham (abbreviated as Da'ish or DAESH). In the West, it is commonly referred to as the Islamic State of Iraq and the Levant (ISIL), the Islamic State of Iraq and Syria, the Islamic State of Iraq and the Sham (both abbreviated as ISIS), or simply as the Islamic State (IS). Arguments abound as to which is the most accurate translation, but here we refer to the group as ISIS.

[8]   As many of our interviewees pointed out, the nature of local responses to CVE and, by extension, terrorism prevention (including the preference to incorporate it into programs that are responsive to a wide range of violence prevention goals) means that initiatives to strengthen the national system also will contribute to responding to other pressing concerns, like school shootings and other mass-targeted violence.

Table S.1
Summary of Policy Options by Terrorism Prevention Activity and Category

Category	Countering Extremist Messaging Online	Community Education, Engagement, Resilience, and Risk-Factor Reduction	Referral Promotion	Intervention	Recidivism Reduction
Situational Awareness	• Sustain efforts to characterize the extent of extremist content online on an ongoing basis. • Publicly release results of the content census to enable public action.	• N/A	• Support periodic, publicly released national surveys to assess public willingness to refer individuals because of concern regarding early mobilization activities.	• Gather data on existing capabilities relevant to terrorism prevention intervention nationally to help facilitate network development and identify shortfalls.	• Develop and maintain a centralized database of individuals incarcerated for ideological violence–related offenses to support program development and implementation.
Awareness and Training	• Provide threat information to technology firms to support their countermessaging efforts. • Increase technical staff in government terrorism prevention efforts to support outreach to industry. • Increase transparency of efforts and broadly share information for terrorism prevention purposes.	• Continue and expand outreach and local coordination efforts through CABs and CREXs.	• Continue and expand outreach and local coordination efforts through CABs and CREXs.	• Continue federal efforts to assemble and disseminate best practices and standards for intervention programs.	• Develop a customized CAB for corrections staff at the federal, state, and local levels. • When appropriate, develop training to disseminate best practices and new evidence-based practices in the corrections sector.

Table S.1—Continued

Category	Countering Extremist Messaging Online	Community Education, Engagement, Resilience, and Risk-Factor Reduction	Referral Promotion	Intervention	Recidivism Reduction
Federal Program Development	• N/A	• Reconstitute and expand federal field staff to act as primary focal points for terrorism prevention at the local level.	• N/A	• Reconstitute and expand federal field staff to act as primary focal points for terrorism prevention at the local level.	• Coordinate with (and assist, as appropriate) federal corrections agencies developing recidivism reduction programming. • Support the development of program standards for intervention efforts to maintain effectiveness in decentralized implementation across the country.

Table S.1—Continued

Category	Countering Extremist Messaging Online	Community Education, Engagement, Resilience, and Risk-Factor Reduction	Referral Promotion	Intervention	Recidivism Reduction
Federal Support of Local Initiatives	• Use grant funding to support counternarrative activities outside government.	• Make "on-call experts" with knowledge, program design, and evaluation expertise available to support local terrorism prevention initiatives. • Use grant funding to support local and NGO early-phase terrorism prevention activities. • Expand use of tabletop exercises to assist localities in developing acceptable and practical local approaches to terrorism prevention.	• Continue to support efforts to develop national-level hotlines for referral of at-risk individuals. • Use grant funding to support local and NGO referral promotion efforts, but recognize that substantial trust-building may be required.	• Use grant funding to support local and NGO intervention models and networks. • Make "on-call experts" with knowledge, program design, and evaluation expertise available to support local terrorism prevention initiatives. • Prioritize supporting intervention capacity separate from law enforcement organizations, particularly in areas where trust is weakened. • Explore alternative funding mechanisms for local initiatives.	• Use grant funding to support state, local, and NGO implementation of recidivism-reduction programs.

Table S.1—Continued

Category	Countering Extremist Messaging Online	Community Education, Engagement, Resilience, and Risk-Factor Reduction	Referral Promotion	Intervention	Recidivism Reduction
Regulatory and Legal Issues	• N/A	• N/A	• Address perceived legal and regulatory barriers to interagency collaboration in terrorism prevention referral and intervention.	• Address perceived legal and liability barriers to nongovernmental intervention activities.	• N/A
Research and Evaluation	• Continue to invest in evaluation of counternarrative efforts.	• Support periodic, publicly released national surveys to assess knowledge and awareness about radicalization and mobilization to violence.	• Continue research focused on improving risk-assessment methods, but manage expectations for their possible accuracy.	• Continue to invest in evaluation of intervention programs. • Prioritize research and evaluation efforts to better understand factors affecting the sustainability of terrorism prevention intervention programs.	• Continue to invest in evaluation of recidivism-reduction programs. • Continue research focused on improving risk-assessment methods, but manage expectations for their possible accuracy. • Prioritize focused research and evaluation efforts to better understand the effect of incarceration on radicalization and violence risk.

Table S.1—Continued

Category	Countering Extremist Messaging Online	Community Education, Engagement, Resilience, and Risk-Factor Reduction	Referral Promotion	Intervention	Recidivism Reduction
Auxiliary Federal Activities	• N/A	• Recognize and proactively manage effects that other DHS and federal programs can have on community trust to support terrorism prevention initiatives. • Increase interagency investment separate from terrorism prevention initiatives to address community concerns and reduce risk factors related to radicalization to violence.	• N/A	• N/A	• N/A

NOTE: N/A = not applicable.

ing violence inspired by ideological causes. Individuals and organizations from the national to the local levels viewed this policy area as an important one, and strongly argued that national approaches to violence prevention need to address ideological violence and terrorism—even though the absolute risk of terrorism to any locality might be quite small.

However, previous CVE programs, and, by extension, terrorism prevention programs, have garnered significant controversy because of legitimate and important civil rights and civil liberties concerns, as well as criticism of the ways in which previous CVE efforts were implemented—including whether they were intended to achieve something quite different than their stated goals. If greater consensus can be achieved regarding appropriate ways to build approaches to dealing with terrorism risk beyond traditional criminal justice tools of arrest, prosecution, and incarceration that process could help move toward better national policies. To that end, the federal policy options laid out in this report has in part responded to issues raised during early efforts to develop then-CVE programs, drawing on examples from localities that have built approaches that seek to safeguard the rights and meet the needs of individuals potentially at risk of committing ideological violence, while still protecting society from potential terrorist attack. In doing so, the goal is to identify *effective* policies and intervention options, but also *practical* ones, which respond appropriately to terrorism risk but do so in a way that simultaneously minimizes the manifold costs to the individuals affected and the society that terrorism prevention efforts aim to protect.

Acknowledgments

In the course of this research effort, the HSOAC team reached out to a wide range of individuals and organizations to gather data and expert views to inform our work. We contacted groups that are directly involved in CVE or terrorism prevention and ones whose efforts, programs, and expertise—although not CVE or terrorism prevention–focused—could provide valuable insight and input for our work. In our interviews, we included current and former members of federal, state, and local government agencies and NGOs, as well as individuals with relevant expertise, experiences, or perspectives.

Not all of the organizations and individuals whose input we sought were comfortable participating in the study because of the sensitivity of terrorism prevention and CVE and the controversy surrounding government activities in this area. Although this made the research team all the more appreciative of the individuals who gave generously of their time, we are also grateful to those who provided frank feedback on why they felt they could not participate. That feedback provided us with critical context on the policy challenge in this area. We have sought to approach our analysis—based not only on the data collected in our interviews, but also on the breadth of published analysis and debate on the topic—in a way that discusses and respects the full range of views, whether or not individuals or organizations holding those views directly participated in our interview process.

Where participants were comfortable with us doing so, we list below the organizations where we spoke with current or former members, to both express our thanks publicly and provide a window on the range of entities consulted during the project. We are extremely grateful to the more than 175 people from these and other organizations who contributed to our work, and hope that the product can help to contribute to a policy area to which many of them have devoted considerable time, effort, and professional passion.

Organization	City
U.S. Department of Homeland Security (current and former)	
• Office of Terrorism Prevention Partnerships	Washington, D.C.
• Office of Strategy, Policy, and Plans	Washington, D.C.
• Office of Intelligence and Analysis	Washington, D.C.

Organization	City
• Office of Counterterrorism	Washington, D.C.
• Office of Civil Rights and Civil Liberties	Washington, D.C.
• Directorate of Science and Technology	Washington, D.C.
• Homeland Security Advisory Committee CVE Subcommittee	Washington, D.C.
Interagency CVE Task Force (current and former)	Washington, D.C.
National Security Council (current and former)	Washington, D.C.
U.S. Department of Justice (current and former)	Washington, D.C.
• State and Local Anti-Terrorism Training Program (former)	Washington, D.C.
• Federal Bureau of Investigation (former)	Washington, D.C.
Administrative Office of the U.S. Courts	Washington, D.C.
National Counter Terrorism Center (current and former)	McLean, Va.
U.S. Department of Defense	Arlington, Va.
U.S. Department of State (current and former)	Washington, D.C.
U.S. Agency for International Development	Washington, D.C.
George Washington University Program on Extremism	Washington, D.C.
University of Maryland, National Consortium for the Study of Terrorism and Responses to Terrorism (START)	College Park, Md.
University of Maryland, Center for Health and Homeland Security	Baltimore, Md.
Counter Extremism Project	New York, N.Y.
Washington Institute for Near East Policy	Washington, D.C.
Middle East Institute	Washington, D.C.
The Soufan Center	New York, N.Y.
Cambridge Global Advisors	Washington, D.C.
Heritage Foundation	Washington, D.C.
Police Foundation	Washington, D.C.
Gen Next Foundation	Washington, D.C.
Twitter	San Francisco, Calif.
Moonshot CVE	London, UK
EdVenture Partners	Orinda, Calif.
Omelas	New York, N.Y.
The Prevention Project	Washington, D.C.
American Islamic Forum for Democracy	Phoenix, Ariz.
Islamic Center of Southern California	Los Angeles, Calif.
All Dulles Area Muslim Society (ADAMS)	Sterling, Va.
Islamic Center of Southern California	Los Angeles, Calif.
Los Angeles Department of Mental Health	Los Angeles, Calif.
Los Angeles Mayor's Office of Public Safety	Los Angeles, Calif.
Los Angeles Police Department	Los Angeles, Calif.
Los Angeles Sheriff's Department	Los Angeles, Calif.
Muslim Public Affairs Council	Los Angeles, Calif.

Organization	City
University of California, Los Angeles	Los Angeles, Calif.
Alliance for Compassion and Tolerance	Houston, Tex.
Anti-Defamation League Southwest Region	Houston, Tex.
Crisis Intervention of Houston, Inc.	Houston, Tex.
Harris County Sheriff's Office (former)	Houston, Tex.
Houston Mayor's Office of Public Safety and Homeland Security	Houston, Tex.
Houston Police Department	Houston, Tex.
Islamic Society of Greater Houston	Houston, Tex.
Outreach Strategists	Houston, Tex.
University of Houston	Houston, Tex.
Anti-Defamation League New England Region	Boston, Mass.
Boston Children's Hospital	Boston, Mass.
Boston Police Department	Boston, Mass.
Boston Public Schools Counseling and Intervention Center	Boston, Mass.
Cambridge Safety Net Collaborative	Boston, Mass.
Empower Peace	Boston, Mass.
Massachusetts Department of Corrections	Boston, Mass.
Massachusetts Executive Office of Public Safety and Security	Boston, Mass.
Parents for Peace	Boston, Mass.
Somali Development Center	Boston, Mass.
United States Attorney's Office District of Massachusetts	Boston, Mass.
Average Mohamed	Minneapolis, Minn.
Hennepin County Sheriff's Office	Minneapolis, Minn.
Minneapolis Police Department	Minneapolis, Minn.
Somali American Parent Association	Minneapolis, Minn.
St. Paul Police Department	St. Paul, Minn.
United States Attorney's Office District of Minnesota	Minneapolis, Minn.
United States District Court District of Minnesota	Minneapolis, Minn.
United States Probation and Pretrial Services District of Minnesota	Minneapolis, Minn.
Aurora Office of the City Manager	Aurora, Colo.
Aurora Police Department	Aurora, Colo.
Aurora Public Schools	Aurora, Colo.
Colorado Department of Human Services	Denver, Colo.
Colorado Department of Public Safety	Centennial, Colo.
Colorado Resilience Collaborative	Denver, Colo.
Counterterrorism Education Learning Lab	Denver, Colo.
Denver Islamic Society	Denver, Colo.
Denver Police Department	Denver, Colo.
United States Attorney's Office District of Colorado	Denver, Colo.

We would also like to acknowledge the contributions of several RAND colleagues. Brian Michael Jenkins gave generously of his time and insight during early discussions on the project. Jennifer D. P. Moroney drove the drafting of the project's case study of CVE efforts in Australia (included in Appendix A to this document). James Ryseff assisted in gathering information on the technology industry and efforts in the online space aimed at extremist communication. Todd Helmus, Andrew Liepman, and Bob Harrison served as peer reviewers for the study. Kristin Leuschner of RAND's Research Communications Group helped us craft the project products. Blair Smith, a research editor in RAND's Publications Department, was critical to the process of finalizing the multiple products that came out of the effort, and made major contributions to improving their quality and readability. Joseph Russo of the University of Denver provided insights on corrections system issues related to terrorism prevention. We also are grateful for the contributions of DHS personnel in the Office of Policy and the Office of Partner Engagement (including the Office of Terrorism Prevention Partnerships) who provided insight and materials for the project and feedback on our research products.

Abbreviations

9/11	September 11, 2001, terrorist attacks
ACLU	American Civil Liberties Union
ADL	Anti-Defamation League
AHRC	American Human Rights Council
AIC	American Islamic Congress
AOUSC	Administrative Office of U.S. Courts
AVE	Against Violent Extremism
BCOT	Building Communities of Trust
BJA	Bureau of Justice Assistance
BOP	Bureau of Prisons
BRAVE	Build Resilience Against Violent Extremism
CAB	Community Awareness Briefing
CAIR	Council on American-Islamic Relations
CAP	Community Awareness Program
CELL	Counterterrorism Education Learning Lab
CEP	Counter Extremism Project
CIT	Crisis Intervention Team
CRCL	Office for Civil Rights and Civil Liberties
CREX	Community Resilience Exercise
CSCC	Center for Strategic Counterterrorism Communications

CT	counterterrorism
CVE	countering violent extremism
CVEO	Countering Violent Extremism Office
DEEP	Disruption and Early Engagement Program
DHS	U.S. Department of Homeland Security
DOJ	U.S. Department of Justice
DOS	U.S. Department of State
DT	domestic terrorism
ED	U.S. Department of Education
EOP	Executive Office of the President
ESF	Emergency Support Function
EU	European Union
FBI	Federal Bureau of Investigation
FEMA	Federal Emergency Management Agency
FERPA	Family Educational Rights and Privacy Act
FFRDC	federally funded research and development center
FLETC	Federal Law Enforcement Training Center
FOIA	Freedom of Information Act
FY	fiscal year
GAO	U.S. Government Accountability Office
GCTF	Global Counterterrorism Forum
GEC	Global Engagement Center
GIFCT	Global Internet Forum to Counter Terrorism
GTD	Global Terrorism Database
GWU	George Washington University
HHS	U.S. Department of Health and Human Services

HIPAA	Health Insurance Portability and Accountability Act
HSAC	Homeland Security Advisory Council
HSOAC	Homeland Security Operational Analysis Center
INSA	Intelligence and National Security Alliance
IPC	Interagency Policy Committee
ISD	Institute for Strategic Dialogue
ISIS	Islamic State of Iraq and Syria
IT	International Terrorism
JTTF	Joint Terrorism Task Force
LAB	Law Enforcement Awareness Briefing
LAPD	Los Angeles Police Department
M-DT	multidisciplinary team
MPAC	Muslim Public Affairs Council
MSA	Muslim Students' Association
NCTC	National Counterterrorism Center
NGO	nongovernmental organization
NSC	National Security Council
NSI	Nationwide Suspicious Activity Reporting Initiative
NTAC	National Threat Assessment Center
OCCI	Online Civil Courage Initiative
OCP	Office of Community Partnerships
OJP	Office of Justice Programs
OLA	Office of Legislative Affairs
OMB	Office of Management and Budget
OPE	Office of Partnerships and Engagement
OTPP	Office of Terrorism Prevention Partnerships

P2P	Peer2Peer
PATHE	Providing Alternatives to Hinder Extremism
PCC	Policy Coordination Committee
PIRUS	Profiles of Individual Radicalization in the United States
RAN	Radicalisation Awareness Network
S&T	Science and Technology Directorate
SAFETY	Supporting Antiterrorism by Fostering Effective Technologies (Act of 2002)
SIP	Strategic Implementation Plan
SLATT	State and Local Anti-Terrorism Training
SPLC	Southern Poverty Law Center
SRC	Shared Responsibility Committee
START	National Consortium for the Study of Terrorism and Responses to Terrorism
STRIVE	Strategic, Tactical, and Resilient Interdiction of Violent Extremism
UK	United Kingdom
UNODC	United Nations Office of Drugs and Crime
USCIS	United States Citizenship and Immigration Services
VCPI	Virginia Community Policing Institute
WHTI	Western Hemisphere Travel Initiative
WORDE	World Organization for Resource Development and Education

CHAPTER ONE

Introduction

Terrorism prevention (superseding the programs and activities previously known as countering violent extremism [CVE]) is one component of the nation's response to the risk of terrorism and extremist or ideologically motivated violence.[1] The development of CVE policy and programming in many countries has been driven by concerns about international terrorist threats "coming home." These threats arise from local individuals inspired by messages transmitted on the internet, from direct recruitment efforts by representatives of such groups, or from the return of individuals who went to fight in conflicts abroad (such as in Iraq or Syria). However, CVE efforts also have sought to respond to domestic threats of ideologically driven violence from the far right or far left, driven largely by racial, economic, or environmental concerns. The main terrorist threats in the United States have come from the radicalization of individuals through exposure to content on the internet, interaction with representatives of international terrorist organizations abroad, and attacks and attempted attacks by individuals inspired by either foreign terrorist organizations or ideologies of domestic origin.[2] Concern about returning foreign fighters persists, but has not been realized as a major source of threat. The United States has been fortunate in that the level of terrorist threat has been considerably lower than that faced by many other countries, providing space for a deliberate approach to management but creating the policy challenge of appropriately crafting responses for a relatively low-incidence, but still consequential, threat.

---

[1] A note on terminology: During the period of this study, the federal government was in the process of transitioning from CVE (which was used for most of the last decade and ended in January 2017) to terrorism prevention. Other nations still use the term *CVE* to describe their programming. To inform our analysis of prospective terrorism prevention policy, however, we drew on the experience of other nations; on the experience of federal, state, and local entities involved in CVE; and on literature analyses published before 2017. In this report, we have sought to use the appropriate term when referring to other nation's policies and programming, and to distinguish U.S. efforts before and after the transition.

[2] See the discussion in U.S. House of Representatives, Committee on Homeland Security, *The Evolving Nature of Terrorism: Nine Years After the 9/11 Attacks*, Washington, D.C.: U.S. Government Printing Office, September 15, 2010.

Terrorism prevention policies and programs aim to reduce the risk of terrorism in ways *other than* investigating and incarcerating the perpetrators of attempted or completed attacks. These policies also provide alternative ways to respond to individuals who have provided direct support to either individual perpetrators or foreign terrorist organizations. Tools to reduce these risks include activities aimed at addressing efforts by groups to recruit members or influence lone actors through extremist messages on websites or social media, efforts to intervene with individuals who are at risk of radicalization through counseling and other programs (often in collaboration with nongovernment or community groups), and—for individuals who have passed through the criminal justice system already for terrorist or extremist crimes—efforts that seek to limit recidivism once they are released.

Successful terrorism prevention requires capabilities and activities that fall outside traditional criminal justice enforcement, where the focus is on addressing the potential threat posed by an individual of concern by arrest, prosecution for crimes related to the support of or perpetration of terrorist acts, and incarceration. Terrorism prevention therefore explicitly seeks to intervene with individuals who have not yet committed any crime. For example, a program might seek to persuade individuals who are searching for extremist content online not to pursue a violent path themselves, or to counsel a youth who is considering traveling abroad to fight or staging a terrorist attack at home to instead pursue education, seek out employment, or channel his or her concerns about domestic or world events into political activism rather than violence. In both of these examples, the person has not yet done anything illegal, meaning that such intervention—and government, and particularly law enforcement, involvement—is both a controversial and sensitive endeavor. But, successful intervention could be beneficial not only to reduce the future risk of terrorist activity, but also for the at-risk individuals themselves, who would be steered toward paths that will be more beneficial to them over the long term.

Law enforcement organizations will always bear a heavy responsibility to maintain awareness of and to act decisively to address imminent threats of terrorist attack. However, in assessing individual threats, it can be difficult to distinguish individuals who pose such a serious threat that they should be arrested from those who do not. This judgment is a high-stakes decision: Errors where true threats are not recognized are easy to see, when individuals who have had previous contact with law enforcement go on to carry out attacks, but errors in the other direction are harder to definitively identify. However, the history of counterterrorism efforts in the United States since 2001 includes individuals arrested and prosecuted where at least some observers viewed such action as unwarranted and have not been persuaded by the information made available in the course of the criminal justice process.[3]

---

[3]   For a review, see Antony Field, "Ethics and Entrapment: Understanding Counterterrorism Stings," *Terrorism and Political Violence*, August 22, 2016.

Whatever the circumstances of individual cases, the reality is that the costs of each type of error are considerable. A missed prevention opportunity means costs in damages and lives from an attempted or successful attack, and damage to the credibility of governments' ability to protect the public. But the application of aggressive criminal justice approaches where they are not warranted has its own set of costs, including the consumption of resources that might be applied to other problems or threats and damage to community trust that could undermine future prevention efforts. Action may even reinforce future threats, if incarceration cements the individuals' commitment to violence rather than reducing it. Terrorism prevention programs therefore could expand the options available to law enforcement organizations, particularly for cases in which the immediacy of the threat posed by an individual is not clear, lowering the stakes of the decision and enabling more effective and efficient use of scarce resources.

The history of past CVE efforts in the United States is one of controversy. Extremity of thought is not a crime in the United States, and actions and statements that can be interpreted as indications of extremism that could lead to violence are protected by rights guaranteed under the U.S. Constitution, Bill of Rights, and other federal laws. Historical actions taken in the name of protecting the country that were later viewed as unacceptable trespasses on the rights of individuals or specific racial or ethnic groups have created a perception for some that terrorism prevention programs "are not what they say that they are." Based on the information available, some have reached the conclusion that, rather than seeking to provide alternatives to intelligence or law enforcement tools for addressing terrorist threats, past CVE programs and, by extension, current terrorism prevention efforts in fact seek to enable their application. During the period of most intense controversy surrounding CVE in the last administration, high-profile arrests of individuals on suspicion of terrorism and undeniable limits in the availability of alternative programs and nonpunitive intervention approaches reinforced these views, creating a significant trust deficit that challenges initiatives in this area now and going forward.[4]

Designing effective terrorism prevention efforts and navigating concerns that have been raised about them are further complicated by the number of entities and organizations that have roles to play in the process. Implementing governmental terrorism prevention efforts has involved a composite effort within the federal government and between the federal and local levels. But although much of the focus of these activities is centered on the role of government organizations, and particularly law enforcement, from the Federal Bureau of Investigation (FBI) down to local police, nongovernmental organizations (NGOs) have played and likely will have to play significant future roles in a practical, acceptable, and effective national terrorism prevention effort. Some NGO efforts have been connected to government (e.g., through

---

[4] Interviews with nongovernmental representatives at the national level and in U.S. cities, 2018.

multidisciplinary teams that include government social-services providers, police, and other agencies), while others have been designed to be separate from government (and law enforcement in particular), meaning that concerns about the effect of terrorism prevention efforts on the threat of terrorism and on individual rights can vary dramatically from program to program.

There is also great diversity in approach. Some programs have been designed specifically for terrorism or ideologically motivated violence, while others have drawn on and repurposed existing programs and interorganizational infrastructures built to address such societal problems as gang violence, police response to the mentally ill, risk of mass shootings, drugs, human trafficking, and other types of individual violence. These other problems have characteristics in common with the threat of individual radicalization and mobilization to extremist violence, including both the attractiveness and the challenges associated with identifying problematic individuals before they act, the nexus between online information and individual behavior, and concerns about individuals returning to the same activities that landed them in jail or prison after their release.

The complexity and controversy inherent in terrorism prevention will likely catalyze a spirited debate about appropriate programs, which agencies should and should not participate, how information is collected and shared, and the balance between the intended benefits of such programs against their unintended consequences. The research reported here seeks to contribute to policy development in this area, taking lessons learned from past efforts focused on terrorism and ideologically motivated violence as well as those aimed at other societal challenges, and exploring possible paths forward to *effective* but, potentially more importantly, *practical* federal and, by extension, national terrorism prevention efforts.

History of Countering Violent Extremism Activity at the Federal Level

In the United States, focus on CVE (and now on terrorism prevention) has increased over time. This focus has responded to changes in the threat environment, with the federal government adopting different roles and approaches to building national programs and capacities. We outline these major events in terrorism prevention in Figure 1.1. Federal efforts can be viewed as falling into three main phases: initial CVE efforts; the CVE Pilot Period, which involved three federally driven pilot initiatives in U.S. cities; and the period after the creation of the CVE Task Force and implementation of the federal grant program in fiscal year (FY) 2016, leading to the transition to terrorism prevention efforts after January 2017.

Initial U.S. CVE Efforts

Some efforts focused on CVE in the years immediately after the September 11, 2001, terrorist attacks (9/11). However, with increasing focus on threats within the United States in the aftermath of the 2009 attack at Fort Hood and the attempted bombing in Times Square in 2010, the U.S. government accelerated efforts designed to counter violent extremism in 2010. During the same time frame, the core of al Qaeda was significantly weakened, leading to its decentralization and its employment of increasingly effective social media efforts (including the activities of al Qaeda in the Arabian Peninsula's Anwar al-Awlaki). This decentralizing and moving online increased concern about homegrown violent extremism. In December 2010, the National Engagement Task Force (co-led by the U.S. Department of Homeland Security [DHS] and the U.S. Department of Justice [DOJ]) began to coordinate community engagement efforts, disseminating best practices to field-based federal components and providing a mechanism through which relevant components could communicate and coordinate.[5] In 2011, the Obama administration issued its first national-level strategy on countering violent extremism, which was focused on empowering local partners.[6] Shortly thereafter, the administration issued its first *Strategic Implementation Plan (SIP) for Empowering Local Partners to Prevent Violent Extremism in the United States* (hereafter referred to as the 2011 SIP) to implement the national-level strategy.[7] In the 2011 SIP, federal departments and agencies, including DHS; DOJ; FBI; and the National Counterterrorism Center (NCTC), which worked with the National Engagement Task Force as appropriate, were tasked with 44 specific tasks to develop or increase their ongoing CVE community engagement, capacity-building, and research and training efforts.[8]

The CVE Pilot Period

Concern over homegrown extremism and radicalization gained renewed and heightened attention after the Boston Marathon bombing in 2013. This concern was exacerbated by the rise of the Islamic State in Iraq and Syria (ISIS) in 2014, with its propaganda efforts encouraging attacks on civilians in the United States and Europe for

---

[5]   Executive Office of the President (EOP), *Strategic Implementation Plan for Empowering Local Partners to Prevent Violent Extremism in the United States*, Washington, D.C.: White House, December 2011b, p. 8; Government Accountability Office (GAO), *Countering Violent Extremism: Actions Needed to Define Strategy and Assess Progress of Federal Efforts*, Washington, D.C., GAO-17-300, April 6, 2017, pp. 8–9.

[6]   EOP, *Empowering Local Partners to Prevent Violent Extremism in the United States*, Washington, D.C.: White House, August 2011a.

[7]   EOP, 2011b.

[8]   EOP, 2011b.

Figure 1.1
Major Federal-Level Events in Terrorism Prevention/CVE, 2009–2018

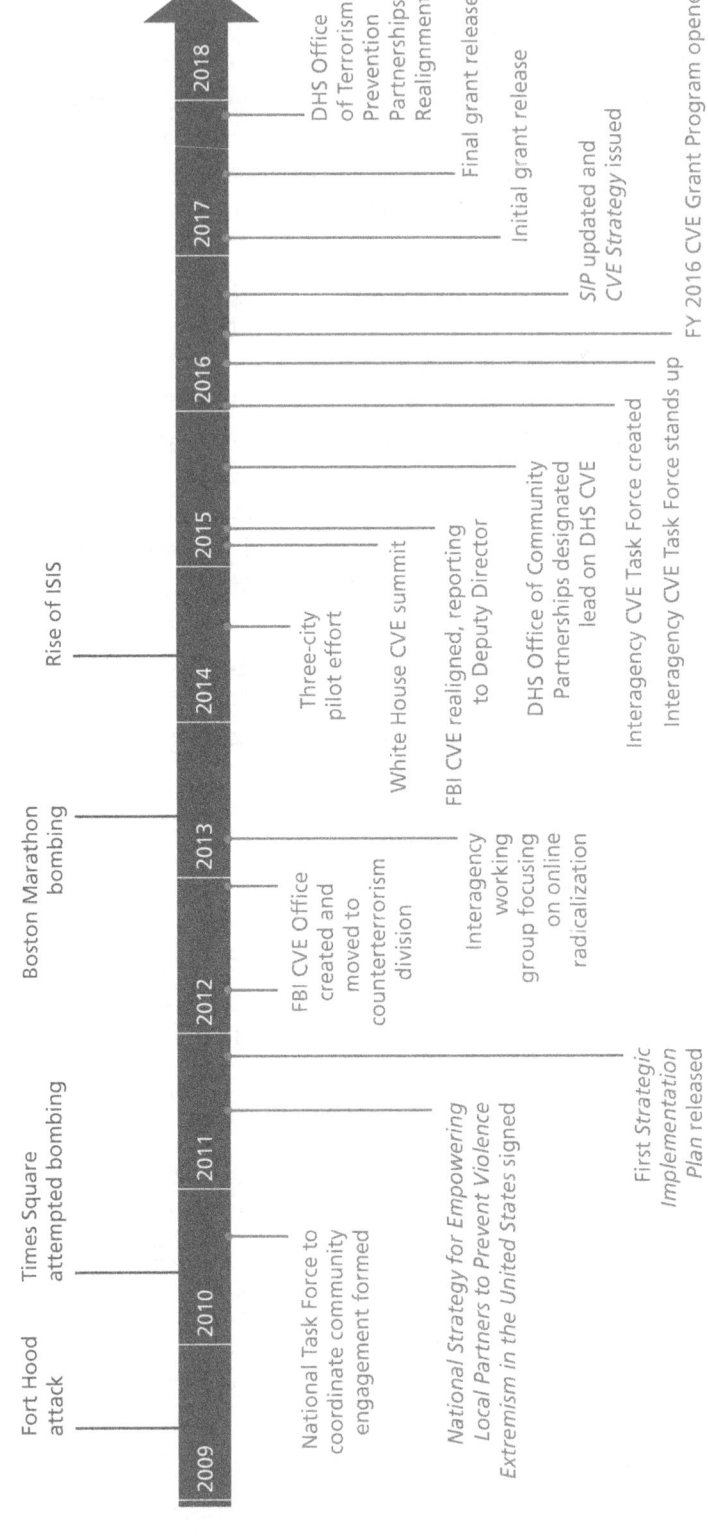

SOURCE: Adapted from GAO, 2017.

RAND RR2647-1.1

those sympathizers unable to travel to Iraq and Syria.[9] Accordingly, additional U.S. government efforts were undertaken to address the threat.

In September 2014, DOJ launched a series of pilot programs (in partnership with the White House, DHS, and NCTC) in three major regional metropolitan areas: Boston, Los Angeles, and the Twin Cities of Minneapolis and St. Paul. These cities were chosen in part based on their achievements with community engagement.[10] In February 2015, the White House held a CVE Summit led by President Obama where local, federal, and international stakeholders met to discuss CVE strategies and approaches, and where the work of the three pilot cities to develop frameworks to address issues facing their communities and prevent violent extremism were highlighted.[11] The White House also announced the first ever full-time CVE coordinator at DHS, although that role transitioned in September of that year with the creation of the DHS Office of Community Partnerships (OCP) and the appointment of its first Director and Deputy Director.[12] OCP was charged with countering violent extremism, building community partnerships and trust, and finding ways to support communities that are taking actions to discourage violent extremism.[13]

The CVE Task Force and Grant Period

In January 2016, DHS and DOJ announced the establishment of a permanent interagency CVE Task Force in recognition of the need for coordination to work more effectively across the U.S. government (especially after the stand-down of the National Engagement Task Force years earlier). The Task Force would be administratively housed by DHS, led by DHS and DOJ, and staffed with representatives from the FBI, NCTC, and other agencies.[14] Resource adjustments were made in addition to these organizational changes. In July 2016, DHS announced the FY 2016 CVE Grant Program, which was appropriated by the *Department of Homeland Security Act of 2016*

---

[9] Josh Levs and Holly Yan, "Western Allies Reject ISIS Leader's Threats Against Their Civilians," *CNN*, September 22, 2014. A note on ISIS: The organization's name transliterates from Arabic as al-Dawlah al-Islamiyah fi al-'Iraq wa al-Sham (abbreviated as Da'ish or DAESH). In the West, it is commonly referred to as the Islamic State of Iraq and the Levant (ISIL), the Islamic State of Iraq and Syria, the Islamic State of Iraq and the Sham (both abbreviated as ISIS), or simply as the Islamic State (IS). Arguments abound as to which is the most accurate translation, but here we refer to the group as ISIS.

[10] DOJ, "Attorney General Holder Announces Pilot Program to Counter Violent Extremists," press release, September 15, 2014; DOJ, "Pilot Programs Are Key to Our Countering Violent Extremism Efforts," press release, February 18, 2015b.

[11] White House, Office of the Press Secretary, "Fact Sheet: The White House Summit on Countering Violent Extremism," Washington, D.C., February 18, 2015.

[12] White House, Office of the Press Secretary, 2015.

[13] DHS, "Statement by Secretary Jeh C. Johnson on DHS's New Office for Community Partnership," DHS News Archive, September 28, 2015a.

[14] DHS and DOJ, "Countering Violent Extremism Task Force," press release, January 8, 2016.

and provided dedicated grant money to support CVE programming for the first time, namely $10 million in available funds. State, local, and tribal governments; nonprofit organizations; and institutions of higher learning could apply to help support community-led initiatives in five categories: (1) developing resilience, (2) training and engaging the community, (3) managing interventions, (4) challenging the narrative, and (5) building capacity.[15]

In October 2016, the White House issued an updated *Strategic Implementation Plan for Empowering Local Partners to Prevent Violent Extremism* in the United States (hereafter, the 2016 SIP). It focused on the implementation of 14 tasks (consolidated from 44 in the 2011 SIP) and aligned them with four CVE Task Force lines of effort: (1) engagement and technical assistance, (2) interventions, (3) communications and digital strategy, and (4) research and analysis.[16] In the last days of the Obama administration, on January 13, 2017, DHS announced an initial list of CVE grant program award recipients;[17] however, after the Trump administration took office, it undertook a review of the CVE grant program and, in June 2017, announced a revised set of award recipients following the review's completion.[18]

In November 2017 testimony to the Senate Committee on Homeland Security and Governmental Affairs, DHS Acting Secretary Elaine Duke stated that DHS was rededicating itself to *terrorism prevention* and announced that DHS was launching an end-to-end review of all CVE programs, projects, and activities to ensure that the approach to terrorism is "risk-based and intelligence-driven, focused on effectiveness, and provides the appropriate support to those on the frontlines who we rely on to spot signs of terrorist activity" and is flexible enough to address all forms of extremism, which she defined as "any ideologically motivated violence designed to coerce people or their governments."[19] In accordance with the shift to terrorism prevention, on November 30, 2017, DHS announced the renaming and transition of OCP to the Office of Terrorism Prevention Partnerships, or OTPP.[20]

---

[15] DHS and DOJ, 2016; DHS, "The Department of Homeland Security Announces the Countering Violent Extremism Grant Program," press release, July 6, 2016b; DHS, "Fact Sheet: FY 2016 Countering Violent Extremism (CVE) Grants," press release, July 6, 2016c.

[16] EOP, *Strategic Implementation Plan for Empowering Local Partners to Prevent Violent Extremism in the United States*, Washington, D.C.: White House, October 2016.

[17] DHS, "Statement by Secretary Jeh Johnson Announcing First Round of DHS's Countering Violent Extremism Grants," press release, January 13, 2017a.

[18] Amy B. Wang, "Muslim Nonprofit Groups Are Rejecting Federal Funds Because of Trump," *Washington Post*, February 11, 2017.

[19] Elaine C. Duke, "Threats to the Homeland," testimony before the Senate Committee on Homeland Security and Government Affairs, September 27, 2017, pp. 7–11.

[20] DHS, "Terrorism Prevention Partnerships," webpage, December 7, 2017b.

Study Context and Approach

In support of DHS planning and strategy development efforts, the DHS Office of Policy asked the Homeland Security Operational Analysis Center (HSOAC) to carry out a research effort to examine the state of knowledge regarding terrorism prevention organization, coordination, programming, and policy. To structure that effort, DHS defined four main lines of effort within terrorism prevention:

1. promoting education and community awareness
2. countering terrorist recruitment and propaganda
3. providing early warning of individuals who have radicalized and responding to cases of radicalization to violence
4. keeping suspects and individuals convicted of terrorism-related offenses from returning to violence.

As part of this effort, HSOAC examined past CVE efforts by DHS and its interagency partners, and explored options for terrorism prevention policy going forward.[21] The basis for this analysis was a set of research questions posed to HSOAC by DHS.

- Questions on current terrorism prevention efforts were
  - How is the department currently postured in terms of structure, personnel, resources, and programs to counter domestic and international terrorist radicalization and recruitment?
  - How is the interagency postured?
  - Is the current posture commensurate with the threat?
- Questions on potential changes to terrorism prevention efforts in the future were
  - What measures overall have proven effective in terrorism prevention?
  - How can success be best measured? What metrics should the department put in place?
  - How does the DHS approach compare with that of foreign partners, and what lessons can be learned from their terrorism prevention activities?
  - What organizational changes, if any, should DHS consider to best prevent terror threats?
  - What programmatic changes, if any, should DHS consider in the relevant terrorism prevention lines of effort?

---

[21] At the time this study was initiated, there was no set federal government definition of terrorism prevention beyond the lines of effort described here. As a result, to provide a foundation for our data-gathering and analysis, HSOAC developed a definition informed by, but not limited to, these four components. We intentionally framed our definition broadly to encompasses the full range of policy approaches used in past CVE efforts, both in the United States and internationally (as well as the literature examining those policies). It is our understanding that DHS is continuing to revise its definitions, goals, and objectives as the development of terrorism prevention policy and programming continues.

To address these questions, HSOAC carried out the following six research tasks:

- **A review of published literature on policy options, evidence for effectiveness, measures and metrics, and international terrorism prevention and CVE programs.** The literature review covered sources specific to terrorism prevention (and CVE) as well as those covering policies and interventions aimed at other problems, including violence, gangs, drugs, individual violence, and suicide. The policy problems covered in the other literature have characteristics in common with terrorism, particularly lone actor–inspired terrorism, and some policy problems have a deeper literature of intervention options and evaluation methods.

- **An examination of current DHS and interagency activities related to terrorism prevention.** HSOAC developed a picture of the current DHS and interagency posture for terrorism prevention by drawing on documentary material provided by DHS and others, the results of the literature review, and interviews with current and former members of the U.S. government and analysts who have focused on terrorism prevention and violent extremism issues.

- **Field visits with state, local, and nongovernmental organizations in five U.S. cities.** To gather perspectives and insights from individuals with experience implementing programs relevant to terrorism prevention, HSOAC visited five U.S. cities and their surrounding areas—Boston, Denver, Houston, Los Angeles, and Minneapolis–St. Paul. The cities were chosen using a set of structured criteria, which we describe in more detail in Appendix B, and in each city, the research team members held discussions with locally based federal staff, state and local government entities, community organizations, and other relevant individuals. Depending on the city, the contacted organizations included those directly involved in past CVE and current terrorism prevention efforts, as well as those with programs or activities that might provide relevant insights for terrorism and extremism-focused policy. The organizations interviewed for the study are listed in the Acknowledgments section, unless individuals requested anonymity.

- **International case studies.** HSOAC developed case studies of seven nations to identify lessons from the experiences of other countries that had designed and implemented terrorism prevention and CVE programs. The countries were selected using a set of structured criteria, which we describe in more detail in Appendix A. Case study preparation drew on the results of the literature review and focused data-gathering on the case countries. The countries examined were Australia, Belgium, Canada, Denmark, France, Germany, and the United Kingdom. The group of case studies was analyzed to identify lessons from single countries (e.g., experiences that were parallel to terrorism prevention challenges encountered by the United States or that seemed particularly relevant to U.S. circumstances) as well as lessons across groups of countries.

- **Threat analysis.** HSOAC gathered available open-source data on radicalization and terrorist activity in the United States to examine whether past CVE and current terrorism prevention efforts are commensurate to the threat posed by both internationally inspired and domestic terrorist groups and movements. Where appropriate, analysts consulted with relevant DHS and other federal organizations and staff to contribute to the study's threat picture. In addition to traditional measures of threat, HSOAC explored ways to consider the effect of terrorist threats on the country (e.g., costs associated with criminal justice responses to radicalization) and how they might inform an assessment of terrorism prevention activities.

- **Analysis and identification of policy options.** Based on the results of the different data-gathering approaches, HSOAC developed answers to the questions posed by DHS detailed above. Where necessary, the team developed a range of approaches to guide consideration of the available options.

In this research, our focus was explicitly on efforts within the United States—with our primary goal being options for DHS policies, activities, and interagency coordination to support national terrorism prevention policy—but we touched on U.S. terrorism prevention efforts abroad from the perspective of understanding coordination and potential synergy between the streams of activity.

About This Report

The results of our analysis, including the goals of terrorism prevention efforts and the range of approaches to achieve those goals, the current state of DHS and interagency activities and the policy history that got us where we are today, and options for terrorism prevention efforts going forward are documented in this report. Because of the wide range of policy tools and issues that touch on different facets of terrorism prevention, the material included in this report is fairly broad. As a result, different readers may find it useful to approach the report in different ways.

Chapters Two and Three are overarching in focus and set the stage for national terrorism prevention policies and federal investments in those policies. Specifically, Chapter Two provides an overview of the level of threat from radicalization and mobilization to violence in the U.S. homeland, framing the risk that terrorism prevention is intended to mitigate. Chapter Three presents our framework for the study, laying out the components of terrorism prevention and linking DHS's lines of effort to that framework. It then frames the larger issues surrounding terrorism prevention policy design by describing measures and metrics for success from a national perspective and laying out ten core design challenges for terrorism prevention policy that arose from the research.

Chapters Four through Eight look in depth at each of the different pieces of terrorism prevention policy that are defined and described in Chapter Three. The goal of each chapter is to focus on facets of the policy space (e.g., messaging, intervention, correctional programming) and look at specific issues, challenges, activities, and options in order to make sure that we have done justice to each piece. Thus, Chapters Four through Eight adopt a common structure. Each chapter starts by looking at the spectrum of approaches to achieving the goals of terrorism prevention in each policy area where our perspective is *national*, including—but not limited to—approaches that could be adopted by the federal government. We then describe what is currently being done in each area, both at the federal level and—to the extent it could be explored—at the state, local, private, and NGO levels as well. Each chapter ends with a discussion of federal options based on policy recommendations in the literature as well as options from other relevant policy areas, the study interviews, and HSOAC analysis.

Readers with particular interests might want to explore these chapters selectively, focusing on the subset of terrorism prevention policies relevant to them.

- Chapter Four covers online countermessaging efforts, where the national effort is the combination of both government and private-sector activities.
- Chapter Five examines broader community education, engagement, resilience, and risk factor–reduction efforts aimed at terrorism risk reduction, covering activities relevant to both community policing and public health approaches to terrorism prevention.
- Chapter Six focuses on the first requirement for intervention to address individuals at risk of perpetrating ideological violence: referring them to sources of counseling and assistance. It addresses both challenges with referral promotion and the limits of threat and risk assessment.
- Chapter Seven covers intervention programs, the most complex part of terrorism prevention. It examines the challenges that have resulted in limited current national capacity to intervene, as well as promising models based on local initiatives in the cities visited during the study.
- Chapter Eight looks at programming to address individuals who have been incarcerated for terrorism-related offenses and what is needed to support their reentry and desistance from violence.

Chapters Nine and Ten return explicitly to a federal focus. Chapter Nine discusses the specific question of resourcing terrorism prevention efforts in the United States, exploring available data on current spending on terrorism prevention. To provide points of comparison, the chapter also examines spending in other Western democracies and explores how "break-even points" for terrorism prevention might be defined based on the costs of alternative approaches to terrorism or the costs associated with small-scale terrorist attacks. Chapter Ten examines the organization of the federal interagency effort for terrorism prevention, drawing on insights from participants in those efforts over the last several years who were interviewed for this research.

Chapter Eleven concludes by bringing together a summary of options for terrorism prevention policy and programming going forward. These options seek to reverse the process outlined in the chapters in the core of the report, reassembling the pieces of the puzzle into an integrated picture of an effective and practical approach to terrorism prevention policy.

Four appendixes to the report provide more in-depth supporting material for the analysis. They are available for download at www.rand.org/t/RR2647.[22]

---

[22] Appendix A presents the international case studies, including a detailed discussion of their selection. Appendix B presents summaries of the lessons learned in each of the U.S. cities visited during the study, and includes a discussion of how the cities were chosen. Appendix C includes a more substantial discussion of measures and metrics for terrorism prevention, and Appendix D provides more detail on the spending calculations discussed in Chapter Nine.

CHAPTER TWO

The Goal of Terrorism Prevention: Examining the Level of Terrorist Threat Inside the United States

In order to design effective programs to counter violent extremism and prevent acts of terrorism within the United States, it is important to appreciate the nature and parameters of the threat those efforts are seeking to address. The history of terrorism in the United States is a long one: The country has experienced attacks originating from groups and individuals inspired by varied ideologies and pursuing vastly different goals through violence. Mass-casualty attacks resulting in the death or injury of large numbers of people have been prominent in the national experience of terrorism, for example, the 1995 bombing of the Alfred P. Murrah Federal Building in Oklahoma City that killed 168 people and the 9/11 attacks, which resulted in the death of almost 3,000 individuals and the injury of many more people, including those with long-term health issues from the attacks themselves and from subsequent response operations. 9/11 galvanized the national response to terrorism and led to the formation of DHS, which is charged with addressing not only the risk of similar large-scale attacks, but also smaller-scale and more-frequent terrorist threats. Although concern about individuals radicalizing to violence existed previously, efforts in the wake of 9/11 built the foundation for CVE in the United States and the subsequent expansion in later years.

In considering terrorism prevention policy, establishing a baseline measure of threat allows us to assess whether terrorism prevention efforts are commensurate with the level and seriousness of the threat and serves as a point of departure for conceptualizing and assessing the goals that future programming can achieve. HSOAC developed an overarching assessment of the terrorist threat in the United States based solely on open-source information, providing a starting point for considering terrorism prevention policy in response.

Definitions of Terrorism

The focus of terrorism prevention is on threats arising *in the United States*, whether they are inspired by ideologies promulgated by international actors—i.e., emerging out of international or foreign-origin terrorist threats to the country—or from domestic or homegrown sources—i.e., those without an obvious foreign nexus. Although the distinction between *geography*—whether the threat originates within the United States or comes from a foreign party entering the country—and *ideological source*—whether the source of inspiration for a terrorist actor emanates from a foreign or domestic group—might seem academic, the distinction is of practical importance because it defines the legal authorities for intelligence collection and actions that can be taken in response. Authorities for NCTC and intelligence agencies other than the FBI or the DHS Office of Intelligence and Analysis (DHS I&A), for instance, are mostly internationally focused, and thus are constrained in terms of responding to domestic terrorism. Foreign threats are more readily defined in a national security framework, where responses would reasonably involve bringing to bear the formidable capabilities of intelligence and other well-developed response options. Domestic threats are immediately more problematic, given constitutional protections of speech, association, and thought, even if individuals' activities spark concern about their potential future behavior. But because individuals—who are now connected globally through modern technology—may become radicalized by either foreign or domestic sources, maintaining distinctions can seem like drawing a blurry line. As a recent commentary in *The University of Chicago Law Review* argues:[1]

> The proliferation of modern communication technologies has caused increasing slippage between the definitions of domestic and international terrorism. For example, many homegrown terrorists are inspired by international groups to commit attacks in the United States. In many cases, the government seems to classify these actors as international terrorists based on Internet activity that ranges from viewing and posting jihadist YouTube videos to planning attacks with suspected foreign terrorists in chat rooms, thus using [the Foreign Intelligence Surveillance Act]'s formidable investigatory weapons against them.

Legal Definitions

Turning to the legal texts themselves, 18 U.S. Code Section 2331 defines *domestic terrorism* as "activities that:

(A)   involve acts dangerous to human life that are a violation of the criminal laws of the United States or of any State;

(B)   appear to be intended—

   i.   to intimidate or coerce a civilian population;

---

[1]   Nick Harper, "FISA's Fuzzy Line Between Domestic and International Terrorism," *The University of Chicago Law Review*, Vol. 81, 2014, pp. 1123–1164.

ii.   to influence the policy of a government by intimidation or coercion; or

iii.   to affect the conduct of a government by mass destruction, assassination, or kidnapping; and

(C)   occur primarily within the territorial jurisdiction of the United States."[2]

By contrast, *international terrorism* is defined as "activities that:

(A)   involve violent acts or acts dangerous to human life that are a violation of the criminal laws of the United States or of any State, or that would be a criminal violation if committed within the jurisdiction of the United States or of any State;

(B)   appear to be intended—

i.   to intimidate or coerce a civilian population;

ii.   to influence the policy of a government by intimidation or coercion; or

iii.   to affect the conduct of a government by mass destruction, assassination, or kidnapping; and

(C)   occur primarily outside the territorial jurisdiction of the United States, or transcend national boundaries in terms of the means by which they are accomplished, the persons they appear intended to intimidate or coerce, or the locale in which their perpetrators operate or seek asylum."[3]

When we compare these two definitions, it becomes clear that the key differentiating factors between international and domestic terrorism as defined in U.S. law are the territorial jurisdiction in which the attack occurred, whether the target(s) of the attack were contained within one nation or transcended national boundaries, and whether the primary area of operations of the perpetrator was constrained within one nation or transcended national boundaries. Notably, the definition of domestic terrorism does *not* specify that the perpetrator of the attack must be a U.S. citizen or an organization of U.S. origin. To further complicate matters, while there is a federal *definition* of domestic terrorism, there is no official list of domestic terrorist organizations maintained by the U.S. government. Although the FBI does keep a list of *indi-*

---

[2]   U.S. Code, Title 18, Crimes and Criminal Procedure, Part I, Crimes, Chapter 113B, Terrorism, Section 2331, Definitions, undated.

[3]   U.S. Code, undated.

viduals most wanted for domestic terrorism crimes, and both it and DHS I&A publish information on domestic extremist ideologies, the government stops short of designating actual terrorist *groups*. As such, these lists are not comparable with the U.S. State Department's "legally and procedurally proscribed . . . regimen regarding the identification of foreign terrorist organizations."[4] Moreover, domestic terrorism is not an independent chargeable federal offense under U.S. criminal law.[5]

As a result, options for responding legally to international and domestic terrorism differ, with options like charging individuals for providing material support to a designated terrorist organization available for one but not the other. However, several states have their own terrorism statutes and some—among them Alabama, Arizona, and New York—have domestic terrorism laws and have prosecuted ISIS-related cases as such when the federal government declined to or was unable to mount a case.[6] Although there has been some examination in the literature of whether there should be a separate domestic terrorism statute or whether domestic terrorism should be treated more comparably to international terrorism, a consensus on the most appropriate path has not emerged.[7] Differences in the way that the federal government in particular talks about terrorism and terrorist incidents—which have had an impact on the perceived fairness of government approaches to the issue—have been attributed to these legal discrepancies. Specifically, it is more straightforward to label incidents as terrorism if they are associated with a designated foreign terrorist organization because they have a legal charge associated with them. This means that incidents connected to jihadist groups and ideologies are more readily recognized as terrorism than are domestic threats originating from right-wing, left-wing, or other ideological sources.[8]

The Blurring of Definitions and Its Consequences

Beyond legal distinctions, the perceived scope of the threat, and, therefore, the problem set terrorism prevention should be viewed as addressing, is also shaped by which types of violent incidents are labeled as terrorism or ideological violence, and which are not. The difference between *terrorist* incidents and *terrifying* incidents that are more appropriately classified as violent or hate crimes has been a concern since the examination of terrorism as a distinct threat began several decades ago. This issue has

---

[4]   Jerome P. Bjelopera, *Domestic Terrorism: An Overview*, Washington, D.C.: Congressional Research Service, R44921, August 21, 2017, p. 57.

[5]   Daniel Byman, "Should We Treat Domestic Terrorists the Way We Treat ISIS? What Works—and What Doesn't," *Foreign Affairs*, October 3, 2017.

[6]   Byman, 2017; Wesley S. McCann and Nicholas Pimley, "Mixed Mandates: Issues Concerning Organizational and Statutory Definitions of Terrorism in the United States," *Terrorism and Political Violence*, 2018.

[7]   Byman, 2017.

[8]   For a summary of a DOJ discussion of this issue, see Ryan J. Reilly, "There's a Good Reason Feds Don't Call White Guys Terrorists, Says DOJ Domestic Terror Chief," *Huffington Post*, January 11, 2018.

reemerged in recent years in the context of large-scale mass shootings like the attack in Las Vegas in 2017. For some audiences, the decision to label certain attacks as terrorism and others as various forms of violent crime is interpreted as reflecting bias in the way this problem is approached, which in turn undermines trust and willingness to participate in terrorism prevention efforts. Academic definitions of terrorism focus on intent and largely echo the legal language above: Where criminals use violence instrumentally to meet their own needs or achieve their own goals, terrorists strategically engage in violence to send a political message and influence an audience that is broader than those directly affected by their act.[9] Even though this focus on intent seems to draw a clear line, that line can blur in practice. In some cases, blurring can occur because of uncertainty about the true motive behind an attack, particularly in cases where some combination of mental health, ideological, or personal factors might influence an individual's actions. In other cases, the nature of an attack may be clearly ideological—as is the case for racist and other types of hate crimes—but the desire to impact an audience *beyond the direct victims of the attack* may be less credible or clear.[10]

Just as is the case for differences in legal definitions, differences in what is counted as terrorism shape perceptions of the scale of threats. Incidents defined as terrorism are recorded as such by analysts and researchers tasked to study them, and therefore data are readily available about them to characterize the threat to the nation. Incidents defined as hate crimes or falling in other categories often are less systematically captured and available data about these incidents are incomplete and difficult to locate.[11] This poses a challenge for analysts seeking to understand terrorism risk to the United States and shape responses appropriately: As multiple interviewees told us during our

---

[9] For more on academic definitions of terrorism, see Bruce Hoffman, *Inside Terrorism*, New York: Columbia University Press, 2006.

[10] These differences are not unreasonably read as inferring priority and making judgments about the relative importance of different incidents—i.e., an incident labeled as terrorism is more important than one viewed as "just" a hate crime or a violent act perpetrated by a disturbed individual. This led some interviewees to argue for approaching violent incidents in a more inclusive way and reducing the distinctions drawn among them. As one community leader we interviewed put it: "Generalizing the term is important but also the messaging—preventing hate crimes is a national security issue. They are committing these crimes to destabilize communities and society. Communities are on edge [that] they are going to be attacked. The church in [specific town] wasn't a hate crime, but an act of revenge violence. When DHS looks at everything differently, you create stigmatization."

[11] In part because of the persistence of differing notions of what counts as terrorism, data on incidents of domestic terrorism and violent extremism are inconsistent—or, in the worst cases, directly contradictory. For instance, some sources include foreign-directed terrorism on U.S. soil in their calculations of total attacks and casualties, while others exclude 9/11, the largest-scale terrorist attack to happen within the United States. Different sources also classify the same incident differently: For example, the 1995 Timothy McVeigh bombing is sometimes classified as a white supremacy–driven act, while in other cases it is identified as an antigovernment attack. Other studies do not apply the same standards within their own research, dismissing some ideologically motivated shootings as murder, while classifying others as acts of terrorism, depending on the ideology in question. We have endeavored to draw our data from balanced sources and to avoid clearly biased interpretations or analyses based on selectively assembled data wherever possible.

study, uncertainty about what hate crimes count as ideological violence or terrorism makes accurately describing the relative importance of different types of threats an arduous task.[12] That uncertainty shapes how threats are discussed in policy debates, which can have a cascading effect on community trust levels, which in turn damages the effectiveness of terrorism prevention efforts.[13] These distinctions might be more academic than practical in import: One study comparing mass murderers and terrorists found that "both offenders are very similar in terms of their behaviors—this in turn suggests that similar threat and risk assessment frameworks may be applicable to both types of offenders."[14] Another study saw parallels in risk factors and behavior between suicide terrorists and school shooters.[15] And, as will become clear in later chapters, which focus on terrorism prevention program options and their implementation, approaches for responding to individuals at risk of perpetrating violence actually are quite similar and systems put in place to address one source of violence can be applied to others as well.

The Nature of the Threat

Ideological Sources of Violence

Although there has been a heavy focus on countering terrorist threats originating from al Qaeda and, subsequently, ISIS in the post–September 11, 2001, era and during military engagements in the Middle East, the United States has faced threats of terrorism and ideologically motivated violence originating from a range of sources. Figure 2.1 shows the percentage of incidents originating from different ideological sources by decade using data categories and terms from the National Consortium for the Study of Terrorism and Responses to Terrorism (START) Profiles of Individual Radicalization in the United States (PIRUS) database. The START PIRUS database examines cases of

---

[12] Interviews with federal representatives, 2018. Those interviewees also flagged differences in capacity to do analysis to navigate these complexities: Many analysts in DHS and in the broader intelligence community are focused on internationally originating terrorism issues. Within DHS, there are many fewer analysts focused on domestic violent movements. Although interviewees indicated that the FBI has significant capability and focus on domestic threats, there are still barriers to information-sharing that mean that, for DHS in particular, there is an asymmetry in the level of analytic capability focused on domestic terrorism (and, therefore, in the capabilities to navigate the complexities associated with it) versus international threats.

[13] Interviews with local representatives in multiple U.S. cities, 2018.

[14] John G. Horgan, Paul Gill, Noemie Bouhana, James Silver, and Emily Corner, *Across the Universe? A Comparative Analysis of Violent Behavior and Radicalization Across Three Offender Types with Implications for Criminal Justice Training and Education*, Washington, D.C.: National Criminal Justice Reference Service, NCJRS 249937, June 2016.

[15] Adam Lankford, "A Comparative Analysis of Suicide Terrorists and Rampage, Workplace, and School Shooters in the United States from 1990 to 2010," *SAGE Publications*, Vol. 17, No. 3, October 12, 2012, pp. 255–274.

radicalization in the United States.[16] Although the draw of some ideologies remained relatively stable over time (e.g., white supremacism), others changed significantly from decade to decade (e.g., the surge in Islamist radicalization from the 1980s to the present) or disappeared entirely (e.g., Irish Republican Army–inspired incidents).[17] Accordingly, attacks in recent years represent a range in both perpetrator ideologies and targets.

Although attacks linked to right-wing extremism have been on the rise and have reportedly been more frequent than other forms of ideologically based violence in the years since 2016,[18] data show that jihadist-inspired terrorist attacks in the United States have been more lethal than any other form of violent extremism, even when excluding the foreign-perpetrated 9/11 attacks.[19] For instance, an ADL report examining how the sources of ideologically inspired violence fluctuate from year to year found that the highest-casualty attack in 2016 was the Pulse nightclub shooting in Orlando (nominally an Islamic extremist attack), while 2017 was dominated by right-wing extremist killings.[20] Still, the attack with the highest number of fatalities in 2017 was an Islamic extremist attack: the New York City bike path attack that killed eight people.[21] In recent years, we have seen increased activity from left-wing extremist groups, with the ADL report finding that 2017 "was the second year in a row in which Black nationalists have committed murders in the United States. Combined with other violent acts by Black nationalists in recent years, these murders suggest the possibility of an emerging problem."[22] In a similar study on the sources of terrorism in the United States, a recent New America report found that, in the post-9/11 period from late September 2001 through March 2018, jihadist attacks caused 104 deaths in the United States.[23] In comparison, right-wing extremist attacks caused 73 deaths, while Black national-

---

[16] PIRUS defines its inclusion criteria as ". . . a sample of individuals espousing Islamist, far right, far left, or single-issue ideologies who have radicalized within the United States to the point of committing ideologically motivated illegal violent or non-violent acts, joining a designated terrorist organization, or associating with an extremist organization whose leader(s) has/have been indicted of an ideologically motivated violent offense." See START, *Profiles of Individual Radicalization in the United States (PIRUS) Codebook: Public Release Version*, College Park, Md., January 2018.

[17] START, "Profiles of Individual Radicalization in the United States (PIRUS)," dataset, undated(b); Anti-Defamation League (ADL), *Murder and Extremism in the United States in 2017: An ADL Center on Extremism Report*, New York, 2017.

[18] Figure 2.1 does not reflect this reported rise because data for the figure ended in 2016.

[19] ADL, 2017a; Peter Bergen, Albert Ford, Alyssa Sims, and David Sterman, *Terrorism in America After 9/11*, Washington, D.C.: New America, undated.

[20] ADL, 2017a, p. 3.

[21] ADL, 2017a, p. 3.

[22] ADL, 2017a, p. 3. In placing Black nationalist violence on the left wing of the spectrum of ideological violence, the ADL acknowledges that "that black nationalists include some adherents who don't necessarily fit neatly within that category." See ADL, 2017a, p. 9.

[23] Bergen et al., undated.

Figure 2.1
Ideological Basis for Radicalization of Individuals in the United States, by Decade

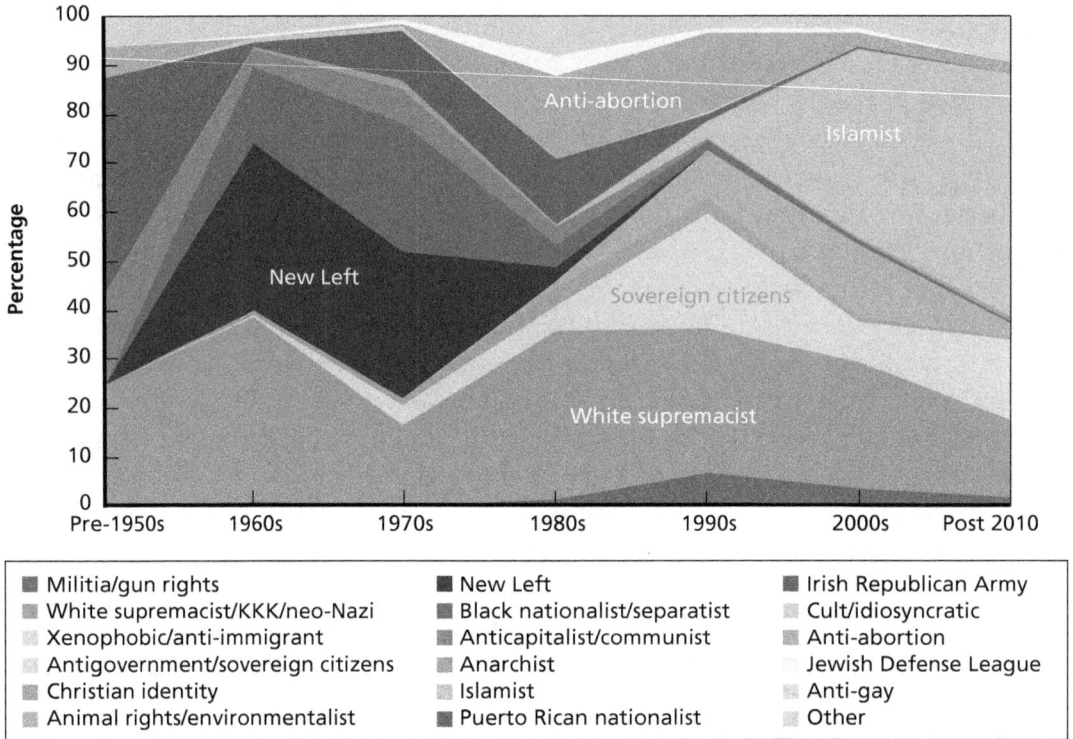

SOURCE: Data and ideology categories were drawn from the START PIRUS database. See START, undated(b).
NOTE: Data available at this writing end in 2016 and therefore do not reflect shifts occurring in 2017–2018. KKK = Ku Klux Klan.
RAND RR2647-2.1

ist attacks caused eight deaths.[24] The number of people injured in these attacks has been much higher (e.g., the Boston Marathon bombing resulted in four fatalities and 170 injuries, and the Charlottesville ramming attack killed one person and injured 19). Figure 2.2, which is drawn from the New America analysis, shows the trends in incidents resulting in fatalities from 2002 through 2018.[25] Other studies have reached similar conclusions.[26]

---

[24] Bergen et al., undated.

[25] See Figure 2.3 for the total number of terrorist incidents each year over this period, including attacks by all perpetrators, regardless of ideology.

[26] See, for example, William Adair Davies, "Counterterrorism Effectiveness to Jihadists in Western Europe and the United States: We Are Losing the War on Terror," *Studies in Conflict and Terrorism*, Vol. 41, No. 4, 2018, pp. 281–296.

Figure 2.2
Cumulative Fatalities from Terrorist Attacks in the United States, by Ideology and Year, 2000–2018

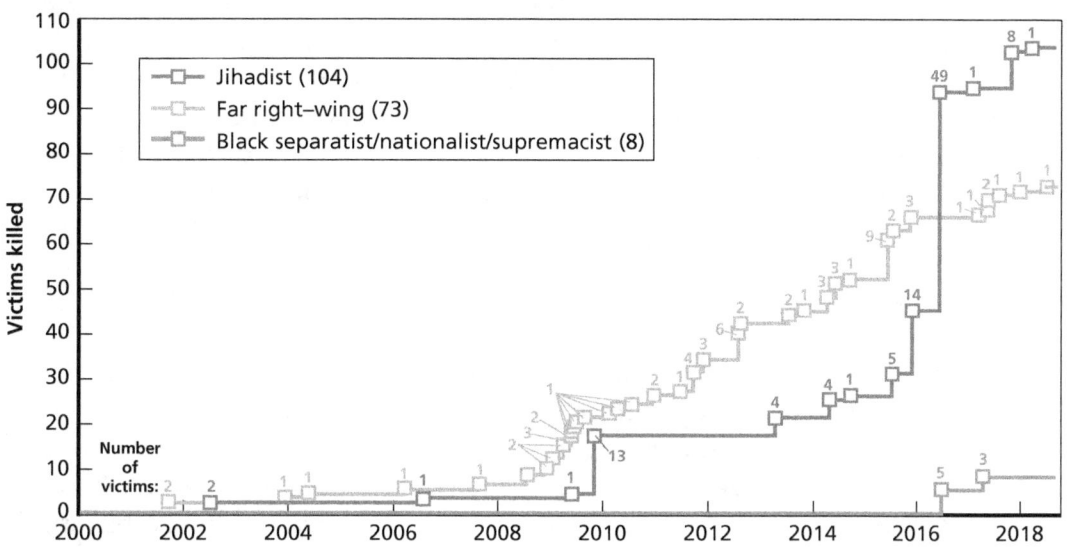

SOURCE: Adapted from Bergen et al., undated.
RAND RR2647-2.2

Available information suggests that (1) the ideologies driving radicalization vary and have shifted in relative influence over time; (2) since 9/11, jihadist-inspired attacks remain the most lethal form of terrorism; (3) right-wing attacks have been the most frequent form of violent extremism in recent years; and (4) incidents perpetrated by Black nationalist groups and left-wing anti-fascist/Antifa groups represent an emerging trend that may grow in prominence.[27] As a result, efforts to respond to the risk of such violence must be responsive to the ideological sources supporting violence and designed in a way that is not ideologically restricted; otherwise, policymakers will run the risk of developing approaches that do not stand the test of time as sources of threat shift.

Types of Threat Actors

Different types of terrorist actors can represent different levels of threat within individual ideologies. Although foreign individuals who are associated with international terrorist networks present a challenge for border security and intelligence efforts, they are outside the scope of this analysis, which focuses on terrorism prevention efforts implemented inside the United States. However, we include in our scope citizens who are returning foreign fighters—i.e., individuals with U.S. citizenship who have trav-

---

[27] Press reporting indicated that these groups have been designated as sources of domestic terrorist violence as of April 2016. See, for example, Josh Meyer, "FBI, Homeland Security Warn of More 'Antifa' Attacks," *Politico*, September 1, 2017.

eled abroad to train and fight with terrorist groups (primarily ISIS) and who have returned to the United States.[28] Returning foreign fighters are also a significant focus of CVE efforts in other countries. The majority of terrorist actors responsible for the recent attacks in the United States discussed in the previous section are homegrown violent extremists, meaning that they are solo actors who are inspired by a terrorist organization or other source of violent ideology to conduct attacks, but are not recognized members of these groups.[29] These distinctions among categories of potential terrorist actors are important because each type poses a different threat to the United States, and thus different solutions are required to respond effectively.

The Scale of the Threat

Terrorism is a low-probability, but potentially high-impact event in the United States. Although terrorist attacks in the United States are rare, the consequences of even one attack conducted by a perpetrator that "slipped through the cracks" can be severe, as terrorist attacks have an outsized impact on the target country compared with other forms of violence. The U.S. government has had an active terrorist threat bulletin in place for the nation as a whole from December 2015 until the time of this writing, reflecting concern about the potential for attack by actors across ideological sources.[30]

We examined five separate measures to characterize the scale of the threat to the United States as relevant to the design and implementation of terrorism prevention efforts: the number and frequency of attacks and plots; fatalities resulting from executed attacks; geographic distribution of all terrorist incidents in the United States; measures for radicalization intensity available in open-source data; and numbers of terrorism-related investigations, arrests, and prosecutions. The different measures have different strengths and weaknesses based on the data available to inform them. Some measures combine foreign-initiated and U.S.-based incidents, meaning that they blur the boundary between threats directly relevant to terrorism prevention initiatives and those that are tangentially related. Some also have embedded assumptions based on current responses to terrorism risk—for example, one critique of using investigation or arrest data as a measure is that counting investigations of individuals who may not actually represent real threats (an issue that we will discuss in more detail in subsequent chapters) risks allowing an existing perception of threat to bias analysis and policy

---

[28] See Brian Michael Jenkins, *The Origins of America's Jihadists*, Santa Monica, Calif.: RAND Corporation, PE-251-RC, 2017; and Richard Barrett, *Beyond the Caliphate: Foreign Fighters and the Threat of Returnees*, New York: The Soufan Center, October 2017.

[29] See Jenkins, 2017; and Mark Pitcavage, "Cerberus Unleashed: The Three Faces of the Lone Wolf Terrorist," *American Behavioral Scientist*, Vol. 59, No. 13, 2015, pp. 1655–1680.

[30] For DHS's National Terrorism Advisory System Bulletin, see DHS, U.S. Department of Homeland Security, "National Terrorism Advisory System (NTAS)," webpage, undated.

design. As a result, consideration of threat must draw on multiple types and sources of data, so the strengths of some sources can help offset limitations of others.

Number and Frequency of Attacks and Plots

The most unambiguous indicators of threat level are the number and frequency of attacks and plots, because these data points are more quantifiable than other metrics. According to open-source data, there have been 329 incidents of terrorism in the United States from all ideological sources between 2002 and 2016, with about half of these attacks occurring after 2011.[31] Over the period of 2002 to 2016, there has been an average of approximately 22 attacks per year. From 2011 to 2016, this rate increased to about 33 attacks per year (see Figure 2.3).[32] The highest frequency of attack occurred between 2010 and 2015, while the percentage of plots thwarted diminished, from approximately 82 percent in 2010–2012 to 61 percent in 2013–2015.[33]

Figure 2.3
Total Terrorist Incidents in the United States, by Year, 2002–2016

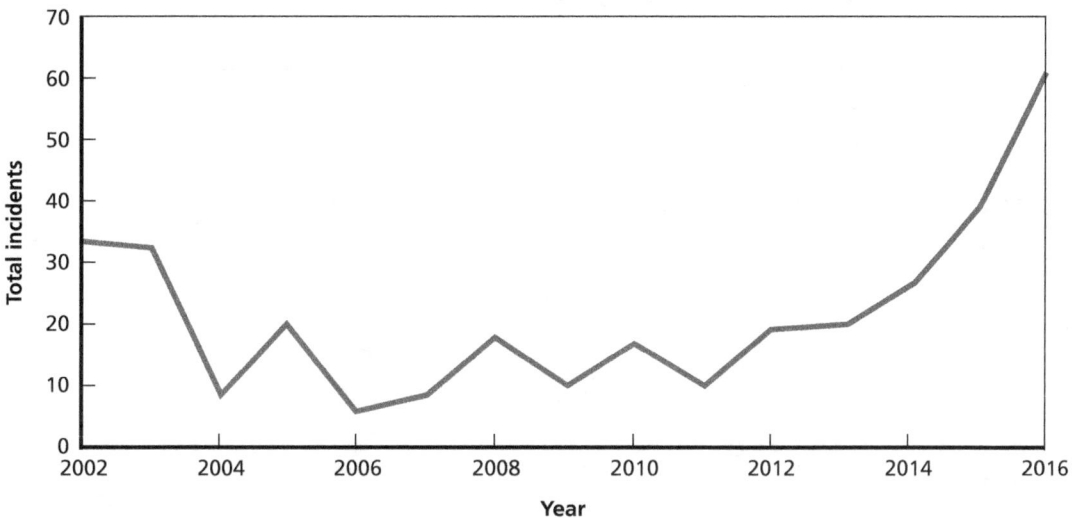

SOURCE: Data are from START, undated(a).
RAND *RR2647-2.3*

---

[31] START, "Global Terrorism Database," database, undated(a).

[32] As previously noted, because START data did not extend past 2016 at the time of this writing, Figure 2.3 does not reflect terrorist attacks occurring in 2017 or 2018, although press accounts seem to indicate that the upward trend has continued.

[33] Davies, 2018.

In absolute numbers, the scale of the terrorist threat in the United States is relatively small, particularly when compared with the severity of the threat facing some countries in Europe.[34] In recent years, however, the difference in total numbers of attacks between the United States and European countries has fallen. Figure 2.4 plots the numbers of annual attacks in all of the Western democracy case study countries examined during this study, illustrating both the general trend of attack numbers in the United States and the comparison with frequencies in other nations.

Fatalities Resulting from Terrorist Attacks

According to the New America report on terrorism in America, which provided the most up-to-date data available at the time of this study, 185 people have been killed in terrorist attacks on U.S. soil from late 2001 to 2018.[35] This corresponds to approximately ten people killed per year as a result of terrorism, although as previously noted, the number of injuries caused by attacks is usually higher than the number of fatalities. (Note that this figure does not include the fatalities incurred by the attacks of 9/11, in

Figure 2.4
Number of Attacks in Case Study Countries, 2002–2016

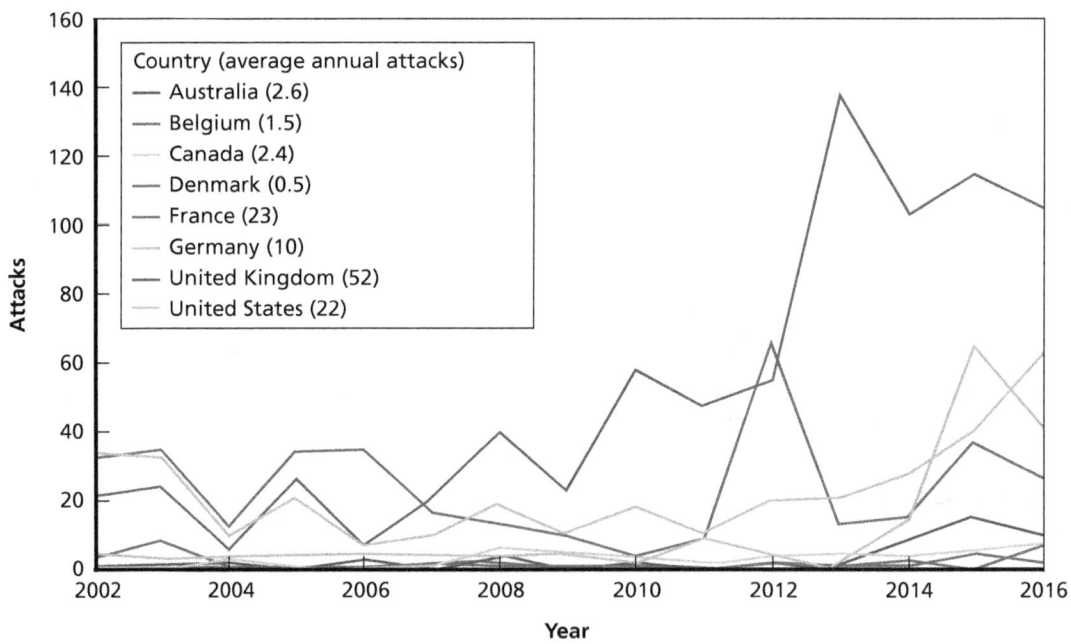

SOURCE: Data are from START, undated(a).
RAND RR2647-2.4

---

[34] Interviews with federal representatives, 2018.

[35] Bergen et al., undated.

which nearly 3,000 people were killed and hundreds more were injured).[36] Although it is beyond the scope of this effort, a fatality rate of ten people per year nationally is a much lower risk than many other sources of harm to people in the United States, both from violent and nonviolent sources.[37]

The relatively low number of total deaths associated with attacks in the United States reflects the recent rarity of large-scale, mass-casualty events since 9/11, a period during which there have been incidents with more than 100 fatalities in other countries. For example, the total number of U.S. fatalities over this period is less than the number of people killed in the March 2004 Madrid train bombings alone, in which 192 people died.[38] More recently, 137 people perished in the November 2015 Paris attacks.[39]

Geographic Distribution of All Terrorist Incidents in the United States
Terrorist incidents associated with both domestic and international terrorism have occurred in nearly every state. There does not seem to be a clear pattern for targets of terrorist attacks apart from clustering in large cities. Figure 2.5 maps START Global Terrorism Database (GTD) data (by city, state pair) for all incidents from 2002 through 2016 in the continental United States.

Radicalization Intensity
Because the goal of terrorism prevention is to respond to radicalization to violence and not to completed terrorist attacks, a better measure of threat for the purposes of designing terrorism prevention policy would be how many individuals were at risk of radicalization and mobilization to violence in different geographic areas of the country. Because many aspects of radicalization (e.g., sympathy with extremist ideas) are both legal and potentially unobservable (with the exception of the online sphere, which we discuss in later chapters), rigorous and reliable measures are not readily available. Work by multiple researchers has shown that trying to assess radicalization through polling is difficult and fraught with analytic challenges. Moreover, distinguishing between

---

[36] See Bruce Hoffman, "A Growing Terrorist Threat on Another 9/11: Al Qaeda Has Regrouped Even as the Battered Islamic State Remains Lethal," *Wall Street Journal*, September 8, 2017b.

[37] If 9/11 is included in the calculation of annual fatalities from terrorism in the United States—rather than limiting the scope to the period after those attacks, when CVE efforts in the United States were initiated and subsequently expanded (see Chapter One)—the average annual fatality rate increases to more than 170 people per year. Such a calculation clearly demonstrates the seriousness and scale of that event, but it also shows that simply averaging in such an incident with the subsequent 17 years, during which total fatalities were just more than 5 percent of the total number of individuals lost on 9/11 risks misrepresenting the intensity of ongoing terrorist risk to the country versus the risk of low-probability but high-consequence incidents.

[38] Bruce Hoffman, "The Evolving Terrorist Threat and Counterterrorism Options of the Trump Administration," *The Georgetown Security Studies Review*, February 24, 2017a, pp. 6–14.

[39] Hoffman, 2017a.

Figure 2.5
Geographic Locations of Terrorist Incidents in the United States, 2002–2016

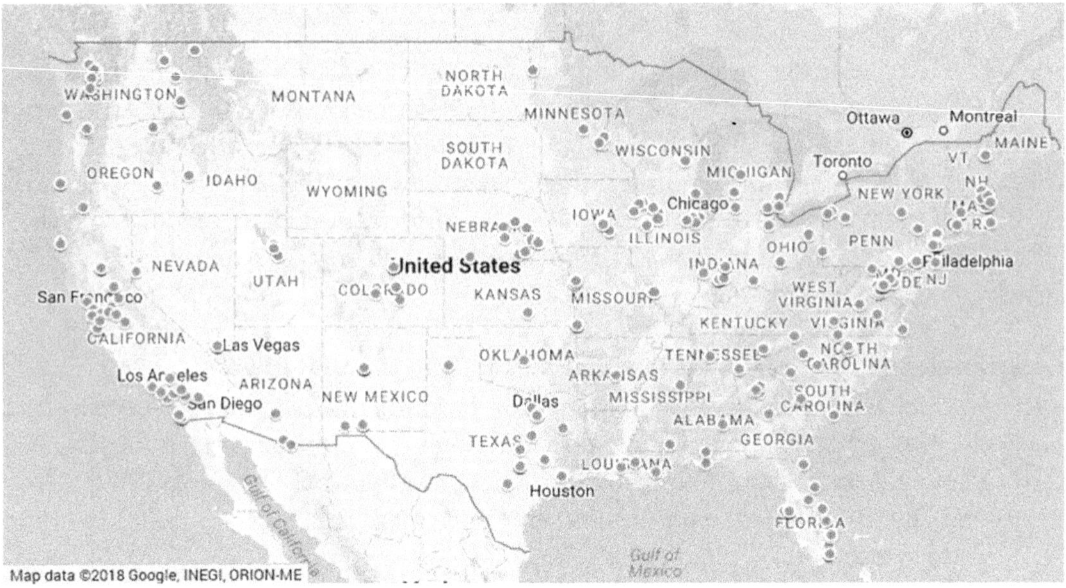

Map data ©2018 Google, INEGI, ORION-ME

SOURCE: Data are from START, undated(a).
RAND *RR2647-2.5*

people who passively or "harmlessly" hold extremist beliefs and those who are likely to act violently based on these beliefs is even more complex.[40] For example, in a recent discussion of the issue in the U.S. context, Jenkins highlighted the difference between answering abstract poll questions about sympathy for abstract ideas and actual mobilization to violence in the name of those ideas.[41]

In an effort to address the need for insight into radicalization levels and processes, the START PIRUS database gathers publicly available data on individuals who have radicalized and have taken violent or other illegal supportive action.[42] Based on those data, there were 943 such individuals in the United States in the period of 2002–2016,

---

[40] See Clark McCauley, "Testing Theories of Radicalization in Polls of U.S. Muslims," *Analyses of Social Issues and Public Policy*, Vol. 12, No. 1, 2012, pp. 296–311; Craig McGarty, Emma F. Thomas, and Winnifred R. Louis, "Are They Terrorist Sympathizers or Do They Just Disagree with the War on Terror? A Comment on Testing Theories of Radicalization in Polls of U.S. Muslims," *Analyses of Social Issues and Public Policy*, Vol. 12, No. 1, 2012, pp. 316–319; Sam Mullins, "Radical Attitudes and Jihad: A Commentary on the Article by Clark McCauley (2012) Testing Theories of Radicalization in Polls of U.S. Muslims," *Analyses of Social Issues and Public Policy*, Vol. 12, No. 1, 2012, pp. 312–315; and Clark McCauley, "Ideas Versus Actions in Relation to Polls of U.S. Muslims," *Analyses of Social Issues and Public Policy*, Vol. 13, No. 1, 2013, pp. 70–76.

[41] Jenkins, 2017.

[42] START, 2018, p. 3.

with 382 (roughly 40 percent) of these cases occurring in 2012 or later.[43] The rate of radicalization in the United States, like the increase in the overall numbers and frequency of attacks in recent years, went from an average of 56 per year from 2002 to 2011 to 76 per year from 2012 to 2016.

Figure 2.6 maps the PIRUS incidents of radicalization in 2002 through 2016 by city-state pair of the residence location of the individuals for all ideological motivations. Instances of radicalization documented in PIRUS have occurred in virtually all 50 states, in both high– and low–population density areas. Although certain communities or populations in the United States may be more susceptible to radicalization based on factors like poverty and lack of education, radicalization in the United States is more evenly distributed than it is in Europe, where identifiable pockets or neighborhoods are highly problematic and poorly integrated into the rest of society.[44]

Figure 2.6
Locations of Individual Cases of Radicalization in the Continental United States Included in the PIRUS Database, 2002–2016

NOTE: Incidents since 2000 are from START, undated(b), and are overlaid on U.S. Census population density by county.
RAND RR2647-2.6

---

[43] START, undated(b).

[44] START analysis of the characteristics of areas in which individuals who had planned and carried out violent incidents in the United States shows statistically significant differences between census tracts where their pre-

For the relevant ideologies (largely jihadist-inspired), the number of outgoing foreign fighters is a useful indicator of the level of radicalization in a given country, and the number of returning foreign fighters provides a baseline for latent terrorism threat, as that group represents a body of potentially still radicalized and trained individuals within the country. As of January 2016, some estimates indicated that ISIS had added 25,000 fighters from outside its territory to its ranks in Iraq and Syria.[45] These foreign fighters included more than 4,500 individuals from Western nations who traveled to the Middle East to fight under the ISIS banner.[46] Despite the magnitude of this threat internationally, the United States has largely been spared from this phenomenon thus far, having produced far fewer foreign fighters than other Western countries.[47] The United States also has one of the lowest rates of *returning* foreign fighters of any country. According to the most recent report from The Soufan Center, only seven foreign fighters have returned to the United States, which represents about 5 percent of those who left the United States to fight abroad.[48] Table 2.1 provides a comparison of the foreign fighter flows in our international case study countries.

Internationally, about 30 percent of the total number of foreign fighters who left to fight in Iraq or Syria have returned to their countries of origin.[49] Only a small number of those who have returned have been arrested by law enforcement in their respective countries. According to a New America study that included all foreign fighters of Western origin, about 18 percent of returnees are in custody; 40 percent have been reported dead; 3 percent have returned but have not been arrested; and the remaining 39 percent are still at large, likely in Iraq or Syria.[50] In stark contrast, the United States arrested 71 percent of its outgoing foreign fighters before they were able

---

incident activity had occurred and census tracts without such activity. Tracts with activity were lower in median income, had greater unemployment, and had a lower percentage of high school graduates. Although the differences were statistically significant, in most cases they were quite small. See START, *From Extremist to Terrorist: Identifying the Characteristics of Communities Where Perpetrators Live and Pre-Incident Activity Occurs Prior to Attacks: Report to the Resilient Systems Division, Science and Technology Directorate, U.S. Department of Homeland Security*, College Park, Md., April 2013.

[45] U.S. House of Representatives, Homeland Security Committee, *Final Report of the Task Force on Combating Terrorist and Foreign Fighter Travel*, Washington, D.C., September 2015.

[46] Lisa Curtis, Luke Coffey, David Inserra, Daniel Kochis, Walter Lohman, Joshua Meservey, James Phillips, and Robin Simcox, *Combatting the ISIS Foreign Fighter Pipeline: A Global Approach*, Washington, D.C.: Heritage Foundation, January 6, 2016.

[47] This point was reinforced by a number of interviewees at the national level, both inside and outside of government.

[48] Barrett, 2017.

[49] Barrett, 2017.

[50] Bergen et al., undated.

Table 2.1
Radicalization Intensity, by Foreign Fighter Flows

Country	Reported Number of Outgoing Foreign Fighters to Iraq and Syria	Approximate Number of Foreign Fighter Returnees	Outgoing Foreign Fighters per Capita	Returning Foreign Fighters per Capita
France	1,910	302	2.86	0.45
Germany	915	300	1.11	0.36
United Kingdom	850	425	1.29	0.65
Belgium	528	123	4.65	1.08
Canada	185	60	0.51	0.17
Australia	165	40	0.68	0.17
Denmark	145	67	2.53	1.17
United States	129	7	0.04	0.002

SOURCE: Foreign fighter statistics were drawn from Barrett, 2017, and were accurate as of October 2017.

NOTE: Per capita numbers were calculated as the relevant number of foreign fighters per 100,000 people.

to reach Iraq or Syria, and only 9 percent of American foreign fighters are still at large based on open source data.[51]

The level of threat posed by the relatively few U.S. foreign fighters who have returned is a matter of debate. On one hand, returning foreign fighters have orchestrated large-scale attacks in Europe—including the November 2015 Paris attacks and the March 2016 Brussels attacks—and some research has linked returning foreign fighters to an increased threat of terrorist attacks in their home countries.[52] Foreign fighters who remain alive abroad also can play roles as propagandists and participants in group social media campaigns for recruitment or mobilization. However, some scholars have argued that, of the foreign fighters who do return, many are "disillusioned" with the jihadi movement and their experiences abroad and thus have no intention of committing violent acts. They also argue that the act of traveling actually increases the likelihood that would-be terrorists will come to the attention of security agencies, thereby reducing their chances of successfully carrying out an attack.[53] Nonetheless, the phenomenon of ISIS foreign fighters returning to their countries of citizenship poses worrisome parallels to al Qaeda's training of foreign nationals in Afghanistan in

---

[51] Bergen et al., undated.

[52] Bruce Hoffman, "The Global Terror Threat and Counterterrorism Challenges Facing the Next Administration," *CTC Sentinel*, Vol. 9, No. 11, November/December 2016.

[53] Daniel Byman and Jeremy Shapiro, *Be Afraid. Be a Little Afraid: The Threat of Terrorism from Western Foreign Fighters in Syria and Iraq*, Washington, D.C.: Brookings Institution, Policy Paper No. 34, November 2014.

the years leading up to 9/11, which suggests that the United States should monitor the potential threats associated with returning foreign fighters carefully.[54]

Numbers of Terrorism-Related Investigations, Arrests, and Prosecutions

The numbers of investigations, arrests, and prosecutions for terrorism-related activities in the United States are useful metrics for determining both the level of radicalization and the number of potential terrorist attacks that have been prevented. According to George Washington University (GWU) researchers' data as of May 2018, there have been 161 arrests related to individuals connected to ISIS in the United States since March 2014, yielding an average of approximately 40 arrests per year.[55] For comparison, New America's survey of cases related to jihadist terrorism found that there were 408 individuals killed or charged with jihadist terrorism–related offenses between 2001 and 2018, with a high of 80 individuals charged in a single year. Over approximately the same period as that covered by the GWU data, New America's data suggest an average of approximately 45 cases per year.[56] As a result, depending on the relative contributions of other ideological sources of violence (e.g., applying data from PIRUS discussed above), these sources would suggest average numbers of incidents between 50 and 100 per year.

More-recent public statements and testimony by members of federal law enforcement and the intelligence community claim higher numbers of arrests and ongoing investigations. For instance, 2017 testimony by FBI Director Christopher Wray cited a higher number than the academic literature of 176 arrests in the approximately 12 months preceding his remarks.[57] In March 2018, Director Wray stated that there were 1,000 open jihadist-inspired homegrown extremist investigations as well as another 1,000 domestic investigations focused on threats from other ideologies.[58]

---

[54] Bruce Hoffman, Edwin Meese, III, and Timothy J. Roemer, *The FBI: Protecting the Homeland in the 21st Century: Report of the Congressionally-directed 9/11 Review Commission*, Washington, D.C., March 2015.

[55] GWU, Program on Extremism, "GW Extremism Tracker: The Islamic State in America," infographic, May 7, 2018a.

[56] Bergen et al., undated.

[57] Christopher A. Wray, "Responses to Congressional Questions: Homeland Security Threats," video testimony before the Senate Homeland Security and Governmental Affairs Committee, video, September 27, 2017a; Christopher A. Wray, "Threats to the Homeland: Statement of Christopher A. Wray, Director, Federal Bureau of Investigation," testimony before the Senate Homeland Security and Government Affairs Committee, September 27, 2017b.

[58] FBI Director Wray noted:

> We have around a thousand what I would call homegrown violent extremists which are basically people here inspired by the various global jihadist movements to commit terrorist acts. We have about another thousand domestic terrorism investigations which cover the water front from everything from white supremacists to all the way to anarchists to everything in between. So these are very active investigations. We have them in all 50 states. This is no longer something that is just in major cities—it's in small towns.

Investigative activity is shaped by the perceived level of threat in addition to the actual level of threat, as increased tips to law enforcement would result in a spike in investigative activity. Indeed, a majority of individuals who are the subject of terrorism investigations never commit an attack and are never arrested for ideologically motivated activity. As such, the number of investigations does not necessarily provide an independent measure of threat. However, investigations divert law enforcement resources from responding to other types of violence and crime, and thus can pose a different kind of threat to overall domestic security. Threat assessment based on investigative activity has also been criticized as potentially being distorted if aggressive investigation techniques (e.g., confidential informants) cause plots to progress further than they would have otherwise (as discussed elsewhere in this document), and therefore simultaneously increase perceived threat and damage the community trust needed to identify and respond to genuine threats.

Conclusion

At present, the level of threat from terrorism in the United States is significant but not disproportionate in frequency or scale to other security and nonsecurity risks that the country faces. The number of terrorist incidents occurring in the country per year from all ideological sources is relatively low. The consequences of those incidents, while concerning, are of commensurate scale—with an average of approximately ten Americans killed per year in terrorist incidents since 9/11.[59] This conclusion is driven in part by the relative scarcity of individual attacks that have killed large numbers of people in the United States. The United States has had incidents with more than ten fatalities since 9/11, including the San Bernardino and Pulse nightclub attacks. However, the United States has not had to endure multiple attacks killing hundreds of people, as has been the case for other nations in recent years, which has helped to limit the average annual burden of terrorism for the country. However, the total number of terrorist incidents and their cumulative lethality—as well as the number of investigations and arrests for terrorism-related offenses—have been increasing in recent years. But, from

---

FBI Director Christopher Wray, quoted in Pete Williams, "FBI Chief on Biggest Threats: China Spies, Terror, Rise in Violent Crime," *NBC News*, March 21, 2018. He also cited another approximately 1,000 ISIS-related investigations, which if originating internationally might fall outside the scope of terrorism prevention or CVE activities.

[59] Several of our interviewees emphasized keeping the level of terrorist threat—which has fortunately been comparatively low—in the United States in perspective when considering responses. As one federal law enforcement interviewee summed it up:

> Let's just be honest, the last year I was in [federal law enforcement], I think there were 19–21 people who had been killed in the U.S. as a result of terrorism and some overseas for a total of less than 50. If you compare this to homicide in the city of Chicago. . . . I almost feel like we have turned terrorism into an unrealistic thing. There is an expectation we have zero terrorist incidents per year, and one is a failure.

the perspective of an individual state or locality, which will experience only a fraction of the total threat facing the nation as a whole, terrorism will always be one among a set of risks that local government and law enforcement agencies must address, including crime, accidents, and weather or natural disasters.

The level of threat the United States has experienced is also a testament to the effectiveness of law enforcement responses, as reflected in the investigation and arrest numbers discussed above.[60] However, as we will discuss in Chapter Nine, that success has not been without significant costs—costs that terrorism prevention programming could minimize, both for the country and for individuals affected by investigative activity. As a result, the consensus across our interviews (at both the national and local levels) was that the current terrorist threat to the United States is genuine but manageable, and that terrorism prevention could help to respond in more efficient and practical ways.

As with any consideration of threats and risks based on historical data, a reasonable question to ask is whether threats are likely to change going forward, prompting shifts in views about their gravity and appropriate responses to them. Our discussions with government organizations and our review of the literature did not point to trends that would change the nature or intensity of the threat in the United States in the near to midterm. Nonetheless, all interviewees added the appropriate caveat that it is difficult to project such changes with any degree of certainty, and that past difficulties in projecting trends in terrorism over even short timelines meant that any prediction had to be made with an appropriate level of analytical modesty.[61]

---

[60] Given the challenges discussed in the opening of this chapter relative to definitions and the types of ideologically related crime that are counted as terrorism, one federal interviewee emphasized that there is a real need for objective, apolitical, and accurate numbers describing threat.

[61] Interviews with federal intelligence representatives and analysts outside government, 2018. For example, an outside analyst who supported the current threat from ISIS framed this issue as follows: "Knowing where the threat is going to be five years from now is hard. You're trying to stop some people from engaging in terrorism, but who? The Islamist threat is the right focus now, but will that be true in five years? [We] don't know what the next wave will be." Similar arguments have been made in the literature, for example, Nicholas J. Rasmussen, "Threats to the Homeland," Hearing Before the Senate Committee on Homeland Security and Governmental Affairs, Washington, D.C., September 27, 2017.

CHAPTER THREE
How Does Terrorism Prevention Policy Seek to Reduce Risk?

What is the role that terrorism prevention policy serves in addressing the risk of individuals radicalizing and mobilizing to violence? Because terrorist violence is an illegal act and some activities during mobilization and preparation for violence are also against the law, the country *could* choose to rely solely on traditional law enforcement to address this risk. To date, such law enforcement activity has been a major—and, some argue, the primary—element of the U.S. national response to terrorism risk, including both traditional law enforcement tools of arrest, prosecution, and incarceration and the post-9/11 transition in focus to more intelligence-led and national security–focused policing.

As a result, addressing the specifics of future terrorism prevention policy requires clarity about what it is and what it is intended to do, as well as clearly distinguishing it from traditional law enforcement approaches to responding to other crime. The need for such clarity was raised in a number of the discussions during the project, both by advocates of such efforts who felt that past failures to appropriately frame what CVE really meant had hurt implementation activities, and by critics of CVE, some of whom had interpreted the lack of clarity as meaning that it, and, by extension, terrorism prevention, was not actually distinct from coercive and enforcement-based strategies. These concerns have resulted in strains of policy debate since the initial CVE efforts began in the United States that have explored whether efforts to address ideological violence should be reframed as public health interventions or as elements of community policing.[1]

---

[1] For more on public health interventions, see Stevan Weine, David P. Eisenman, Janni Kinsler, Deborak C. Glik, and Chloe Polutnik, "Addressing Violent Extremism as Public Health Policy and Practice," *Behavioral Sciences of Terrorism and Political Aggression*, Vol. 9, No. 3, 2017, pp. 208–221; and Shannon N. Green and Keith Proctor, *Turning Point: A New Comprehensive Strategy for Countering Violent Extremism*, Washington, D.C.: Center for Strategic and International Studies, November 2016. For community policing, see David Schanzer, Charles Kurzman, Jessica Toliver, and Elizabeth Miller, *The Challenge and Promise of Using Community Policing Strategies to Prevent Violent Extremism: A Call for Community Partnerships with Law Enforcement to Enhance Public Safety, Final Report*, Durham, N.C.: Triangle Center on Terrorism and Homeland Security, Sanford School of Public Policy, Duke University, January 2016; and recommendations in Stevan Weine and William Braniff, *Report on the National Summit on Empowering Communities to Prevent Violent Extremism*, Washington, D.C.: Office of Community Oriented Policing Services, 2015. Note that there have been cautions regarding viewing

Although a range of definitions exist for what policies in this area are intended to do (generally discussed using the terminology of CVE),[2] for the purposes of our work, we constructed a baseline definition that drew on elements from definitions in the literature and from discussions with interviewees:

> Terrorism prevention policy seeks to reduce the incidence of violence inspired by ideology and extremist causes, and to expand the range of options for responding to that risk. It includes efforts—either alone or in collaboration—by such government entities as law enforcement, social services, and mental health agencies; non-governmental organizations; civil society; community groups; and the private sector.

> By building options beyond the traditional criminal justice tools of arrest, prosecution, and incarceration—and involving organizations and capabilities outside the organizational boundaries of government—terrorism prevention programs seek to enable action earlier, before individuals have taken illegal actions that could pose imminent danger and have lasting consequences both for themselves and others.[3]

Our definition focuses specifically on violence rather than beliefs because individuals' freedom of beliefs, religion, and political views is protected.[4] Extremity of belief—i.e., radicalization of viewpoint versus radicalization to violence[5]—is also not the point because, in strong democracies, individuals and movements with beliefs that

---

CVE and, by extension, terrorism prevention, as simply part of community policing out of concern of situating too strongly in the law enforcement sphere. See Bipartisan Policy Center, National Security Preparedness Group, *Preventing Violent Radicalization in America*, Washington, D.C., June 2011.

[2]   Others in the literature have used other terminology, such as "preventing and countering violent extremism," see Matthew Levitt, ed., *Defeating Ideologically Inspired Violent Extremism: A Strategy to Build Strong Communities and Protect the U.S. Homeland*, Washington, D.C.: Washington Institute for Near East Policy, No. 37, March 2017.

[3]   For clarity, this definition of terrorism prevention was developed by HSOAC, and informed by the DHS lines of effort discussed in Chapter One, but explicitly seeks to reflect a broader national perspective on terrorism prevention. We were informed by both past literature and debate surrounding CVE, in which definitions were central. As a result, definitions of this policy area produced or used by multiple entities—not only DHS, but also individual law enforcement organizations, civil society organizations, and others—could be narrower than our intentionally inclusive framing. It is our understanding that DHS is continuing to revise its definitions, goals, and objectives as the development of terrorism prevention policy and programming continues.

[4]   In the lexicon of the academic and policy literatures, we are therefore focusing on *disengagement* or *demobilization* when considering the goals of government efforts, rather than *deradicalization*. However, because we are considering the placement of those government efforts in the broader context of a national terrorism prevention, efforts by others (e.g., religious leaders, NGOs, families) might attempt to change individuals' views, and government efforts might involve linkages to such entities (e.g., participation of NGOs or religious leaders as part of a corrections reentry counseling program).

[5]   See, for example, discussion in J.M. Berger, *Making CVE Work: A Focused Approach Based on Process Disruption*, International Centre for Counter-Terrorism—The Hague, May 2016.

differ considerably from the status quo are a part of a healthy political and social dynamic, and can be drivers of innovation and change.[6] Our definition also explicitly distinguishes terrorism prevention from the operational and enforcement actions taken by law enforcement organizations, although this is not to say that law enforcement or criminal justice agencies will not be central to terrorism prevention efforts. It is not government-centric, since some important options to enable early action are nongovernmental, reflecting where it is most practical to build capability and the real and important civil liberties concerns inherent in governmental intervention with individuals who have not committed any crime. The definition also reflects the complexity that terrorism prevention is threat- and violence-focused, but more closely resembles service provision in response to a social problem than it does sharp-edged counterterrorism.[7]

The full range of national—not just federal, or governmental—terrorism prevention initiatives can therefore be viewed as falling along a spectrum.[8] At one end are *indirect and community-centered efforts* that may be entirely outside of government and may not even be focused on terrorism risk. An example of such an initiative is a counseling program managed by a community or religious organization aimed at youth issues including extremism and violence. Other indirect or community terrorism prevention approaches—many of which fall under the rubric of public health approaches to extremist violence—are focused on addressing risk factors in society rather than on specific individuals at risk of violent behavior. At the other end of the spectrum are *direct and government-driven efforts* in which government agencies and law enforcement are involved or even central to terrorism prevention efforts. An analogous exam-

---

[6] One example of extremity of viewpoint cited in project interviews was the civil rights movement in the 1960s, where beliefs different from the status quo drove positive societal change.

[7] In the policy literature surrounding CVE, there have been various labeling and conceptual debates about the value of framing it as a public health activity versus a law enforcement or security-focused activity. For example, see the discussion in Weine, Eisenman, and Kinsler et al., 2017. In our work and in this definition, we do not take either position, in part because of a strong message from interviewees that these activities need to be locally defined, but also because it is not clear how much a "disciplinary label redefinition" of the activity would address the policy challenges in this area. However, much of the way we have defined terrorism prevention efforts—including explicitly distinguishing them from law enforcement counterterrorism activities—is consistent with public health approaches to the issue.

[8] One example of a national (rather than federal) initiative centered on local government (which was initiated after the attack in Charlottesville, Va.) is the ADL-managed compact of mayors committed to taking steps locally with respect to extremism, hate, and bias crimes, including activities that readily link to the policy framework described in this document. For more information, see ADL, "Responding to Charlottesville, U.S. Conference of Mayors and ADL Join on Action Plan to Combat Hate, Extremism and Discrimination," press release, August 18, 2017b. The United States Conference of Mayors also had its own initiative related to these issues, which focused broadly on partnership with relevant groups (including the Strong Cites Network and ADL) and elected leaders from Canada, the United Kingdom, and Germany, as well as on "coordinated effort to align and work with corporations, community groups, and the philanthropic sector." United States Conference of Mayors, "Taking Action Against Hate Crime and Violent Extremism by Supporting Robust City Partnerships with the Private Sector for the Safety and Cohesion of Our Societies," Boston, Mass., 86th Annual Meeting, June 8–11, 2018.

ple at that extreme—but with the same goal as the indirect or community counseling program above—would be a police-managed program that connects troubled youth who come into contact with law enforcement with counseling efforts in an effort to change their behavior and keep them out of the criminal justice system.

In areas or communities where trust of government or law enforcement is limited, indirect and community-centered options may increase the chance that at-risk individuals will be referred for help. In areas where trust and collaboration between the public and government are high, there may be limited barriers to reaching out and programs inside and outside government could collaborate or even merge.

Building a Framework for Terrorism Prevention Policy

Although DHS's four lines of effort specified at the initiation of this study—promoting education and community awareness; countering terrorist recruitment and propaganda; providing early warning of individuals who have radicalized and responding to cases of radicalization to violence; and keeping individuals convicted of offenses from returning to violence—provided an initial breakdown of the different components of terrorism prevention programming, we mapped those lines of effort to a simple process model of radicalization for the purposes of this study.

The process of radicalization and mobilization to violence for individuals has been the focus of considerable research attention and policy debate for many years.[9] Early attempts to understand the process posited well-defined steps and a progression of individuals from their starting point through adoption of extremist views and increasing levels of commitment culminating in violence. Different models have focused on different contributors to or risk factors of radicalization, ranging from the ideological to the individual, and have ascribed varied relative weights to different factors. Models have also disagreed on how deterministic or predictable the radicalization of an individual is, and therefore whether concepts like "an individual on the path to violence"

---

[9]   Academic researchers have pointed out that the concept of radicalization is a relatively new one, even within the field of terrorism research:

> No one talked of the [Irish Republican Army] being radicalized, or Shining Path, or [the Basque terrorist group] ETA or the Red Army Faction—though they all certainly were by our modern understanding. After 9/11 it became awkward to talk about people "becoming" terrorists, "joining" terrorist groups, or being "recruited." Those terms were too banal, too ordinary. Ordinary terms might imply ordinary processes, and worse, ordinary solutions (Andrew Silke, "Terrorists, Extremists and Prison: An Introduction and Critical Issues," in Andrew Silke, ed., *Prisons, Terrorism and Extremism: Critical Issues in Management, Radicalization and Reform*, New York: Routledge, 2014c, p. 7).

This echoes ideas expressed by some of our national-level interviewees about the downsides of viewing terrorism prevention as something too distinct from overarching violence prevention activities.

have any objective meaning.[10] More-recent studies of radicalization paint a more complex and diverse picture, noting the potential influence of many factors simultaneously, even for individuals nominally radicalized by the same ideological cause. Timelines can differ considerably. Even the role of ideology and extremism is complicated: A person can be an extremist without being violent (which is not only legal but constitutionally protected in the United States),[11] and can be violent in the name of a cause without being particularly fervent regarding—or without correctly understanding—the tenets of the cause itself.[12] Studies by the FBI have gone even further, pointing out that even when individuals are *making threats*, it is not necessarily definitive: "[M]any persons who make threats do not pose a threat."[13]

Given our current understanding of radicalization processes—and the near certainty of great diversity across individuals and among different causes and ideologies that might inspire violence—we chose to use a very basic model to anchor our work. We thus divided the people involved in radicalization processes into three relevant populations (see Figure 3.1):

- vulnerable population—i.e., all the people who might radicalize to violence
- individuals who are radical of thought but may or may not become violent[14]

---

[10] This lack of a well-defined and readily predictable path to violence and, therefore, a lack of clear markers for individuals at risk of violence apart from individuals who may be adopting radical ideas has been a core part of critiques of CVE that argue that it lacks scientific basis. See Brennan Center for Justice, *Countering Violent Extremism: Myths and Fact*, undated.

[11] Horgan, Shortland, and Abbasciano have also explored different types of involvement in terrorism rather than viewing it as a binary distinction (John G. Horgan, Neil Shortland, and Suzzette Abbasciano, "Towards a Typology of Terrorism Involvement: A Behavioral Differentiation of Violent Extremist Offenders," *Journal of Threat Assessment and Management*, Vol. 5, No. 2, 2018, pp. 84–102).

[12] For a comprehensive review of both historical and recent literature, see Daniel Koehler, *Understanding Deradicalization: Methods, Tools and Programs for Countering Violent Extremism*, New York: Routledge, 2017, Chapter 3; Mohammed Hafez and Creighton Mullins, "The Radicalization Puzzle: A Theoretical Synthesis of Empirical Approaches to Homegrown Extremism," *Studies in Conflict and Terrorism*, Vol. 38, 2015; Clark McCauley and Sophia Moskalenko, "Mechanisms of Political Radicalization: Pathways Toward Terrorism," *Terrorism and Political Violence*, Vol. 20, 2008; Clark McCauley and Sophia Moskalenko, "Toward a Profile of Lone Wolf Terrorists: What Moves an Individual from Radical Opinion to Radical Action," *Terrorism and Political Violence*, Vol. 26, 2014; Gary LaFree, Michael A. Jensen, Patrick A. James, and Aaron Safer-Lichtenstein, "Correlates of Violent Political Extremism in the United States," *Criminology*, Vol. 56, No. 2, 2018; Katarzyna Jasko, Gary LaFree, and Arie Kruglanski, "Quest for Significance and Violent Extremism: The Case of Domestic Radicalization," *Political Psychology*, Vol. 38, No. 5, 2017; and Angela McGilloway, Priyo Ghosh, and Kamaldeep Bhui, "A Systematic Review of Pathways to and Processes Associated with Radicalization and Extremism Amongst Muslims in Western Societies," *International Review of Psychiatry*, Vol. 27, No. 1, February 2015

[13] FBI Behavioral Analysis Unit, *Making Prevention a Reality: Identifying, Assessing, and Managing the Threat of Targeted Attacks*, undated, p. 15.

[14] For a discussion of individuals who are radical of thought but may or may not become violent, see Koehler, 2017, pp. 74–80.

- individuals actually involved in attempted attacks (denoted by the red starburst in the figure).

The three populations are connected by two processes:

- radicalization to extremism (which, again, may or may not mean a greater chance of the individual becoming violent)
- mobilization to violence.

Given the level of threat in the United States, each successive population is much smaller than the population preceding it, with only a small percentage of any vulnerable population radicalizing and only a percentage of that population escalating to violence.[15] This basic model is not specific to any given ideology or population.[16]

Because different points of the process involve distinct terrorism prevention activities, we divided the process into three phases:[17] *early*, which focuses more broadly on vulnerable populations either to increase resistance to radicalization or reduce factors

Figure 3.1
Radicalization and Mobilization States, with Phases of Terrorism Prevention

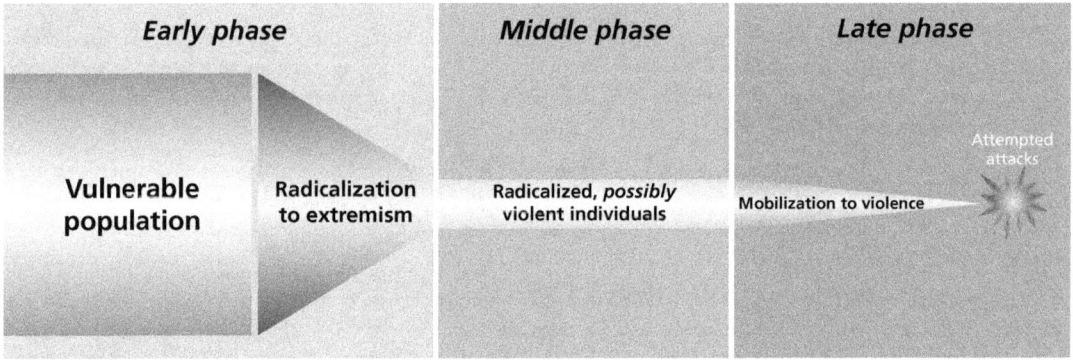

RAND RR2647-3.1

like extremist messages in the environment; *middle*, which focuses on individuals at

---

[15] See the discussion in Justin Snair, Anna Nicholson, and Clair Giammaria, *Countering Violent Extremism Through Public Health Practice: Proceedings of a Workshop*, Washington, D.C.: National Academies Press, 2017.

[16] Based on some of the feedback that we received from interviewees, this basic "transition to a potentially violent state" and then some subset of individuals from that state carrying out violence is also similar to nonideological violence, including school shootings and some types of workplace violence.

[17] These phases are parallel to those used in Levitt (2017) to divide the CVE policy space, although there the terminology used is *prevention* (our early phase), *intervention* (our middle phase), and *rehabilitation/reintegration* (our late phase).

risk of carrying out violence; and *late*, which addresses efforts aimed at individuals who have broken the law and are already involved in the criminal justice system.[18]

Early-Phase Terrorism Prevention

What we have labeled early phase terrorism prevention captures a set of policies that seeks to reduce the rate at which individuals from a vulnerable population become radicalized, and therefore are at risk of mobilization to violence. Policies relevant to this phase fall into DHS's first two lines of effort that were defined at the initiation of the study—i.e., promoting education and community awareness and countering terrorist recruitment and propaganda—and are mapped onto the relevant portion of the framework in Figure 3.2. We cover these activities in more detail in Chapters Four and Five.

Activities in this space can be very focused and terrorism-specific, like the delivery of education programming intended to delegitimize messages disseminated by extremist groups to make them less persuasive or counter those messages directly (e.g., efforts by internet and social media firms to remove extremist content from their platforms). In our model, these activities are aimed at the process of radicalization that links members of the vulnerable population to the next group of radicalized, potentially violent individuals. These types of efforts can include government but also rely on actions by the private sector (particularly in the online space), NGOs, and others.

To achieve the goal of limiting individual radicalization, programs could also focus on the vulnerable population to address broader factors that might facilitate individual radicalization.[19] For example, if a risk factor for radicalization is a sense of grievance or disconnection from the community, programs aimed at addressing those grievances or promoting community strength would be another route to reducing radicalization.[20] Arguments for this more indirect, broader-framed approach have come from the public health field, which largely views ideologically motivated violence as

---

[18] Koehler (2017) has an alternative formulation distinguishing prevention (roughly our early phase) from intervention (which includes our middle and late phases, as well as counternarrative efforts, which we place in the early phase). In his comprehensive review of relevant programming, he breaks apart programs by nongovernmental versus governmental status, whether they are active or passive (e.g., are delivering programming or waiting for people to come to them), and whether they include ideological components. For our analysis, we do not subdivide these different categories within our phases but discuss some of the distinctions between them as we present current programming and future options.

[19] For example, the Boston strategy developed to guide the city's CVE efforts in 2015 and 2016 focused on (1) "building trust and earning social support," (2) "fostering civic engagement and cultural awareness," (3) "treat[ing] the root causes of violence and violent extremists by improving conditions to the extent that people can reach their full potentials." This strategy is described in Snair, Nicholson, and Giammaria, 2017, p. 83.

[20] Several sources reviewed a wide variety of potential risk factors for radicalization to violence. See, for example, David P. Eisenman and Louise Flavahan, "Canaries in the Coal Mine: Interpersonal Violence, Gang Violence, and Violent Extremism Through a Public Health Prevention Lens," *International Review of Psychiatry*, Vol. 29, No. 4, 2017; and Ross Owens, Jonathan Evans, Jennifer Foley, and Ji Sun Lee, *Countering Violent Extremism—Developing a Research Roadmap: Literature Review*, North Triangle Park, N.C.: RTI International, April 2016. In a risk-factor approach, the presence of more risk factors would increase the chance of an individual radicalizing.

Figure 3.2
Radicalization and Terrorism Prevention Framework, with DHS's Terrorism Prevention Lines of Effort

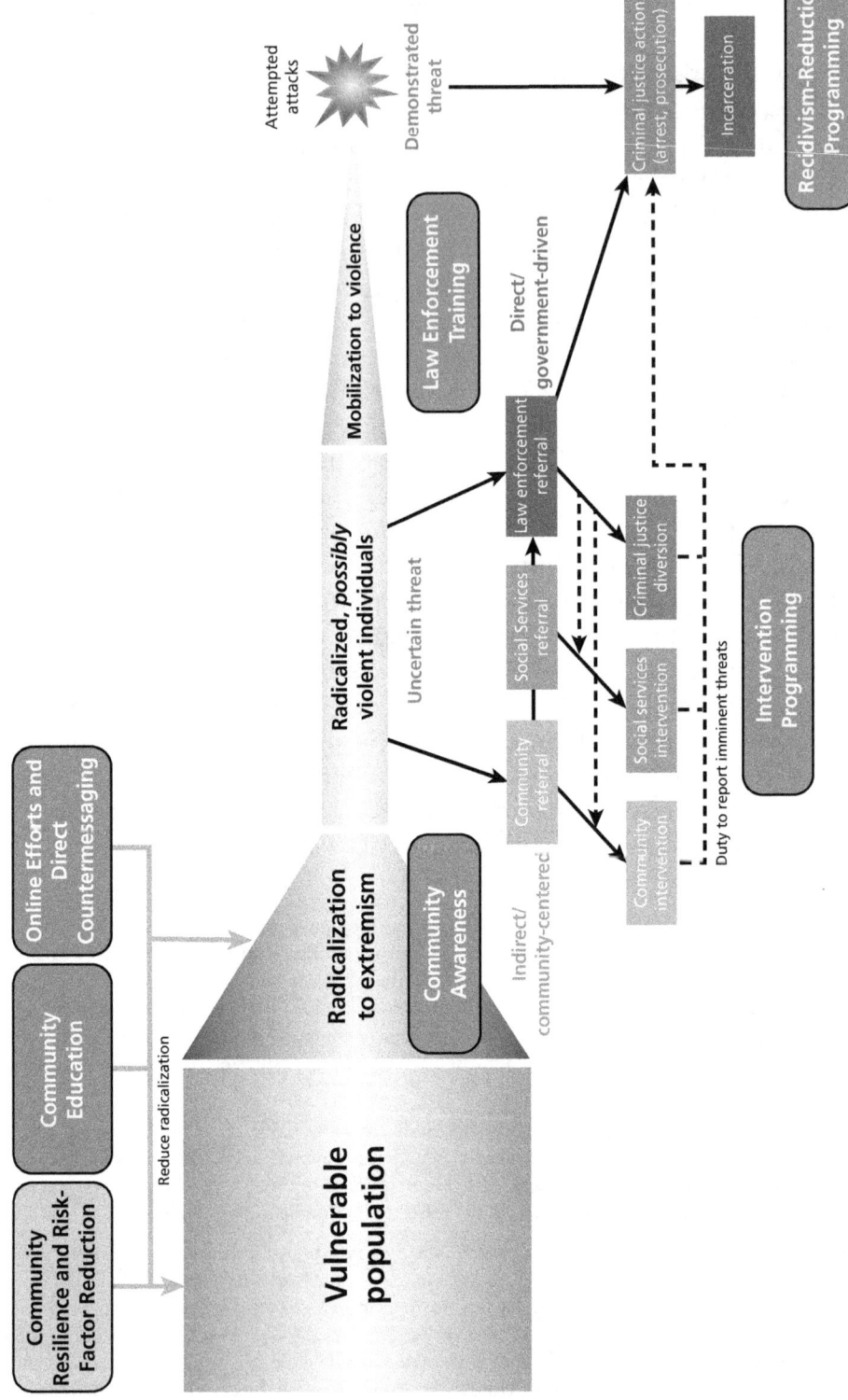

a type of public health concern.[21] In the language of public health, such efforts constitute "primary prevention" efforts aimed at preventing a problem before it arises.[22] Such programming could be aimed at making medical and mental health treatment resources available, providing broad youth services, increasing connection and investment between communities and government (including police), and other "good governance–type" activities. Such efforts also are a less controversial route to addressing terrorism risk, because their breadth reduces potential stigma associated with terrorism and they can be clearly separated from any enforcement-focused activity.[23] Given the potential breadth of these programs, the types of entities and actors both inside and outside government that could be involved are also very broad.

Although such broadly focused programming can help reduce terrorism risk, there is not consensus on the extent to which such activities should be defined as part of terrorism prevention policy and programming—and the framing of DHS lines of effort for this study did not definitively include them.[24] For example, because mental health and wellness issues have been associated with some individuals' radicalization, increasing availability of mental health services could contribute to reducing the risk of ideological violence.[25] However, few would argue that it follows from that conclusion that all efforts to increase the availability of mental health services should be defined as terrorism prevention, funded from terrorism prevention resources, or managed as part of federal efforts designed around national security and terrorism goals. Although we acknowledge the value of risk-factor reduction, there is still the hard question of where to draw the boundary of terrorism prevention. Doing so too narrowly risks excluding practical ways to reduce terrorism risk that are both supportive of and acceptable to communities. However, being too expansive immediately pushes into areas of

---

[21] Weine, Eisenman, and Kinsler et al., 2017; discussion in Snair, Nicholson, and Giammaria, 2017; Green and Procter, 2016. Note that this type of argument has not been unique to CVE. It has also been argued that criminal justice generally could benefit from being viewed from a public health perspective. See, for example, Roberto Hugh Potter and Jeffrey W. Rosky, "The Iron Fist in the Latex Glove: The Intersection of Public Health and Criminal Justice," *American Journal of Criminal Justice*, Vol. 38, 2013.

[22] In public health terminology, our middle-phase terrorism prevention is either "secondary prevention, which aims to reduce the impact of a [problem] that has already occurred, or tertiary prevention which aims to soften the impact of an ongoing [problem] that has lasting effects." See Weine, Eisenman, and Kinsler et al., 2017, p. 210.

[23] Interviewees in multiple cities we visited were very positive about these types of broadly framed and foundational programs, in some cases arguing that they were the only viable approach to implementing *any* terrorism prevention programming, given opposition to efforts viewed as connected to enforcement mechanisms. These points have been echoed in other examinations of CVE, e.g., discussion in Snair, Nicholson, and Giammaria, 2017.

[24] Although "promoting education and community awareness" could capture risk-factor reduction that was done through educational mechanisms, it would not capture programming to address many of the other identified risk factors for radicalization.

[25] This point was argued by Weine, Eisenman, and Kinsler et al., 2017.

responsibility and policy that are much larger than terrorism prevention, which would immediately overwhelm any pool of resources likely to be allocated to this mission and could create new challenges of stigma and discrimination across mission areas. We will return to this boundary issue later in the report as a challenge without an obvious answer that creates both difficulties and potential opportunities for designing effective terrorism prevention policy.

Middle-Phase Terrorism Prevention

The middle phase of terrorism prevention captures the challenges of (1) identification and referral of individuals who may be at risk of violent action, (2) risk/threat assessment to make a decision about whether an individual does indeed pose a threat, and (3) interventions of various types designed to reduce the risks they pose. This phase includes the second part of DHS's first line of effort for the study (promoting education and community awareness, which includes recognition of warning signs) and its third line of effort, providing early warning of individuals who have radicalized and responding to cases of radicalization. As a component of that third line of effort, we have broken out law enforcement training, given the number of efforts that have been specifically devoted to that activity in the past. These activities are shown in the middle and lower middle of Figure 3.2 and are mapped to the relevant portions of the framework. This phase of terrorism prevention is conceptually and practically the most complex, as many individuals for whom intervention might be warranted will not have broken any laws, and government activity in this area is controversial, given constitutional protections of freedoms of speech, religion, thought, and association. We cover these activities in more detail in Chapters Six and Seven.

Several different terms have been used for activities captured in this middle phase of terrorism prevention, including *intervention* and *off-ramping*. The goal is to help an individual move away from violence through noncoercive counseling, service provision, and other resources. Although some of the elements of intervention (which is the term we use in this report) may be specific to individuals at risk of perpetrating violence who are driven by particular ideologies (e.g., religious counseling, tolerance-focused programming), many of the elements are not.[26] As many of our interviewees emphasized, key elements of terrorism prevention intervention include job training, mental health services, life skills counseling, and other services that might be provided

---

[26] Several researchers and practitioners in the field have argued that there are substantial lessons to be learned for CVE and, by extension, terrorism prevention from related fields that have a longer history of interventions intended to achieve similar goals. See Owens et al., 2016; Adrian Cherney, "Designing and Implementing Programmes to Tackle Radicalization and Violent Extremism: Lessons from Criminology," *Dynamics of Asymmetric Conflict*, Vol. 9, 2016; Eisenman and Flavahan, 2017; and Stevan M. Weine, B. Heidi Ellis, Ron Haddad, Alisa B. Miller, Rebecca Lowenhaupt, and Chloe Polutnik, *Lessons Learned from Mental Health and Education: Identifying Best Practices for Addressing Violent Extremism*, College Park, Md.: National Consortium for the Study of Terrorism and Responses to Terrorism, October 2015.

to at-risk youth because of concern about gang involvement, as components of sub-stance abuse treatment, or through programs aimed at addressing other social ills.[27] As is the case in those areas, entities involved in intervention can be government agencies, including law enforcement; social service agencies and NGOs; and community and other groups.

Figure 3.2 shows three different variants for identification of individuals at risk of radicalizing to violence and referral falling across our indirect/community-centered to direct/government-driven terrorism prevention spectrum:

1. community models (i.e., an at-risk individual is identified by a family member, friend, or other community member and referred for help)
2. social services models (identification is made by a service provider either inside or outside government)
3. law enforcement models (identification might be made through law enforce-ment investigative activities).

Depending on the options available to make referrals, community members could call a private-sector resource (e.g., an NGO helpline); a government service provider (e.g., a social services agency or multiorganization coordinating body); or the police or security-focused agency at the federal level, such as DHS or the FBI. Whether a com-munity member is willing to make a referral will be determined by trust of whatever organization(s) are available, because such a call for help potentially involves personal and relationship risks. A similar dynamic could exist for other entities (e.g., schools, medical providers) because there will always be uncertainty in the threat posed by a specific individual, and the consequences of making or not making a referral could affect an organization's ability to achieve its primary missions. We show intervention itself falling across a similar indirect/community-centered to direct/government-driven spectrum, including options that are community driven (e.g., an NGO model that is separate from government), managed by social services, or connected to the criminal justice system. At the community end, any intervention effort would be entirely vol-untary and noncoercive. At the other end of the spectrum, criminal justice–based pro-grams *could* be mandatory as a condition of diversion from prosecution.[28]

---

[27] One governmental interviewee emphasized this very strongly, reporting that the perception that terrorism prevention or CVE programming was somehow unique had been an impediment to developing and sustaining practical approaches to policy in this area.

[28] There appears to be little current activity in the United States that is focused on diversion in lieu of prosecu-tion for any terrorism-related offenses, in contrast to some other types of crimes (according to multiple interviews with government representatives at the federal and local levels, 2018). The one possible exception is the Disrup-tion and Early Engagement Program (DEEP) run by the U.S. Attorney's Office in the Eastern District of New York. For a description of DEEP, see Barrett Devlin, "Some Terror Sympathizers to Get Counseling—FBI Tries New Approach as It Faces Surge in Americans Tempted by Islamic State Messages," *Wall Street Journal*, August 6, 2015. During our research, however, sufficiently detailed information was not available on the program to char-

An area could theoretically be served by a single program drawn from these options. For example, in situations of high trust among communities, law enforcement, and service providers, members of the public might be entirely comfortable with law enforcement being the referral point for at-risk individuals. In such circumstances, law enforcement might be comfortable handing off cases to social services or other organizations to manage, knowing they will call them back in if intervention is not working. Terrorism prevention in this area could be very efficient, maintaining single points of contact and a single program for intervention. In areas of low trust, it is possible that multiple referring options and programs would need to exist (e.g., a poor relationship between the community and police might mean that some people would not be comfortable with law enforcement involvement in referral and intervention). Damaged trust is therefore a source of inefficiency, requiring a more extensive and potentially redundant set of activities for effectiveness. An intermediate case might have multiple programs in place but that share information among organizations, as shown by the dashed lines in Figure 3.2.

In this phase, perhaps the most difficult challenge is risk assessment—making a judgment about whether a particular individual represents a threat—which we have emphasized in Figure 3.2.[29] The best current understandings of radicalization processes show that there are no unambiguous risk factors for those who will progress to violence, and questions have been raised about whether it is possible to identify any such factors specific and diagnostic enough to be useful.[30] As a result, individuals in this phase pose uncertain levels of threat, and the decision of whether an individual is dangerous will always be a judgment call. It is a consequential and high-stakes decision, particularly when that decision might trigger high-cost processes for both the individual and society. The consequences to individuals flagged as risks based on uncertain factors is a key criticism of CVE efforts.[31]

Multiple government interviewees in our study emphasized that this was a particularly difficult challenge for law enforcement organizations applying traditional enforcement-based approaches to counterterrorism: For each person who comes to the attention of police, a decision must be made about whether that person merits inten-

---

acterize its scope and activities. Others have recommended the development of greater options for diversion from prosecution for such activities as attempting to travel abroad to areas of conflict (e.g., Levitt, 2017).

[29] Challenges in risk assessment are not unique to terrorism. The use of risk assessment tools, as well as their perceived fairness, is a concern for criminal justice more broadly.

[30] For example, see Snair, Nicholson, and Giammaria, 2017; and Matthew K. Wynia, David Eisenman, and Dan Hanfling, "Ideologically Motivated Violence: A Public Health Approach to Prevention," *American Journal of Public Health*, Vol. 107, No. 8, August 2017. One federal-level interviewee asked the question of whether there might be clear indicators in the data about individuals' online behavior that would allow experts to distinguish between someone who was just curious about terrorism versus becoming radicalized and mobilized for violence. Interview with a federal representative, 2018.

[31] Faiza Patel and Meghan Koushik, *Countering Violent Extremism*, New York: Brennan Center for Justice, 2017.

sive investigation (and potentially arrest and prosecution). Halting investigation into an individual means that police will get no further information about that person or their behavior, which will involve accepting some risk that that person will take action in the future. However, attempting to pay attention to too many potential threats will rapidly deplete criminal justice resources.[32] Organizational consequences are also asymmetric: An agency will receive heavy blame for any individuals who are subsequently involved in criminal behavior (because they are viewed as missed opportunities, intelligence failures, or worse), driven by the unrealistic goal of preventing every potential terrorist event. However, those same organizations receive no credit for all the individuals who are "appropriately cut loose" and never do anything of concern again, because such outcomes are never counted. These combined pressures can push toward intensive investigation to allow rapid arrest, letting a suspected threat be *definitively* cleared through incarceration without any uncertainty about the future behavior of the individuals involved.[33] This strategy sidesteps the shortcomings of risk assessment, but can be costly both monetarily (which we explore in detail in Chapter Nine) and in organizational credibility and trust if there are concerns that aggressive investigative techniques push people toward violence and into illegal acts that they would not have otherwise committed.[34]

Effective middle-phase terrorism prevention programming, and particularly more-collaborative intervention programming that is service delivery–focused, can help to lower the stakes for individual decisions by adding options that are less stark than "arrest or cut loose." Although participation in an intervention program could have some negative consequences for an individual, those consequences would almost certainly be less serious than arrest and conviction for a terrorism-related offense.[35] Intervention programming is intended to produce changes in behaviors that should benefit the individuals involved (e.g., although the goal of providing employment counseling as part of a violence-reduction intervention might be to reduce the chance of individual

---

[32] This point has been made about individuals at risk of perpetrating other types of targeted violence as well: "Most uniformed law enforcement organizations are stretched thin as it is. It can be difficult to devote resources to preventing something that may or may not happen" (FBI Behavioral Analysis Unit, undated, p. 6).

[33] As one federal interviewee put it, "And even if the folks are on radicalization radar but not indicating that they are moving towards mobilization, [the preferred path] is to close the case. . . . So that is a really big challenge for the FBI, and there's no alternative right now other than investigation and arrest. . . . FBI field offices do thing[s] a little differently, but nationally there is not an option. And I think that's a problem—that's a [counterterrorism] problem even if you don't like [terrorism prevention]."

[34] Some scholars come at this problem from another direction, making the analogy to drug courts and "therapeutic jurisprudence" as a model for considering the intersection of intervention with criminal justice (Weine et al., 2015). That said, a government interviewee pointed out that it is easier to think about such models for offenses like drugs (where the main harm is to the individual) than it is for something like terrorism.

[35] One interviewee framed this in terms of the potential stigma for participating in the "terrorist counseling program" similar to the way that stigma from substance abuse treatment or mental health counseling is a concern for individuals' future employability or reputations.

illegal behavior, the immediate effect will be to get the individuals involved jobs). This lowers the stakes for the individuals involved, making the shortcomings in risk assessment—and the almost inevitable outcome that some people will be viewed as potential risks who would never progress to violence on their own—less serious. However, it also lowers the stakes for government and law enforcement organizations. Referral of an individual to an intervention program provides a path that is not just "arrest or cut loose" while still allowing criminal justice resources to be freed up to address other concerns.[36] Continued contact between the at-risk individuals and program staff also means that there will be people in positions to assess their progress, almost certainly based on much better and more nuanced understanding of their circumstances and behavior than what is available to a law enforcement investigator.[37] That relationship transforms what was a single high-stakes decision into a stream of decision opportunities, where action can be taken if concern about their behavior increases rather than fades away over time.[38]

Late-Phase Terrorism Prevention

The late phase of terrorism prevention captures activities and programming aimed at individuals who have been convicted of terrorism-related offenses. Such offenses can result in individuals in custody (i.e., sentenced to prison terms) or to supervision in the community for some types of activity that are not directly violent. Individuals who are incarcerated would transition to supervision after release. This phase of effort corresponds to DHS's fourth line of effort defined for the study, keeping suspects and individuals convicted of terrorism-related offenses from returning to violence. These efforts appear in the lower-right portion of Figure 3.2. We cover these activities in more detail in Chapter Eight.

The goal of these efforts is to reduce recidivism, which, for ideological violence and terrorism, could include returning to violence personally or to activities supporting violent action by others. This means that terrorism prevention in this phase is quite distinct from the early and middle phases, where activity is focused on individuals who have not committed a crime. Another factor emphasized by interviewees was that strong reliance on enforcement-based approaches to reducing terrorism risk (i.e., arrest and prosecution for such offenses as material support) drives the necessity and scope of terrorism prevention activities of this type. The greater the number of individuals in

---

[36] Some have argued for the need to message that there are good reasons for these programs and that they are not being "soft" on terrorism (e.g., Eric Rosand, *Communities First: A Blueprint for Organizing and Sustaining a Global Movement Against Violent Extremism*, Washington, D.C.: The Prevention Project, December 2016).

[37] See, for example, FBI Behavioral Analysis Unit, undated, p. 67.

[38] Although the focus of this discussion is on risk from ideological violence, this same dynamic—i.e., concern about the consequences of individuals being viewed as threats incorrectly balanced against organizational imperatives to protect the public—exists for other types of violence, including school shootings and workplace violence.

the criminal justice system for ideologically involved offenses, the greater the need for programming focused on their desistance from violence.

Efforts in this phase of terrorism prevention include programming inside correctional institutions and for individuals after release. Inside institutions, there is concern about inmates spreading extremist beliefs among the population to the detriment of prison security conditions, but there is also programming that focuses on the individuals' desistance from future violence or on supporting reevaluation of their beliefs. After release, programming is designed to support reentry and manage the potential for these individuals to pose a risk to the community.[39] The types of activities in this phase of terrorism prevention have significant commonality to programming that is traditionally provided in correctional institutions and in the context of post-release supervision, including various types of counseling, education, vocational training, and other support (e.g., substance abuse programming). Specific types of counseling may be required for individuals associated with specific ideologies, including religious counseling or counseling related to tolerance and hate crime.[40]

Translating Terrorism Prevention Goals to Measures of Success

Although it is not unknown for programs responding to immediate problems of concern to be implemented before we know how to rigorously analyze their effects, it is essential to develop and implement assessment and performance monitoring as experience is built and knowledge is gained.[41]

Since CVE efforts became a focus in federal-level policy, there has been recurring concern about whether investments in policy and programs are achieving their intended goals.[42] Outside government, think tanks and other organizations focused on federal initiatives in this area have described the need for measures and metrics, and many have flagged the development and validation of metrics as a valuable federal role even for prevention efforts implemented at the state and local levels or outside of government.[43] Both the need for metrics and the complexity of developing them

---

[39] The FBI Behavioral Analysis Unit describes this as "protecting public safety and caring for persons of concern [being] heavily intertwined" (undated, p. 51).

[40] As one of our interviewees pointed out, the types of programming and counseling capabilities needed to meet the needs of post-release individuals have much in common with those required for intervention with an individual at risk of perpetrating ideologically motivated violence, so there may be efficiencies in developing common infrastructures for both phases of terrorism prevention.

[41] Snair, Nicholson, and Giammaria, 2017, pp. 78–79.

[42] For more on these concerns, see GAO, 2017; H. Rept. 114-344, "Countering Violent Extremism Act of 2015, Report to Accompany H.R. 2899," November 19, 2015.

[43] Examples of policy reports calling out the need for high-quality metrics for CVE and analytical work to develop and validate them include Bipartisan Policy Center, 2011, pp. 22–24; Lorenzo Vidino and Seamus

were recurring themes in interviews at all levels during our study.[44] Aside from a general consensus for the need for metrics, however, some interviewees cautioned that it was important to "do metrics right" in terrorism prevention in order to avoid pitfalls that have affected the drive toward measurement in other policy areas. Interviewees expressed concerns that it is easier to measure some variables than others (e.g., arrests associated with enforcement-focused counterterrorism[45] versus successful cooperation with communities in the course of past CVE or current and future terrorism prevention initiatives) and that the design of metrics could limit innovation and local flexibility in designing new prevention efforts.[46] They emphasized that efforts to measure terrorism prevention have to be resourced appropriately or it is unrealistic to expect them to be successful.[47] Time is also an issue: Local practitioners argued that many initiatives (particularly early-phase ones) might "take years to bear fruit" and "so to evaluate something after six months is unfair."[48]

The desired outcome of terrorism prevention efforts is clear: fewer, or ideally no, terrorist attacks. Anchoring measurement and program evaluation only to that final outcome is difficult, however, because of the fortunate reality that there have been relatively few individuals who have been radicalized in the United States.[49] When we

---

Hughes, *Countering Violent Extremism in America*, Washington, D.C.: George Washington University, Center for Cyber and Homeland Security, Program on Extremism, June 2015, p. 16; Weine and Braniff, 2015, p. 14; Green and Procter, 2016, p. 24; Todd C. Helmus, Miriam Matthews, Rajeev Ramchand, Sina Beaghley, David Stebbins, Amanda Kadlec, Michael A. Brown, Aaron Kofner, and Joie D. Acosta, *RAND Program Evaluation Toolkit for Countering Violent Extremism*, Santa Monica, Calif.: RAND Corporation, TL-243-DHS, 2017; Heritage Foundation, *Defending the Homeland: The Future of U.S. Countering Violent Extremism Policy*, video, August 8, 2017; Levitt, 2017, pp. 21–22; Snair, Nicholson, and Giammaria, 2017; Bipartisan Policy Center, 2011.

[44] To this end, the IMPACT Europe project made available a database of evaluated CVE programs, including ratings of the strength of the evidence for their success (IMPACT Europe, homepage, undated).

[45] For example, in DOJ performance reporting, the FBI sets goals for the numbers of terrorist plots disrupted as a forward-looking performance measure (see U.S. Department of Justice, Office of the Attorney General, *FY 2016 Annual Performance Report and FY 2018 Annual Performance Plan*, Washington, D.C., May 2017), which could result in incentives for enforcement-focused counterterrorism versus terrorism prevention. Viewed from the terrorism prevention perspective, an arrest of an individual inspired to violence inside the United States would be a *negative* measure indicating failure to identify and intervene effectively.

[46] A more in-depth discussion of measures and metrics related to terrorism prevention is included in Appendix C to this report.

[47] According to a former federal interviewee, measurement here is "no different from crime prevention [or] drug prevention. The problem isn't that we don't do it, we aren't given the resources to measure and then we give up on measurement. I don't buy into naïve metrics. I think people don't understand metrics or just aren't given the money to do it well. You can't say if this is good or bad if you don't resource it" (2018).

[48] Interviews with community organization representatives in two U.S. cities, 2018.

[49] This challenge is not unique to terrorism prevention. The FBI has made similar points with respect to the prevention of other types of targeted violence: Audiences must be "mindful that statistics rarely provide proof of successful prevention; only tragedies make the headlines, whereas successful prevention efforts are difficult to measure" (FBI Behavioral Analysis Unit, undated, p. 7).

think about this issue from the "bottom up"—i.e., looking at a single terrorism prevention program implemented in one geographic area—it is essentially impossible to definitively prove the negative: that a terrorist attack that would have happened in the absence of the program did not happen as a result of its efforts. Measuring the effects of terrorism prevention is further complicated because doing so requires reflecting the *national* terrorism prevention effort. Because any activities carried out or supported by the federal government take place in concert with state and local as well as nongovernmental and community activities, thinking about measurement only from the point of view of federal programming would risk creating a partial or skewed picture of performance.

From the national perspective, measuring terrorism prevention capability and effectiveness is not only about whether a specific area (e.g., one city) has sufficient terrorism prevention capability or whether an individual program is effective. If terrorism prevention programming is to play a role in addressing the risk of terrorism, capability needs to be available where and when it is needed, and it must be effective when it is used. Because concern about different types of ideological violence exists across the country (see, e.g., Figures 2.5 and 2.6 in Chapter Two), measurement must therefore consider the "national coverage" of terrorism prevention capability. This echoes the finding of the DHS Homeland Security Advisory Council (HSAC), CVE Subcommittee, of the need to "build an architecture for all 50 states" for CVE.[50]

The three phases of terrorism prevention defined in the previous section are useful in considering the range of terrorism prevention activities that could be part of a national effort because they queue up reasonable ways of thinking about the top-down policy goals that programs are trying to achieve. Evaluation can be viewed from two national-level perspectives: (1) a current-level-of-performance perspective, which seeks to measure how well the country is reducing threats or meeting terrorism prevention needs with programming already in place; and (2) a change-over-time perspective, which seeks to measure how programs and investments are either increasing or decreasing terrorism prevention capability in different ways. In the early, middle, and late phases of terrorism prevention, these two ways of thinking about measurement can mean quite different things:

- In the early phase, the goal is essentially countercommunication, by messaging or message removal in the online space or—via education or risk factor–reduction efforts—making messages ineffective in inspiring individuals to act violently. Success is defined in the same way evaluation of a marketing or public health messaging campaign might be defined—i.e., in terms of reducing the resonance of competing (in this case violence-inciting) messages or changing the behavior

---

[50] DHS HSAC, "Interim Report and Recommendations," Washington, D.C., Countering Violent Extremism (CVE) Subcommittee, June 2016, p. 15.

of the intended audience. Both can be framed in probabilistic terms based on how their combined effort reduces the chance that individuals in an area will be inspired to ideologically driven violence.

From the "current stock perspective," assessment would involve seeking to measure the intensity and scope of the threat environment (e.g., the volume and persuasiveness of threat messages online). At any given time, the effects of any implemented, content-focused messaging or educational effort would be reflected in current conditions. That baseline would then be the measure against which the effects of any new efforts could be assessed, assuming that other factors remained constant. Complete assessment would also reflect whether there were unintended consequences of efforts (e.g., potential backlash against messaging efforts, producing or strengthening stigma). Broader risk reduction efforts are different, but there is existing program evaluation infrastructure relevant to measurement for such programs.

- In the middle phase, intervention is essentially "service delivery," where the customers for that service must be found (i.e., identifying individuals at risk of violent radicalization) and successfully marketed to and served through delivery of counseling and related programming. Probabilistically, the desired outcome is a high probability that (1) an individual at risk of perpetrating ideological violence in an area will be identified and connected to services and (2) that those services will be effective in turning them away from violence.

  Assessing the stock of terrorism prevention capacity in an area would involve thinking about the likelihood that both steps would happen as well as the measurement of capacity—i.e., how many individuals could be served and how that amount compared with the perceived need. Flow measures would focus on individual programs and whether they were increasing that likelihood or capacity over time. Holistic measurement also would be needed to measure the broader effects of programming on populations, perceptions of effectiveness and unintended consequences, and perceptions of participants in programming.

- In the late phase, programmatic activity is analogous to standard offender reentry services and supervision intended to reduce recidivism for all crime, but the goal is the delivery of effective services to terrorism-related offenders such that the likelihood of their return to violence after release is reduced.

Although framing metrics in the way in which we have here is one step removed from the ideal of being able to directly measure prevented terrorist incidents, framing the goal as estimating likelihoods of success at each step defines a logical linkage to that goal. For example, if an area can defensibly estimate that the probability that at-risk individuals would be referred for intervention was high and that the services available to intervene were of high quality, then it would be reasonable to conclude that the combination of the two was reducing relative terrorism risk. This approach also provides a way to link program-level outputs to local or national outcome performance (which we discuss in greater detail in later chapters and in Appendix C).[51] In addition, anchoring assessment in terms of overall likelihoods of success reflects another point made by interviewees: that in even the best of circumstances, no intervention mode will be perfectly effective and so "failures" should be expected, just as is the case for treatment-based interventions in other areas.

Design Challenges in Terrorism Prevention Policy

We asked our interviewees about major issues or problems that future programs would need to address to be effective in order to provide a basis for both assessing current terrorism prevention efforts and proposing future directions. We distilled that input into ten significant "design challenges," which we list here and discuss in more detail in the subsequent sections.

1. Responding practically to the relatively low rate of radicalization, while also addressing the wide national dispersion of need
2. Navigating the tension between a need for efficiency, which could lead to an emphasis on specific communities, and the risk of stigmatizing communities and alienating key allies
3. Responding to variations in public trust, which can range from enthusiastic to strongly opposed
4. Managing the fact that the "damaged CVE brand" has frightened away important partners
5. Standardizing approaches in useful ways while acknowledging that terrorism prevention activities must be highly specific to local circumstances
6. Coordinating independent multidisciplinary organizations with overlapping responsibilities while avoiding conflict between operational demands and more-collaborative terrorism prevention approaches
7. Mitigating risk aversion (including fears of failure and liability), which can limit experimentation and innovation
8. Developing terrorism prevention approaches that are not dependent on specific individuals and that can be sustained through staffing changes
9. Balancing the demand for data collection and measurement in terrorism prevention with the need to avoid reinforcing community perceptions of being surveilled and stigmatized

---

[51] "You can't monitor every action—there is no perfect baseline. . . . The former secretary asked me, how can you isolate that something reduced terrorism? We will probably never be able to demonstrate that writ large, but we can for the projects" (Interview with a federal representative, 2018).

10. Using traditional federal policy levers of funding and influence in the controversial environment that surrounds terrorism prevention efforts.

Although some of the challenges are specific to the federal context, most come from differences between the federal and local contexts that create the potential for conflicts in approach or requirements. Depending on the segment of terrorism prevention—where, in some cases, centralized lead or action (e.g., online efforts, recidivism reduction) is appropriate and sometimes focus at the local level is needed—whether federal or local level concern should dominate may differ.

Among our interviewees, views also differed on the seriousness of individual challenges. In our assessment, each of the following subsections represents an issue that, if it could be resolved to the satisfaction of both supporters and critics of CVE and terrorism prevention efforts, is an opportunity to strengthen not only the performance of terrorism prevention efforts, but also their practicality.

Responding Practically to the Relatively Low Rate of Radicalization, While Also Addressing the Wide National Dispersion of Need

As described in Chapter Two, although the numbers of terrorist incidents, events of radicalization, and potential threats may add up to an appreciable total for the nation overall, numbers observed in any local area—even for most large cities—will be relatively small. This creates a mismatch between the view from the federal level, where addressing the national problem requires taking a broad perspective, and the local level, where individuals at risk of perpetrating ideological violence are often a small slice of a larger set of risks that are of concern to communities and must be managed.[52] We heard this in our interviews with government representatives and community members, and it has been observed by other researchers as well.[53]

As a result, the design challenge for terrorism prevention is crafting policies that are *effective* at responding to the risk of ideological violence, but doing so in a way that is *practical* at the level at which the programs must be implemented. For example, although programs that are specific to ideological violence may be viable when the right implementation point is the national level (e.g., programming for all individuals in federal prisons on terrorism-related charges), at the local level, building and sustain-

---

[52] See arguments on this issue in Weine and Braniff, 2015; Patel and Koushik, 2017. One interviewee put it this way: "If the federal government comes and tells you to spend money on terrorism but your problems are drugs, gangs, car thefts. . . it's not that the cops don't want to counter terrorism, but if their essential problem is drugs, it's crazy" (Interview with a policy researcher, 2018).

[53] See, for example, the discussion in Snair, Nicholson, and Giammaria, 2017, p. 78; and Weine, Eisenman, and Kinsler et al., 2017.

ing capability to intervene with at-risk individuals may only be viable in the context of existing service-provision systems and programs.[54]

Navigating the Tension Between a Need for Efficiency, Which Could Lead to an Emphasis on Specific Communities, and the Risk of Stigmatizing Communities and Alienating Key Allies

In spite of the fact that federal CVE initiatives have for many years been framed as responding to all types of extremism, a theme in many of our interviews was that efforts were still perceived by many as focusing on the Muslim community and neglecting other potential sources of domestic ideological violence. This concern appears in much of the public debate by critics of past CVE and current terrorism prevention policies.[55] The view of communities is that these programs have been stigmatizing, have alienated communities from participating, and have hurt their relationships with government and law enforcement.[56] Stigmatization has been a significant issue in other countries studied in this effort, including France and the United Kingdom (see Appendix A for more information). Interviewees from government to community groups emphasized that terrorism prevention policies need to be designed in a broad-based way; address all types of potential radicalization to violence, from religious to right- and left-wing sources; and be implemented in such a way that communities are not stigmatized as a result of programming.

At the same time, there are clearly good reasons to be "specific rather than general" in approaches to particular communities. Part of building effective partnerships between communities and government is "government bringing something to the table," or collaborating with communities and taking action in response to their priorities, not expecting them to be responsive to the government's needs.[57] Initiatives designed to achieve this goal are common at the local level and exist at the federal level

---

[54] There is a deep literature on the problems of sustaining initiatives aimed at specific problems, particularly if they are funded externally through mechanisms like time-limited grants. See discussion in Cherney, 2016; Mary Ann Scheirer, "Is Sustainability Possible? A Review and Commentary on Empirical Studies of Program Sustainability," *American Journal of Evaluation*, Vol. 26, No. 3, 2005; Shannon Wiltsey Stirman, John Kimberly, Natasha Cook, Amber Calloway, Frank Castro, and Martin Charns, "The Sustainability of New Programs and Innovations: A Review of the Empirical Literature and Recommendations for Future Research," *Implementation Science*, Vol. 7, No. 17, 2012; and Eyal Aharoni, Lila Rabinovich, Joshua Mallett, and Andrew R. Morral, *An Assessment of Program Sustainability in Three Bureau of Justice Assistance Criminal Justice Domains*, Santa Monica, Calif.: RAND Corporation, RR-550-BJA, 2014. This was recently argued in guidance from NCTC, DHS, and FBI to local first responders as well (NCTC, DHS, and FBI, "First Responders Toolbox: Terrorism Prevention— A Form of Violence Reduction," October 30, 2017).

[55] See, for example, Patel and Koushik, 2017; American Civil Liberties Union (ACLU), "The Problem with 'Countering Violent Extremism' Programs," webpage, undated(c).

[56] Patel and Koushik, 2017.

[57] This is a core component of participatory governance in general, as well as of initiatives like community policing.

as well (e.g., DHS programs that provide services to houses of worship on their security needs). To be effective, however, such programs need to be responsive to the needs of the community, which vary from area to area and group to group.

As a result, there is a tension between "targeting communities" and "collaborating with and serving specific communities effectively." In our discussions in cities around the country, we saw this tension in the way that outreach and programming were described. From government interviewees, concerns about being broad-based and general in approach to avoid alienating communities were juxtaposed with statements about the value of dedicated outreach to individual ethnic or religious communities to maintain strong connections and collaboration. From community interviewees, the critique that CVE (and, by extension, terrorism prevention) efforts stigmatized individual communities by implying that they were homogeneous[58] or that "they all were potential terrorists" was balanced with praise for dedicated law enforcement or government outreach efforts.[59]

This issue appeared easier to navigate at the local level than with respect to federal programming, presumably because of the opportunity for extended interaction and relationship-building at the local level. Even if stigmatizing communities was not the intent, addressing the fact that they have felt stigmatized by these efforts is important for the effectiveness of terrorism prevention going forward. Researchers examining causes of radicalization in U.S. cases noted that "almost every individual had a sense of community victimization, feeling deeply that they were members of communities being targeted and victimized."[60] If the implementation of terrorism prevention efforts themselves creates that sense of targeting or victimization, it will work at cross purposes with its intended outcomes.[61]

Responding to Variations in Public Trust, Which Can Range from Enthusiastic to Strongly Opposed

Across our interviewees outside of government—with representatives of community organizations, social services providers, and researchers—there was a wide variation of trust in government CVE efforts.[62] There was relatively strong consensus that the stated outcomes of the government's CVE efforts would be beneficial. The difference

---

[58]   See, for example, Weine, Eisenman, and Kinsler et al., 2017.

[59]   Interviews with community leaders, 2018.

[60]   Snair, Nicholson, and Giammaria, 2017, p. 15.

[61]   This potential for CVE or terrorism prevention efforts to be self-undermining was also discussed in other literature, and not only with respect to post-9/11 activities, but also with respect to the ideologies of domestic violent movements that have victimization by government as central to their narratives (RTI International, *Countering Violent Extremism: The Use of Assessment Tools for Measuring Violence Risk, Literature Review*, Research Triangle Park, N.C., March 2017a, p. R-30). It is also similar to effects observed with interventions aimed at crime more generally (e.g., the labeling of youth as "at risk" affecting their behavior in a negative way) (Cherney, 2016).

[62]   Green and Procter (2016) make this point more broadly across countries.

was in whether interviewees believed that the programs were designed to achieve the stated outcomes versus actually being designed to facilitate prosecution and enforcement approaches. A similar dichotomy exists in the published policy debate surrounding past CVE efforts and therefore future terrorism prevention activities, starting with U.S. efforts even before the 2015 White House Summit and intensifying afterward.[63]

Individuals make their own decisions about who and what government programs they trust, and concerns about the consequences of damaged trust are not unique to terrorism prevention. In the words of an interviewee at the federal level, "When communities fear that government programs are directed at them, all these issues are conflated. Then it's impossible to galvanize that community. . . . If people don't trust that you won't harm them, that you will protect their privacy, they won't trust you."[64] Trust and the perceived legitimacy of government action has been an ongoing issue for law enforcement, particularly in recent years, when a desire for greater police-community collaboration through community policing has been a priority.[65] Issues with terrorism prevention have much in common with challenges to building trust between law enforcement and the communities they police. Past actions have resonance for and shape public views, and can make it difficult to establish trust going forward. Some examples cited during our interviews as affecting the trust and legitimacy of past CVE and future terrorism prevention activities included enforcement actions taken by the FBI—in particular, what the interviewees referred to as counterterrorism "stings," using informants in communities—but also events that reached back into history, with domestic surveillance actions taken by federal law enforcement in the 1960s and 1970s resurfacing in the current discussion of terrorism prevention.[66]

As has been observed in law enforcement more generally, trust can be particularly fragile for activities that are not transparent, because, in the absence of data, individuals will draw conclusions based on the information available and make assumptions about what is going on that they cannot see.[67] Differences in terminology and disciplinary

---

[63] Weine, Eisenman, and Kinsler et al., 2017.

[64] Interview with a federal representative, 2018.

[65] For a review, see Brian A. Jackson, *Respect and Legitimacy—A Two-Way Street: Strengthening Trust Between Police and the Public in an Era of Increasing Transparency*, Santa Monica, Calif.: RAND Corporation, PE-154,-RC, 2015.

[66] See also, for example, similar discussion in Neil Krishan Aggarwal, "Questioning the Current Public Health Approach to Countering Violent Extremism," *Global Public Health*, May 11, 2018; and Patel and Koushik, 2017.

[67] See, for example, ACLU, "ACLU Briefing Paper: What Is Wrong with the Government's 'Countering Violent Extremism' Programs," undated(a); and CAIR California, "L.A. Based Organizations' Statement on Federal Government CVE Programs," webpage, undated. A tangible example cited by entities critical of CVE in the past is that the FBI's strategic plan for its Countering Violent Extremism Office, an important component of whose activities were aimed at partnerships and engagement, was a classified document and was released under the Freedom of Information Act with significant redactions (FBI, *FBI Strategic Plan to Curb Violent Extremism: Countering Violent Extremism Office*, Washington, D.C., [as redacted and publicly released under the Freedom of Information Act (FOIA)], original classification date, March 12, 2015). The slide deck describing the FBI Field

language can lead to questions about whether activities really are what they say they are (e.g., in our interviews, we had discussions where participants emphasized that different definitions of such terms as *case management* or *intelligence*[68] had very different implications for organizations collaborating on terrorism prevention efforts). Even the term *community policing*—a movement in law enforcement going back decades with the goal of connecting law enforcement agencies to communities to better serve their needs—has been interpreted critically and some of our interviewees suggested that terminology (and community policing activities, as interpreted by concerned groups) can have the potential to undermine trust.[69]

Our interviewees emphasized that trust is also affected by the national environment and by political discourse around topics specific to terrorism prevention and relevant to the affected communities.[70] This is a major challenge in that the effectiveness of many terrorism prevention options depends on people believing in the system and being willing to call on programs when they have concerns. Even enforcement-focused approaches to managing terrorism risk depend on public trust. The disruption of ter-

---

Office CVE Model was released with the entirety of the content redacted (FBI, *Field Office CVE Model*, slide deck, [redacted and released under the Freedom of Information Act], undated[b]).

[68] The use of the term *intelligence* with respect to terrorism prevention is particularly challenging. Long before attempts to build a coherent CVE effort in the United States, police departments were adopting the term (e.g., intelligence-led policing). This was initially part of the branding of a movement to make greater use of data on criminal activity in policing in the early 1990s, but was reinforced in the post-9/11 era as law enforcement responded to the threat of terrorism. See Jerry H. Ratcliffe, "Intelligence-Led Policing," *Australian Institute of Criminology: Trends and Issues in Crime and Criminal Justice*, Vol. 248, April 2003; Bureau of Justice Assistance (BJA), *Intelligence-Led Policing: The New Intelligence Architecture*, Washington, D.C.: U.S. Department of Justice, NCJ 210681, September 2005. Even before significant implementation of CVE activities, the linkage of the term to policing was flagged as risking creating the wrong impression among the public in particular. For example, according to Ratcliffe, "To the public it can suggest subterfuge, a clandestine and covert activity conducted by officers of a shady disposition and involving a degree of moral ambiguity" (Jerry H. Ratcliffe, "Intelligence-Led Policing," in Richard Wortley and Lorraine Mazerolle, eds., *Environmental Criminology and Crime Analysis*, Cullompton, UK: Willan Publishing, 2008, p. 263). Other researchers have argued for intensifying use of the terminology and more national security–like intelligence practices (e.g., increased focus on programs like suspicious activity reporting). See Jeremy G. Carter and David L. Carter, "Law Enforcement Intelligence: Implications for Self-Radicalized Terrorism," *Police Practice and Research*, Vol. 13, No. 2, 2012, pp. 138–154.

[69] See Aggarwal, 2018. A government representative in another U.S. city we visited gave a similar critique of some police departments' implementation of community policing:

> While I understand why people call it community policing, it's a very misunderstood term in the community *and* law enforcement. I've had conversations with line-level cops who say, "It's my responsibility to make relationships to get information and intelligence," whereas I've heard others who do it frame it properly. Using the phrase "community policing"—it's poorly understood and means different things to different people.

[70] Some published assessments and interviewees we spoke with at the local level argued that, depending on the national discourse around terrorism prevention and related issues, it could be necessary for local areas (e.g., a city where approaches are incompatible with national discourse) or individual organizations to establish independence from federal efforts to remain able to effectively address this risk in their areas. For example, Eric Rosand, "Fixing CVE in the United States Requires More than Just a Name Change," Brookings Institution blog, February 16, 2017a.

rorist plots by arrest often hinges on tips made by members of the public, and lack of trust or damaged police legitimacy can reduce the willingness to call police.[71] In some discussions of trust and terrorism prevention efforts, researchers have emphasized that trust is a two-way street—i.e., government expectations that the community should trust them with intervention for early-stage threats must be accompanied by government trust in community groups or NGOs as well.[72]

As a result, a significant design challenge is how to address trust issues, not only in pursuit of public support for terrorism prevention, but also for the effectiveness of the programs themselves. Although seeking designs that are welcomed by all is likely unrealistic, to the extent that policies can be built that improve perceptions of procedural justice, protection of the privacy of participants, and the legitimacy and trustworthiness of the organizations implementing terrorism prevention over time, both performance and efficiency will likely improve going forward.

Managing the Fact that the "Damaged CVE Brand" Has Frightened Away Important Partners

Damaged trust can reduce the willingness of organizations to participate in terrorism prevention efforts. Across our interviews, a subset of individuals drawn from different types of organizations used similar language to describe CVE (and by extension terrorism prevention) as a "damaged brand" that many agencies and entities did not want to be associated with.[73] This was a potent concern at the state and local levels, driven by perceptions about what the reactions of communities and nongovernmental funders

---

[71] For discussions on tips by members of the public, see Kevin J. Strom, John S. Hollywood, and Mark W. Pope, "Terrorist Plots Against the United States: What We Have Really Faced, and How We Might Best Defend Against It," in Gary LaFree and Joshua D. Freilich, eds., *The Handbook of the Criminology of Terrorism*, Hoboken, N.J.: Wiley, 2017. For discussions of reduced willingness to call the police, see Emily Ekins, *Policing in America: Understanding Public Attitudes Toward the Police: Results from a National Survey*, Washington, D.C.: Cato Institute, 2017; Tom R. Tyler, Stephen Schulhofer, and Aziz Z. Huq, "Legitimacy and Deterrence Effects in Counterterrorism Policing: A Study of Muslim Americans," *Law and Society Review*, Vol. 44, No. 2, 2010; Aziz Z. Huq, Tom R. Tyler, and Stephen Schulhofer, "Why Does the Public Cooperate with Law Enforcement? The Influence of the Purposes and Targets of Policing," *Psychology, Public Policy, and Law*, Vol. 17, No. 3, 2011.

[72] See, for example, Basia Spalek and Douglas Weeks, "The Role of Communities in Counterterrorism: Analyzing Policy and Exploring Psychotherapeutic Approaches Within Community Settings," *Studies in Conflict and Terrorism*, Vol. 40, No. 12, 2017; Adrian Cherney and Jason Hartley, "Community Engagement to Tackle Terrorism and Violent Extremism: Challenges, Tensions and Pitfalls," *Policing and Society*, Vol. 27, No. 7, 2017, pp. 755–756; and Jackson, 2015. As one federal law enforcement interviewee put it, "[communities and community organizations] want to work with people but they want to be respected. It comes down to trust and respect." From the law enforcement perspective, a policy researcher interviewee said: "A less law enforcement-centric approach means they're giving their responsibilities to someone else, they're never going be happy about that especially if they have so much riding on them if something goes wrong."

[73] See the discussion in Snair, Nicholson, and Giammaria, 2017, pp. 82–83.

might be to association with terrorism-related efforts. These concerns also have been documented in the academic literature:[74]

> For example, during the formative evaluation of a CVE program in Boston, Massachusetts, after visiting 45 organizations and interviewing more than 50 stakeholders, the evaluator reported "98 percent of interviewees stated bluntly that they would not take part in a program with the 'CVE' label, because it would risk undermining the trust and relationships they had worked to build with the communities they serve."

In our work, similar concerns were raised by representatives of some organizations, including groups contacted by the team in the course of our broader outreach efforts. For some organizations, even participating in a study focused on CVE or terrorism prevention was viewed as a potential risk to their future ability to achieve their core missions.[75] Particularly in the area of intervention, the common requirements for terrorism prevention and other intervention programs mean that significant "opt out" by service providers, NGOs, and others can limit the ability to deliver and maintain the availability of programming for individuals at risk of perpetrating ideological violence.[76]

This is also an issue at the federal level. Since the beginning of CVE initiatives in the United States, one issue that has been raised in published policy analysis (as well as by a number of our interviewees) is the reticence of nonsecurity federal agencies (including the U.S. Department of Health and Human Services [HHS], the U.S. Department of Education, and the U.S. Department of Labor) to be substantially and publicly involved in CVE efforts.[77] As is the case when local service providers opt out

---

[74] Wynia, Eisenman, and Hanfling, 2017, p. 1245.

[75] Entities critical of CVE efforts have highlighted this risk more broadly, as part of linking CVE and, by extension, terrorism prevention to surveillance: "expecting people like teachers, social services, and healthcare providers to report youth turn[s] trusted adult role models into informants" (Patel and Koushik, 2017, p. 17).

[76] For example, "[public health professionals] want to do something but they don't want to be tainted by the national security element of this topic, or other communities won't trust them if they see they are involved here" (Interview with federal representatives, 2018).

[77] DHS HSAC identified a range of opportunities for education-focused initiatives that could be spearheaded by the Department of Education in its recommendations for this issue. (DHS HSAC, 2016, p. 23). In his critique of federal efforts, Rosand (2017a) illustrates the consequences of this disengagement with the strong pushback from education and community groups to the FBI's "Don't Be a Puppet" campaign, suggesting that the situation would have been very different if the effort had been spearheaded by the Department of Education. Interviewees echoed similar sentiments at the federal level: "On a federal level, I've never known HHS or [the U.S. Department of Education] to jump in. . . . [CVE] always made them uncomfortable" and "Get entities like HHS on board. That was a failure of the [CVE Task Force]. No one from civil society or the communities [was] on the [Task Force]." In contrast, other federal representatives stated that HHS was involved in Task Force activities, including attending meetings and participating in working groups on intervention and research and evaluation (Interviews with and feedback from nongovernmental representative and federal representatives, 2018). The vast

of terrorism prevention, limited or no involvement by federal social services–focused agencies means that existing initiatives, grant programs, knowledge, and capabilities that might be able to help respond to concerns about individuals at risk of perpetrating ideological violence (and do so in a way that would be trust-enhancing and more acceptable to affected communities) are not available.

Standardizing Approaches in Useful Ways While Acknowledging that Terrorism Prevention Activities Must Be Highly Specific to Local Circumstances

Another "design tension" affecting terrorism prevention policy is the extent to which it makes sense to standardize approaches or have common programming nationally versus terrorism prevention efforts being customized to local environments. Interviewees in all five cities consistently argued that terrorism prevention policy must be designed to match the needs and practicalities of a local area: Different cities face different distributions of threats, have different levels of existing capability, have different community dynamics, and so on.[78] Even within a metropolitan area, requirements can differ from suburb to suburb.[79] Local realities may also constrain terrorism prevention options: In some cities, interviewees bluntly stated that *any* intervention effort would have to be clearly separated from law enforcement, while in others there is tight cooperation between police and other groups. Those different realities led to widely varying proposals for terrorism prevention models, including law enforcement–centric, public health, community-led, and even emergency preparedness–framed approaches. As a result, any effort by the federal government to impose a "cookie cutter" approach to terrorism prevention across the country was viewed as problematic.[80]

At the same time, interviewees saw benefits in standardizing some elements of terrorism prevention policy and practice. The most common issue that was raised was the need to treat at-risk individuals comparably across different ideological sources of violence. The core driver of this critique was the perception that terrorism linked to international groups (e.g., jihadist groups like al Qaeda or ISIS) was treated differently than threats inspired by domestic ideological causes.[81] To illustrate how regional variation

---

differences in view on the involvement of nonsecurity agencies in the Task Force and the barriers to civil-society and community involvement in the Task Force are discussed in Chapter Ten.

[78] For example, a researcher at a policy organization distilled this issue as follows: "It's very important to think about this from a state and local/federal perspective. Even at the end of the Obama administration, who made their share of mistakes, there were different reasons for letting this be locally driven. . . . This is something that happens in local communities so they are best situated to address these issues. Nobody likes the federal government coming in to dictate what they should do" (Interview with a policy researcher, 2018).

[79] Interview with a federal government representative in a U.S. city, 2018.

[80] Scholars have made the point that difficulty with a "top down" approach has been common in other areas as well, such as crime prevention, where centralization breeds resistance and lack of local buy-in (Cherney, 2016).

[81] This perception was frequently ascribed to differences in federal statutes that resulted in different charging strategies, meaning that individuals connected to international groups were more likely to be charged with

could create credibility problems for terrorism prevention, interviewees cited examples from prosecution (e.g., individuals who did comparable things in different areas of the country being charged differently) and enforcement (e.g., different FBI field offices adopting different strategies with respect to investigation tactics). Others suggested that standard guidelines (e.g., common privacy protection requirements) could be useful to build and sustain trust.[82] Standardization also makes it more straightforward to think about building a common national-level capability (as discussed previously regarding metrics).

Coordinating Independent Multidisciplinary Organizations with Overlapping Responsibilities While Avoiding Conflict Between Operational Demands and More-Collaborative Terrorism Prevention Approaches

Terrorism prevention interventions frequently require a coordinated multidisciplinary approach. Interviewees emphasized that this was often extremely beneficial, since it meant that different people with different expertise were brought to bear on addressing individuals at risk of perpetrating ideological violence.[83] However, the different agencies involved will likely not always see eye to eye, and some may determine that they have the responsibility to act unilaterally. This was most often flagged as a challenge for intervention activities involving law enforcement. As one of our interviewees put it:[84]

> That [juvenile] would still come to the counseling center but the police retain the ability to pursue legal action if the threat is imminent. It's a two-pronged approach. We know they are working collaboratively with us to prevent involvement in the criminal justice system. It's a fine line for law enforcement, I understand that. And sometimes it doesn't settle well with us . . . [but] our history with them has proven that they don't just haul a kid into court and press felony charges . . . without a clear evaluation.

Although this challenge came up in interviews regarding state and local-level programming, it was also flagged at the federal level, where actions taken can have reverberating effects at the local level. At the federal level, the FBI has the responsibility to respond to imminent threats. That responsibility creates potential tension between

---

terrorism-related offenses, although not all of our interviewees agreed with that argument.

[82] This approach was also argued in Patel and Koushik, 2017, p. 37.

[83] For example, one interviewee used a hypothetical case as an illustration: Having someone from a social work perspective and someone from the law enforcement perspective "argue" about and discuss the level of threat posed by a person identified browsing extremist content online would be valuable. While the social work approach to individual cases could limit the risk of escalating too quickly to measures like arrest and prosecution, having law enforcement at the table could help reduce the chances that the potential for the individual to pose an imminent threat would be too quickly discounted.

[84] Interview with a social services provider, 2018.

enforcement-focused action and more-collaborative terrorism prevention programming, particularly given local sensitivities about the FBI's enforcement activities.[85] In interviews at both the federal and local levels, the point was made that this may not be a challenge that can be "resolved" as much as one that must be confronted on an ongoing basis and could constrain the depth at which law enforcement agencies can be integrated into terrorism prevention efforts.

This potential friction between operational responsibilities to act in response to threats and more-collaborative approaches to dealing with social problems is not unique to terrorism. Similar tensions exist in community policing, which pairs interaction and problem-solving with a continuing requirement that police respond to criminal activity and enforce the law.[86] Interventions aimed at gang and drug crime often involve similar tradeoffs and tensions. Outside law enforcement, interventions focused on youth (e.g., intervening to improve family functioning, behavior, violence) can also encounter tension between continuing counseling and programming versus the requirement to act to protect at-risk children.[87]

Mitigating Risk Aversion (Including Fears of Failure and Liability), Which Can Limit Experimentation and Innovation

Because the goal of terrorism prevention efforts is the prevention of *terrorism*, it is not surprising that there are concerns that someone who was the subject of an intervention would later go on to commit a terrorist attack. At the federal level, interviewees described this concern as inhibiting willingness to try new programs or communications strategies that, while minimizing the risk of failure, also minimized the potential for terrorism prevention to make progress to reduce terrorism risk. Others have flagged this concern for nongovernmental funders.[88] This political risk aversion was also raised

---

[85] This tension has been recognized for some time. Bjelopera includes a similar discussion (including from the perspective of FBI officials) about the tension between enforcement and engagement, and the effects of aggressive intelligence-gathering and criminal justice approaches on the potential success of collaborative approaches (Jerome P. Bjelopera, *Countering Violent Extremism in the United States*, Washington, D.C.: Congressional Research Service, 7-5700, February 19, 2014, pp. 10–12). Others have made similar arguments regarding the involvement of U.S. Attorneys. See, e.g., Erroll Southers, "The U.S. Government's Program to Counter Violent Extremism Needs an Overhaul," *Los Angeles Times*, March 21, 2017.

[86] Research on the implementation of community policing has made the point that not all organizations will necessarily be equally adept at managing these internal tensions and competing demands. As a result, taking organizational characteristics into account may be necessary in the implementation of such efforts (e.g., Allison T. Chappell, "The Philosophical Versus Actual Adoption of Community Policing: A Case Study," *Criminal Justice Review*, Vol. 34, No. 1, 2009).

[87] A similar operational tension was raised in project discussions about terrorism prevention–related messaging. There are concerns about interference or conflict between CVE messages aimed internationally (where the U.S. Department of State [DOS] leads) and the homeland messaging space. In spite of these concerns, DOS has a mission responsibility to do that messaging and so the potential interference must be managed.

[88] Rosand, 2016, p. 18.

in describing law enforcement agencies' responses to terrorism—creating the pressure discussed above to arrest and prosecute rather than using more-collaborative, indirect, or community-centered terrorism prevention options. Some interviewees contrasted the United States with the United Kingdom in this respect: "For as much as people slam the UK programs, they try and fail [and learn]. We don't do that here."[89]

At the state, local, and NGO levels, there were other concerns about risk. Interviewees cited concerns about liability associated with intervention where they might be open to civil suit from victims of an attack by someone they sought to redirect from extremism. Questions were also raised about whether they would be subject to criminal exposure under terrorism material support laws if their intervention efforts were interpreted post hoc as having contributed in some way to a perpetrated attack.[90] Both of these types of potential liability exposure—in addition to the same "political liability" relevant at the federal level—were described as strong disincentives for private organizations to become involved in implementing terrorism prevention efforts.

In follow-up discussions of liability concerns, federal representatives argued that such concerns were unlikely to be realized because of the requirement to prove "knowing or intentional" support in the context of criminal prosecution and causation in the course of civil litigation. However, even if neither type of action would ultimately succeed, whether the costs of defense would be covered by liability insurance (as well as whether there would be differences in coverage across disciplines, e.g., between counseling providers versus other types of nonprofit or community organizations) remains unanswered. However, even if civil or criminal action associated with terrorism prevention efforts never occurs, concern leading organizations to opt out from participating still represents a design challenge that must be addressed.

Developing Terrorism Prevention Approaches that Are Not Dependent on Specific Individuals and that Can Be Sustained Through Staffing Changes

The scarcity of qualified individuals with the mix of skills and knowledge needed to make terrorism prevention efforts function effectively was a consistent theme in interviews. At the federal level, terrorism prevention efforts have been spearheaded by a cadre of staff who have committed a significant percentage of their government careers to the topic. These staff populated the CVE Task Force and drove activity at their respective agencies. Federal representatives in states and localities—from DHS, the U.S. Attorney's offices, the FBI, and others—were described as critical for building local implementation efforts and negotiating what has been a controversial and contentious policy area from the start.

---

[89] Interview with an academic researcher, 2018.

[90] For example: "[T]hey are trying to help, but if that person does something, there's a concern about liability. . . . [We] worried about a DOJ implication or in the community, the victim's families. If I intervene, am I providing material support?" (Interview with a federal representative, 2018).

Because federal CVE efforts have been relatively modest in scope and were implemented with greater focus on immediate priorities, interviewees flagged challenges in sustaining a federal CVE—and now terrorism prevention—enterprise over the long term. Over the course of past CVE efforts, many of these staff moved to other roles inside and outside government, and, in the words of more than one of our interviewees, "there was not a strong bench to draw from to replace them." The period of transition between CVE and terrorism prevention efforts over the last two years was also raised as a driver of migration of staff from this policy area. Although it is not surprising that in such a complex policy area the departure of a central person could be very disruptive to trust and weaken interagency and interorganizational relationships, the reality meant that past CVE efforts were—and terrorism prevention efforts are—vulnerable to the departure of key staff. State and local interviewees made similar points about key individuals, although they were less prominent than in our federal and national-level interviews.

Balancing the Demand for Data Collection and Measurement in Terrorism Prevention with the Need to Avoid Reinforcing Community Perceptions of Being Surveilled and Stigmatized

The development of measures and metrics and, in particular, collecting data to support evaluation could reinforce the perception by some that past CVE and current terrorism prevention efforts are actually surveillance programs. Data collection could therefore serve to directly reinforce that narrative and undermine the success of such efforts.[91] Developing an approach that allows data collection for evaluation and continuous improvement in terrorism prevention efforts over time while not undermining program success is a design and implementation challenge. Although mechanisms and structures exist in research contexts to take on these questions and craft approaches to address the concerns (e.g., regulatory and oversight structures for the protection of human subjects in research), whether those structures will be enough to overcome this hurdle may differ among different communities and populations. One part of that process could be increasing transparency about what is being collected and shared for evaluation purposes so that the community has an accurate picture of program activities and processes.[92]

---

[91] Interview with a federal representative in one U.S. city, 2018.

[92] In one city we visited (separate from the one in which this concern was specifically raised), the following was suggested:

> So, what does it look like? So, what are you reporting to DHS? There's a quarterly reporting process, but it's not like a list of people who we met. *So, we're meeting with DHS in terms of what we can share [with the community about what their reporting looks like].* We report like number of groups met, number of [law enforcement] briefings. *So how much can we share the actual report with the community to alleviate their concerns?* And we're also toying with the idea of having quarterly consultations where we say how much outreach we did, briefings we gave, but so that people can see. So we're looking at what methodology would look like to meet those goals. *And*

Using Traditional Policy Levers of Funding and Influence in the Controversial Environment that Surrounds Terrorism Prevention Efforts

Finally, controversy has made the implementation of past federal CVE initiatives more complex, and will likely remain a challenge to terrorism prevention going forward. Several interviewees emphasized that controversy around federal involvement required the government to adopt a "first do no harm" approach to not hinder progress made on terrorism prevention at the local level. In contrast to most policy areas, federal funding of terrorism prevention efforts is, in the words of more than one of our interviewees, "complicated." Sources of funding for terrorism prevention were described as sparse by interviewees involved in the implementation of local-level programs from both government and nongovernmental sources.[93] However, there were concerns about potential blowback from accepting federal funding, meaning that the traditional policy lever for strengthening local efforts is less straightforward for terrorism prevention. In the words of a local level community leader, "if funding . . . comes through CVE it kind of negates its legitimacy." Although relatively few organizations turned away federal grant dollars during the FY 2016 DHS grant solicitation, interviewees did suggest that concerns about controversy had reduced the number of organizations willing to compete for funds. Other interviewees were optimistic that the issue could be overcome, but that it was a design challenge to explore how increases in transparency and other trust-building activities could do so.

Summary

The goal of terrorism prevention efforts is to build alternatives to traditional counterterrorism and law enforcement–based approaches to addressing the risk of terrorist violence in the United States. However, doing so must respect that efforts are focused on individuals who have not broken any laws, but rather *may* be on a path that could lead to extremism and violence. Examination of past cases of radicalization and attempted attacks has shown that what "on a path that will lead to violence" means is difficult to define. This ambiguity reinforces the need for options other than aggressive investigation and prosecution, but it also means that terrorism prevention efforts must be designed with an eye to their effects on the individuals who become subject to them, because a significant number of those individuals are likely to be "false positives" who would not have carried out future violence. Finding options that meet that challenge— and the range of other design challenges that exist for this policy area—is what is

---

asking [the]community what they do want to see and know. We want them to know we're here to work with them not surveil them. (Emphasis added.)

[93] As we discuss in Chapter Nine, relatively modest amounts of funding have been allocated to CVE (now terrorism prevention) efforts, even after federal interest in the mission area increased. The exception to that funding reality was the FY 2016 grant program that made $10 million available to fund local efforts.

needed to move toward a more effective and practical national terrorism prevention enterprise.

CHAPTER FOUR

Early-Phase Terrorism Prevention: Countering Extremist Messaging Online

The internet has become a powerful tool to spread messages about violent ideologies. The growth of mobile phone usage, first seen in developed countries, has spread extensively across the world, including to underdeveloped areas in Africa and Southeast Asia with limited wiring and other infrastructure. This trend means that people are better connected worldwide—and that extremists can exploit this connectivity to reach new audiences. The problem is exacerbated by the diversity of platforms on which extremist content is shared. Large technology companies like Alphabet (which operates Google and YouTube), Facebook, and Twitter run platforms that are only the tip of the online iceberg. Some extremists have become adept at using encrypted platforms like Telegram, WhatsApp (now owned by Facebook), and others to share messages that can evade detection more easily.

Online platforms also have improved terrorists' ability to recruit new members from all over the world. This has been especially problematic in Western European countries, where foreign fighter recruitment—through a combination of online and in-person mechanisms—has been a major issue (see Table 2.1 in Chapter Two).[1] Digital platforms make it easy to spread ideas to wide swaths of the population, including ideas pertaining to violent or extreme ideologies. At its peak, ISIS's social media campaign consisted of between 40,000 and 90,000 individuals—including active propagandists and participants in the group's larger "social media echo chamber," which aims to reinforce and spread the group's messages.[2] These accounts tend to have substantially more followers than a typical Twitter account and they tweeted far more often, expanding their reach.[3] The United States has experienced much less foreign recruitment

---

[1] This threat has been a driver of focus in the United Kingdom on extremist content online, and the country has taken a leading role in international discussions of the issue.

[2] J. M. Berger and Jonathon Morgan, *The ISIS Twitter Census: Defining and Describing the Population of ISIS Supporters on Twitter*, Washington, D.C.: The Brookings Institution, No. 20, March 2015, pp. 2–3.

[3] Elizabeth Bodine-Baron, Todd C. Helmus, Madeline Magnuson, and Zev Winkelman, *Examining ISIS Support and Opposition Networks on Twitter*, Santa Monica, Calif.: RAND Corporation, RR-1328-RC, August 2016, pp. 8–11.

than many allies and partners, but there have been some notable cases, including al-Shabab's "active and deliberate attempt" to recruit Somali youth in the United States in part through distributing recruitment materials online.[4] Such cases represent threats to young people in America because they reach across national borders via the internet, creating threats here and exacerbating threats abroad.[5]

Similar concerns exist wholly within our national borders. Domestic white nationalist groups were responsible for violence at the alt-right "Unite the Right" rally in Charlottesville, Va., in 2017. Such groups have used Twitter and other platforms to promote their ideals: Social media was integral in attracting participants to Charlottesville and has been used to catalyze other coordinated activities, like flash mobs.[6] As a result, taking a holistic view of the range of ideologies that can incite violent action, whether through recruitment to well-defined organizations or by inspiring actions by individuals independently, is an issue within the United States as well. Activities falling within this facet of terrorism prevention are captured in the upper part of our mapping, the relevant section of which is reproduced in Figure 4.1.

The complexities associated with online communication contribute to the idea that the "messaging conflict" in the online space must be a central focus of national terrorism prevention activity, but it is complicated by its direct relation to constitutionally protected rights of free speech. Thus, the line between legal, protected activity and illegal behavior can be difficult to draw. U.S. government leaders we spoke to for this study are well aware of the challenges posed by extremist content on online platforms and how difficult it can be to respond to it. In the United States and abroad, there are many efforts dedicated to stopping the spread of online extremist messaging. It is important to examine these issues through a global lens because online content does not observe boundaries, and we should expect that content created anywhere in the world can reach a U.S. audience and vice versa. Nongovernmental interviewees who are working on these problems also emphasized the issues of balance and expressed concern about acting in response to individuals' statements online, given the difficulty in discerning real and true threats from the potentially misguided behavior of youths trying to get attention by being extreme. As a result, and echoing language with respect to physical world intervention efforts (which we discuss in more detail in Chapter Seven), an NGO leader framed their active efforts to respond to extremism online

---

[4]   ADL, *Al Shabab's American Recruits*, New York, February 2015.

[5]   A federal intelligence community interviewee pointed out that one way to think about this facet of the threat was "people out there trying to poison kids' minds" here at home, reflecting the duality that young people exposed to extremist propaganda online may eventually become threats, but they are also victims (e.g., this is analogous in some respects to youth recruited by human traffickers). Interview with a federal representative, 2018.

[6]   Jane Coaston, "The Alt-Right Is Going on Trial in Charlottesville," *Vox*, March 8, 2018; Michael Edison Hayden, "Richard Spencer: Prepare for More White Nationalist Flash Mobs," *Newsweek*, October 10, 2017.

Figure 4.1
Online Countermessaging Within the Terrorism Prevention Policy Space

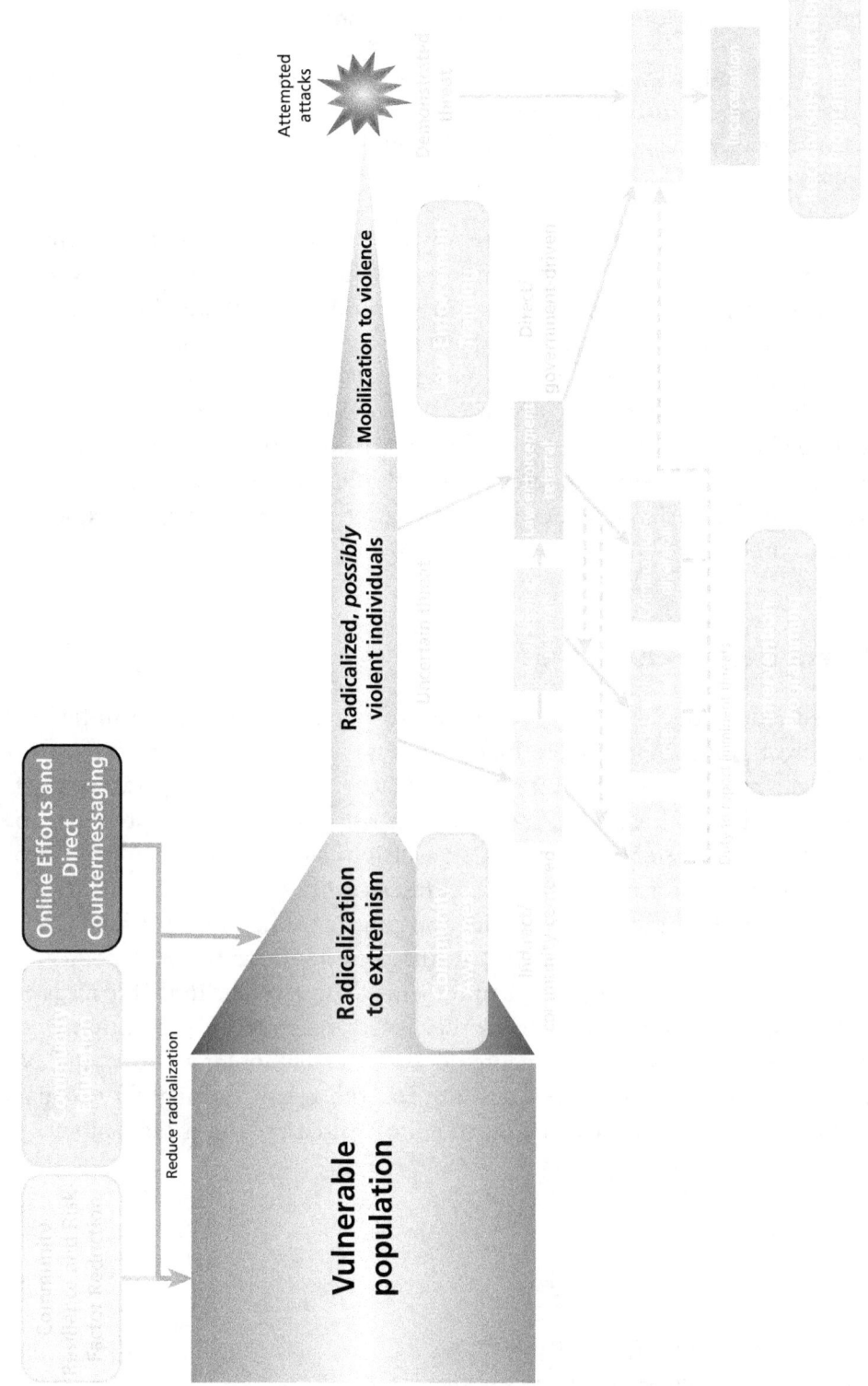

as focused not only on responding to threats, but also on responding to the potential law enforcement response to such communication:

> If a 15-year-old is posting pro-extremist material online, there are two people looking: the extremist trying to recruit them and the [law enforcement official] trying to arrest them. Digital CVE is the third option. The aim of our work is to stop both parties.[7]

Such framing has parallels to the way that a group of law enforcement interviewees framed their intervention efforts in one of the cities we visited. They argued that, in addition to preventing harm to the community, they were also trying to prevent the often young individuals involved from escalating to a point where law enforcement had no choice but to make an arrest.[8] Within the United States, government and public-private partnerships focused on online countermessaging have achieved varying degrees of success. We observed two major types of interventions to respond to extremist content online: content removal and countermessaging. The former has proven somewhat easier to achieve than the latter, for reasons we will explore throughout this chapter.

Relevant Design Challenges

Damaged trust (coupled with a sensitivity to potential impacts on individual rights) makes direct government involvement in messaging activities very difficult. Furthermore, legal restrictions prohibiting government use of propaganda prevent certain activities outright. This makes the area high risk politically and presents a barrier to efforts' success, therefore increasing risk aversion. Multiple agencies have responsibilities and authorities for messaging and online activities that also could come into conflict—notably DOS messaging outside the country. The potential for those messages to diffuse back into the United States can create tensions between coordination/collaboration and individual agency requirements. Effectiveness in this space is even more dependent on outside partners than other facets of terrorism prevention, where those partners are technology platform providers, other technology firms, and NGOs. In contrast to other terrorism prevention areas, the relative availability of data in the online and messaging space can contribute to evaluation and measurement.

---

[7]   Interview with an NGO representative, 2018.

[8]   Interview with law enforcement representatives in a U.S. city, 2018.

Approaches to Countering Extremist Messaging Online

Given the importance of the online space for the development of threats, it has been crucial that the government and private sector alike consider appropriate responses to extremist messaging online.[9] DOS creates countermessaging content for its overseas CVE programs, but the goals for these interventions may be different than goals for interventions focused within the United States. Furthermore, federal and private-sector stakeholders we spoke to for this study expressed concern over the risks associated with attempting counternarrative efforts aimed within the United States. Although it is much less controversial than countermessaging, the removal of extremist content from circulation is not universally viewed as acceptable, especially when the government is driving the process. For example, the perception of the federal government monitoring or ordering the removal of objectionable content could be viewed as overreach and raise concerns about free speech.[10] Damaged trust between the federal government and members of the public makes credible interventions difficult to achieve.[11] As a report from the University of Washington notes, "Individuals inclined toward extremism often already have poor relationships with their governments due to the structural polices that perpetuate their desperation. For this reason, governments are not always the best arbiters of counter-narrative programs. . . ."[12] This lack of trust has made it even more important for the federal government to attract credible private-sector partners to assist in their countermessaging efforts. One notable program that government leaders cite as effective in this regard is the Peer2Peer or P2P program, which we will discuss later in this chapter.

Policies and Programming

Challenges of operating in the online space notwithstanding, there are several options for the federal government to implement policies and programming to counter extremism online.[13] One option is the removal of content advocating violence.[14] Content

---

[9] Other assessments of needs and proposals for improving then-CVE efforts have focused on the need to motivate private-sector actors to innovate in this space. See, e.g., Green and Proctor, 2016.

[10] Interviews with an NGO representative, 2018, and interviews with current government officials, 2018.

[11] Interviews with federal government representatives, 2018.

[12] Angela Kim, Stacia Lee, Oliver Marguleas, and Jessica L. Beyer, *JSIS Cybersecurity Report: Do Counter-Narrative Programs Slow Terrorist Recruiting?* Seattle, Wash.: University of Washington Jackson School of International Studies, October 3, 2016.

[13] For a review, see Benjamin Ducol, Martin Bouchard, Garth Davies, Marie Ouellet, and Christine Neudecker, *Assessment of the State of Knowledge: Connections Between Research on the Social Psychology of the Internet and Violent Extremism*, Waterloo, ON: Canadian Network for Research on Terrorism, Security and Society, Working Paper 16-05, May 2016.

[14] Federal interviewees conceded that, as was the case for local law enforcement, major technology firms must view extremist content as one among a group of threat and risk issues that they need to address to respond to the

removal has become a focus in some of the countries we examined, most notably the United Kingdom and at the European Union (EU) level.[15] Conversely, messaging could focus on community engagement to "detect" radicalized individuals who require intervention or "immunize" at-risk populations to reduce their susceptibility to radicalization. The goals and factors affecting success are different for each class of activity, however, which must be considered when contemplating programming. The private sector largely has been responsible for content removal, while federal government efforts have been more focused on countermessaging through such programs as "Don't Be a Puppet" and "Think Again, Turn Away," which we will discuss later in this chapter.

International terrorism prevention messaging interventions include media or organizationally delivered messaging that focuses on nonviolence or nonradicalization, or alternative grievance-resolution approaches. Domestically, media and organizationally delivered messaging also have been implemented for terrorism prevention, as well as gang and violence prevention. For example, the Cure Violence program has been implemented in several American cities, including Chicago and Baltimore, to build a social consensus against gun violence. It relies on in-person interventions and media campaigns to build relationships with community leaders and law enforcement alike.[16] However, there is mixed evidence for evaluating the effectiveness of messaging efforts aimed at specific problems. It is often difficult to determine whether these messages are received by the target audience, which is integral to assess the effectiveness of messaging efforts.

Evidence for Effectiveness

Academics have criticized CVE messaging interventions for relying on expert opinion instead of evaluating their approaches scientifically. As Kate Ferguson of the University of East Anglia puts it, "the absence of methodologically robust monitoring and evaluation practices with regard to CVE counter-narratives is striking."[17] Maura Conway, of the University of Dublin and the EU-funded think tank VOX-Pol, argues that the

---

needs of their community. Other examples cited were issues with human trafficking and attempts to groom individuals to be trafficked via social media, content advocating or documenting self-harm, and other hate material (Interview with a federal representative, 2018).

[15] Natasha Lomas, "UK Outs Extremism Blocking Tool and Could Force Tech Firms to Use It," *Tech Crunch*, February 13, 2018.

[16] Jeffrey A. Butts, Caterina Gouvis Roman, Lindsay Bostwick, and Jeremy R. Porter, "Cure Violence: A Public Health Model to Reduce Gun Violence," *Annual Review of Public Health*, Vol. 36, 2015; Daniel W. Webster, Jennifer Mendel Whitehill, Jon S. Vernick, and Elizabeth M. Parker, *Evaluation of Baltimore's Safe Streets Program: Effects on Attitudes, Participants' Experiences, and Gun Violence*, Baltimore, Md.: Johns Hopkins Center for the Prevention of Youth Violence, Johns Hopkins Bloomberg School of Public Health, January 11, 2012.

[17] Kate Ferguson, *Countering Violent Extremism Through Media and Communication Strategies*, Norwich, UK: University of East Anglia, Partnership for Conflict, Crime, and Security Research, March 1, 2016.

lack of scientifically valid research into the mechanics of the online radicalization process means that attempts to develop online CVE programs are essentially futile. As she explains, "How can we develop and deploy effective online CVE projects absent knowing who precisely these should be targeted at, what types of content are attractive to them, and what platforms are trafficked by these users? These are the kinds of answers that nobody appears to have at the present time."[18] It remains unclear whether counternarratives should focus on countering specific extremist claims or supplanting extremist narratives, or whether offline activities will ultimately be more important than any online activities.

Some stakeholders we interviewed for this project believed that online counter-messaging was one place where quantitative metrics could be more easily developed.[19] For example, Jigsaw, Google's "think and do" tank, found that several hundred thousand visitors spent half a million minutes viewing videos that counter ISIS narratives in 2016.[20] However, statistics that track how many individual clicks a link gets or minutes a video is watched only provide a glimpse into how people engage with online content. Tracking whether behavior changes based on this engagement has proven to be a more intractable problem.

Although evidence regarding the effectiveness of initiatives to counter online extremism is sparse, there are some examples. In general, the best evidence for effectiveness comes from prevention campaigns that target individuals in the process of radicalizing. For example, the Institute for Strategic Dialogue's (ISD)'s One to One project identified a small number of violent extremists from white nationalist groups in the United States and Islamist groups in the United Kingdom and had former extremists directly message them via Facebook.[21] The sample size from the intervention was small—only 76 extremists received messages—but, of those reached, slightly more than 60 percent of the extremists saw the messages, and 63 percent of white nationalists and 42 percent of Islamists actually responded to the message. Sixty percent of those who responded sustained the engagement for five or more messages.

Although these numbers exceed the industry average for email marketing campaigns, as is the case for most evaluations of messaging campaigns, the assessment had a limited pool of responses from which to draw conclusions. As covered elsewhere in our broader examination of metrics, the study also experienced the common challenge of getting to outcomes, as there was no way to measure whether those who received the intervention left extremist groups or avoided violent behavior. Google's evaluation of

---

[18] Maura Conway, "Determining the Role of the Internet in Violent Extremism and Terrorism: Six Suggestions for Progressing Research," *Studies in Conflict and Terrorism*, Vol. 40, No. 1, 2017a.

[19] Interviews with former and current government officials, 2018.

[20] Andy Greenberg, "Google's Clever Plan to Stop Aspiring ISIS Recruits," *Wired*, September 7, 2016.

[21] Ross Frenett and Moli Dow, *One to One Online Interventions: A Pilot CVE Methodology*, London: Institute for Strategic Dialogue, 2015.

its Redirect Method takes a comparable approach and offers similar research positives and negatives, which we will discuss later in this chapter.[22]

Evaluations of online initiatives to prevent hate crimes, suicide, and substance abuse that also use internet or media-based tactics to reach and influence at-risk youth have experienced similar challenges. The effects of online initiatives can take time to demonstrate results. It is often not possible to isolate the effects of one particular online intervention from another, or from an offline intervention. Researchers from the University of Washington note that similar anti-gang messaging efforts are often successful because they are linked to the broader network of community programs designed to discourage gang involvement.[23] Regarding evaluation for a related social issue, hate crimes, Perry notes that "[cyberhate scholarship] is an area that is only just emerging in the broader literature on hate crime. Sadly, relatively little attention has been paid to either developing or evaluating social policy initiatives. The primary cause for optimism has been the work on school-based anti-hate programming."[24]

A 2015 review of web-based suicide prevention interventions targeted at youth found some benefits to these types of approaches, but cautioned that additional research is needed to fully understand the benefits and risks. Youth surveyed found web-based interventions enjoyable to engage with, but concerns persist about the volume of content to which they can be exposed online and whether that might affect them in ways counter to the interventions. The authors note the emergence of web-based interventions because of the popularity of these platforms, but caution against the lack of literature that assesses these interventions. In this growing field, there are many opportunities for further study that can appropriately shape antisuicide campaigns.[25] The same sentiment was echoed in another review of research related to adolescent use of the internet for suicide or self-harm. The authors found that youth who use online platforms to seek help are also susceptible to cyber-bullying, which can have harmful consequences on young people who are already in a fragile state. However, given the proclivity of young people to seek information or help from the internet, there appears to be promise in using online platforms to deliver interventions that can steer at-risk youth away from suicide or self-harm.[26]

---

[22] The Redirect Method, "About the Method," webpage, undated(a).

[23] Kim et al., 2016.

[24] Barbara Perry, "The More Things Change. . . Post 9/11 Trends in Hate Crime Scholarship," in Neil Chakraborti, ed., *Hate Crime: Concepts, Policy, Future Directions*, New York: Routledge, 2010, p. 29.

[25] Yael Perry, Aliza Werner-Seidler, Alison L. Calear, and Helen Christensen, "Web-Based and Mobile Suicide Prevention Interventions for Young People: A Systematic Review," *Journal of the Canadian Academy of Child and Adolescent Psychiatry*, Vol. 25, No. 2, 2016.

[26] Kate Daine, Keith Hawton, Vinod Singaravelu, Anne Stewart, Sue Simkin, and Paul Montgomery, "The Power of the Web: A Systematic Review of Studies of the Influence of the Internet on Self-Harm and Suicide in Young People," *PLOS One*, Vol. 8, No. 10, 2013.

A review of interventions to reduce substance abuse in youth came to similar conclusions regarding digital interventions. Media campaigns against smoking, which have a longer history than mobile content, demonstrated effectiveness in influencing adolescents away from smoking. Content created for mobile phones in particular appeared promising, but the existing research is scant. Researchers observed generally positive or neutral indications from youth who interacted with internet-based interventions about the negative effects of smoking, drugs, and alcohol, but more-rigorous evaluation is needed.[27]

In short, young people especially are active online, which may necessitate interventions to reach them there for a variety of disciplines aimed at improving public health and safety. Narratives that counter extremist messaging will benefit from further analysis to determine whether their programming reaches target audiences, and whether those audiences are affected by the messages.

Current U.S. Terrorism Prevention and Related Efforts to Counter Online Extremist Messaging

Government Initiatives

Federal efforts to counter extremist messaging within the United States have focused mainly on coordination with technology and other platforms where messages are transmitted, with extremely limited direct-messaging activity. One exception is the FBI's "Don't Be a Puppet" campaign, which tries to explain terrorist recruitment pathways but has been broadly criticized for perpetuating stereotypes against Muslims and breeding suspicion over potentially innocuous activities, such as travel to countries like Germany, France, and Saudi Arabia.[28] At the local-government level, some city law enforcement officials we spoke to include internet safety training as part of community outreach efforts. These measures were viewed as promising for increasing resilience against extremist messaging without prompting anti-CVE, and now, anti–terrorism prevention, backlash.[29]

In contrast to the paucity of its U.S.-focused countermessaging activity, the U.S. government has engaged in internationally focused CVE-messaging efforts led by DOS for years. However, government officials recognize the spillover potential, given the borderless online space in which some of these messages are created and shared.

---

[27] Jai K. Das, Rehana A. Salam, Ahmed Arshad, Yaron Finkelstein, and Zulfiqar A. Bhutta, "Interventions for Adolescent Substance Abuse: An Overview of Systematic Reviews," *Journal of Adolescent Health*, Vol. 59, No. 4, 2016.

[28] Lauren Camera, "FBI's Anti-Extremism Website Should Be Scrapped, Groups Say," *U.S. News and World Report*, April 6, 2016.

[29] Interview with a local NGO representative, 2018.

The Global Engagement Center (GEC) leads DOS's counterpropaganda efforts, which were expanded with the FY 2017 National Defense Authorization Act to include state-sponsored disinformation.[30] The GEC supersedes DOS's Center for Strategic Counterterrorism Communications (CSCC), which was originally tasked with coordinating public communications against terrorism and extremism with NCTC and other government entities as appropriate.[31] Both GEC and CSCC have historically sponsored a range of countermessaging activities in languages native to their target populations. These engagements include advertisements targeted at youth in North Africa who sought to engage with ISIS content, and social media campaigns on platforms like Twitter including direct messaging with extremists.[32] In 2013, CSCC launched the "Think Again, Turn Away" campaign, which included the graphic and critically received "Welcome to ISIS Land" video. As is the case for all terrorism prevention initiatives and discussed in our examination of metrics, the difficulty of "proving a negative"—i.e., the notion that it is impossible to truly know whether someone decided not to join ISIS *because* of watching CSCC content—became a major barrier to assessing the effectiveness of CSCC countermessaging.[33] Other elements of the U.S. government, including the Broadcasting Board of Governors, with its mission to "inform, engage, and connect people around the world in support of freedom and democracy," also play central roles in the international components of this policy area.[34]

Public-Private Partnerships

There has been outside interest in federal grants for producing countermessaging content. In the FY 2016 funded grants, online and counternarrative activities received approximately 16 percent of the funding across eight separate grant awards.[35] There also were a substantial number of unfunded submissions to the solicitation in this category, suggesting greater demand for implementing programming in this facet of terrorism prevention.

---

[30] DOS, "Global Engagement Center," webpage, undated.

[31] White House, Office of the Press Secretary, *Executive Order 13584—Developing an Integrated Strategic Counterterrorism Communications Initiative*, Washington, D.C., September 9, 2011.

[32] Joby Warrick, "How a U.S. Team Uses Facebook, Guerrilla Marketing to Peel Off Potential ISIS Recruits," *Washington Post*, February 6, 2017. GEC reports that its "direct engagement with violent extremists has been reduced in favor of partner-driven messaging and enhancing the content capabilities of our partners." It is also increasing use of analytics to "understand radicalization dynamics online, to guide and inform our messaging efforts, and to measure. . . effectiveness" (DOS, undated).

[33] Greg Miller and Scott Higham, "In a Propaganda War Against ISIS, the U.S. Tried to Play by the Enemy's Rules," *The Washington Post*, May 8, 2015.

[34] Broadcasting Board of Governors, "Mission," homepage, undated.

[35] Some awards that fell into categories outside the "Challenging the Narrative" component of the FY 2016 solicitation included relevant activities.

DHS's former Peer2Peer program was cited repeatedly by interviewees as a success story in government cooperation with the private sector on countermessaging efforts, leading many to view the defunding of its U.S-oriented component as a significant missed opportunity to build on that success. P2P was cosponsored at different times by DHS, DOS, and the U.S. Department of Defense. The program funded university students to create campaigns to counter extremist narratives.[36] Because supporting student efforts is relatively low cost, the program produced some countermessaging initiatives in a way that averted government concerns and risk aversion in this area for relatively little investment. It also had established interest in CVE in student and faculty populations, and many schools repeated the program for new classes.[37] The overall program and its activities are still active, although it is no longer affiliated with the U.S. government. EdVenture Partners, the firm that manages the program, now implements a version of the U.S.-focused effort with the support and collaboration of the ADL. Facebook partners with EdVenture on global student-run counternarrative campaigns.[38]

P2P may be a good way to generate new ideas for public- or private-sector consideration, but evaluation of the long-term effects of the campaigns launched through the program is still a challenge. Although P2P built goodwill between government and academic communities, a report from the University of Washington critiqued P2P for failing to demonstrate that it reached its target audience—youth vulnerable to radicalization.[39] Furthermore, approximately 75 percent of campaigns end when students move on, creating a lack of consistency that makes program evaluation even more challenging. EdVenture is working on developing an evidence-based evaluation to address some of these challenges.[40]

Contacts between the government and technology firms to remove extremist content are another way government cooperates with the private sector to counter extremist messaging. These interactions—in which DHS plays a lead role—often take place through such forums as the Global Internet Forum to Counter Terrorism (GIFCT), the EU Internet Forum, or the Global Coalition against Daesh;[41] in some cases, tech-

---

[36] DHS Office of Academic Engagement, "How DHS Partnerships Help Counter Violent Extremism," DHS Study in the States Blog, July 20, 2016.

[37] This effect was flagged by interviewees as an important outcome of the program, since a viable route to strengthening human capital for terrorism prevention efforts (which we discuss in greater detail elsewhere in this report) would be to stimulate interest in the area and its challenge in college and graduate student populations (Interview with a federal representative, 2018).

[38] Interview with NGO representatives, 2018.

[39] Kim et al., 2016.

[40] Interview with NGO representatives, May 2018.

[41] Although interviewees inside and outside the federal government were very positive about these types of forums, some federal interviewees in particular still suggested there were "translation problems" between federal staff and technology companies because of their different perspectives—and that such interactions could help

nology companies have identified individual agencies of the government they collaborate with, such as NCTC in the United States or the Home Office in the United Kingdom.[42] Interaction with technology firms was a core line of activity under the CVE Task Force (with dedicated individuals responsible for that role). Efforts included the *Digital Forum on Terrorism Prevention*, an event that involved representatives from the technology industry and government. A Community Awareness Briefing (CAB) focusing on terrorist use of social media was developed under the auspices of the Task Force as well, designed to be delivered to technology-sector partners via online distribution. Significant DHS outreach and coordination activities with the private sector are ongoing.

YouTube has the most-extensive collaboration with third-party organizations. Its "trusted flagger" program provides government and nongovernmental organizations who are approved for participation with more-advanced tools to report videos they believe violate the site's terms of use. Flagged content goes into a priority queue where YouTube's content moderation team will quickly respond to these takedown requests.[43] Although YouTube does not publicly list these organizations, the involvement of some (such as the Southern Poverty Law Center) have been criticized by some groups as potentially resulting in bias in moderation activities.[44]

Private-Sector Efforts to Counter Online Extremist Messaging

Numerous counternarrative initiatives have been driven by large technology companies and smaller NGOs, including redirection efforts, content removal, presentation of contextualizing content alongside extremist messages, hashtag campaigns against extremism and hate, and the creation of countercontent by students and other entities. Internet safety campaigns and content—i.e., teaching parents about online extremist content as part of informing them how to watch out for their children—were cited by interviewees as part of their community outreach activities and a response to online threats.[45] Private-sector initiatives apply to platforms run by technology companies as well as tools for broader use. In addition to well-known companies like Facebook, Twitter, and Google, organizations like the ISD, the Gen Next Foundation, Moon-

---

continue to address extremist content online (supplemented by federal human capital concerns, which we discuss in Chapter Ten).

[42] Monika Bickert and Brian Fishman, "Hard Questions: How We Counter Terrorism," *Facebook Newsroom*, June 15, 2017; Colin Stretch, "Testimony Before the Senate Judiciary Subcommittee on Crime and Terrorism," United States Senate Committee on the Judiciary Subcommittee on Crime and Terrorism, October 31, 2017.

[43] YouTube, "Trusted Flagger Program," undated.

[44] Ben Kamisar, "Conservatives Cry Foul over Controversial Group's Role in YouTube Moderation," *The Hill*, March 8, 2018.

[45] Interviews with local law enforcement officials in U.S. cities, 2018.

shot CVE, and others produce counternarratives, analyze these efforts, or both.[46] The following section presents an overview of the work these entities are performing to counter extremist messaging online. Given the breadth of organizations around the world involved in these and similar efforts—and how quickly new organizations can emerge—we present this as an illustrative sample of organizations involved in producing national or global counternarratives, not a definitive account of countermessaging initiatives.

Major Technology Companies

To counter the spread of extremist content, Google, Facebook, and Twitter have turned primarily to artificial intelligence and machine learning algorithms. According to internal data from these firms, such tools have made a dramatic difference in the fight against ISIS online in particular. Machine-learning algorithms now detect and remove 83 percent of all YouTube videos that violate its violent extremism policies.[47] Twitter now credits similar algorithms with identifying and suspending 95 percent of all accounts flagged for violating their terrorism policies; 75 percent of those suspensions occurred before the account has made a single tweet.[48] Facebook claims a 99-percent success rate in its own similar efforts.[49]

Although these companies credit autonomous algorithms with the bulk of their success, they also acknowledge the need to supplement these approaches with a human touch. To ensure that context is taken into consideration when making determinations about content violations, Google, Facebook, and Twitter have invested in expanding their content moderation teams. YouTube—which is owned by Google—has boosted their content moderation team to more than 10,000 people, while Facebook has nearly doubled its team from 4,500 to 7,500 people.[50] Twitter has fewer content moderators, given that the company's total staff of 4,000 employees is smaller than the number of *moderators* in each of the other two firms. Additionally, Facebook has a dedicated counterterrorism team of 150 experts, including former FBI agents, academics, and

---

[46] Federal interviewees who were involved in the technology side of CVE over the years praised early efforts by large technology firms (during the period when the main concern was al Qaeda and responding to Anwar al-Awlaki's communication efforts) for training and building the capacity of community organizations to broaden the bench of entities that were active in this space (Interviews with federal representatives, 2018).

[47] Richard Salgado, "Written Testimony Before the Senate Judiciary Subcommittee on Crime and Terrorism," Washington, D.C., October 31, 2017.

[48] Sean J. Edgett, "Testimony Before the Senate Judiciary Subcommittee on Crime and Terrorism," Washington, D.C., October 31, 2017.

[49] Bickert and Fishman, 2017.

[50] For YouTube, see Sam Levin, "Google to Hire Thousands of Moderators After Outcry over YouTube Abuse Videos," *The Guardian*, December 5, 2017. For Facebook, see Alexis C. Madrigal, "Inside Facebook's Fast-Growing Content-Moderation Effort," *The Atlantic*, February 7, 2018.

analysts who assist other Facebook teams with understanding terrorist behavior on the platform so they can build tools to combat it.[51]

In addition to filtering content, both Google and Facebook have initiatives to expose people searching for jihadist content to alternative narratives. Google implemented a pilot effort under the brand "Redirect Method" to describe this, while Facebook calls its initiative "Counter-speech."[52] Google provides statistics to gauge the effectiveness of this program, demonstrating that users engaged with these ads more frequently and for a longer period than typical online advertisements. Jigsaw's anti-jihadi content has been informed by research into ISIS's particular appeal and seems to follow best practices in this sphere. Redirect videos employ ISIS defectors who can personally and specifically counter ISIS's propaganda, documentary footage showing the reality of ISIS rule, and credible religious figures to undermine ISIS's interpretation of Islam.[53] However, a recent study by the Counter Extremism Project (CEP) found that a user searching for extremist content on YouTube was almost three times more likely to see that content instead of counternarratives, suggesting that Redirect may not be as effective as previously thought.[54] Facebook's approach is less centralized, involving partnerships with a wide variety of NGOs expressing general anti-violence/pro-tolerance messages.

Despite positive engagement metrics for some initiatives, overall user engagement was still low, and these metrics track only engagement, not effectiveness.[55] For example, only about 4 percent of users clicked on Redirect ads. As with other online counternarrative initiatives, it remains exceptionally difficult to determine effectiveness. An ISD study that examined three counternarrative campaigns over the course of one year found that engagement with content, such as liking, sharing, or commenting, did not necessarily correlate with how long a video was viewed, pointing to difficulty determining whether someone engaging with the video absorbed its message and modified (or failed to modify) their behavior accordingly.[56]

In addition to their individual efforts, Google, Facebook, Twitter, and Microsoft collaborated to found GIFCT in 2017. GIFCT works with a range of stakeholders, including the UN, ICT4Peace Foundation, and Tech Against Terrorism, to share information and best practices, and to conduct and fund research.[57] Initially, their pri-

---

[51] Seth Fiegerman, "Facebook Grows Its Counterterrorism Team," *CNN*, June 15, 2017.

[52] The Redirect Method, undated(a); Facebook, "Counterspeech," webpage, undated.

[53] The Redirect Method, "The Pilot Experiment," webpage, undated(b).

[54] CEP, *OK Google, Show Me Extremism: Analysis of YouTube's Extremist Video Takedown Policy and Counter-Narrative Program*, 2018.

[55] The Redirect Method, "The Pilot Experiment: Results," webpage, undated(c).

[56] Tanya Silverman, Christopher J. Stewart, Zahed Amanullah, and Jonathan Birdwell, *The Impact of Counter-Narratives*, London: Institute for Strategic Dialogue, 2016.

[57] GIFCT, "About," homepage, undated.

mary contribution was to create a shared database of video "hashes" that would allow all participating members of the alliance to identify duplicate copies of a video banned by any of the participating services.[58] Hash codes are calculated by a mathematical function that ensures that the hash function will always generate the same number for the same input. Identifying a hash function with these properties for slight variations of the same video is a particularly difficult problem.

GIFCT has now expanded to assist smaller technology companies with adopting best practices to disrupt the hosting of extremist content.[59] It is unclear how far this collaboration goes. For example, JustPaste.it has reportedly become one of ISIS's favorite hosting sites, yet it likely lacks the resources and technical staff to implement industry best practices on its own.[60] Any significant decrease in ISIS content hosted on the site may indicate more-robust cooperation with larger technology companies.

Other NGOs and Initiatives

The ISD responds to challenges posed by all forms of extremism through research, evaluation, and content generation. ISD, which is an independent organization based in London with offices worldwide, works with public- and private-sector entities to counter extremist content "through cutting-edge research, analysis, data management, and capacity building."[61] ISD claims to have engaged 4,800,800 "at-risk" individuals online as of June 2018.[62] In addition to the One to One program, described earlier in this chapter, ISD supports the Counter-Narrative Toolkit, which is a website with how-to guides for creating and promoting campaigns and content. The website also includes case studies with best practices, although it is unclear whether any rigorous evaluation of the campaigns the site highlights has been conducted.[63] ISD also manages counterextremism.org, which is part of a wider project funded by the European Commission to "support the dissemination and exchange of best practice[s] in the field of counter-radicalisation work across Europe." Through this program, ISD has completed three cross-country evaluations of counterextremism programming, sponsored two exchanges for practitioners working in the field, and advises member nations on counterextremism and counterradicalization.[64]

---

[58] Kent Walker, "Working Together to Combat Terrorists Online," *The Keyword*, September 20, 2017.

[59] The Keyword, "Update on the Global Internet Forum to Counter Terrorism," Google blog, December 4, 2017.

[60] Ahmad Shehabat and Teodor Mitew, "Black-Boxing the Black Flag: Anonymous Sharing Platforms and ISIS Content Distribution Tactics," *Perspectives on Terrorism*, Vol. 12, No. 1, 2018.

[61] ISD, *About: the IDS Approach*, undated(a).

[62] ISD, *Work*, undated(d).

[63] For more, see "Counter-Narrative Toolkit," homepage, undated.

[64] CEP, homepage, undated(a).

ISD also runs the Online Civil Courage Initiative (OCCI), a partnership with Facebook, and the Innovation Hub. OCCI is "the first strategic non-governmental effort to mount a proportional response to the propagation of hate, violence and terrorism online, across Europe. It delivers models that combine expertise from the technology, communications and marketing, and academic sectors to 'upskill and upscale' the civic response to online hate and extremism." OCCI provides research on extremist trends and potential responses, grants to NGOs seeking to create online countermessaging, and training. OCCI also runs conferences and other engagements to support a community of interest. OCCI has 500 members and claims to have reached 15 million people online, although it is unclear what the outcomes of these engagements have been.[65]

ISD's Innovation Hub brings together partners from around the world to create replicable, data-driven counternarratives designed to build off of existing content and strengthen future efforts. These counternarratives are informed by the Innovation Hub's mapping and research capabilities that identify current and new platforms extremists are using to spread propaganda.[66] One of the organizations the Innovation Hub has worked with is Average Mohamed, a Minneapolis-based nonprofit run by Mohamed Ahmed, a Somali immigrant (see Figure 4.2). Ahmed produces cartoons with simple messages that seek to counter ISIS narratives and promote more-peaceful dialogue on matters of race, religion, family, and other issues of importance to youth

Figure 4.2
Average Mohamed

SOURCE: "Average Mohamed," homepage, undated. Used with permission.
RAND RR2647-4.2

---

[65] ISD, *Online Civil Courage Initiative*, undated(c).

[66] ISD, *Innovation Hub*, undated(b).

worldwide.[67] Ahmed's work has been publicized by major media outlets, but he relies on donations and grants for much of his funding. When those opportunities are scarce, he uses his own money to produce his campaigns.[68]

ISD supports the members of Against Violent Extremism (AVE; see Figure 4.3) alongside the Gen Next Foundation on producing and distributing online counternarratives and on conducting interventions both offline and online. AVE was created jointly by Jigsaw (formerly Google Ideas), ISD, and the Gen Next Foundation in 2011. AVE runs several online platforms where "formers" and other survivors of all forms of violent extremism can engage with at-risk populations to share their experiences, including a website and YouTube channel. According to its website, AVE has made 2,635 connections since its founding, onboarding more than 309 formers and 164 survivors.[69] Network members have partnered with community groups, academic institutions, and law enforcement, and have appeared on 60 Minutes, MSNBC, CNN, and other major media outlets. Gen Next engages in philanthropy to online and offline CVE content, including producing counternarratives to violent ideologies. Gen Next

Figure 4.3
Against Violent Extremism

SOURCE: "Against Violent Extremism," homepage, undated. Used with permission.
RAND RR2647-4.3

---

[67] Average Mohamed marketing materials obtained by the study team, 2018.

[68] Interview with an NGO representative, 2018.

[69] "Against Violent Extremism," homepage, undated.

distributes this content via well-used platforms like Twitter, YouTube, and Facebook, and through more-sophisticated means like professionally produced videos and film festivals.[70]

ISD has had a prolific reach worldwide through the various initiatives it sponsors and other organizations with which it partners. Another UK-based organization, Moonshot CVE, also works globally to counter violent extremism of all kinds. Moonshot conducts three primary areas of work: *intervention* to identify individuals on their way to joining extremist networks to stop them from joining, which takes on- and offline forms; *communications and messaging*, which includes analysis, mapping demographics of those engaging in interventions, and other attempts to understand drivers toward extremism; and *capacity building* both for large organizations who need assistance and smaller community organizations who are engaging in CVE but need help.[71] These three areas also feed a research and development arm, where Moonshot develops and tests technologies that governments or other private companies could invest in. At a public Brookings Institution event in 2016, Moonshot co-founder Ross Frenett emphasized that effective countermessaging does not begin with condemning extremist sympathizers, but rather, understanding their points of view. "If you try and engage someone," Frenett said, "if you meet them where they are, even if you don't completely agree with them, then they will want to engage in [a] conversation, and that is step one . . . in getting them on a more peaceful path."[72]

Another organization, CEP, describes itself as "a not-for-profit, non-partisan, international policy organization formed to combat the growing threat from extremist ideologies." Part of its mission focuses on counternarratives and stopping online extremist recruitment. It maintains a public database of extremist groups and support networks to help inform public- and private-sector actors alike.[73] CEP is active on social media, especially Twitter. One of its campaigns, Digital Disruption, began in 2014. It is a crowdsourced approach that seeks to expose extremist content by linking it to the hashtag #CEPDigitalDisruption so that Twitter can remove the offending content (see Figure 4.4).[74] In 2016, CEP announced that it had developed an algorithm that could make content removal more expedient, and proposed that a new organization, which it named the National Office for Reporting Extremism (NORex), be created to operate the technology. The technology was codeveloped with a Dartmouth professor who created a similar algorithm for detecting child pornography, but tech

---

[70] Gen Next Foundation, homepage, 2016.

[71] Interview with an NGO representative, 2018.

[72] Dana Hadra, "What Tech Companies Can Do to Counter Violent Extremism," Brookings Institution blog, September 13, 2016.

[73] CEP, homepage, undated(a).

[74] CEP, "Digital Disruption: Fighting Online Extremism," undated(b).

Figure 4.4
Example of a #CEPDigitalDisruption Tag on Twitter

SOURCE: CEP, #cepdigitaldisruption, Twitter, July 21, 2017.
RAND *RR2647-4.4*

company executives were skeptical that NORex could implement such technology for extremist content, which can be less obvious to recognize.[75]

As discussed in our section on public-private partnerships, EdVenture Partners ran DHS's P2P program until funding expired in 2016. Student campaigns focused on a wide range of extremism. The winning campaign for the Spring 2017 semester was the University of Maryland's "It Takes Just One," which encouraged students not to remain bystanders to violent extremism or radicalization (see Figure 4.5).[76] EdVenture's new domestic program, run through the ADL, also engages students to create campaigns against violent extremism of all kinds. The students receive $1,000 and 750 Facebook advertising credits to create and run their campaign. EdVenture also runs this program internationally, sponsored by Facebook's Counterspeech initiative. Its hope is that content created by students to appeal to other young people will have a better chance of reaching target audiences. Under ADL, the renamed Innovate Against

---

[75] Patrick Tucker, "How to Stop the Next Viral Jihadi Video," *Defense One*, June 17, 2016.

[76] EdVenture Partners, "It Takes Just One," Spring 2017.

Figure 4.5
Spring 2017 P2P Challenging Extremism Winner

SOURCE: University of Maryland, "It Takes Just One," undated. Used with permission.
RAND *RR2647-4.5*

Hate program has more leeway to tackle all forms of extremism, which means that students can design a campaign to appeal to the specific challenges of their communities.[77]

Assessment

Many respondents we interviewed for this study noted that the federal government's somewhat limited U.S.-focused role was appropriate—even if they also argued that not having robust voices to counter online narratives in chat platforms and other forums was a challenge and serious shortfall.[78] Privacy, free speech, and civil liberty concerns are critical boundaries that U.S. leaders must respect when deciding whether to produce and distribute counternarratives. The risks posed by crossing these boundaries have proven too great for some government agencies, including DHS, which interviewees indicated has simply not been active in direct-messaging efforts. Legal restrictions, including appropriations act riders prohibiting propaganda in the United States, also limit available options.

The exceptions have been efforts by the FBI (focused inside the United States) and DOS (focused internationally), both of which have been criticized for perceived missteps in their messaging efforts. Counternarratives run by these organizations have been met with such wide backlash that they served to undermine the ability of U.S. government messaging to win the attention of those drawn to extremist content. Going up against an organization like ISIS, which has none of the same obligations to respect privacy or justify its messaging to constituents, has meant that U.S. government efforts consistently fall behind.

This experience was viewed as contributing to risk aversion by government in this space, which was repeatedly cited as a barrier to a further federal role in producing or distributing counternarrative content. Recent EU policy shifts mandating that such content come down quickly were also cited as a driver that may limit the need

---

[77] Interview with NGO representatives, 2018.

[78] Interviews with multiple federal representatives, 2018.

for as much U.S. action in this area.[79] Additionally, the UK government unveiled its own machine-learning tool designed to identify ISIS content online and remove it, but this has drawn criticism for censorship of free speech—a major concern in the United States as well, and one that has led to the relatively more modest approach of the U.S. government.[80]

Public-private partnerships, on the other hand, allow time and space for dedicated technology organizations to think creatively about counternarratives. Outside expertise can provide an advantage in proposing content targeted to specific audiences and removing objectionable content. Any countermessaging plan, whether strictly government, a public-private partnership, or a wholly private endeavor, must include evaluation measures during the program to identify whether content needs to be adjusted, and after the lifecycle of the message, to determine whether it reached its target audience. Measures to evaluate resulting behavior change may be more difficult to identify, which appears to be a common problem in hate crime, suicide, and substance abuse prevention interventions as well. However, the preponderance of interventions creates opportunities for researchers to begin creating and implementing more-robust evaluations to ensure that counternarratives are reaching and influencing their target audiences.

Regarding private-sector efforts, independent research has confirmed technology companies' claims that social media sites have become less hospitable to organizations of violent extremists, such as ISIS. For example, VOX-Pol, an EU-funded think tank, found that the number of ISIS accounts with at least one follower has decreased from 40,000–90,000 accounts (per Brookings' aforementioned estimate) to fewer than 1,000 between February and April 2017, although the drop is likely a result of multiple factors beyond increased policing of content.[81] Other reports and data back up the narrative of ISIS retreating from public-facing, searchable social media in favor of private channels on services such as Telegram.[82] Even organizations that continue to voice concerns about the jihadist threat agree with this overall narrative; they simply assign greater importance to the utility of these private communication channels and content.[83] However, there are more-recent attempts to understand extremist use of private

---

[79] Reuters, "EU Piles Pressure on Internet Giants to Remove Extremist Content," March 1, 2018.

[80] Lomas, 2018.

[81] Maura Conway, "Islamic State's Social Media Moment Has Passed," *Demos Quarterly*, November 1, 2017b.

[82] J. M. Berger and Heather Perez, *The Islamic State's Diminishing Returns on Twitter: How Suspensions Are Limiting the Social Networks of English-Speaking ISIS Supporters*, Washington, D.C.: George Washington University Program on Extremism, February 2016; Cole Bunzel, "Come Back to Twitter: A Jihadi Warning Against Telegram," *Jihadica*, July 18, 2016; Maura Conway, Moign Khawaja, Suraj Lakhani, Jeremy Reffin, Andrew Robertson, and David Weir, "Disrupting Daesh: Measuring Takedown of Online Terrorist Material and Its Impacts," *VOX-Pol*, Policy Report, 2017.

[83] Martyn Frampton, Ali Fisher, and Nico Prucha, *The New Netwar: Countering Extremism Online*, UK: Policy Exchange, 2017.

communication services. GWU's Program on Extremism began tracking content that espoused pro-ISIS messages on Telegram in 2017. Their Spring 2018 Telegram Tracker found that 689 channels—34.8 percent of which were public—contained English-language pro-ISIS content.[84]

Although technology companies have improved their responsiveness in this area a great deal, some demand further progress. Social media companies have improved their takedown rates such that 81 percent of complaints about extremist content are reviewed within 24 hours (up from 51 percent in 2017).[85] The March 2018 action by the EU Commission, cited previously, demanded more-aggressive action, proposing a one-hour turnaround deadline and an additional expansion of content moderation teams.[86] Legal changes have been made in individual countries as well, including Germany's implementation of its Network Enforcement Act (NetzDG) in January 2018. That law also requires rapid takedown of content by providers, and not doing so risks significant fines.[87] Policy Exchange, a think tank based in the United Kingdom, has offered the most far-reaching solutions, arguing that the UK government should force technology companies to pay for an expanded Counter Terrorism Referral Unit and prosecute corporations that are deemed to "willfully neglect" their responsibility to remove content in violation of British law.[88] These kinds of policy proposals remain outliers, however; most proposals seem designed to simply encourage technology companies to do as much as they can.

Major distributors of online advertisements such as Alphabet, Facebook, and Microsoft all collect immense amounts of data about the activities of users online and track metrics that measure the effectiveness of online advertisements and not simply user engagement. By examining best practices from related established disciplines and designing and measuring metrics for its specific purposes, CVE counternarrative campaigns should be able to achieve a similar level of scientific rigor and proven effectiveness.

Federal Options for Online and Countermessaging-Focused Policy and Programming

Among our interviewees, there was consensus that a federal role in countermessaging is necessary, as online propaganda is a central driver of terrorist threats in the country

---

[84] GWU, Program on Extremism, "Telegram Tracker," infographic. Spring 2018b.

[85] Julia Fioretti, "Social Media Companies Accelerate Removals of Online Hate Speech—EU," Reuters, January 18, 2018.

[86] Charles Riley, "EU Gives Tech Companies 1 Hour to Remove Terrorist Content," *CNN*, March 1, 2018.

[87] BBC, "Germany Starts Enforcing Hate Speech Law," January 1, 2018.

[88] Frampton, Fisher, and Prucha, 2017.

from all ideological sources. Coordination is also critical, since having many federal actors reaching out to the same players in the technology community was viewed as confusing and potentially alienating for those receiving the outreach.[89] The CVE Task Force (which we will discuss in greater detail in Chapter Ten), which coordinated multiple interagency engagements with private technology companies, is less able to do so since its personnel and resources were diminished.

The absence of a substantial U.S.-focused messaging effort was viewed by some interviewees as a serious gap because it is an important tool for terrorism prevention that is essentially not applied at the federal level. However, even those who support federal messaging efforts were circumspect about how controversial those efforts could be because of trust and credibility issues. As a result, in direct countermessaging, interviewees had different views on useful federal roles. For example, if advertisements can be targeted based on profiles, why not do the same with government-disseminated counternarratives (as is being done in NGO and private efforts)? But even proponents of more-robust activity cautioned that federal involvement would be complex, given privacy concerns. One possible suggestion was substantial government funding of an outside entity to take on U.S.-focused countermessaging that would "firewall" the data involved in such activities from the government, but would still be able to coordinate concerns between U.S.-focused and international messaging as needed.

Interviewees expressed concern that there is no good way to connect individuals to offline help, an important component to a holistic terrorism prevention strategy. There are some embryonic efforts at national helplines that we will discuss later in this report, which could play that role, but none are well-developed.

Given the volume of private-sector efforts to produce and disseminate counternarratives, the need to evaluate these initiatives more systematically, and the desire for some federal role in this area, in this facet of terrorism prevention, federal options identified from the literature and interviews focused on

- **Situational Awareness**
  - **Sustain efforts to characterize the extent of extremist content online on an ongoing basis.** While this is a complex issue in the current information and political environment, one approach could be a sustained or ideally automated effort to characterize the extent of extremist content online (e.g., measures of the intensity of hate or violent content on different platforms).[90] Although this would be a higher-cost activity, it could be run outside government (and might

---

[89] For example, one federal interviewee who had been involved in these efforts summed it up as, "Everyone and their brother is talking to industry, because 'tech solves everything!' and so that means the tech people are legitimately overwhelmed."

[90] This is similar to a recommendation made by Rachel Briggs and Sebastien Feve, *Review of Programs to Counter Narratives of Violent Extremism: What Works and What Are the Implications for Government?* London: Institute for Strategic Dialogue, 2013, p. 27.

be more effective as an independent effort). The GWU Program on Extremism's Telegram Tracker may be a step in this direction. However, since that effort does not address all ideological sources of threat to the United States, parallel efforts would be needed to complete the picture and allow comparison across threats. This reflected the strong message from interviewees that terrorism prevention must address the full range of ideological sources of violence. Routine collection of these data could provide a foundation for the evaluation of messaging and countermessage efforts.

— **Publicly release results of the content census to enable public action.** Providing data to inform and catalyze "digital grass roots pushback"[91] may be valuable, given the perceived potency of public action, as seen with reactions to CEP's Digital Disruption campaign, for example.

- **Awareness and Training**
  - **Provide threat information to technology firms to support their countermessaging efforts.** The role of the federal government in providing information to technology firms was emphasized by interviewees as valuable, and the general view was that interaction with technology firms was proceeding relatively effectively. Specific examples of current efforts in this space include DHS outreach efforts and the online-delivered CAB specifically focused on issues of technology firms. One interviewee we spoke to noted that large technology companies are not so dissimilar from governments with respect to the large bureaucracies that govern them both, and therefore have some similar needs and challenges for interaction and coordination.[92] Practical issues regarding the needs of small firms managing content removal challenges (which might not have staff or resources comparable to large established platforms) was an issue and a potential focus of research and development. Multiple interviewees emphasized that the role of government in providing information to those firms was valuable, even as efforts within industry to forge communal responses to these problems are underway.[93]
  - **Increase technical staff in government terrorism prevention efforts to support outreach to industry.** The federal government needs more permanent technical staff members who understand both the relevant technologies and the industries involved in terrorism prevention. Past use of fellows and individuals rotating through government were viewed as promising approaches,

---

[91] In the words of an interviewee from an NGO, "We need to have it as a grassroots movement. Include pillars of communities, celebrities, platforms, everyone. Have a slogan, a campaign. We can make a movement out of this against hate in all its forms. We need to reach outside the government sometimes, to Madison Avenue, Hollywood, entities in Silicon Valley. We need to reach out to organizations, celebrities and make the stand against hate cool. Make a brand out of it."

[92] Interview with an NGO representative, 2018.

[93] Interviews with NGO and technology firm representatives, 2018.

but having technically experienced individuals as permanent staff would be valuable to sustain activities.

– **Increase transparency of efforts and broadly share information for terrorism prevention purposes.** Similar to other facets of terrorism prevention, interviewees in this space emphasized the importance of transparency of information.[94] One of our interviewees noted that the government holds a lot of information that could be relevant to those attempting to track and counter extremist threats.[95] Of course, classified information must be protected, but the intelligence community and other federal agencies should consider how to expediently release information that could inform a broader understanding of extremist threats, social media use, and potential trends. If reliance on classified or otherwise protected information prevents or slows the ability to share widely with technology firms, it could put the private sector behind the curve when it comes to responding quickly. Providing security clearances to select individuals in the private sector only goes so far. It enables select individuals to see information, but they cannot use it to inform or explain their activities. It could improve government credibility to be transparent with information that could assist in the development of counternarratives.

- **Federal Support of Local Initiatives**
  – **Use grant funding to support counternarrative activities outside government.** Government-sponsored counternarratives have proved problematic in the past, especially those focused on domestic extremism. Third-party organizations can be effective with less complexity than government involvement in these activities, and can help information to be disseminated publicly through an independent source that might have more credibility with a broader audience. As a result, as is the case in other facets of terrorism prevention, partnering with other nonprofits and NGOs to inform their counternarratives and ensure that content is timely, relevant, and reaches its intended audience appears preferred to a major national messaging activity. Such an approach is also likely comparatively low cost. Although some organizations may be sensitive to working with the government or accepting government grant money because of political optics, such views are likely not universal. Local options for countering extremist messaging include grant funding, where there was considerable interest in FY 2016 unfunded proposals, and through funding of programs like P2P to create countermessaging content. Although individual initiatives would likely be threat- or ideology-specific, government investments

---

[94] This was also a core recommendation of Patel and Koushick, 2017, p. 38.

[95] Interview with NGO representatives and a former government official, 2018.

as a portfolio should be balanced across ideological sources of violence, based on objective data on relative threat and prevalence.[96]

- **Research and Evaluation**
  - **Continue to invest in evaluation of counternarrative efforts.** A specific area where federal support could be useful is funding evaluations for counternarrative campaigns. Scholars in many disciplines note the challenge of conducting rigorous evaluations of media influence campaigns, including how to determine whether those who received it acted (or failed to act) based on engaging with the campaign. However, the volume of anti-extremist messaging means that there is a plethora of data to assess—but those who fund such assessments must be patient. Metrics that demonstrate how many times users engage with content might demonstrate frequency, which is important to know, but they do not track long-term behavior. To do so, rigorous evaluations should be deployed that allow researchers to fully understand how counternarratives affect recipients' choices.[97]

Because of the focus on extremist messaging online—which is driven in large part by the effectiveness of international terrorist groups and movements in the space—there is considerable activity both in removing content focused on inspiring violent action and in counternarrative efforts. Given the sensitivity of government intervention in or near activities that are constitutionally protected, this is a space where the center of gravity is in the private and NGO sectors, with a wide variety of initiatives focused on responding to the threat. Although government may not be the primary actor, both the literature and our study interviews identified a range of options available for federal efforts in this area, many of which build on existing efforts or past successes.

---

[96] Funding and convening members of the tech community to create counternarrative campaigns was also noted as an important role for government by the EU's Radicalisation Awareness Network (RAN) in 2015. See RAN, *Counter Narratives and Alternative Narratives*, Brussels, Belgium, 2015, p. 2.

[97] In its 2016 report, DHS HSAC recommended the creation of a government-led "Innovation Lab" to "facilitate the full range of efforts related to innovation and partnerships with technology innovators" (DHS HSAC, 2016, p. 9).

CHAPTER FIVE

Early-Phase Terrorism Prevention: Community Education, Engagement, Resilience, and Risk-Factor Reduction

Community education, engagement, resilience, and risk factor–reduction efforts seek to affect early-stage radicalization by either (1) reducing the persuasive power of messages through education and interaction, or (2) strengthening the community and individuals so that they are less open to the messages in the first place. This can include education (e.g., providing information for parents to help their children), engagement and coordination activities to promote information-sharing and collaboration among organizations inside and outside government, and programs that try to build up communities with youth programming or economic development. Across this full spectrum of activities, the intended outcome is the same: reducing the likelihood that individuals in the communities will mobilize to ideological violence, even if messages or influences to do so are present in their environment. Given that the overall national terrorism prevention effort involves the activities of a wide range of groups, government can either implement programs directly, or it can build capacity in outside groups or assist such organizations to implement programs independently.[1] Activities falling within this facet of terrorism prevention are captured in the upper part of our mapping presented in Chapter Three, the relevant section of which is reproduced in Figure 5.1.

As introduced in Chapter Three, there are elements of this facet of terrorism prevention that are unambiguously threat-focused and clearly fall within DHS's defined lines of effort for terrorism prevention, specifically community education and engagement activities. Such activities seek to reduce risk directly, but are also important approaches for building the trust and collaboration needed for the success of other terrorism prevention activities.[2] However, there is less agreement on whether broader-framed initiatives—i.e., programming focused on strengthening communities and

---

[1] This is important because, as an interviewee in the study summarized, although it is constitutionally prohibited for the government to try to shape individuals' views of their religion or other beliefs, their parents and religious leaders are not only *able* to do so, they *are expected to* as part of the roles they play in individuals' lives.

[2] There is a clear analogy to community policing for dealing with everyday crime issues, which involves education and engagement not only to help agencies identify what problems the community cares about, but also as a way to help solve them.

Figure 5.1
Community Education, Engagement, Resilience, and Risk-Factor Reduction Within the Terrorism Prevention Policy Space

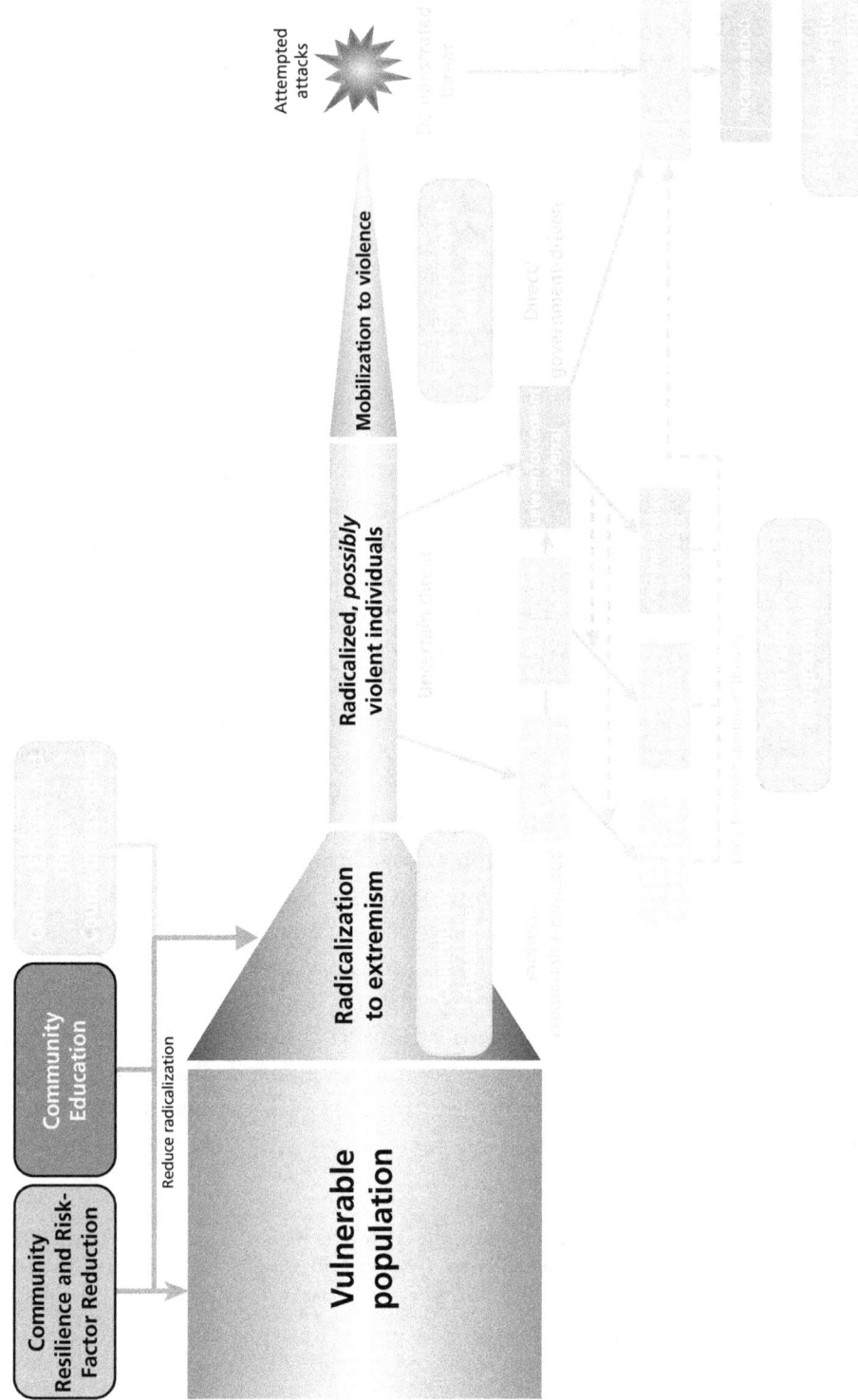

addressing violence risk factors via public health approaches—should be defined as terrorism prevention. Many risk factors identified with respect to violent extremism can be wide-reaching (e.g., family functioning and communication, individual identity and mental wellness, youth with unsupervised time to engage in delinquent behavior, political disengagement or breakdowns in communication around social or crime issues). Consequently, programs to address these issues are not terrorism-specific and might be framed as having nothing to do with terrorism at all. As a result, in this facet of terrorism prevention, there is essentially a boundary question regarding what activities should be viewed as threat-focused terrorism prevention policy versus which are good-governance initiatives that should be pursued independent of concerns about terrorism.

In the literature, and for a number of our state and local interviewees, the fact that such programing was not terrorism-specific was viewed as positive, because such efforts can reduce terrorism risk (and contribute to other policy goals) while sidestepping concerns about stigma or barriers to participation in terrorism-related programing. These are key drivers of the proposal that terrorism prevention (and previously CVE) should be approached from a public health perspective.[3] The counterargument to that view is based on the concern that such an approach could undermine terrorism prevention effectiveness, but also on questions regarding how labeling such programs as terrorism prevention might affect them. The first concern is largely one of focus: If the concept of terrorism prevention is stretched sufficiently so that it can include the full range of such programs, the resulting breadth will make it more difficult to define achievable and evaluable goals for terrorism prevention—essentially, "if CVE is everything, it is nothing."[4] The second concern is driven by the weight of the CVE brand discussed previously: Labeling a youth development program as terrorism prevention (or previously as CVE) may risk poisoning otherwise uncontroversial programs with the controversy surrounding terrorism and security-focused initiatives.[5] These types of

---

[3] For example, Snair, Nicholson, and Giammaria, 2017; Wynia, Eisenman, and Hanfling, 2017; Weine et al., 2015; Stevan Weine, David P. Eisenman, La Tina Jackson, Janni Kinsler, and Chloe Polutnik, "Utilizing Mental Health Professionals to Help Prevent the Next Attacks," *International Review of Psychiatry*, Vol. 29, No. 4, 2017; Weine, Eisenman, and Kinsler et al., 2017; Green and Procter, 2016.

[4] However, even in this report, we argue that terrorism prevention activity should occur "within the larger context of building community resilience against violence extremism . . . [and should] balance the good governance and security sides of [terrorism prevention] to create space for a whole-of society [terrorism prevention] strategy that allows for the commonsense application of a public-health-style model to community-led prevention while maintaining strong connective tissue between law enforcement and community service organizations when it comes to interventions" (Levitt, 2017, p. 20).

[5] Paraphrasing one of our interviewees, this argument was also made from the perspective that communities, particularly minority or immigrant communities, should be supported and these types of programs put in place simply as part of good government and a desire to address problems affecting those communities, rather than only being motivated by the issue of terrorism and threat (Interview with a community organization representative, 2018).

initiatives have been argued to be an effective role for the private sector, because investments in communities can help address many risk factors in a way that is congruent with business interests or to achieve corporate social responsibility goals.[6]

Other countries made different decisions regarding where their efforts fell on the spectrum between (1) focusing on risk factors in general versus terrorism-specific programming, and (2) regarding their mix of programs aimed at populations overall (e.g., employment programs at the city level) or individuals (e.g., employment counseling for at-risk individuals). We therefore went to our international case studies (which we include in Appendix A) for points of comparison to see if there had been a preferred combination of strategies in other Western democracies. The basic answer is that there is not: Across the countries, programs varied in their focus on risk factors versus terrorism specificity. Essentially all of the countries took a balanced approach between population-focused and individually focused programs as well.[7] As a result, in our discussion here, we address the range of options but also explore reasons for varied "placement" of the boundary of terrorism prevention on this spectrum of policy and programming options.

Relevant Design Challenges

Early-stage activities involving both education and risk factor–focused programming are affected by almost all of the design challenges identified for terrorism prevention activities, although with the different ends of the spectrum of options affected to differing extents. Interviewees flagged challenges within maintaining engagement and knowledge given the low base rate of terrorism incidents in any specific area, and given changes in personnel and people involved in government, community, and other organizations. Interviewees raised concerns about the potential for education and resilience efforts to create stigma and be affected by concerns about surveillance, although more for terrorism-specific than for more broadly focused activities. Even for such broad risk factor–focused activities, concerns about the CVE brand and trust were viewed as barriers for some potential partners participating, and creating sensitivity regarding federal funding of these initiatives. Federal interviewees also expressed concerns about the historical reticence of nonsecurity agencies to be involved substantially in CVE. Barri-

---

[6] See, for example, Rosand, 2016. However, the experience in Minneapolis–St. Paul is cautionary. Considerable private funding was assembled for CVE programs that had a strong, early-phase focus. However, when controversy around then-CVE efforts intensified, it was difficult to maintain the support (Interviews with multiple stakeholders in one U.S. city, 2018).

[7] One caveat regarding this international comparison is that we did not do a comprehensive review of all types of programs that *could* address risk factors for ideological violence, and particularly, programs that were not labeled as having any connection to the country's terrorism strategies. As a result, we almost certainly underweight broad-based and population-targeted social programming.

ers to participation were also flagged as drivers for flexibility in local implementation of programming, so initiatives to contribute to terrorism prevention could be designed in ways that were acceptable and practical to local conditions. Finally, measurement was raised as a particular challenge in this area of terrorism prevention because the effects of both terrorism-specific community engagement and public health risk factor–reduction programming can be subtle and manifest over long periods of time.

Approaches for Community Education, Engagement, Resilience, and Risk-Factor Reduction

Early-phase terrorism prevention activities are anchored by community outreach and policies designed to reduce vulnerability of communities to either active recruitment or mobilization to self-directed ideological violence. Approaches to do so can be drawn on from a wide variety of fields and communities of practice. Practitioners and researchers have designed similar early stage–type activities and initiatives aimed at social problems, including violence prevention (e.g., initiatives focused on gang violence, intimate partner violence, and child abuse), substance abuse, and a range of public health and safety problems. Law enforcement community policing initiatives apply these techniques to address criminal behavior and other issues of neighborhood or community disorder.[8] As a result, in considering the palette of options available for terrorism prevention policy and program design, there is a body of both practice and evaluation literature available to draw on.

Policies and Programming

In considering the range of options available in this facet of terrorism prevention, it is easiest to separate the community education and engagement end of the spectrum (where efforts *can* focus specifically on terrorism concerns, but do not have to) from the broader resilience and risk factor–focused efforts that are likely not terrorism-specific.

Community Education and Engagement

In past CVE efforts and ongoing terrorism prevention efforts, a wide variety of approaches and options have been used for community education and engagement (outside the online space discussed in the previous chapter). Community education and engagement have been central components of government efforts, both in the United States and in other countries. These efforts have focused on making communities aware of threats, building relationships and coalitions, and laying the groundwork

---

[8] See the discussion in Cynthia Lum, Christopher S. Koper, Charlotte Gill, Julie Hibdon, Cody W. Telep, and Laurie O. Robinson, *An Evidence-Assessment of the Recommendations of the President's Task Force on 21st Century Policing—Implementation and Research Priorities*, Fairfax, Va.: George Mason University, Center for Evidence-Based Crime Policy, International Association of Chiefs of Police, 2016.

for collaboration on CVE and terrorism prevention efforts and in pursuit of other risk-reduction goals. The government or other agencies that publish information regarding threats and terrorism risk contribute to this facet of terrorism prevention including release of research that contributes to in-depth public understanding of the nature of threats, responses, and levels of risk. Just as is the case in the online space, education and engagement efforts can include explicit countermessaging—i.e., seeking to respond to or undermine messages used by ideologically extremist organizations in recruiting or influence efforts. The general consensus view is that for such "messaging immunization" efforts to be effective, the people delivering the message must be credible to their audience, leading in some cases to employment of former extremist group members to do so.[9]

The spectrum of approaches for offline delivery of such programs is straightforward, including using media channels and direct person-to-person efforts (e.g., community briefings) and building institutions or groups (e.g., ongoing advisory mechanisms, like community councils). Efforts can also be provided in different contexts, including schools, community organizations, and workplaces.[10] The approaches vary to the extent that they are one-way (or "broadcast only") versus two-way modes for the exchange of information and interaction over time. The latter have the potential to achieve a wider range of goals than the former (e.g., trust building, improving effectiveness of initiatives over time, addressing controversy or emergent events). Such community education and engagement activities have been an element of initiatives in the criminal justice (e.g., community policing efforts), public health (e.g., participatory research models, community-level interventions), and substance abuse intervention spaces. The breadth of examples across fields is vast.

There are examples of community education and engagement efforts that are specific to terrorism concerns, including DHS's CABs (which we discuss in greater detail below) and the formation of specific councils in the course of past CVE initiatives (e.g., the advisory groups that were associated with CVE efforts in the three Pilot Cities). However, there are also analogous examples of more broadly framed structures or efforts that either can be or have been used to address concerns about ideologically motivated violence. These efforts were viewed as ways to address issues without creating stigma by being perceived as singling out individual communities. In multiple

---

[9] Involvement of former group members in that communication role is not without risk. In the countergang space, concerns have been raised regarding the potential for "inverse effects" where, rather than persuading at-risk individuals that gang life was not for them, instead inadvertently glamorize it and make it more attractive. See the discussion in Malcolm W. Klein, "Comprehensive Gang and Violence Reduction Programs: Reinventing the Square Wheel," *Criminology and Public Policy*, Vol. 10, No. 4, 2011. These types of effects have been observed for terrorism in Northern Ireland (Gordon Clubb, "The Role of Former Combatants in Preventing Youth Involvement in Terrorism in Northern Ireland: A Framework for Assessing Former Islamic State Combatants," *Studies in Conflict and Terrorism*, Vol. 39, No. 9, 2016). See also the recommendations in DHS HSAC, 2016.

[10] See, for example, FBI, Office of Partner Engagement, *Preventing Violent Extremism in Schools*, Washington, D.C., January 2016.

cities we visited, there was significant focus among law enforcement organizations on their capacity for community outreach in general, separate from any concerns about terrorism.[11] Such outreach is aligned with the tenets of community policing and helps departments meet the needs of the communities at the same time as it provides a structure and builds strong enough relationships that communities will collaborate with law enforcement on difficult issues like violent extremism.[12] We heard similar messages from federal staff who had been involved in outreach efforts: "We started a lot of our outreach with 'we want people to report hate crimes more, we want to see how we can be a resource.'"[13] State and local law enforcement also argued that interfaith outreach about hate crime is a productive way to broach issues related to ideological violence with communities. Doing so is responsive to a problem they viewed as important, and stimulates conversation and interaction in a way that is not alienating.[14] Although creating a broad program is one way to avoid stigma, a former law enforcement interviewee emphasized that just "doing better outreach" on specific issues can work: "If we're talking about the violence threat posed by MS-13, we don't talk about El Salvadorians, we talk about MS-13. . . . [We] need to do that with terrorism. Don't paint communities with a broad brush."[15] Another example from the health, academic, and NGO sectors is the model of community-based participatory research that has been applied in a wide range of contexts and has been a productive approach for dealing with a variety of issues, including violence.[16]

---

[11] For example, one law enforcement interviewee in a U.S. city said, "It's about relationship building. Our officers need to be sensitive to communities" and in another interview, "The new word I like is trust. It's on our business cards. Building on that trust—anything you deal with in this country comes back to trust."
Others have argued that a similar approach should be adopted at the national level:

> To be clear, the FBI and local law enforcement should continue to engage Muslim religious, business, civic, and community leaders to maintain a network of contacts across the country. This allows for open lines of communications, which is vital for when there are problems and also helps demystify the important work of federal and local law enforcement. However, this type of engagement should be decoupled from CVE efforts. Otherwise, it will continue to strain relations with Muslims and reinforce the impression—rightly or wrongly—that the government views them writ large as a potential security problem (Robert L. McKenzie, *Countering Violent Extremism in America: Policy Recommendations for the Next President*, Washington, D.C.: Brookings Institution, October 18, 2016).

[12] For an overview, see Gary Cordner, "Community Policing," in Michael D. Reisig and Robert J. Kane, eds., *The Oxford Handbook of Police and Policing*, Oxford, UK: Oxford University Press, 2014; or Lum et al., 2016.

[13] Interview with a federal representative in one U.S. city, 2018.

[14] Interviews with local law enforcement representatives in multiple cities, 2018. An NGO representative described an initiative where prominent members of the Muslim community in a city traveled with an interfaith group to Germany, where they learned about the indoctrination of young people by neo-Nazi groups there—and that the experience of seeing how youth radicalization had common elements across ideologies (i.e., that it was not a "Muslim issue") made it easier to address similar issues locally.

[15] Interview with a former law enforcement leader, 2018.

[16] For an in-depth discussion, see, B. Heidi Ellis and Saida Abdi, "Building Community Resilience to Violent Extremism Through Genuine Partnerships," *American Psychologist*, Vol. 72, No. 3, 2017.

We noted strong tension in the interviews between the desire of government to focus education or engagement efforts and feelings of stigmatization among community members. Broader-based or non–terrorism specific models reduce the potential for creating stigma, although in doing so can add complexities in implementation.[17]

Resilience and Risk Factor–Focused Approaches

Previous research efforts have identified a broad scope of risk factors that may contribute to individuals being at risk of carrying out ideological violence. Eisenman and Flavahan reviewed the range of factors, drawing on research specific to extremism threats and broader violence prevention literature.[18] Their results are shown in Figure 5.2.[19] In the public health approach, such risk factors are targets of intervention, not to assess threats posed by an individual. Such initiatives seek to address the risk factors in the absence of any prediction of whether the people being served will or will not become violent in the future. In considering options for addressing risk factors, they encompass virtually the entirety of the social policy space. These risk factors include mental health and wellness (e.g., individual anger or identity issues); economic development; family health and abuse; crime and local governance; and large-scale societal issues like discrimination, inequality, and social change.

Although this framing of CVE risk factors comes from the public health field, it should be noted that there are approaches within criminology that are similar, notably the concept that the "collective efficacy" of a community is related to the incidence of crime and options available for its control.[20] Public health approaches have been applied to other types of violence as well.[21] Programming in these areas can be aimed at

---

[17] Ellis and Abdi (2017) explore how community-based participatory research models can be a way to navigate this issue, where a general and collaborative structure for program design and implementation can make it possible to address potentially stigmatizing health and other problems. Similar arguments have been made for the BRAVE (Build Resilience Against Violent Extremism) model developed in Montgomery County, Md., by ensuring that community engagement efforts to build a coalition of stakeholders were not restricted to terrorism concerns (Hedieh Mirahmadi, "Building Resilience Against Violent Extremism: A Community-Based Approach," *The ANNALS of the American Academy of Political and Social Science*, Vol. 668, November 2016).

[18] Eisenman and Flavahan, 2017. Practitioners we interviewed also drew explicit parallels between risk factors for gang involvement and extremism, particularly via youth exposed online: "The system doesn't do a good job of raising kids. A lot of our foster kids are trying to grab onto anything that they can to feel loved and connected. It's a lot of foster youth who are connecting with the wrong youth or feeling disconnected. [This is the] same reason people join gangs. Someone will care about them" (Interview with an NGO representative, 2018). Others also drew parallels to the process that traffickers and abusers use to groom and recruit children through online communication channels (Interview with a federal representative, 2018).

[19] Such listings are not unique to public health approaches to violence. For a set of risk factors framed from a law enforcement perspective, see FBI Behavioral Analysis Unit, undated.

[20] See, for example, Robert J. Sampson, Stephen W. Raudenbush, and Felton Earls, "Neighborhoods and Violent Crime: A Multilevel Study of Collective Efficacy," *Science*, Vol. 277, No. 5328, August 15, 1997.

[21] Reviewed in Elena Savoia, Marcia A. Testa, Jessica Stern, Leesa Lin, Souleymane Konate, and Noah Klein, *Evaluation of the Greater Boston Countering Violent Extremism (CVE) Pilot Program*, Boston, Mass.: Harvard T.H.

Figure 5.2
Risk Factors Identified for Ideologically Motivated Violence

Individual

- Fragmented cultural identity
- Anger or hostility to others
- Psychological/personality disturbances
- Alcohol/substance misuse
- Victim of child maltreatment
- Violent or suicidal behavior—past or current
- Contact with charismatic leaders justifying violence
- Access to lethal means

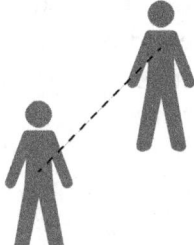

Relationship

- Fractured family structures
- Family history of violence or suicide
- Current relationship/marital turmoil; intimate partner violence
- Financial, work stress
- Friends and family who engage in violence
- Association with aggressive or delinquent peers
- Emotionally unsupportive family

Community

- Poverty; poor education systems
- Limited economic opportunities
- High local crime levels
- Low social cohesion/connectedness
- Inadequate social services
- Situational factors

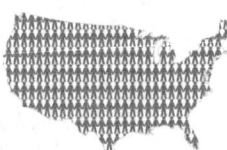

Societal

- Rapid social change
- Economic inequality
- Gender inequality
- Stigma regarding mental distress and help-seeking
- Cultural norms that support violence
- Discrimination
- Access to lethal methods (firearms)
- Global, national, or regional armed conflict

SOURCE: Figure adapted from Eisenman and Flavahan, 2017.
RAND *RR2647-5.2*

addressing trust issues between government and communities (e.g., police-youth sports to build rapport, efforts to create or strengthen links between adults and the police). These types of risk factor–reduction efforts are an established component of interventions aimed at issues like gangs and gang violence.[22]

As a result, one effect of stretching terrorism prevention to this more public health–framed approach is to vastly increase the range of policy options that are available in principle to respond to terrorism concerns. In their work, Eisenman and Flavahan explore the variety that ranges from individual mental health and substance abuse intervention to societal-level policies aimed at ensuring the availability of food, housing, health, and education.[23] In the literature on broader CVE policies drawing from these strategies, there are examples of programs focused at the individual level (e.g., sports leagues to engage and occupy adolescents), relationship level (e.g., family focused efforts), and higher, although, echoing the views expressed by our interviewees, broader programs may be less likely to be viewed as terrorism prevention efforts.[24]

Evidence for Effectiveness

Although assessing the available literature on the effectiveness of all possible interventions aimed at risk-factor reduction would be a Herculean undertaking, the broad body of evaluation literature across multiple fields provides a foundation to consider the potential effectiveness for terrorism prevention. The evaluation of prevention programs for criminality, gang, and other violence is most analogous to terrorism prevention, and a variety of programs in these areas have shown desirable effects.[25] However, assessing the terrorism prevention outcome effects of these types of interventions is even more of a challenge than other terrorism prevention activities, reflecting not only

---

[22] For a review, see Jason Gravel, Martin Bouchard, Karine Descormiers, Jennifer S. Wong, and Carlo Morselli, "Keeping Promises: A Systematic Review and a New Classification of Gang Control Strategies," *Journal of Criminal Justice*, Vol. 41, 2013; or Butts et al., 2015. It should also be noted that there is some "crosstalk" between education and engagement activities and risk factor reduction–type efforts. For example, in published literature on CVE and education, the roles of both education in making violent extremism less attractive (risk-factor reduction) and the delivery of information about violent extremist risk (education and engagement) are important (e.g., Naureen Chowdhury Fink, Ivo VeenKamp. Wedad Alhassen, Rafia Barakat, and Sara Zeiger, *The Role of Education in Countering Violent Extremism*, Center on Global Counterterrorism Cooperation and Hedayah, December 2013).

[23] Eisenman and Flavahan, 2017, p. 344.

[24] A START effort applied this thinking about risk factors in another way: It used data on the geographic variation in risk factors to identify locations in the United States that might be at greater risk for producing individuals vulnerable to perpetrating ideologically motivated violence, which could then be used to guide resource allocation (Shira Fishman, *Community-Level Indicators of Radicalization: A Data and Methods Task Force*, College Park, Md.: National Consortium for the Study of Terrorism and Responses to Terrorism, February 16, 2010).

[25] This point is reviewed in Charlotte Gill, "Community Interventions," in David Weisburd, David P. Farrington, and Charlotte Gill, eds., *What Works in Crime Prevention and Rehabilitation: Lessons from Systematic Reviews*, New York: Springer, 2016.

the difficulties associated with evaluating terrorism interventions, but also those assessing the effects of broad and diffusely acting social programs.

Of the handful of CVE efforts that have been evaluated, most are broad-based programs with significant engagement and education components. In a review supporting the development of an evaluation toolkit in 2017, RAND researchers identified only four rigorous studies examining interventions in the United States or Europe.[26] One of those four studies was of the BRAVE program in Montgomery County, Md., which included several components that fall within this facet of terrorism prevention. The quantitative evaluation of that effort showed reported improvements in a range of variables related to social integration and empowerment, although strong evaluation designs could not be used.[27] Qualitative and case study–type evaluations of options in this area are often positive, but, as discussed elsewhere in this report, the ability to connect them to direct security outcomes is tenuous.[28] Mitts produced an exploratory analysis using online activity (pro-ISIS Twitter posts from accounts that appeared to be located inside the United States) to see whether community engagement events resulted in less pro-ISIS discussion.[29] The analysis did suggest a beneficial effect of the events. There are also examples of evaluations of international programs suggesting that programs make it easier for individuals to participate in legal work (i.e., address a risk factor) and reduce participation in illegal, including violent, activity.[30]

Cherney reviews lessons from broad-based programming aimed at diverting youth from risky activities (e.g., sports programs) and other community-level interventions focused on crime to inform thinking about CVE, and, by extension, terrorism prevention, efforts. The assessment is positive, but cautious:[31]

> While there is little doubt that the immediate experience of participating in a diversionary programme can have positive benefits, the evidence indicates [that] diversion can have time-limited outcomes. . . . That is, the effects can wear off over

---

[26] Sina Beaghley, Todd C. Helmus, Miriam Matthews, Rajeev Ramchand, David Stebbins, Amanda Kadlec, and Michael A. Brown, *Development and Pilot Test of the RAND Program Evaluation Toolkit for Countering Violent Extremism*, Santa Monica, Calif.: RAND Corporation, RR-1799-DHS, 2017.

[27] Summarized in Mirahmadi, 2016.

[28] For example, White and McEvoy (2012) include a case study of CVE efforts aimed at terrorism in Northern Ireland in the context of both the peace process there and dissident violent groups from that process (Stephen White and Kieran McEvoy, *Countering Violent Extremism: Community Engagement Programmes in Europe*, Qatar International Academy for Security Studies, February 2012).

[29] Tamar Mitts, *Do Community Engagement Efforts Reduce Extremist Rhetoric on Social Media?* New York: Columbia University, Department of Political Science, April 6, 2017.

[30] See, for example, Christopher Blattman and Jeannie Annan, "Can Employment Reduce Lawlessness and Rebellion? A Field Experiment with High-Risk Men in a Fragile State," *American Political Science Review*, Vol. 110, No. 1, February 2016.

[31] Cherney, 2016, p. 86.

time, which is more likely if there is no follow-up with participants. Hence, diversionary programmes that remain one-off experiences can have limited outcomes in the medium or long term because participants (e.g., young people) can simply return to their negative environments or peer contexts that reinforce an extremist ideology.

Others also have mined the literature for practices that have been evaluated or that showed promise in other contexts (e.g., violence prevention efforts in the mental health or education sectors). These efforts have involved more-focused education and engagement and broader programs and included end goals similar to early-phase terrorism prevention, such as channeling community concern into productive civic engagement and away from destructive activities.[32] Education and messaging efforts can have specific evaluation concerns, in part because of their broad focus. For example, even if a message is broadcast widely, it does not mean that it was received by the intended audience. Morris et al. review this issue with respect to community health education efforts as part of measuring the effectiveness of the problems they targeted.[33]

When we take community policing as an analogous example (and one promoted as a model or foundation for community-focused terrorism prevention efforts), the evaluation literature is not as deep as might be expected, but efforts to evaluate programs have shown benefits.[34] Evaluations of very early forays into community policing showed beneficial effects on perceived relationships between police and communities, even if their effect on crime was unclear.[35] Others have shown both improvements in community relations and reductions in disorder, and some have shown crime reductions as well.[36] Surveys have been used to examine effects on public views of the police and how different engagement and policies change those views. For example, in a

---

[32] This point is reviewed in Weine et al., 2015.

[33] Daniel S. Morris, Meagan P. Rooney, Ricardo J. Wray, and Matthew W. Kreuter, "Measuring Exposure to Health Messages in Community-Based Intervention Studies: A Systematic Review of Current Practices," *Health Education and Behavior*, Vol. 36, No. 6, December 2009.

[34] DHS CVE Curriculum Working Group, *Community Policing and Countering Violent Extremism: Draft of Curriculum Components* (redacted and released under FOIA, 2015-CRCL-00011-000026–000040), January 2011; Schanzer et al., 2016.

[35] Susan Sadd and Randolph M. Grinc, *Implementation Challenges in Community Policing Innovative Neighborhood-Oriented Policing in Eight Cities*, Washington, D.C.: National Institute of Justice, February 1996.

[36] Nadine M. Connell, Kristen Miggans, and Jean Marie McGloin, "Can a Community Policing Initiative Reduce Serious Crime? A Local Evaluation," *Police Quarterly*, Vol. 11, No. 2, June 2008, and references therein; Jihong "Solomon" Zhao, Matthew C. Scheider, and Quint Thurman, "Funding Community Policing to Reduce Crime: Have COPS Grants Made a Difference?" *Criminology and Public Policy*, Vol. 2, No. 1, 2002. An evaluation of problem-oriented policing (which has some overlap with community policing in approach) also showed beneficial effects (David Weisburd, Cody W. Telep, Joshua C. Hickle, and John E. Eck, "Is Problem-Oriented Policing Effective in Reducing Crime and Disorder? Findings from a Campbell Systematic Review," *Criminology and Public Policy*, Vol. 9, No. 1, 2010).

department that had focused on community policing programs, survey data measuring public satisfaction with the department showed community members with higher perceptions of police performance than officers had, even while they thought the department still needed to improve its community relations overall and with minority groups in particular.[37]

Current U.S. Terrorism Prevention and Related Efforts for Community Education, Engagement, Resilience, and Risk-Factor Reduction

Terrorism prevention efforts as broad community engagement activities (e.g., outreach activities to connect government to communities, build trust) and resilience-building (including programs as varied as community dialogues, programs that occupy youths' time to keep them from extremist activities, etc.) are part of existing programming at all levels. Both activities were cited as important in the literature and in our discussions with state and local organizations, federal representatives directly involved in terrorism prevention efforts, and NGOs and community groups.

At the federal level, the DHS Civil Rights and Civil Liberties (CRCL) office was an early adopter of community engagement: It had been conducting outreach informally since 2003.[38] CRCL continues to hold regular roundtables with community leaders and federal, state, and local government officials regarding community civil rights concerns. DHS has held roundtables recently in Washington, D.C.; Chicago; Los Angeles; San Diego; Boston; Detroit; Tampa; Orlando; Columbus; Seattle; Atlanta; Denver; Houston; New York; Phoenix; Tucson; Portland; and Minneapolis. DHS also has held roundtables focused on young leader and campus engagement in Los Angeles, Houston, and Washington, D.C.[39] Community and specific advisory committees are also used. For example, in 2012, DHS created a faith-based Security and Communications Advisory Committee—with membership from law enforcement, religious groups, and community organizations around the country—to advise on issues related to information-sharing between DHS and faith-based organizations.[40] There also have been efforts to improve trust between DHS and the public, such as the "Every Inter-

---

[37] John Liederbach, Eric J. Fritsch, David L. Carter, and Andra Bannister, "Exploring the Limits of Collaboration in Community Policing: A Direct Comparison of Police and Citizen Views," *Policing: An International Journal of Police Strategies and Management*, Vol. 31, No. 2, 2008.

[38] DHS CRCL, "Newsletter," Vol. 2, No. 1, September 2011.

[39] DHS CRCL, "Community Engagement," webpage, undated.

[40] DHS HSAC, "Faith-Based Security and Communications Advisory Committee Membership List," undated.

action Counts" campaign that was designed to "increase DHS employee awareness of their critical role in building trust among those that they serve."[41]

DHS and DOJ worked together on the Building Communities of Trust (BCOT) program, which is administered by the Nationwide Suspicious Activity Reporting Initiative (NSI). The program provides roundtables in urban areas to establish and develop trust among law enforcement, fusion centers, and the communities they serve in order to address protection of communities from violence, suspicious activity reporting, and protection of civil rights and liberties.[42] The BCOT conducted 21 different events across the country between December 2011 and February 2016.[43]

The 2011 SIP tasked DOJ to expand beyond the 32 U.S. Attorney's Offices conducting community engagement activities to have all U.S. Attorney's Offices serve as the federal engagement leads for CVE to listen to community concerns, seek input on U.S. government policies, and raise awareness about how the U.S. government can protect Americans from discrimination, hate crimes, and other threats.[44] DOJ increased the number of U.S. Attorney's Offices designated as engagement leads and DOJ's Civil Rights Division also continued to hold bimonthly meetings that brought together community leaders and top federal officials to address civil rights issues.[45] A survey effort published in 2016 documented that U.S. Attorney's Offices carried out a wide range of outreach and engagement efforts, spending a reported average of 15 labor hours per week on the activities.[46]

Central programming activities for federal outreach and engagement (done in collaboration with DHS, NCTC, and DOJ) were the CABs and Community Resilience Exercises (CREXs). CABs and CREXs are the main products offered as part of federal outreach and engagement. However, the CABs and CREXs are multipurpose: They educate and seek to provide awareness to help their audiences identify at-risk individuals and promote referral for intervention. Because they are such a prominent component of the federal effort in that facet of terrorism prevention, we will discuss them in more detail in the next chapter.

---

[41] DHS, *DHS Action Plan to Counter Violent Extremism*, Washington, D.C., released under FOIA, DHS-001-425-003550-75, October 20, 2015b, p. 17; DHS, *Department of Homeland Security Countering Violent Extremism Programs and Initiatives*, Washington, D.C., Fiscal Year 2016 Report to Congress, June 14, 2016a.

[42] Information Sharing Environment, Department of Homeland Security, Nationwide SAR Initiative, U.S. Department of Justice Community Oriented Policing Services, *Building Communities of Trust Fact Sheet*, January 2014.

[43] GAO, 2017, Appendix III.

[44] EOP, 2011b; Vidino and Hughes, 2015.

[45] DOJ, *Ten Years Later: The Justice Department After 9/11, Partnering with the Muslim, Arab, and Sikh Communities*, undated.

[46] David Schanzer and Joe Eyerman, *United States Attorneys' Community Outreach and Engagement Efforts to Counter Violent Extremism: Results from a Nationwide Survey*, Durham, N.C.: Triangle Center on Terrorism and Homeland Security, Sanford School of Public Policy, Duke University, December 2016.

FBI outreach efforts have ranged from national-level discussions with established groups to participation in local multicultural boards and engagements, to community and youth activities, as well as grassroots programs in each of its 56 field offices to engage with diverse communities.[47] Most of the current FBI outreach programs are managed by division outreach coordinators and include youth programs and citizens academies, including the "Campus Liaison Initiative, the Private Sector Liaison, the Corrections Initiative, the FBI Citizens Academy, and the Junior G-Man Program." According to the FBI, such engagement programming is intended to "integrate community and law enforcement goals to mitigate local risk factors for violence."[48]

Some federal field staff, such as representatives from U.S. Attorney's Offices and DHS field staff, participate in local community-led and NGO-initiated programs.[49] These programs included efforts initiated locally during the pilot period, which all three of the pilot cities framed around the concepts of resilience and healthy communities. Other federal activities, including efforts by HHS, were described in the 2013 report of the National Engagement Task Force.[50] In addition to the plethora of locally based organizations active here, there are a range of NGOs that conduct community outreach activities nationwide in this space, including the Council on American-Islamic Relations (CAIR), the American Islamic Congress (AIC), the American Human Rights Council (AHRC), the Muslim Public Affairs Council (MPAC), and the Muslim Students' Association (MSA).[51]

Because general "good governance"–type efforts (e.g., initiatives designed to improve relations between communities and law enforcement) can contribute to terrorism prevention goals, the boundary between community engagement under terrorism prevention and efforts that would be viewed as useful, but not as terrorism prevention, is not entirely clear. Indeed, in the CVE analytic literature, the roles and potential outcomes of extremism-focused efforts like these often are framed similarly to those of broader police-community initiatives and other initiatives focused on community engagement and participation in civil society and governance. In discussions with community and state and local groups, these types of initiatives were generally praised as useful based on their own merits and because they were terrorism prevention

---

[47] See, for example, DOJ, undated.

[48] Kerry Sleeper, "Testimony on Combatting Homegrown Terrorism," Hearing Before the Subcommittee on National Security of the Committee on Oversight and Government Reform, U.S. House of Representatives, July 27, 2017.

[49] Interviews with federal representatives in multiple U.S. cities, 2018.

[50] Mell Johnson and David Gersten, "Catalog of Best Practices for Community Engagement: National Engagement Task Force," released under the Freedom of Information Act, DHS-001-425-000785 thru 000831, April 18, 2013.

[51] Descriptions of relevant activities are available on the organizations' websites.

efforts that could be framed broadly and therefore not attract the reflexive opposition that initiatives aimed at terrorism can attract.[52]

This was also a major component of activities funded in the FY 2016 CVE grants, reflecting a significant DHS investment in these efforts.[53] As shown in Figure 5.3, the geographic spread of the funded grants (shown by the red circles) was broad. The black circles are the unfunded grants falling into the categories of "developing resilience," "training and engagement," and "building capacity," which is the best proxy for those covering community education and awareness. They show a much larger demand for involvement in activities in this area and the potential for broader geographic coverage of efforts.

Assessment

Although programs aimed at community engagement and risk factor–focused efforts for other social problems have been rigorously evaluated, similar literature on CVE (and, by extension, terrorism prevention) efforts is largely unavailable. As a result, assessment is limited to the perceptions of interviewees who either participated in or had knowledge of different activities.

Community Education and Engagement
Federal Outreach Approaches and Staffing

Several interviewees viewed current and past DHS and other federal government terrorism-specific community engagement and education as useful. However, there were also concerns expressed about past outreach efforts creating stigma, particularly because of the focus on Muslim communities.[54] Examples cited of useful efforts included CABs, interactions between federal staff—most commonly DHS (including

---

[52] Multiple state- and local-level interviews with government and NGO representatives, 2018. Some examples of these opinions include the following: "We're looking at a broader way that communities interact. It's that notion of building healthy intergroup relations. That takes us from understanding this from within the scope of public health" (Interview with local government representative in one U.S. city, 2018); "We are taking the community-based approach to CVE, which is: filling a gap that needs to be filled. The gap is social services to build resilient communities" (Interview with a community organization representative in one U.S. city, 2018); "It is important for us to know what's going on out there with immigrants and refugees. . . . Everything is about immigrant integration. We believe that this is like a social contract" (Interview with local government representative in one U.S. city, 2018).

[53] Grant initiatives in this area overlap somewhat with those covered in Chapter Six on referral promotion.

[54] In the words of one local leader who was involved in these efforts:

> There's an idea somehow that when we outreach to [a] Muslim community we're outreaching to ISIS. We're not. . . . We're looking at a broader way that communities interact. It's that notion of building healthy intergroup relations. That takes us from understanding this from within the scope of public health. We're essentially doing that in this space. . . . All of that work specifically when it comes to outreach and engagement, some of it comes to interfaith framing. How are we engaging Muslims, Christians, Jews, Sikhs, etc. How do these relationships play out not just [in] times of conflict but before that and how do we engage this to invigorate community resilience?

Figure 5.3
Funded and Unfunded FY 2016 CVE Grant Applications Relevant to Community Education and Building Resilience

NOTES: Red circles show locations of funded grant applications; black circles show locations of proposals that were not funded in the program. Data were provided by DHS, released under the Freedom of Information Act.
RAND *RR2647-5.3*

both field staff and representatives from CRCL) and U.S. Attorney's Office staff—and local communities, and CREXs. Local interviewees did comment specifically on the value of CRCL roundtables as a venue for engagement and trust building. In most of the cities we visited, interviewees argued for expanded efforts. The assessment that "more outreach would be better," was driven by what it could achieve directly and also because building strong relationships (and through them, increasing trust) is necessary for the success of other terrorism prevention initiatives.

Multiple interviewees argued that effective outreach and engagement required federal *field staff* in local areas.[55] Some individuals argued that maintaining engagement and education efforts needed dedicated, full-time staff, while in other cases it was a more general desire for *engaged* federal representatives in the area (i.e., if the individuals involved had other duties, terrorism prevention would have to have high enough priority not to be routinely displaced by other demands on their time). There was general consensus that federal staff members visiting periodically from Washing-

---

[55] This was also a recommendation of DHS HSAC, 2016.

ton, D.C., were insufficient to achieve the engagement outcomes needed.[56] Based on our observations across interviews in different cities, there was considerable difference in perceived terrorism prevention progress and success between areas where there was effective and trusted local federal engagement and where there was not, which supports the judgment that locally placed staff are valuable in these efforts.

There was a period where DHS OTPP (then OCP) had a sizable contract field staff playing this role (and, in other areas, federal staff from the U.S. Attorney's Office did so, reflecting the history of DOJ involvement in terrorism prevention during the period around the pilot efforts). However, that presence has recently shrunk substantially. These staff were involved in both education and outreach activities, including regular meetings with stakeholders, delivering the CABs, and holding CREXs that had been developed by NCTC, DHS, and interagency partners. As a result of the contraction in staffing, interviewees reported that there is considerable unmet demand for these efforts, and that coordination between the federal government and state and local levels is weak in cities without such staff.[57] Multiple interviewees did cite non–terrorism specific engagement (e.g., with DHS CRCL) as effective and useful, and another instance in which there appeared to be unmet demand and potential value in expanding activity.

There was a range of views expressed regarding the strengths and weaknesses of field staff coming from different agencies, with the main concern being that staff from criminal justice entities (sometimes the U.S. Attorney's Office, but more frequently the FBI) would not be able to build sufficient trust with the full range of community organizations needed for success. Across different types of interviewees (government, community, social service, etc.) the strength of the view varied, but this concern was more often seen as a challenge that could be overcome rather than an insurmountable barrier if the main federal representative in an area was drawn from a criminal justice agency.[58]

Looking outside DHS and NCTC engagement efforts to other federal actors, some interviewees during the study spoke positively about FBI community outreach efforts (including one religious leader who cited the Bureau's youth academy and junior special agent programs and a community group leader who pointed to a local

---

[56] This is not a new conclusion. Bipartisan Policy Center (2011, p. 43) put it thus: "Current federal outreach activities are 'no more than touches,' that fail to have any lasting impact. . . . [Unless changes are made,] federal outreach will remain a 'flying circus' while local engagement will continue to be reactive rather than proactive."

According to one interviewee, "I tend to like the model that DHS and NCTC quietly did. Sent a person in L.A., Denver and Houston as their full-time gig. Train the local offices and use that person as a sounding board. Better than fly-in teams from D.C. giving talks. They can't set up the intervention programs" (Interviews with NGO representatives, 2018).

[57] Interviews with a variety of individuals during U.S. city visits, 2018.

[58] Drawing the main federal representative from DOJ might make the likelihood of success dependent on the commitment of that person to build trust. However, it could increase the potential for success to be strongly driven by the specific person in the role, and that person's personality and skills.

advisory committee group).[59] However, broader focused communication activities (e.g., the Bureau's "Don't Be a Puppet" campaign) have been controversial. FBI CVE efforts were examined as part of a 2015 report from the Congressionally directed 9/11 Review Commission based on interviews within the organization. The Commission raised questions about the effectiveness of FBI activities under this facet of terrorism prevention:[60]

> The FBI, like DHS, NCTC, and other agencies, has made an admirable effort to counter violent extremism (CVE) as mandated in the White House's December 2011 strategy, Empowering Local Partners to Prevent Violent Extremism in the United States. In January 2012, the FBI established the Countering Violent Extremism Office (CVEO) under the National Security Branch. The CVEO was re-aligned in January 2013 to CTD's Domestic Terrorism Operations Section, under the National JTTF, to better leverage the collaborative participation of the dozens of participating agencies in FBI's CVE efforts. Yet, even within FBI, there is a misperception by some that CVE efforts are the same as FBI's community outreach efforts. Many field offices remain unaware of the CVE resources available through the CVEO. Because the field offices have to own and integrate the CVE portfolio without the benefit of additional resources from FBI Headquarters, there is understandably inconsistent implementation. The Review Commission, through interviews and meetings, heard doubts expressed by FBI personnel and its partners regarding the FBI's central role in the CVE program. The implementation had been inconsistent and confusing within the FBI, to outside partners, and to local communities. The CVEO's current limited budget and fundamental law enforcement and intelligence responsibilities do not make it an appropriate vehicle for the social and prevention role in the CVE mission. Such initiatives are best undertaken by other government agencies. The Review Commission recommends that the primary social and prevention responsibilities for the CVE mission should be transferred from the FBI to DHS or distributed among other agencies more directly involved with community interaction.

The issue raised by the Commission regarding conflict between intelligence responsibilities and effectiveness in these early-stage engagement efforts echoes points made by our interviewees both inside and outside government. Assessments of federal CVE activities published by civil liberties and academic groups have made similar points, highlighting the fact that outreach and engagement efforts have been described

---

[59] FBI programs are described on the webpage (FBI, "Community Outreach," webpage, undated[a]), and in some materials that have been released under the Freedom of Information Act (FBI, *Domestic Investigations and Operations Guide*, 0667DPG, [as redacted and publicly released under FOIA], October 16, 2013b).

[60] Hoffman, Meese, and Roemer, 2015, pp. 95–96.

in released documents as connected to intelligence efforts.[61] Unfortunately, because of limits on the amount of information that this study was able to gather beyond what was publicly available and the relatively overarching observations by interviewees, it is not possible to further characterize the scope or effectiveness of FBI outreach efforts.

Local Outreach Approaches and Staffing

In multiple cities, the need for greater engagement at the local level (e.g., between local government entities and communities) could be inferred from differences across organizations we interviewed.[62] For example, some members of government organizations indicated that outreach and community relations efforts were very effective in building relationships, while in the same city others said there were high barriers between community and law enforcement. Objective data even on the cities we visited (e.g., surveys that asked questions about levels of trust or engagement) were not available, meaning that alternative sources of insight into the differences could not be identified. Some engagement efforts are part of local grants funded in the FY 2016 program, meaning that DHS has made investments in this area. However, it was not clear what the right division of responsibility should be for "local responsibility to build strong relationships" and supplementation of efforts to do so with federal funds.

In more than one city, there clearly was tension between the desire to target outreach efforts (e.g., sustained activities to connect with specific immigrant or religious communities) and the sensitivity that efforts not stigmatize or be perceived as targeting individual groups, reflecting one of the central terrorism prevention design challenges.[63] Those tensions appeared to be mitigated for community-specific interactions that were not focused on terrorism concerns. As discussed above, although there are education and awareness efforts managed by NGOs both from a range of communities and aimed at different audiences and goals, it was difficult to determine how to think about their level of capacity within an overall national effort.

---

[61] Patel and Koushik, 2017, p. 23. This is an example of how the framing of activities in national security terms and terminology (reflecting the earlier language and terminology of "intelligence-led policing"), which we discussed as a design challenge with respect to law enforcement activities focused on CVE or terrorism prevention, can be a potent shaper of how programs are perceived.

[62] We discuss individual outreach and engagement associated with specific intervention programs in the next chapter.

[63] For example, two interviewees from the same city clearly demonstrate this tension pulling in opposite directions: "After 9/11 we had this problem with alienating Muslim communities. It was really very difficult. We realized that our strategy can't be looking just from law enforcement from one side, but we need to engage communities. So we started an outreach program to regain the trust of the Muslim community. . . . Let's educate the community about law enforcement but let's also educate law enforcement about the community" *versus* "And you can't target one community because they feel stigmatized. You have to generally treat society." An NGO representative in a different city echoed a similar point to the second interviewee: "I do think that when you're trying to do something broad-based and you make it about just one community, then you're less likely to get buy-in because you're accusatory."

Resilience and Risk Factor–Focused Approaches

At the other end of the spectrum, there are resilience-focused efforts (e.g., support of youth sports and community dialogue). It is difficult to make an impartial judgment about (1) how much of such efforts are going on, and (2) whether the "right amount" is being done. As alluded to previously, these activities were cited as valuable by many interviewees, in part because they can be framed as not specific to terrorism prevention, and are therefore a potential strategy to reduce risk in a broad (although rather diffuse) way. In our case studies, we heard about a convenience sample of such activities that are ongoing, some with and some without governmental funding. Finding funding for such activities was characterized as difficult, and that the amount being done now is constrained by available resources rather than by any measure of need or requirement. Efforts in this area have considerable overlap between programs that could be implemented for terrorism prevention purposes and those for other forms of violence (e.g., gangs) since, for example, a sports team to keep youth off the street out of concern for ideological violence would also occupy time during which the same youth could pursue gang membership. As a result, although interviewees did indicate a desire for "more support" for these types of programs, the fact that many such efforts are not terrorism-specific means that desire is not necessarily the same as a call for increased investment within terrorism prevention programs. Indeed, the view that involvement by nonsecurity organizations and non–terrorism specific funding streams is needed was common in our interviews and has been argued in the literature as well.[64] That involvement also has been framed as a potential way to increase available resources for risk factor–focused activities.[65]

Federal Options for Community Education, Engagement, Resilience, and Risk Factor Reduction–Focused Policy and Programming

Defining the scope of terrorism prevention is central to considering how policies and programming might change in the future. Although terrorism-specific education and engagement is clearly within its scope, how much of the broader risk factor reduction–type activity should be considered terrorism prevention (and, therefore, should have its funding come from terrorism prevention–specific pools of resources) is a policy question without a clear answer.[66]

---

[64] See, e.g., Aggarwal, 2018.

[65] Weine, Eisenman, and Kinsler et al., 2017, p. 212.

[66] This is a similar argument to that made in Levitt (2017) regarding CVE-relevant programs versus *CVE-specific* ones. Successful implementation of these programs can absolutely contribute to the goals that terrorism prevention efforts are seeking to achieve, just as similar efforts can for other violence problems, like gangs or juvenile delinquency.

Many of our interviewees viewed such programs positively—some argued that they are the most viable way to approach terrorism prevention, given the controversy and stigma surrounding more-focused past CVE efforts both in the United States and elsewhere.[67] Numerous literature sources also advocate in this direction. A particularly salient example is the initial evaluation done by Savoia et al. based on a very large set of interviews on the CVE effort in Boston.[68] All nine of their recommendations for practice focused on programs that would fall within this facet of terrorism prevention. In their report, they highlighted the focus on such approaches:[69]

> Many of the interviewees refer to the need for implementing basic societal development programs to strengthen opportunities directed to youth. This approach may seem quite different from what is frequently seen in CVE programs, which typically focus on developing interventions aimed at de-radicalization and which, according to project stakeholders, would be narrow in scope, and would not embrace a cost-effective transgenerational approach to the prevention of violent extremism, as is desired.

The belief that risk factor–focused programming should be central to efforts to address the risk of ideological violence is a foundational part of the argument for reframing CVE (and, by extension, terrorism prevention) in a public health and broader violence prevention model, with the expectation that public health–focused agencies like the Centers for Disease Control and Prevention or HHS would then pick up the mantle for such activities.[70] The assumption is that such a rebranding would help to avoid stigma and integrate terrorism prevention into more-acceptable and less controversial programs.[71] Others argue for a balanced approach, including using these types of activities as the backbone of early-phase prevention efforts while having activities specific to terrorism in later phases:[72]

> Strike a healthier balance between security-based and other community-wide efforts to prevent and counter violent extremism, especially in the preventive space. Such efforts are most successful when they address the full spectrum of challenges and needs facing a community or an individual. Desecuritizing such efforts also

---

[67] See, for example, the discussion in Weine et al., 2015.

[68] Savoia et al., 2016.

[69] Savoia et al., 2016, p. 49.

[70] Eisenman and Flavahan, 2017, p. 347.

[71] Weine et al., 2015. Interviewees echoed this point: "I would say if the resources are coming from DHS, they should have an interagency agreement with HHS so that this is looked at as a public health issue. Show that the two agencies are working together. That was done here in [state]. DHS gave it to the State's Attorney, who then gave it to HHS to provide."

[72] See, for example, Levitt, 2017, pp. 20–21.

facilitates the integration of nonsecurity, service-oriented agencies at all levels of government and their community service organization partners.

Rather than trying to reframe all of terrorism prevention by essentially "dissolving it" into public health practice, an alternative would be a division of labor: carving off broad risk factor–focused programs and initiatives for nonsecurity organizations to implement in a way that is not specific to terrorism concern.[73] Such an approach would appear to have several potential advantages: It could (1) provide a path to bring more engagement from nonsecurity agencies into this space, which we discuss in more detail in Chapter Ten; (2) provide a set of activities that would respond to terrorism risk without raising many of the concerns of communities and opponents of terrorism prevention; and (3) concentrate available terrorism prevention funds on more-specific goals that are unlikely to have other willing supporters, including the development of programming for both intervention and recidivism reduction.

As a result, in our examination of federal options in this area, we focus on the education and engagement end of the policy and program spectrum. The options for community engagement that would be most useful are shaped by two related goals: (1) educational outcomes that try to directly reduce risk (i.e., having an effect based on the information that is delivered) and (2) strengthening the relationship between federal actors and others to enable terrorism prevention initiatives and activities (in which the federal government could be a part but more likely, as we discuss in more depth in the next chapter, it acts to facilitate local implementation). The first goal is outcome focused, while the second is a process goal, although one that is particularly important, given the trust issues that are viewed as constraining federal activity and direct involvement in this area.

There is a range of options to deliver information to the public and others, which we order from the least to most costly below:

- technology-mediated approaches (e.g., web-based approaches)[74]
- incentivizing others to act independently (e.g., models similar to the P2P program focused on communication initiatives)
- episodic federal engagement (e.g., Washington D.C.–based individuals traveling to deliver CABs and CREXs)

---

[73] Although the discipline of public health is broad and interventions have been developed that address both violence-related and highly stigmatized problems, it is unclear whether or not "dissolving CVE into public health" would be more likely to wash away the stigma of the damaged "CVE brand" or to transfer that stigma to public health initiatives in which it was integrated. Although we explored whether there were similar historical examples that might lend some insight, none could be identified in the course of the research.

However, the notion of the division of labor is roughly the recommendation made in Patel and Koushik (2017, p. 38) to "delink social and educational programs from counter-terrorism."

[74] Whether or not the criticism it received is viewed as fair or unfair, the response to the FBI's "Don't Be a Puppet" web-based effort suggests caution in relying on web-based efforts aimed at broad audiences.

- funding others to perform similar functions (e.g., via academic models or outside organizations)
- reconstituting substantial staff located across the country for national engagement coverage.

Although all of these options could be successful in conveying information to wide audiences, the less costly options could not achieve trust-building and engagement goals. Given the history and controversy surrounding past CVE efforts, the view of a significant number of interviewees was that both addressing the trust deficit faced by the federal government in this space and having the room to develop locally workable terrorism prevention models required federal representatives that were locally based so that conversation and trust-building could be an ongoing effort. As a result, the most relevant federal options include the following:

- **Awareness and Training**
  - **Continue and expand outreach and local coordination efforts through CABs and CREXs.** The consensus around education and engagement was that past federal efforts and products—notably the CABs and CREXs (which we will discuss in greater detail in Chapter Six)—had been valuable and should be continued. The main concern was the capacity to deliver them to all interested audiences (ideally working toward national coverage, as we discussed in Chapter Three). The education element could be delivered in other ways (e.g., an online version of a CAB, as is being pursued for technology sector outreach) and could contribute to increasing dissemination of information. However, to achieve the goals of engagement, trust-building, and federal-local collaboration, person-to-person interaction is needed. As a result, although technologically mediated approaches might increase scale at low cost, they would not achieve all relevant DHS and federal goals. Past federal efforts to ensure coverage of the range of potential sources of ideological violence in outreach efforts should be continued and reinforced.
- **Federal Program Development**
  - **Reconstitute and expand federal field staff to act as primary focal points for terrorism prevention at the local level.** Given the level of need and the consensus view of most of the interviewees (including national and state and local representatives), significant increases in outreach and engagement supported by field staff appear valuable.[75] Because of the design challenges and sensitivities around federal involvement in terrorism prevention, it is difficult to envision success without a robust outreach effort to build trust and partnership to make federal facilitation of local terrorism prevention initiatives viable.

---

[75] Literature sources also argue for the importance of federal field staff (e.g., Levitt, 2017).

There were a variety of views of who could fill those roles (from local DHS staff to individuals from other federal agencies) and there were both practical and implementation strengths and weaknesses to each of the options.

The outreach efforts need to be approached in a way that does not stigmatize individual communities or groups and the integration of CABs covering both domestic and internationally inspired ideological violence is a step toward that goal. In practice, these outreach roles require individuals both with deep knowledge and specific skills in navigating both complexity and controversy. In planning an effort to rebuild field staff for engagement, location and mobility of those individuals must be a design criterion. Past data (discussed in Chapter Two) have shown that ideological violence can come from a wide range of communities, both urban and rural. As a result, if staff are placed in urban areas, they will need the flexibility to travel throughout their geographic area of responsibility to be effective and responsive to needs.

Interviewees emphasized that success could take time, which was a tenet of the argument that federal staff periodically visiting from Washington was not a viable model: Even rotational postings like those for FBI Field Office leadership (cited by interviewees as between one and two years) were viewed as too short.[76]

- **Auxiliary Federal Activities**
  - **Recognize and proactively manage effects that other DHS and federal programs can have on community trust to support terrorism prevention initiatives.** In some of our interviews, individuals highlighted things the government can and should do that could help build relationships and trust with communities that were absolutely not terrorism prevention–focused. Examples within DHS included *proactive positive programs* (e.g., assistance to houses of worship in security through National Protection and Programs Directorate programs) and *responding to negative effects* of other DHS activities (e.g., more robust community interaction associated with actions like immigration enforcement to explain actions taken, and accessible and navigable redress mechanisms for individuals affected by DHS actions at airports and during international travel). These issues were raised most often in the context of efforts focused on Muslim communities with respect to jihadist threats, but they were also referenced in an interfaith context (e.g., assistance to churches and synagogues) with respect to race or bias crime and violence as well.
  - **Increase interagency investment separate from terrorism prevention initiatives to address community concerns and reduce risk factors related to**

---

[76] From a local-level NGO interviewee: "DHS is better than FBI to send [for community engagement]. FBI is not structured to do . . . engagement—the core is building a relationship. Structurally, FBI moves people every 18 months. They're structured not to build long-term ties with people."

radicalization to violence. To the extent that more-robust risk factor–focused programs funded by interagency nonsecurity partners are implemented and seek to reach communities where there is risk of ideological radicalization to violence, proactive efforts to identify priorities in communities and link them to funding programs for community participatory interventions could also be valuable. Public-private models of funding (e.g., creation of a partnership to manage funding versus direct government support) could be an alternative model. Interviewees from law enforcement noted that these sorts of efforts were consistent with the philosophy behind community policing—i.e., by addressing issues that are important to the community, helping to deliver services and solve problems, and responding to concerns about treatment in citizen-police interactions in a positive way, trust is built and maintained.

- **Federal Support of Local Initiatives**
  - **Make "on-call experts" available to support local terrorism prevention initiatives with knowledge, program design, and evaluation expertise.** One of the roles of locally stationed federal staff is to be sources of expertise to local initiatives, addressing the challenge that terrorism will likely always be one threat among many for local organizations and decisionmakers. Either as a supplement to them or as a substitute in areas without that level of federal engagement, the potential of building a network of "on-call experts" on terrorism prevention (and previously for CVE) has been put forward in both our interviews and the literature.[77] In terms of multidisciplinary models of intervention, which we will discuss in Chapter Seven, developing outreach capabilities and being able to connect to knowledgeable individuals in local areas—where the small scale of the problem of ideological violence may make it impossible to build or maintain a high level of expertise—could be an alternative approach. If a robust field staff model is implemented, the members of that field staff could play this role, both in their areas and more widely.
  - **Use grant funding to support local and NGO early-phase terrorism prevention activities.** Constraints on available resources were cited in a number of our discussions regarding these types of efforts, so federal funding—i.e., the continuation of grants to support terrorism prevention activity—appears to be necessary. There was also significant demand for efforts in this area in the FY 2016 grant program. As framed in the discussion of design challenges, this is not as simple as other policy areas. Some interviewees were very concerned about the consequences on community trust if they accepted federal funds, so even as they needed funding they were at best uneasy about those funds coming from DHS. This is not a new issue: Literature on CVE efforts, particularly with respect to how to enable "credible voices" to respond to messaging

---

[77] See, e.g., Eisenman and Flavahan, 2017, p. 347.

and participate in ideological debates in communities, has long recognized that the act of taking money from government could make a once credible voice appear compromised. One goal of the activities of local field staff is to help navigate the controversy to make it possible for DHS to be a more effective partner supporting local initiatives and activities. As detailed above, public-private partnerships for funding and management of initiatives could be an alternative model, although they would not be expected to completely address trust challenges for terrorism prevention. Although individual initiatives might be threat-specific or ideologically specific, government investments as a portfolio should be balanced across ideological sources of violence, based on objective data on relative threat and prevalence.

- **Expand use of tabletop exercises to assist localities in developing acceptable and practical local approaches to terrorism prevention.** Interviews and our literature review showed that tabletop exercises appear to be a particularly valuable tool. CREXs and other exercises have been a part of federal outreach and education efforts for some years, providing community members with a forum to work through issues and concerns using the game structure to explore how they think their community should respond. Interviewees who had participated in them provided positive feedback on their value. This is consistent with past work at the RAND Corporation that applied exercises in this way to allow decisionmakers and stakeholders who may not agree on policy to work through and debate issues in a neutral environment.

    However, the CREX approach is different from some other exercise programs in ways that would appear to limit its potential impact: (1) CREX has been implemented as a service delivered by government, rather than making materials public so others could use them to guide similar activities in their own areas independently;[78] (2) previous exercise efforts that focused on controversial topics affecting different communities have used the game mechanic to allow (or force) stakeholders to trade roles to better understand the perspectives and constraints of actors on all sides of the problem;[79] and (3) the results of games and the policy lessons learned from them are published as research products, protecting the identities of participants or specifics of the organizations involved—so they can contribute to policy development and learning

---

[78] Some CREX materials were publicly released under the Freedom of Information Act, but this is distinct from designing exercise materials intended for public consumption and decentralized implementation (Office of the Director of National Intelligence, "FOIA—Publicly Released Records," multiple dates).

[79] See discussions on the use of such games to explore different stakeholder and actor roles in drug policy debate and implementation in James P. Kahan, John Setear, Margaret M. Bitzinger, Sinclair B. Coleman, and Joel Feinleib, *Developing Games of Local Drug Policy*, Santa Monica, Calif.: RAND Corporation, N-3395-DPRC, 1992; and James P. Kahan, C. Peter Rydell, and John Setear, "A Game on Urban Drug Policy," *Peace and Conflict: Journal of Peace Psychology*, Vol. 1, No. 3, 1995.

beyond the individuals in the room when the exercises occurred. Integrating such features into the model for CREX or developing exercises that could be used this way could allow more-substantial contributions to terrorism prevention goals in this activity.

- **Research and Evaluation**
  - **Support periodic, publicly released national surveys to assess knowledge and awareness about radicalization and mobilization to violence.** Because the direct goal of education and engagement is to increase knowledge, regular survey measurements of levels of knowledge about terrorist threats could provide a piece of analytic infrastructure for evaluating initiatives. If the results of such surveys were made public, they could be used to trigger media reporting (and therefore use its megaphone to advance education). Such surveys could also assess levels of trust and engagement (which we also explore in the next chapter on referral promotion).

The education and engagement space is also an area where interviewees repeatedly emphasized the need to implement programs—not only from the federal level, but also from local actors—with care not to stigmatize particular communities. Some initiatives in this space are designed to reach broad audiences, but even focused efforts (e.g., on schools) can hit large percentages of a community. As a result, if those initiatives are framed such that the affected communities feel that they are being unfairly characterized, the unintended consequences can be potent. In our interviews, we heard repeatedly that it was important not to design programming such that it was (or was perceived to be) aimed only at Muslim communities. They should instead be designed on interfaith models and anchored with issues (e.g., hate or bias crime) that are concerns across multiple communities while also providing a nonstigmatizing way to address ideological violence risk.

CHAPTER SIX

Middle-Phase Terrorism Prevention: Referral Promotion

One of the central ways terrorism prevention seeks to reduce terrorism risk is by providing services to at-risk individuals who would otherwise not be identified until they were close to or had attempted an attack. Assuming that effective intervention capability is available, such individuals could be redirected from violence before they have committed a crime, potentially avoiding harm and negative consequences to themselves and others. As a result, and as framed in Chapter Three, the central focus for this component of terrorism prevention is understanding the likelihood that an at-risk individual in a given geographic area will be referred for help, and taking steps to increase that likelihood. Activities falling within this facet of terrorism prevention are captured in the center part of our mapping, the relevant section of which is reproduced in Figure 6.1.

The goal of referral promotion is not simply "more referrals." Increasing the likelihood of referrals is only valuable if the people being referred actually pose a risk of violence. Referral of large numbers of people who are not threats could in practice *increase* the risk of successful terrorist attacks: Dealing with these "false positives" could clog up the system in place to follow up, creating unsustainable costs that would threaten the viability of terrorism prevention efforts, obscure real threats in the noise of the false positives, and—depending on the type of actions that are taken—produce significant negative effects on the referred individuals.[1] In an example from one of our international case studies, the sheer number of false positives associated with the Channel program in the United Kingdom has been viewed as undermining its legitimacy (see Appendix A). If the number of false positives and their consequences are perceived as unjust, the effect on the perceived legitimacy of the effort could undermine the willingness of individuals or institutions to make referrals at all. As a result, even if a larger number of referrals meant that a larger percentage of true positives was identified, a sufficient increase in false positives could overwhelm any potential security benefit.

For referral of individuals at risk of carrying out ideological violence, the key elements can be thought through in terms of responses to five questions:

---

[1] As one federal law enforcement interviewee put it, "I don't know the answer. There's a 'see something, say something,' push [to send in] lots of leads. [But] if you miss just one, your organization is crucified."

Figure 6.1
Referral Promotion Within the Terrorism Prevention Policy Space

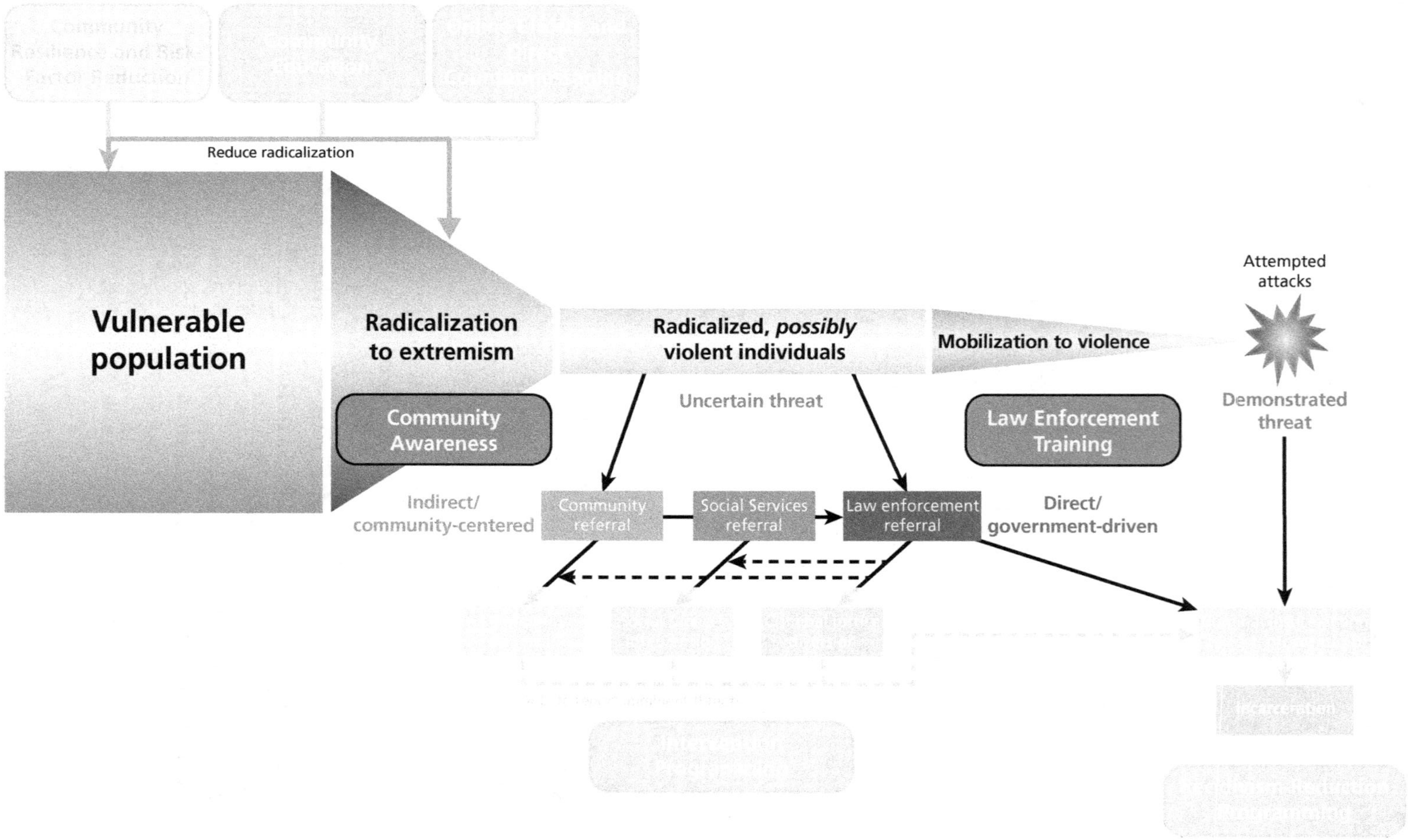

1. Who might be in a position to notice changes in behavior[2] preceding mobilization to violence or other action?
2. Will those people notice the changes (and not misinterpret and refer based on other behaviors or factors that could increase false positives)?
3. Are there ways for them to reach out—whether to authorities, service providers, or community groups—to get advice or make the referral?
4. Are they willing to reach out, and what factors affect their willingness to do so?
5. How will entities that receive referrals assess the threat posed by an individual to distinguish false from true positives?

We take on each of these questions in turn in the subsequent sections.

Who might be in a position to notice changes in behavior preceding mobilization to violence? In the literature on terrorism and individual mobilization to ideological violence, a wide range of potential "bystanders" who might see changes in behavior before an individual takes violent action have been identified. Analysts have flagged the potential for family, peers, professionals (e.g., teachers or health providers), and community or religious leaders—all of whom could have comparatively deep knowledge about a person—to see and be able to recognize changes in behavior.[3] More "distant" bystanders include law enforcement officers during interactions in the course of their duties, other government representatives, workers in businesses that individuals frequent, or even members of the general public. Past successes in disrupting plots through traditional enforcement mechanisms have involved individuals from across these categories: In examinations of disrupted terrorist activity, members of the public provided nearly one in five of the initial leads to law enforcement that lead to disruption, and one in ten was discovered in the investigation of other criminal activity.[4] In one FBI study described in media reporting and Congressional testimony, analysts looking at past incidents identified "peers, family members, authority figures, and strangers" who had some indications of the plot before it was carried out.[5] For earlier-stage intervention, greater reliance on non–law enforcement and nonintelligence sources of information would therefore be expected.

Will those people notice the changes? Referrals can range from highly nuanced and individually focused at one extreme to the much more generic "if you see some-

---

[2] Numerous interviewees and the literature emphasize that risk assessment should be driven by behavior, not personal characteristics or the simple presence of risk factors (e.g., FBI Behavioral Analysis Unit, undated).

[3] An NGO interviewee described this as the "natural ecosystem" that the person is developing (and potentially mobilizing to violence) within.

[4] Strom, Hollywood, and Pope, 2017.

[5] See description of the FBI study included in Peter Bergen, "Who Do Terrorists Confide In?" *CNN*, February 3, 2016. The Bureau has done similar work with respect to other violent incidents, also demonstrating bystander awareness (FBI Behavioral Analysis Unit, undated).

thing, say something" suspicious activity reporting.[6] Although both are relevant and considered in policy discussions of terrorism prevention, there are important differences across this "personal to impersonal continuum," including the factors that shape what will likely be reported and the willingness to do so.

The basis on which someone decides to refer or report behavior also affects the potential security benefit. This is the first point in this stage where "detection performance matters":

- On one hand, there is a need to educate people about behaviors that might indicate mobilization to violence, so that real clues are not missed.[7] This is difficult because, as we discussed in Chapter Three, research has shown that there are no clear and unambiguous indicators for either terrorism or other targeted violence, like school shootings.[8] As a result, teaching members of the public, professionals, and others about the constellation of factors and behaviors that can suggest the potential for future violence is a complex communication and education challenge. Such subtleties and complexity also mean that there will invariably be false positives even in a perfectly functioning and wholly appropriate referral effort.

- On the other hand, there is also a need to teach what *not* to report, and what is not an appropriate basis for reporting.[9] In our interviews across government, community, and research organizations, the real damage that can be done by inappropriate action (e.g., referral because of an individual's race or ethnicity, expression of dissenting views about U.S. policy, or constitutionally protected religious or political behavior) came up repeatedly. The nature of the damage to credibility and trust was illustrated by interviewees and in the literature not only with respect to past cases where terrorism-focused actions were guided by race or religion (e.g., post-9/11 police surveillance of Muslim communities),[10] but also by more common—and often widely reported both in the media and online—situations where calls to police or law enforcement responses were driven by the race or religion of the people involved, rather than their actions.[11]

---

[6] Suspicious activity reporting is clearly a part of this space in which there is some innovation, as two of the law enforcement departments we spoke with talked about use of mobile apps to make the process smoother.

[7] See the discussion in FBI Behavioral Analysis Unit, undated.

[8] Those risk factors can also change over time (Horgan et al., 2016), meaning that the utility of any given set may be perishable.

[9] This has been a concern in the United Kingdom regarding the Channel program and has also been raised by entities critical of CVE over the years (e.g., Patel and Koushik, 2017, pp. 2, 4).

[10] Matt Apuzzo and Adam Goldman, "After Spying on Muslims, New York Police Agree to Greater Oversight," *New York Times*, March 6, 2017.

[11] For example, Snair, Nicholson, and Giammaria (2017, p. 85) describe the assessment model in the Los Angeles area, which drew on the framework used by the existing program focused on school violence. Such approaches were contrasted with those focused on ethnicity, appearance, religious behavior, and other individual characteris-

Are there ways to reach out to get advice or make the referral? The mechanisms available for people to make referrals and their willingness to do so are related.[12] Calling a national "suspicious activity reporting line" about a neighbor's behavior is qualitatively different than reaching out to a religious leader. There are institutional mechanisms on the law enforcement side of counterterrorism with systems in place for officers to make suspicious activity reports (which also act as interagency information-sharing mechanisms for reports submitted by others).[13] In considering the national picture, referral options range from the impersonal to the very personal, and can include governmental (e.g., the local police) and nongovernmental options (e.g., crisis or other NGO hotlines), as well as those where referrers have the option to remain anonymous.[14]

Are they willing to reach out, and what factors affect their willingness to do so? Beyond having referral options available, trust of the organizations involved is important. People differ in whether they will be willing, for example, to reach out directly to law enforcement in such a situation. In the cities we visited, we heard very different assessments regarding the likelihood that members of the public would call local police with concerns about someone radicalizing: In some areas, cases were cited where people had reached out to police for assistance with their own children, while others told us that would never happen and that there would be reticence to reach out to law enforcement with respect to radicalization by anyone, not just a family member. These concerns make it impossible to decouple terrorism prevention from broader police-community relations in the United States. The concerns that communities have about the treatment of their members by law enforcement, along with perceptions of bias or fairness, and procedural justice or injustice will inevitably shape the implementation of terrorism prevention, particularly because of the serious and permanent consequences of prosecution for terrorism-related offenses. This has been a central element of the definitional discussion of CVE from the beginning, including proposals to view these efforts in terms of public health or to "desecuritize" them by managing them separately from law enforcement agencies.

---

tics that had been elements of some post-9/11 counterterrorism training curricula. For examples of these efforts, see Meg Stalcup and Joshua Craze, "How We Train Our Cops to Fear Islam," *Washington Monthly*, March/April 2011.

[12] "[I]n the overwhelming majority of those cases, someone in the person's social or family sphere realized that something was amiss but did not know what to do or where to go (anecdotally, this may be attributable to trepidation in contacting law enforcement for a range of different reasons)" (Snair, Nicholson, and Giammaria, 2017, p. 55).

[13] There have been recurring concerns about the value of the information (essentially the false positive versus true positive ratio) in suspicious activity reports (also referred to as SARs). For a review based on interviews with relevant law enforcement practitioners, see Priscilla M. Regan, Torin Monahan, and Krista Craven, "Constructing the Suspicious: Data Production, Circulation, and Interpretation by DHS Fusion Centers," *Administration and Society*, Vol. 47, No. 6, 2015.

[14] Crisis or NGO hotlines are recommended in Levitt, 2017, p. 21.

Perceptions about the consequences of making a referral—for both the referrer and the person they refer—play an important part in whether people will be willing to make referrals.[15] One interviewee involved in an intervention program summed it up: "people are willing to refer to us because they know we have the capability to actually help."[16] In discussions and in literature critical of terrorism prevention efforts, similar arguments are made, but are inverted: The perceived absence of noncoercive and beneficial intervention options supports a conclusion that the most likely outcome of referral will be prosecution, not help.[17] Thus, some have concluded that CVE (and now terrorism prevention) are surveillance efforts.[18] Referral of individuals by professionals—whether they are school staff, medical providers, or counselors—is also shaped by professional responsibilities and ethical requirements that are themselves affected by expectations about the likely outcome of referral. Responsibilities to contact authorities or, conversely, to *not* do so under specific circumstances are shaped by such professionals' (sometimes complex and conflicting) responsibilities to patients or students individually and as a group.[19] Interviewees also argued that willingness to refer was also tied to whether the program accepting the referral was focused on terrorism specifically or was more general in scope (see Chapter Seven); general programs would be more likely to get referrals.[20]

However, individuals who are in a position to refer often do not reach out regarding concerns about radicalization or mobilization to violence. The FBI study cited pre-

---

[15] Williams, Horgan, and Evans explored this issue, specifically with respect to peers making referrals regarding concerns about radicalization and mobilization to violence (Michael J. Williams, John G. Horgan, and William P. Evans, "The Critical Role of Friends in Networks for Countering Violent Extremism: Toward a Theory of Vicarious Help-Seeking," *Behavioral Sciences of Terrorism and Political Aggression*, Vol. 8, No. 1, 2016).

[16] This "likely outcome-driven" view is not unlike factors that shape whether individuals are willing to call the police when they are the victims of crime.

[17] Or, from a more instrumental law enforcement perspective:

> Federal investigators and prosecutors continue to have limited options other than arresting and prosecuting young people suspected of having travelled or seeking travel to support the Islamic State, but who are judged not to pose a security threat and for whom a 10 to 20-year jail sentence might risk further radicalization. This, despite an increasing awareness, including within the FBI and DOJ, that alternatives to criminal prosecution and incarceration, in certain circumstances, can help facilitate the cooperation of family, friends, and other members of vulnerable communities who may be reluctant to cooperate with law enforcement if they know that any outreach might put their loved one in a prison cell (Rosand, 2017a).

[18] This challenge was also raised in DHS HSAC, 2016; and Rosand, 2017a.

[19] These responsibilities are addressed under the concept of "duty to warn," which was reviewed at the National Conference of State Legislatures with respect to mental health professionals in particular (National Conference of State Legislatures, *Mental Health Professionals' Duty to Warn*, September 28, 2015).

[20] "Referrals are accepted differently when they come from law enforcement versus educators, health professionals, other community members. . . . It can't just be for CVE. No community will create a CVE platform. There's also no evidence that I'm aware of that a broader based targeted violence prevention platform couldn't work on this. There's just this notion that this kind of violence is different" (Interview with a former government official and current NGO representative, 2018).

viously that looked at completed attacks showed that 80 percent of the time there was some leakage of information to bystanders—usually peers and family members—but that many did not take any action based on that information.[21] Comparable academic studies reached similar conclusions (e.g., Gill, Horgan and Deckert [2014] found a total of just more than 60 percent).[22] Researchers at START explored willingness to report *to police* in public surveys fielded in 2012–2014, which showed a relatively high estimated likelihood that individuals would report more unambiguously threatening and likely illegal behavior (e.g., approximately 75 percent indicated that they would call police about someone "talking about planting explosives") but many fewer were willing to do so for more-ambiguous behaviors (e.g., approximately 40 percent said that they would call police about someone "talking about joining a terrorist group" and about 20 percent regarding someone "reading material from terrorist group").[23]

How will entities assess the threat posed by an individual to distinguish false from true positives? After an individual thought to be at risk of committing violence is referred to someone, there is the problem of assessing whether that person poses a threat—i.e., whether he or she is a true positive—or whether he or she is a false positive that should not be engaged further. This is the second point where "detection performance" matters, and the lower the quality of initial referrals, the greater the performance challenge at this later stage. As alluded to previously and in Chapter Three, this is not an easy task. The clearest demonstration of the challenge is illustrated by individuals who were known to law enforcement, had been contacted in the course of investigative activity, and were judged not to be risks, but later went on to carry out attacks.[24] These problems are not new, and are not limited to concerns about assessing the potential for terrorist violence. Challenges assessing the threat posed by individuals go back decades. The issue has been the subject of foundational work done by the U.S.

---

[21] See Horgan et al., 2016, for a discussion of "leakage" of information by different attacker types.

[22] Paul Gill, John Horgan, and Paige Deckert, "Bombing Alone: Tracing the Motivations and Antecedent Behaviors of Lone-Actor Terrorists," *Journal of Forensic Science*, Vol. 59, No. 2, March 2014.

[23] Gary LaFree, Stanley Presser, Roger Tourangeau, and Amy Adamczyk, *U.S. Attitudes Toward Terrorism and Counterterrorism: Examining Results from a Four-Wave Survey Conducted Between September 2012 and July 2014*, College Park, Md.: National Consortium for the Study of Terrorism and Responses to Terrorism, November 2014, p. 5. These findings are consistent with the larger literature on the bystander effect, which has shown that individuals are more willing to intervene in a situation when it is perceived as dangerous and imminent. For a recent comprehensive review of bystander effect research, see Peter Fischer, Joachim I. Krueger, Tobias Greitemeyer, Claudia Vogrincic, Andreas Kastenmüller, Dieter Frey, Moritz Heene, Magdalena Wicher, and Martina Kainbacher, "The Bystander-Effect: A Meta-Analytic Review on Bystander Intervention in Dangerous and Non-Dangerous Emergencies," *Psychological Bulletin*, Vol. 137, No. 4, 2011.

[24] This issue is exacerbated by time and resource pressures, as we discuss in Chapter Nine: "Manpower pressures, for example, encourage agents and Joint Terrorism Task Forces to make quick decisions regarding whether a suspect poses a threat. In many of the thousands of counterterrorism cases the FBI investigates a year, what determines who is merely 'aspirational' and who might someday be 'operational' is often just an agent's or squad's intuition" (Garrett Graff, "The FBI's Growing Surveillance Gap," *Politico*, June 16, 2016).

Secret Service on assessment methods and approaches and of focused studies on assessment in stalking, school violence, sexual offending, and other specialized crimes.[25] There also has been substantial more recent work on the use of violence prediction tools in the broader criminal justice context to inform decisions about pretrial release, sentencing, and probation programming.[26]

Although there are many risk tools that have been developed in the criminal justice context, their performance and, therefore, the consequences of their broad use are quite controversial. Concerns about accuracy and fairness have been raised both for "actuarial" risk assessment tools (which use quantitative data to score or bin offenders by assessed risk using models developed from group data) and for methods of structured professional judgment where clinicians or analysts make an assessment of an individual on a case-by-case basis. Analyses have shown that the performance of these tools is much better than chance, but is far from perfect—meaning that they result in a significant number of false positives.[27] Others have argued that both human and actuarial tools can produce results that embed biases, raising questions about their fairness.[28] Risk assessment in the crime or clinical contexts, where the goal is to predict higher base-rate events (e.g., recidivism) in relatively large populations, is a comparatively easier problem than terrorism, where base rates are very small. As a result, even if tools for risk assessment for ideological violence are available and are as good as those for everyday crime, they would only be partially effective to screen out false positive referrals—meaning that broad use of tools in large populations for referral identification would almost certainly produce unacceptable numbers of false positives.[29] As discussed in Chapter Three, the stakes involved in these risk decisions (i.e., the perceived cost of missing a true positive) create the potential to err on what is seen as the safer

[25] See, for example, Jane Takeuchi, Fredric Solomon, and W. Walter Menninger, eds. *Behavioral Science and the Secret Service: Toward the Prevention of Assassination*, Washington, D.C.: National Academies Press, 1981.

[26] For example, Jay P. Singh, Martin Grann, and Seena Fazel, "A Comparative Study of Violence Risk Assessment Tools: A Systematic Review and Metaregression Analysis of 68 Studies Involving 25,980 Participants," *Clinical Psychology Review*, Vol. 31, 2011, review a number of tools.

[27] See Singh, Grann, and Fazel, 2011, for a review.

[28] For human tools, see Charles Kurzman, Ahsan Kamal, and Hajar Yazdiha, "Ideology and Threat Assessment: Law Enforcement Evaluation of Muslim and Right-Wing Extremism," *Socius: Sociological Research for a Dynamic World*, Vol. 3, 2017; for actuarial tools, see Julia Angwin, Jeff Larson, Surya Mattu, and Lauren Kirchner, "Machine Bias," *ProPublica*, May 23, 2016.

[29] This concept is reviewed in Kiran M. Sarma, "Risk Assessment and the Prevention of Radicalization from Nonviolence into Terrorism," *American Psychologist*, Vol. 72, No. 3, 2017.

side, and accept that some false positives will be treated as true positives.[30] However, doing so has significant costs of its own.[31]

Relevant Design Challenges

In considering the main design challenges affecting terrorism prevention efforts in this phase, the central difficulty comes from the fortunate challenge that radicalization and mobilization to violence inside the United States is a rare problem.[32] This means that maintaining salience and sustaining referral and risk-assessment mechanisms that are *only* relevant to terrorism will be difficult. This is an area where measurement is important. Because this is the first step of a process in which individuals at risk of violent radicalization are connected with assistance, success at this point is a fundamental constraint on performance overall. Measurement to track the ability of a local terrorism prevention effort to distinguish true positives from false ones is critical to monitor. But the most important design challenges at this step and drivers of likely success and failure are public trust and the potential complexities of multiagency coordination and information-sharing—because individual organizations may not possess all of the expertise needed to assess individual cases, it may be unrealistic to expect them to do so on their own. Breakdowns in public trust—whether driven by concerns about local or national law enforcement, government in general, or the federal government in particular—will mean that parts of the population will be unwilling to participate, putting a ceiling on success. To the extent that multiagency mission conflict or information-sharing challenges arise, whether because of perceived obligations to act or not act and share or not share, those challenges could feed back into both performance and trust. Each of these represents a design challenge requiring that referral promotion efforts be

---

[30] In the clinical testing context, there has been significant analysis on the information value of a diagnostic test, and how false positive rates, true positive rates, the relative costs of false positives and false negatives (i.e., missed detections), and the base rate of the event that is being predicted affect how tests should be used. For a low base rate like terrorism, false positive costs (paid by individuals, government, and in terrorism prevention performance as a result of damaged trust) could add up sufficiently to drive the information value of an assessment down significantly (e.g., discussion with respect to violence in Grant T. Harris and Marnie E. Rice, "Characterizing the Value of Actuarial Violence Risk Assessments," *Criminal Justice and Behavior*, Vol. 34, No. 12, 2007; and Richard M. McFall and Teresa A. Treat, "Quantifying the Information Value of Clinical Assessments with Signal Detection Theory," *Annual Reviews of Psychology*, Vol. 50, 1999, more broadly).

[31] This becomes an argument for designing a system of intervention where referrals can be "responded to" in a way that explicitly seeks to minimize the cost if someone is a false positive rather than a real threat. Although doing so can minimize costs for the government (e.g., see discussion in Chapter Nine), reducing costs on the affected individuals—or, in an ideal world, being able to intervene in a way that is actually beneficial to the individual while addressing the uncertainty about societal risk—would make false positives less ethically and practically problematic. We take on this argument in the next chapter on intervention programming.

[32] There are common issues affecting efforts to promote referrals and the systems that will act on that information to manage intervention activity (which we discuss in the next chapter).

shaped in response to the multiple and sometimes conflicting needs and concerns of different government agencies, community organizations, and members of the public.

Approaches for Referral Promotion

Although survey data show that members of the public are relatively likely to report individuals involved in illegal behavior to police, the likelihood of referral supporting earlier intervention is less clear. The question is therefore what options are available that could increase referrals at a stage where intervention could be used to avoid arrest and prosecution.[33]

Policies and Programming

We suggest that there are three categories of approaches to improving referrals of individuals at risk of committing ideological violence: (1) efforts to communicate information about what sorts of behaviors raise concerns;[34] (2) improving individuals' ability, willingness, and incentives to refer; and (3) improving risk assessment of anyone who is referred.

Communicating Information About Behaviors of Concern

In the first category, conveying information about behaviors of concern is differentiated by audience (e.g., the general public; specific institutions, like schools; specific professions, like mental health counselors or law enforcement officers) and by delivery mode (e.g., print, in person, via the media, or online). Such communication and public education campaigns, whether focused or broadly targeted, have been a component of policy responses to everything from health concerns (e.g., general health promotion, prevention campaigns, focused communications during disease outbreaks) to police responses to specific crime problems. Communication and education efforts aimed at specific professions range from broad (e.g., presentations to conventions about national issues) to narrow audiences (e.g., roll call briefings to police officers). Development of print and online resources (e.g., best practices documents produced by federal technical and research agencies on policies or problems) and the use of media campaigns (e.g., online or broadcast public service messages) are similarly differentiated.

---

[33] Such options blur the line between this piece of terrorism prevention and intervention (which we discuss in the next chapter), because the organizations delivering programming will almost invariably be involved in risk-assessment activities. This blurring of the boundaries we have defined for discussion purposes emphasizes, however, that the effect of referral promotion efforts on those organizations must be central to consideration, as significant increases in false positive referrals could have damaging effects on their ability to perform their roles.

[34] Both interviewees (across disciplines) and sources in the literature emphasized that the basis of risk assessment must be behaviors of concern, not individual characteristics or beliefs (e.g., Weine et al., 2015; FBI Behavioral Analysis Unit, undated).

The options within educational programming essentially relate to what to communicate, including how to frame risk factors or behaviors that should raise concerns and potentially prompt referral. There has been significant activity to date focused on communicating signs of concern about radicalization to violence and seeking to encourage referrals from the public (e.g., "See Something, Say Something"), law enforcement, schools, and other institutions. In designing communication and educational materials, the main policy choices are how much to communicate and how much complexity to include. Based on the discussion in the section above, another facet would be how much to communicate about what *not to report* and the potential effects of false positive reports on security. Such programming choices are similar in initiatives for other social problems as well: community outreach as part of community policing often includes information on crime prevention and actions individuals can take in response, in part to encourage crime reporting and enable effective police response.

Addressing the Ability, Willingness, and Incentives to Refer

To increase the likelihood of referral or reporting, options to address the logistical practicalities generally focus on two issues: "refer how" and "to whom." On the first point, most technical options are relatively self-explanatory, although whether a phone hotline or online system feeds into a national, regional, or local entity can vary, and can have different implications. Models can be specific to terrorism (e.g., a radicalization hotline) or can be integrated into other systems (e.g., suicide or family support hotlines).

The full range of options that could be the recipient of referrals or reporting include law enforcement or security organizations (e.g., to local police, or the FBI or DHS at the federal level), to other government agencies (e.g., social services), to entities outside of government (e.g., NGOs), or some combination thereof (e.g., a multidisciplinary team of organizations). Information-sharing mechanisms supporting the multidisciplinary nature of responding to these types of reports (or acting on them when individuals appear to pose immediate threats) can be either technical (e.g., information technology systems linking organizations) or procedural. The expected "access point" for calls has to be staffed with individuals with the right expertise to understand what they are hearing, which was a shortfall we heard in interviews regarding both local options (e.g., 911 calls)[35] and national-level suspicious activity reporting lines.[36]

---

[35] One community organization representative noted: "If a person is calling into 911, those dispatch individuals [need to] know that the suspicious activity report is in fact an actual report . . . [and] to pass that info along. . . . They were like, 'this isn't [an] emergency.' So they would tell the person that was calling in, 'unless it's an emergency, don't call us. Call your nonemergency number.' I guarantee that is still happening. . . . So we work with some of those dispatchers now to train them up" (Interview with a community organization representative in one U.S. city, 2018).

[36] Interview with federal representatives, 2018.

The "to whom" question has been a focus of controversy in the United States, and has had effects on the willingness of individuals and institutions to participate. For example, as cited above, our interviewees varied in their views about whether direct reporting to law enforcement would be a barrier to referral. For areas where this is a barrier, there are a range of approaches under the rubric of "trust building" that have precedents not only in CVE, but also in efforts aimed at other policies.

Part of the process of public collaboration in development of the CVE strategies in the 2015 Pilot Cities was an example from the terrorism/radicalization space. Our interviewees in Boston, for example, cited that process—and the fact that organizations that were both "pro- and anti-CVE" participated and could put their views on record was important. Similar community advisory, coordination, and participation structures are part of many community-policing structures, and interviewees during our study also cited models of participatory research and community-driven interventions in other areas (e.g., health) as models of how trust could be strengthened in what could be controversial interventions. However, such models can only be effective to the extent that the community has influence in shaping the effort and in defining the policies that govern it. Such collaboration can also allow models to evolve as trust and needs evolve. For example, an interviewee who was involved in an intervention effort noted that when they started their effort, members of the community would not accept law enforcement involvement in any form, so at that point there was a hard barrier between the organization's activity and police. But, over time, trust was built and a link was formed, and the organization began accepting referrals from law enforcement entities as well.[37] In some cases, a component of training (e.g., law enforcement cultural awareness and interaction training) is designed to minimize the likelihood that misunderstandings or miscommunications will poison relationships between police and communities and reduce the likelihood of collaboration.

Given particular concerns by critics of past CVE efforts that the program's real focus is surveillance, there is also the challenge of maintaining trust over time. The best option for maintaining trust, as is the case for police agencies in general,[38] is building transparency mechanisms so that critical audiences are reassured that the effort is really doing what it says it is doing.[39] Such mechanisms range from autonomous oversight boards to public disclosure, auditing, and other modes of information release and monitoring.[40] As is the case for police agencies, the need to protect information must

---

[37] Interview with a social services provider, 2018.

[38] See Jackson, 2015, for a review.

[39] One NGO interviewee noted that "[The] White House strategy afterwards was very general. Other countries have published hundreds of pages on what they are doing and why. There's nothing like that here" (Interview with an NGO representative, 2018).

[40] See Lum et al., 2016, for a review of oversight mechanisms and associated evidence.

be balanced against the need for transparency, not just for operational reasons but also to protect the privacy of individuals involved.[41]

These concerns also shape the question of which organizations get access to what types of information when, and how privacy or other information protection requirements are built into local efforts. The sharing of information across organizational boundaries (e.g., between mental health providers and law enforcement) can be a concern that affects individuals' or organizations' willingness to engage in terrorism prevention efforts out of concern that situations that might not have involved police previously would be responded to using criminal justice tools. Similar concerns have been raised about police involvement in schools as a result of school safety threats, and whether their presence increases the chance that situations that would have been framed as discipline problems become criminal matters.[42]

For some of the populations in positions to identify at-risk individuals, efforts to shift cultural and professional norms are a mechanism to increase the likelihood of early detection of potential terrorist activity. As discussed in Chapter Three, in the years after 9/11, there was significant focus on how law enforcement officers' actions could contribute to protecting the country from attack. Although the concept of intelligence-led policing was older, the national security language of intelligence collection, information-sharing, and warning was more extensively integrated into the framing of the roles and functions of local police.[43] In an interview for this study, the concept of "every officer an intelligence collector" came up as an example of what was needed to better detect threats. Although the initial framing of intelligence-led policing was more about the use of data and information to guide law enforcement action, the national security concept of intelligence as an element of law enforcement activity fits readily into thinking about missions and needs after 9/11. The concept of intelligence-led policing was relatively successful in engaging local law enforcement in the counterterrorism mission, but the unintended consequence was alienating some communities

---

[41] In interviews with some representatives of organizations involved in interventions for a variety of issues and concerns, maintaining privacy of the individuals involved was highlighted as absolutely critical. One described a model that can be summarized as "need to know to help": The effort was a multidisciplinary team of many organizations, and in the whole group (which was involved in risk assessment) all cases were discussed anonymously, with the identity of the individual known only to the organization referring the person for help. Once it was decided what programming the person needed, his or her identity was disclosed only to the organizations that would be delivering that programming. Although the police were at the table (and were sometimes sources of referrals), for the cases they did not bring and were not involved in, they had no need to know who the person was.

[42] This has been referred to as "net widening." (See Cherney, 2016, for a discussion of the concept related to radicalization and terrorism prevention.)

[43] For a review, see Carter and Carter, 2012; or Carl J. Jensen III, James L. Regens, and Natalie Griffin, "Intelligence-Led Policing as a Tool for Countering the Terrorism Threat," *Homeland Security Review*, Vol. 7, No. 3, 2013.

who interpreted "intelligence" as "spying," and were therefore less willing to collaborate with police.[44]

One strategy to increase willingness to report is simply to legally require it. A variety of mandating reporting laws exist for criminal victimization, including child abuse, neglect, and elder abuse. In addition, there are legal requirements defining a "duty to warn" for some mental health professionals originating from the 1976 *Tarasoff* legal case with respect to violence risk,[45] and the proceedings of a National Academies workshop on CVE described an upswing in such requirements for health professionals after the Sandy Hook school attack in 2012.[46] With respect to mandated reporting and terrorism risk, the experience of the United Kingdom is cautionary regarding the effects of doing so, where the imposition of a mandate was followed by a large increase in the annual number of reports and concerns from professionals who were obligated to make those reports.[47] Although both literature sources and interviewees from this study indicated that current regulatory structures protecting health (HIPAA) and educational (FERPA) information do not prevent disclosure in situations where individuals are viewed as imminent threats to others,[48] other interviewees did raise concerns about such sharing and viewed regulatory barriers that prevented it as positive rather than negative.[49] Similar to other policy options, there are concerns about tradeoffs here as well, specifically, whether requirements for reporting will lead individuals not seeking help or care, and therefore undermining the goal the reporting is intended to

---

[44] For a review, see Mathew C. Waxman, "Police and National Security: American Local Law Enforcement and Counterterrorism After 9/11," *Journal of National Security Law and Policy*, Vol. 3, 2009. Examinations of the application of intelligence approaches to law enforcement have explicitly called out one benefit of the approach— that "it provides a framework for intelligence professionals and frontline police officers to 'speak the same language'" (Jensen, Regens, and Griffin, 2013, p. 278). Other researchers have framed the challenge as "balancing the priorities of intelligence gathering, community engagement and trust building" (Cherney and Hartley, 2017), although it is not unreasonable to assume that an acceptable balance involving intelligence-gathering might not exist for all communities or individuals.

[45] National Conference of State Legislatures, 2015.

[46] Snair, Nicholson, and Giammaria, 2017, p. 88. Other examinations of the CVE space have argued that greater guidance is needed for relevant professionals regarding where the legal threshold for duty to warn falls in the radicalization and terrorism space (Levitt, 2017; Rosand, 2016). We heard similar things from interviewees: "So when does it cross over into a law enforcement matter where prevention and intervention will no longer work? And then what are the liabilities for the people who work in prevention? . . . I think this is the last ring in the chain. I think that's what we're missing now" (Interview with local-level representative in one U.S. city, 2018).

[47] For example, see Josh Halliday, "Almost 4,000 People Referred to UK Deradicalisation Scheme Last Year," *Guardian*, March 20, 2016.

[48] See, for example, U.S. Department of Health and Human Services, "Health Insurance Portability and Accountability Act (HIPAA) Privacy Rule: A Guide for Law Enforcement," undated.

[49] For example, in a description of the BRAVE program, Mirahmadi states: "In Montgomery County, Maryland, we also integrated a licensed clinical social worker into the police department. . . . *Her case files are subject to protected health information rules, so the community can use her as a resource without worrying that it would lead to a police investigation*" (2016, p. 138, emphasis added).

achieve. In some cases, this has led to the development of anonymous information-sharing mechanisms providing law enforcement with data that can guide protective decisions while protecting individual privacy and seeking to avoid unintended consequences of mandatory reporting.[50]

Assessing the Risk of Anyone Referred

Once individuals of potential concern are referred, the options available to assess the risk that they pose are limited. There are existing risk assessment tools aimed at ideologically motivated violence, although they have been developed with a focus on correctional settings and are discussed further in Chapter Eight.[51] The United Kingdom uses the "Vulnerability Assessment Framework" derived from one of those tools for the Channel referral program.[52] Because of the differences between extremist offending and everyday criminal behavior, risk assessment tools that are not terrorism-specific are not viewed as useful in this policy space.[53]

Evidence for Effectiveness

In our interviews with national-level individuals (federal and researchers) and local representatives, concerns were raised about the effectiveness of past awareness and referral-type training for law enforcement, where biased and inaccurate information provided by a number of sources was not only ineffective, but also undermined efforts by damaging public trust.[54] However, most interviewees assessed that actions that had been taken since then, notably the development of training standards by DHS, had addressed the issue.[55] Literature on evaluation of terrorism prevention training is not robust, where frequently evaluation is focused on perceptions of training by participants rather than on actual measurement of information transferred or later applied.[56]

---

[50] See, for example, Curtis Florence, Jonathan Shepherd, Iain Brennan, and Thomas Simon, "Effectiveness of Anonymised Information Sharing and Use in Health Service, Police, and Local Government Partnership for Preventing Violence Related Injury: Experimental Study and Time Series Analysis," *British Medical Journal*, Vol. 342, 2011; and Alex Sutherland, Lucy Strang, Martin Stepanek, Chris Giacomantonio, and Adrian Boyle, *Using Ambulance Data for Violence Prevention: Technical Report*, Cambridge, UK: RAND Europe, RR-2216-WMPS, 2017.

[51] This concept is reviewed in Martine Herzog-Evans, "A Comparison of Two Structured Professional Judgment Tools for Violent Extremism and Their Relevance in the French Context," *European Journal of Probation*, Vol. 10, No. 1, 2018.

[52] Monica Lloyd and Christopher Dean, "The Development of Structured Guidelines for Assessing Risk in Extremist Offenders," *Journal of Threat Assessment and Management*, Vol. 2, No. 1, 2015, p. 49.

[53] Silke, 2014c, p. 9; Interviews with government representatives, 2018.

[54] Also discussed in Bipartisan Policy Center, 2011, p. 44.

[55] DHS CRCL, 2011; Jerome P. Bjelopera, "Testimony Before the Committee on Homeland Security, Subcommittee on Counterterrorism and Intelligence," U.S. House of Representatives, October 28, 2015.

[56] See, for example, Lois M. Davis, Todd C. Helmus, Priscillia Hunt, Leslie Adrienne Payne, Salar Jahedi, and Flavia Tsang, *Assessment of the State and Local Anti-Terrorism Training (SLATT) Program*, Santa Monica, Calif.:

Some assessments have been done of coverage of different ideologies and potential sources of violence in law enforcement training.[57] In some cases, pre-post type assessment has been done.[58] Evaluations appear more common for training for law enforcement and response to terrorist events (which is not relevant for terrorism prevention). Examples of evaluations of public messaging campaigns (e.g., DHS's See Something, Say Something campaign) have been done as well.[59] Most evaluations of communication efforts show positive assessments from recipients of the information.

There has been limited systematic evaluation of the role of referral efforts in terrorism prevention.[60] In our interviews, individual cases were discussed that provide anecdotal evidence for effectiveness, but evaluation literature for this element of terrorism prevention could not be located. Even on broader programs like the National Suspicious Reporting Initiative (i.e., the infrastructure for law enforcement suspicious activity reporting), most literature that could be identified was conceptual (e.g., discussing the trade between information quality and quantity).[61]

Some data exist in the literature on reported willingness to refer or report suspicious behavior, including the START survey data discussed previously. Raw numbers for suspicious activity reports from industries or other sources are also publicly released.[62] There is limited evaluation, however, on whether terrorism prevention policies have an impact on the willingness to report. There is a more robust literature on willingness to report other criminal activity, both at the individual and societal levels, on how factors like perceptions of organizational legitimacy affect willingness to call

---

RAND Corporation, RR-1276-NIJ, 2016; Mark T. Sedevic, "An Evaluation of the Chicago Police Department's Recruit Curriculum in Emergency Response Week Relating to Terrorism Awareness and Response to Terrorism Incidents," dissertation, Olivet Nazarene University, May 2011; and John Eric Powell, "Terrorism Incident Response Education for Public-Safety Personnel in North Carolina and Tennessee: An Evaluation by Emergency Managers," dissertation, University of Tennessee, Knoxville, December 2008.

[57] For example, Chermak, Freilich, and Shemtob assess the coverage of far-right extremism in law enforcement training (Steven M. Chermak, Joshua D. Freilich, and Zachary Shemtob, "Law Enforcement Training and the Domestic Far Right," *Criminal Justice and Behavior*, Vol. 36, No. 12, December 2009).

[58] See, for example, Randal D. Beaton and L. Clark Johnson, "Instrument Development and Evaluation of Domestic Preparedness Training for First Responders," *Prehospital and Disaster Medicine*, Vol. 17, No. 3, September 2002.

[59] See, for example, Thomas G. Campbell III, "Remaining Vigilant Against Domestic Terrorism: Making Meaning of Counterterrorism in a National Awareness Campaign," thesis, College Park, Md.: University of Maryland, 2011.

[60] Studies cited previously have looked at the roles of reported information from different sources in the disruption of terrorist plots (e.g., Strom, Hollywood, and Pope, 2017), therefore focusing on non-terrorism prevention or enforcement-focused responses to threats.

[61] James E. Steiner, "More Is Better: The Analytic Case for a Robust Suspicious Activity Reports Program," *Homeland Security Affairs*, Vol. 6, No. 3, September 2010.

[62] See, for example, *Wall Street Journal*, "Banks Secretly Report Millions of U.S. Customers," March 30, 2016.

police, and on how the characteristics of individual crimes affect bystander behavior.[63] Literature evaluations also have examined reasons for lack of mandated reporting in other areas and reasons for shortfalls (e.g., reporting of child maltreatment).[64] Literature analyses of the willingness of different communities to collaborate with police and CVE efforts (of which willingness to refer is one component) are available as a result of other policies and actions.[65] In a UK study, researchers showed correlations between geographic areas with low levels of confidence in the police and perceived risk of violent extremism, raising concerns about the potential efficacy of prevention efforts.[66] There have been evaluations of the unintended consequences of mandated reporting in other policy areas, including concerns about whether requirements for notification will affect individuals' decisions to seek care or call law enforcement for help.[67]

Regarding risk assessment, the central challenge is that available tools specific to violent extremism and mobilization to violence have not been validated and there are practical difficulties in doing so because of the fortunately small sample sizes available.[68] Issues have also been raised regarding focusing validation on individuals who

---

[63] For more on organizational legitimacy, see, e.g., Robert C. Davis and Nicole J. Henderson, "Willingness to Report Crimes: The Role of Ethnic Group Membership and Community Efficacy," *Crime and Delinquency*, Vol. 49, No. 4, 2003; Tom R. Tyler and Jeffrey Fagan, "Legitimacy and Cooperation: Why Do People Help the Police Fight Crime in Their Communities?" *Ohio State Journal of Criminal Law*, Vol. 6, 2008; Jackson, 2015; and Nancy La Vigne, Jocelyn Fontaine, and Anamika Dwivedi, *How Do People in High-Crime, Low-Income Communities View the Police?* Washington, D.C.: Urban Institute, 2017 and references therein. For bystander behavior, see, e.g., Sarah C. Niksa, "Bystander's Willingness to Report Theft, Physical Assault, and Sexual Assault the Impact of Gender, Anonymity, and Relationship with the Offender," *Journal of Interpersonal Violence*, Vol. 29, No. 2, 2014.

[64] Krisann M. Alvarez, Maureen C. Kenny, Brad Donohue, and Kimberly M. Carpin, "Why Are Professionals Failing to Initiate Mandated Reports of Child Maltreatment, and Are There Any Empirically Based Training Programs to Assist Professionals in the Reporting Process?" *Aggression and Violent Behavior*, Vol. 9, No. 5, August 2004; Risé Jones, Emalee G. Flaherty, Helen J. Binns, Lori Lyn Price, Eric Slora, Dianna Abney, Donna L. Harris, Katherine Kaufer Christoffel, and Robert D. Sege, "Clinicians' Description of Factors Influencing Their Reporting of Suspected Child Abuse: Report of the Child Abuse Reporting Experience Study Research Group," *Pediatrics*, Vol. 122, No. 2, 2008.

[65] See, for example, Huq, Tyler, and Schulhofer, 2011; Tyler, Schulhofer, and Huq, 2010; and Kristina Murphy, Natasha S. Madon, and Adrian Cherney, "Promoting Muslims' Cooperation with Police in Counter-Terrorism: The Interaction Between Procedural Justice, Police Legitimacy and Law Legitimacy," *Policing: An International Journal*, Vol. 40, No. 3, 2017.

[66] Alex Murray, Katrin Mueller-Johnson, and Lawrence W. Sherman, "Evidence-Based Policing of U.K. Muslim Communities: Linking Confidence in the Police with Area Vulnerability to Violent Extremism," *International Criminal Justice Review*, Vol. 25, No. 1, 2015.

[67] See, for example, Pamela A. Herendeen, Roger Blevins, Elizabeth Anson, and Joyce Smith, "Barriers to and Consequences of Mandated Reporting of Child Abuse by Nurse Practitioners," *Journal of Pediatric Health Care*, Vol. 28, No. 1, 2014; Cathy Humphreys, "Problems in the System of Mandatory Reporting of Children Living with Domestic Violence," *Journal of Family Studies*, Vol. 14, No. 2-3, 2008; J. P. May, D. Hemenway, and A. Hall, "Do Criminals Go to the Hospital When They Are Shot?" *Injury Prevention*, Vol. 8, 2002.

[68] This point is reviewed in RTI International, 2017a.

have carried out attacks compared with members of the general population: Because extremist views are not a crime in the United States, Smith has argued[69] that the comparison group for whether a risk assessment tool effectively predicts risk of ideologically motivated *violence* should be ideologically extreme but nonviolent individuals, therefore limiting the potential for these tools to internalize bias against constitutionally protected activities.[70] As discussed previously, differences between other crimes and ideologically motivated violence mean that evaluation of other tools provides limited insight for terrorism prevention-specific tools, although the challenges encountered in their development are cautionary.

Current U.S. Terrorism Prevention and Related Efforts for Referral Promotion

In support of the need to have community members and government entities make referrals about individuals who exhibit concerning behavior that could be a sign of violent extremism, national efforts have focused on increasing community awareness and administering relevant law enforcement training.

Community Awareness

There has been significant effort over many years in the area of community awareness as it relates to referral promotion for CVE. This effort has been undertaken by different components of the federal government and by other organizations (sometimes with federal support). Successful coordination and deconfliction of these many community awareness efforts was one of the achievements of the CVE Task Force that was regularly cited by interviewees (we discuss this in more detail in Chapter Ten).

Starting in 2010, NCTC, DHS, and other interagency partners developed an international terrorism (IT) CAB, which was created to inform communities about terrorist efforts to recruit Americans and was adapted to different audiences, as appropriate. The purpose of these CABs was to facilitate a discussion about what government entities, communities, and individuals could do to counter the threat of violent extremism.[71] NCTC and DHS provided the IT CAB to communities upon request and, after some feedback that the IT CAB was not tailored to or as helpful for some audiences, a more focused domestic terrorism (DT) CAB was created and delivered

---

[69] Smith is quoted in RTI International, 2017a.

[70] As one of our academic interviewees put it, "we only know about the true positives who get to the end of the process, we never know how many people looked just like them but didn't do anything." This argument also has been raised in critiques of CVE programming and its effect on individual rights—seeing only the true positives leads to confirmation bias regarding factors that are only seen as important for prediction in hindsight (Patel and Koushik, 2017, p. 17).

[71] EOP, 2011b.

to communities around the country.[72] As the CVE Task Force stood up, it took on a greater role in coordinating these CAB engagements and integrated the CABs to produce a briefing covering all forms of violent extremism. In FY 2015 and FY 2016, CABs were held in approximately 10–20 cities for more than 1,000 attendees per year.[73]

Recently, NCTC and DHS transitioned CAB delivery to a "train the presenter" model, which allows community-based individuals to provide the information to multiple groups in the community proactively, or upon request.[74] And NCTC had plans to transition the CABs entirely to other agency-led delivery in part because NCTC's legal authorities and mission are focused on the terrorism threat emanating from outside the United States; NCTC is not authorized to integrate intelligence pertaining exclusively to domestic terrorism threats.[75] NCTC also developed and worked with DHS to implement a half-day CREX, which involves local governments and community members addressing an unfolding scenario of possible violent extremist activity with the goals to improve communication between law enforcement and communities, build trust, and empower communities against violent extremism.[76] Under the auspices of the CVE Task Force, the CREX was expanded at the request of the Attorney General to include scenarios addressing domestic terrorism. As of mid-2016, CREXs appear to have been held in more than ten cities across the country.[77]

Numerous interviewees indicated that federal agencies, including NCTC, DHS, and others were not able to fully meet demand for programming like the CABs and CREXs. This is all the more concerning because of NCTC's planned transition of these activities to DHS, at the same time that DHS staff and resources in this area have been scaled back.[78] This is where other models to try to scale up capacity, including the transition to a "train the presenter" model for the CAB, are intended to fill the gap.

There also has been some experimentation with online models of building community awareness. In FY 2014 and FY 2015, the Federal Emergency Management Agency (FEMA) funded online training through the University of Maryland's START for community members, NGOs, and local government representatives.[79] And, in FY 2017, the CVE Task Force began work with interagency partners to build a Social Media CAB, which has now been developed and is designed to be delivered

---

[72] GAO, 2017, Appendix III.

[73] NCTC, "CVE Tools and Training," publicly released under FOIA DF-2015-00215, April 14, 2016.

[74] NCTC, 2016.

[75] Interview with a federal government representative, 2018.

[76] Levitt, 2017, p. 8; NCTC, "CVE Engagement Activities: NCTC Directorate for Strategic Operational Planning Domestic Countering Violent Extremism (CVE) Team," undated.

[77] NCTC, 2016.

[78] Interview with a federal government representative, 2018.

[79] GAO, 2017, Appendix III; Interview with an academic representative, 2018.

remotely online.[80] Although online delivery is well suited for the intended audience of that CAB, broader use of purely online delivery modes should likely be approached cautiously: As discussed with respect to online messaging efforts, some federal efforts to use online models have had difficulty achieving success. One example of this is the FBI's 2015 "Don't Be a Puppet" campaign (discussed previously), which is a website with videos and games designed for use by educators and community leaders and organizations to divert youth from violent extremism and provide training to identify signs of radicalization.[81] However, the campaign has received criticism as to its approach for potentially stereotyping certain individuals, singling out religious radicalization, and oversimplifying how radicalization occurs.[82]

There are several other initiatives to develop awareness training for educational settings. The FBI provides education sector–specific violent extremism–related materials, including various media-based products and documentaries aimed at educating and preventing violent extremism at schools.[83] NCTC and DHS also have briefed the CAB to educators.[84] Other work in this area is being conducted by NGOs. The University of Maryland's START is developing school-focused training related to countering violent extremism.[85] NGOs such as the AIC, ADL, Average Mohamed, and CAIR (which we discussed in Chapter Four) conduct direct outreach to schools and community groups as part of their engagement programming, which can take the form of lectures or town hall meetings.[86] The Counterterrorism Education Learning Lab (CELL) in Denver, Colo., has a Community Awareness Program (CAP), which is taught by members of the public safety community and provides members of the public with the tools needed to recognize and help prevent terrorism.[87]

Beyond efforts to promote awareness and referrals through increasing knowledge, there are also ongoing efforts aimed at developing national referral lines. DHS Science and Technology Directorate (S&T) has research underway to increase knowledge about the nature of the threat and potential engagements to address it. DHS S&T also has specific work underway to assess local call centers and their networks of providers with regard to terrorism prevention, and to identify protocols for safe referral systems

---

[80] Interview with federal government representative, 2018; RTI International, *Countering Violent Extremism (CVE)—Developing a Research Roadmap: Final Report*, Research Triangle Park, N.C., October 2017b, p. 8.

[81] Sleeper, 2017.

[82] RTI International, 2017b; Camera, 2016.

[83] Sleeper, 2017.

[84] GAO, 2017, Appendix III.

[85] Interview with an academic representative, 2018.

[86] RTI International, 2017b, p. 9.

[87] Counterterrorism Education Learning Lab, homepage, 2012.

for friends, family, and others to connect individuals with social-service providers.[88] There are federal contact lines, such as the "See Something, Say Something" line, which allows an individual to report suspicious activity.

As is the case for intervention activities more broadly, some efforts seek to integrate terrorism prevention into existing crisis intervention infrastructures. There are 2-1-1 community information and referral service lines in some communities that field calls related to violent extremism. In Los Angeles, the 2-1-1 line is already dedicated to providing information and referrals for all health and human services in LA County. Los Angeles planned to integrate referrals for targeted violence into that same platform, supported by FY 2016 CVE grant money,[89] but controversy surrounding CVE and terrorism prevention led the city to halt the effort and reject the DHS grant.[90] There also are efforts in the NGO sector related to telephone and IT referral lines. For example, the Crisis Intervention Hotline of Houston was awarded FY 2016 CVE grant money to launch a hotline to provide mental health and other referrals, including to community groups who have programming in place to counter violent extremism.[91] Parents for Peace also is implementing a hotline for the referral of at-risk individuals.[92]

Law Enforcement Training

Given the role of local law enforcement in responding to incidents of violence, as well as in identifying at-risk individuals through day-to-day policing activities, training officers to recognize signs of radicalization has been a prominent concern, particularly as the occurrence of individual radicalization within the United States has increased. Based on discussions with our interviewees, there appears to be less current concern with the availability of training for law enforcement, suggesting that efforts to make training more accessible have been beneficial.[93] We have identified several efforts both within government and outside of it that were focused on law enforcement training.

---

[88] GAO, 2017, Appendix III; Owens et al., 2016; DHS S&T, *Terrorism Prevention*, undated(b); Interview with federal government representative, 2018.

[89] Interviews with multiple representatives in Los Angeles, 2018. See also, City of Los Angeles, Mayor's Office of Public Safety, "Building Healthy Communities in Los Angeles; Managing Intervention Activities," DHS Grant Application EMW-2016-CA-APP-00294, 2016.

[90] Subsequent to completion of the data gathering for this study, the Mayor's Office in Los Angeles made the decision to decline the grant award as a result of delay caused by intense local debate surrounding the issue (Emily Alpert Reyes, "L.A. Turns Away Federal Grant to Combat Extremism Amid Concerns of Unfairly Targeting Muslims," *Los Angeles Times*, August 16, 2018).

[91] Interviews with local NGO representatives, 2018. See also, Crisis Intervention of Houston, Inc., "Building a Resilient Community to Counter Violent Extremism: Houston/Harris County," DHS Grant Application EMW-2016-CA-APP-00188, released under the Freedom of Information Act, 2016.

[92] Parents for Peace, homepage, undated.

[93] There are recommendations in the literature for greater law enforcement training (e.g., Rosand, 2017a) but the focus is framed as enabling police roles in "whole of community" responses and to provide "local police with

At the federal level, one of the earliest programs to conduct law enforcement training in this area was the State and Local Anti-Terrorism Training (SLATT) program, administered by DOJ's Bureau of Justice Assistance (BJA), which provided train-the-trainer, on-site, and online training to state and local law enforcement on terrorism-related issues.[94] The SLATT program was defunded for a period of time, although there was a solicitation for continuation released in 2018.[95] In 2011, DHS completed training guidance, with the FBI and NCTC involved in training quality assurance efforts.[96] DOJ also produced training principles and accompanying guidance.[97] In 2016, the FBI was reported to have hosted a CVE conference with state and local participants and briefed more than a dozen police departments and numerous police organizations with state and local sheriffs and police chiefs.[98]

More recently, DHS OTPP and CRCL worked with the Federal Law Enforcement Training Center (FLETC) to develop a Law Enforcement Awareness Briefing (LAB).[99] The LAB was piloted in 2017 and 2018 in law enforcement training for the Denver area, as part of the Denver Police Department's FY 2016 CVE grant.[100] FLETC also has integrated issues related to violent extremism into its overall training.[101] Additionally, the U.S. Secret Service's National Threat Assessment Center (NTAC) provides training related to terrorism prevention to universities, law enforcement, and security agencies when requested.[102]

Law enforcement training was part of six grant awards in the funded CVE FY 2016 grants and represented a relatively modest percentage of the resources allocated. This seems appropriate, given that this area was not called out as a major short-

---

the skills and knowledge to engage effectively with rather than alienate community members" rather than threat recognition training.

[94] BJA, *State and Local Anti-Terrorism Training (SLATT) Program*, Washington, D.C.: U.S. Department of Justice, undated.

[95] DOJ, Office of Justice Programs (OJP), *State and Local Anti-Terrorism Training (SLATT) Program, undated*; *DOJ OJP, Information Regarding a Change to the State and Local Anti-Terrorism Training (SLATT) FY 2018 Competitive Grant Solicitation*, March 14, 2018.

[96] Johnson and Gersten, 2013.

[97] James M. Cole, "Training Guiding Principles," memorandum for Heads of Components and United States Attorneys, Washington, D.C.: U.S. Department of Justice, Office of the Deputy Attorney General, March 20, 2012.

[98] GAO, 2017, Appendix III.

[99] RTI International, 2017b, p. 8; DHS, *DHS Countering Violent Extremism Programs and Initiatives*, Washington, D.C., Fiscal Year 2017 Report to Congress, January 2018.

[100] Interviews with local government representatives, 2018.

[101] GAO, 2017, Appendix III.

[102] RTI International, 2017b, p. 8.

fall in our interviews, and a variety of other government and non-government training efforts were identified.

There also have been activities by NGOs related to law enforcement training. The International Association of Chiefs of Police has provided short online training modules on community, cultural awareness, and various forms of violent extremism, and received funding through FEMA to design in-person training modules.[103] Both the ADL and the Southern Poverty Law Center (SPLC) provide training to law enforcement groups on working with diverse communities and identifying violent extremism, and the SPLC also produces videos on officer safety protocols to deal with extremist groups.[104] Earlier sources cite efforts by the Los Angeles Police Department (LAPD) and Major City Chiefs in developing and piloting training for local law enforcement.[105] In 2014, the Intelligence and National Security Alliance (INSA) conducted a Homegrown Violent Extremism Homeland Security Exercise, which included the participation of government and law enforcement agencies to discuss information-sharing policies between the public and private sectors to address the homegrown violent extremist threat.[106]

Some efforts have been underway locally as well. In 2010, LAPD established the HYDRA simulation training for command-level officers to simulate critical incidents, including terrorism-related ones. In one exercise, religious leaders also participated in the training.[107] The Virginia Community Policing Institute (VCPI) developed the Strategic, Tactical, and Resilient Interdiction of Violent Extremism (STRIVE) program with FEMA FY 2015 funds, which focuses on community policing and approaches to "detect, deter, disrupt, and deny violent extremism."[108]

Assessment

Our interviewees rated past and ongoing referral promotion programs as positive and helpful. Interviewees believed that there was unmet demand for CABs as a result of staffing contraction in DHS and NCTC shifts in activity. Although it was possible to identify nonfederal efforts aimed at increasing awareness and promoting referral, it was not clear how significant they were or what their level of capability was. A

---

[103] International Association of Chiefs of Police, "The Role of Community Policing in Homeland Security and Preventing Radicalization to Violence," undated; RTI International, 2017b.

[104] RTI International, 2017b.

[105] Johnson and Gersten, 2013.

[106] INSA, Homeland Security Intelligence Council, "After Action Report: Homegrown Violent Extremism Homeland Security Exercise," September 2014.

[107] Elaine Pittman, "Los Angeles Police Department Hydra System Promotes Simulation Training for Command-Level Officers," *Government Technology*, October 4, 2010; Interview with an NGO representative in Los Angeles, 2018.

[108] VCPI, "Experience and Expertise," webpage, 2018.

detailed review of the content of the briefings was outside the scope of this study, but the material across CABs that focuses on threats from internationally inspired individuals and domestic violent movements covers what is known about factors that can lead to radicalization and mobilization to violence, as well as what is known about responding to individuals of potential concern within legal and constitutional boundaries. If shortfalls in government capability to deliver CABs continue, interviewees expressed concern about low-quality external trainers meeting that unmet demand. Concerns about training quality and bias were prominent in the early years of CVE and undermined trust in federal efforts. Although there are some alternatives available (e.g., online training initiatives funded by government and otherwise), it is unclear how broadly they are used.

National-level interviewees raised information sensitivity as a serious issue and barrier in this area. In an effort to make briefings relevant and useful (in particular to law enforcement audiences), information is often included that is considered For Official Use Only or Law Enforcement Sensitive (e.g., discussions of recent cases). This makes sense, but it means that briefings containing that information cannot be broadly released, potentially contributing to the impression that terrorism prevention efforts are not transparent.[109] Moreover, the perception that law enforcement entities receive more or different briefings from others in the course of terrorism prevention efforts could also reinforce some of the central critiques put forward of past CVE efforts. Among interviewees for the project, this is an issue on which there was not unanimity. Some federal-level interviewees characterized this as a barrier that made it difficult to deliver training broadly outside law enforcement agencies. At the same time, there is ongoing effort to create a specific LAB distinct from the CABs.[110]

Different agencies—even different components within DHS—have adopted strategies that avoid these types of information sensitivity concerns. Notably, the work done by NTAC within the United States Secret Service, which also addresses violent threats, threat assessment, and potential intervention approaches, is produced using only open source information and is published on the web.[111]

---

[109] For example, redacted CAB materials have been released under the Freedom of Information Act versus being created in a form where they could be made fully publicly available (ACLU, "CVE FOIA Documents," webpage, undated[b]).

[110] There has been at least one research effort that sought to assess a group of law enforcement officers' likelihood of recognizing behaviors associated with terrorist activity (James K. Regens, Nick Mould, Carl J. Jensen III, and Melissa A. Graves, "Terrorism-Centric Behaviors and Adversarial Threat Awareness," *Social Science Quarterly*, Vol. 97, No. 3, September 2016) and on the effect of training on their capability to do so (James K. Regens, Nick Mould, Carl J. Jensen III, David N. Edger, David Cid, and Melissa A. Graves, "Effect of Intelligence Collection Training on Suspicious Activity Recognition by Front Line Police Officers," *Security Journal*, Vol. 30, No. 3, 2017).

[111] See NTAC, "NTAC Research and Publications," webpage, undated, which includes publications on threat assessment and warning signs for violence inspired by a range of factors using open source information that can be widely shared. One example is a publication on threat assessment using the case of Jared Lee Loughner, who

Similar points are relevant to the CREXs. Interviewees who had experienced them, both inside and outside government, described them as very valuable. The structure of the exercise—which gets diverse government, service provider, and community groups together to game out a hypothetical scenario of someone radicalizing in their community—was viewed as a useful way to work through issues, explore what type of terrorism prevention model was viewed as workable for their area, and to build relationships and trust. The same DHS staffing contraction and changes at NCTC have affected the capacity to deliver CREXs as well, meaning that there is unmet demand. Although our discussions during the project and literature research identified a few examples of similar exercises done by others, the capacity for these activities appears to be insufficient and their potential value underutilized. Details relating to the CREX and its associated materials also appear to have been treated as sensitive information to date, with materials only openly available on the Office of the Director of National Intelligence and outside organizations' Freedom of Information Act–related sites.

With respect to mechanisms for referrals, there are clearly robust systems inside governments for suspicious activity–type reporting, which, while related to the referrals relevant for terrorism prevention, is not the full picture (and, in the absence of connections between organizations with access to those systems and intervention capability, may not actually constitute a route for referral). On a national basis, it is clear that there is no operational "help line" or other established mechanism for referral of individuals seeking help for themselves or others.[112] In our interviews, examples were cited of different types of call-in lines (e.g., for family issues, suicide prevention) where a person with concerns about radicalization might be able to be connected to assistance. Although our interviewees identified some examples where terrorism prevention expertise was being built into existing crisis lines, new national call-in resources were being developed, and initiatives were focused on linking people browsing online to phone-based or other outside support, the level of capability currently in place is minimal.[113]

More-localized intervention initiatives have their own mechanisms in place for referral (e.g., through the participating organizations, schools, law enforcement organizations, community and religious organizations, and others). Examples from the cities

---

targeted U.S. Representative Gabrielle Giffords (NTAC, *Using a Systems Approach for Threat Assessment Investigations: A Case Study on Jared Lee Loughner*, Washington, D.C.: U.S. Secret Service, Department of Homeland Security, 2015).

[112] Assessments in the literature have argued that there are relatively few options for referral or reporting other than calling law enforcement (Rosand, 2017a).

[113] As discussed above, some of these efforts are supported through DHS grant funding. DHS S&T also has done research and development work focused on assessing capabilities for call-in assistance related to violent radicalization (John G. Horgan, Michael J. Williams, William P. Evans, and Jocelyn J. Bélanger, *Assessment Report: Current Capabilities of 2-1-1 Call Centers and Local Service Providers. Text-Enabled CVE Gatekeeper Intervention Help-Line and Referral System*, Georgia State University Research Foundation, Inc., Contract Report HSHQDC-16-C-B0028, undated).

we visited are discussed in the next section. Although the programs we learned about have referral capacity and networks commensurate with their level of capability to intervene, there was no way to assess whether that capability "fully met the needs" in the programs' catchment areas.[114] Indeed, the same statement can be made from a national perspective: The fundamental assessment question for referral (as introduced in Chapter Three) is to provide a high probability that an at-risk individual in an area will be referred for help.[115] In the course of this research, we could not identify data sources that would allow that question to be answered in a rigorous way, either for a specific area or nationally.

With respect to risk assessment, if the standard against which the current situation is measured is whether a given individual's propensity for future ideological violence can be readily and reliably assessed, then current capabilities are clearly lacking.[116] This lack of capabilities is relevant not only for supporting efficient referral efforts and screening out false positives, but also for intervention and recidivism-reduction efforts as part of monitoring individual progress and guiding programming. However, just as local intervention efforts have referral paths in place, the programs that were operating in the cities we visited (which we discuss in more detail in the next chapter) also had risk assessment processes that were viewed as practical and workable for terrorism prevention. The assessment approaches were essentially all implemented with multidisciplinary teams, where different types of expertise were brought to bear to evaluate cases. As we discuss in the next chapter, most of these efforts were not specific to extremist violence concerns, and their case-by-case, individualized risk assessment processes built on previous research on a broad range of threat types.[117] There are efforts to examine violent extremism–specific risk-assessment tools in the U.S. context (in corrections, which we discuss in Chapter Eight). However, these efforts are not focused on the requirements of assessment of initial referrals or screening out false positives from such processes.

---

[114] Others made similar observations regarding the absence of resources based on interviews in Los Angeles and Minneapolis: "Community members report that if one sees something suspicious or communications that suggest a risk for ideological violence, there often are not clear pathways to get advice from trusted persons in their community. They add that there are not enough programs and practitioners where the potential bystander can find others who can help them to interpret and problem solve and put a stop to activities before they become crimes" (Weine, Eisenman, and Kinsler et al., 2017, p. 209).

[115] Green and Procter (2016, pp. 37–39) make this point globally with respect to awareness of risk and referral efforts.

[116] RTI International, 2017a.

[117] For a comprehensive review, see Andre Simons and J. Reid Meloy, "Foundations of Threat Assessment and Management," in V. B. Van Hasselt and M. L. Bourke, eds., *Handbook of Behavioral Criminology*, Chan, Switzerland: Springer, 2017.

Federal Options for Referral Promotion–Focused Policy and Programming

Options at the federal level related to referral promotion have some overlap with those for broader community education, given common mechanisms for information dissemination and community engagement. Given that the locus of most intervention activity is at the state and local (and nongovernmental) levels, most referral promotion activity will likely occur locally, even if actions taken to strengthen it (e.g., the CABs and CREXs) are delivered from the national level. The main exceptions to this are national-level crisis lines or other mechanisms, but even those referral options would need to connect at-risk individuals or their families to local resources for intervention. Federal options, based on published policy proposals, input from interviewees during the study, and analysis include

- **Awareness and Training**
  - **Continue and expand outreach and local coordination efforts through CABs and CREXs.** According to the views of interviewees on the value of federally delivered briefings and exercises for threat awareness (specifically, DHS and NCTC briefings), continuing and expanding those efforts appear warranted. Both the CAB and the CREX generate opportunities for interaction and engagement among federal participants, local entities, communities, and members of the public, and convey information and catalyze activity on terrorism prevention. This type of programming, particularly if delivered by local federal staff (versus individuals coming to the area for short periods of time), provides opportunities to build trust between federal representatives and local organizations through an activity that is less controversial than other facets of terrorism prevention.

    As described above, with respect to broader community education, broader dissemination of the materials used in these efforts would contribute to achieving the policy goals (similar to NTAC's model for information dissemination).
- **Situational Awareness**
  - **Support periodic, publicly released national surveys to measure public willingness to refer individuals because of concern regarding early mobilization activities.** The only data on individual willingness to report mobilization behaviors that we could identify in our work came from DHS S&T–funded survey research. Repeated surveys either at the national level or in subsets of the country could provide an ongoing picture of where the nation stands both on overall trust measures and on willingness to refer, and could act as intellectual infrastructure for the evaluation of efforts to improve.

- **Federal Support of Local Initiatives**
  - **Continue to support efforts to develop national-level hotlines for referral of at-risk individuals.** Given trust and sensitivity issues, local implementation of intervention—and therefore, most referral for intervention—would likely be most efficient and practical. National-level hotlines that connect individuals to local programming could play a role, particularly in providing a bridge between the online space and offline capability.[118] Because initial activity aimed at such referral lines is already a part of more than one DHS-funded grant, however, little additional federal action appears needed other than continued support of those initiatives.
  - **Use grant funding to support local and NGO referral promotion efforts, but recognize that substantial trust-building may be required.** Given trust concerns and the controversy around terrorism prevention, direct federal support of local initiatives touching on referral promotion (whether separately or as part of an intervention delivery effort) will likely be complex in some areas. To the extent that there are concerns that CVE and, by extension, terrorism prevention efforts are actually intelligence collection or surveillance focused, referral promotion activities could strengthen those narratives and concerns. As a result, relationship- and trust-building might be needed to make federal support of activities in this area viable (e.g., as part of awareness and training efforts) or developing privacy protections or other processes sufficient to address critical concerns.

    However, in our interviews, state and local representatives also emphasized that federal support of local initiatives in part can be viewed as what DHS and its interagency partners do *not* do. Numerous interviewees emphasized that there must be flexibility in designing efforts at the local level so that they can both match local requirements and respond to local concerns, so federal mandates (e.g., that terrorism prevention efforts *must* involve law enforcement agencies directly) could reduce the willingness of organizations and members of the public to participate in referral efforts and undermine their potential success. To the extent that referral promotion efforts cannot be framed as relevant across threats—i.e., that they must be ideologically specific to be effective—federal efforts overall must address the range of potential sources of ideological violence in order to maintain credibility and trust.
- **Regulatory and Legal Issues**
  - **Address perceived legal and regulatory barriers to interagency collaboration in terrorism prevention referral and intervention.** Concerns about regulatory barriers (specifically HIPAA and FERPA) getting in the way of referral and intervention were raised by some interviewees. There was not consensus

---

[118] These were also recommended in DHS HSAC, 2016.

that there are indeed barriers: Other interviewees argued that exceptions to relevant privacy regulations already allow for the necessary information-sharing. In some cases, limits on sharing from those rules were also viewed as positive (e.g., by interviewees who were concerned about law enforcement gaining access to data from health providers). Clarification of what sharing is permissible under the regulations and what types of protections should be implemented as part of referral and intervention efforts could help address uncertainty that may be a barrier to some local implementation efforts.

- **Research and Evaluation**
  - **Continue research focused on improving risk assessment methods, but realistically manage expectations for their possible accuracy.** Risk assessment tools for violent extremism are clearly still limited in capability. However, the challenges to their improvement suggest the need to manage expectations that their performance can be raised to a level where they would be suitable for risk assessment across sizable populations of referrals. In the event that risk assessment for early-stage intervention will always be imperfect, research into developing intervention models that are programmed accordingly will be needed.

Given the limitations of risk assessment, national performance for terrorism prevention would benefit most from efforts that increase true positive referrals more than simply increasing the total volume of referrals (i.e., true and false positives). As described in the discussion of the FBI bystander study earlier in the chapter, the individuals who are most likely to know that an individual is at risk of carrying out violence are family, friends, and other individuals or professionals with close relationships with the person. As a result, the fundamental goal in referral promotion should be increasing referrals from them, rather than seeking more referrals or suspicious activity reporting from strangers. The willingness of family to make such referrals is the highest bar of trust, and, as cited above, our interviewees argued that it is possible only if they have confidence that the programs they were referring the individuals to would be able to help them.[119] As a result, the potential to increase the probability that true at-risk individuals are referred will be affected by whether intervention capability is in place—which we turn to in the next chapter—and whether that capability is viewed as valuable and acceptable.

---

[119] Interview with a local law enforcement representative in a U.S. city, 2018. Another local law enforcement representative made a related point in response to transparency: Even though there are requirements not to release certain types of information, either because of pending cases or to protect the privacy of individuals involved, providing some level of feedback when individuals make referrals is needed to maintain confidence that making future referrals is "worth doing."

CHAPTER SEVEN

Middle-Phase Terrorism Prevention: Intervention

Intervention is a central piece of what is required for terrorism prevention to achieve its goals and on which the benefits of other components depend: Without the capacity and capability to *help* an individual at risk of perpetrating ideological violence, success in community education, awareness, and referral promotion will have nothing to connect to, and the only option available to respond to someone will be the coercive route, from arrest to prosecution and incarceration. Since CVE's inception, critics have characterized it as programming whose end effect is to put individuals who may or may not pose actual risk on a path into the criminal justice system. That is not what CVE or terrorism prevention is supposed to do, but to make this a reality, a path must be available that can take those individuals somewhere else. Activities falling within this facet of terrorism prevention are captured in the center part of our mapping, the relevant section of which is reproduced in Figure 7.1.

In order for terrorism prevention to be successful, the path needs to lead to a system that can deliver services to individuals at risk that reduce their chances of perpetrating violence. From our interviews and review of the literature, that system needs a core "decisionmaking node" where the activities described in the previous chapter try to assess the level of risk an individual might pose. More importantly, this decisionmaking node must decide what the individual needs in terms of help to reduce risk. As we discussed in the previous chapter, our interviewees and sources in the literature—drawing on both experience with CVE and similar interventions for other problem types—reflected a general consensus that the preferred model is a multidisciplinary team (M-DT) structure[1] where all relevant organizations collaborate in risk assess-

---

[1] Similar models exist in other countries, including the Hub Model used in Canada, Denmark, and Australia (Michele T. Pathé, Debbie J. Haworth, Terri-Ann Goodwin, Amanda G. Holman, Stephen J. Amos, Paul Winterbourne, and Leanne Day, "Establishing a Joint Agency Response to the Threat of Lone-Actor Grievance-Fuelled Violence," *Journal of Forensic Psychiatry and Psychology*, Vol. 29, No. 1, 2018; Dale R. McFee, and Norman E. Taylor, "The Prince Albert Hub and the Emergence of Collaborative Risk-Driven Community Safety," Canadian Police College Discussion Paper Series, 2014, pp. 7, 14; see Appendix A of this report). International multilateral organizations also have collected best practices on the approach (RAN, *Ex Post Paper: Handbook on How to Set Up a Multi-Agency Structure that Includes the Health and Social Care Sectors?* Copenhagen, Denmark: meeting on multi-agency structures, May 18–19, 2016b).

Figure 7.1
Intervention Within the Terrorism Prevention Policy Space

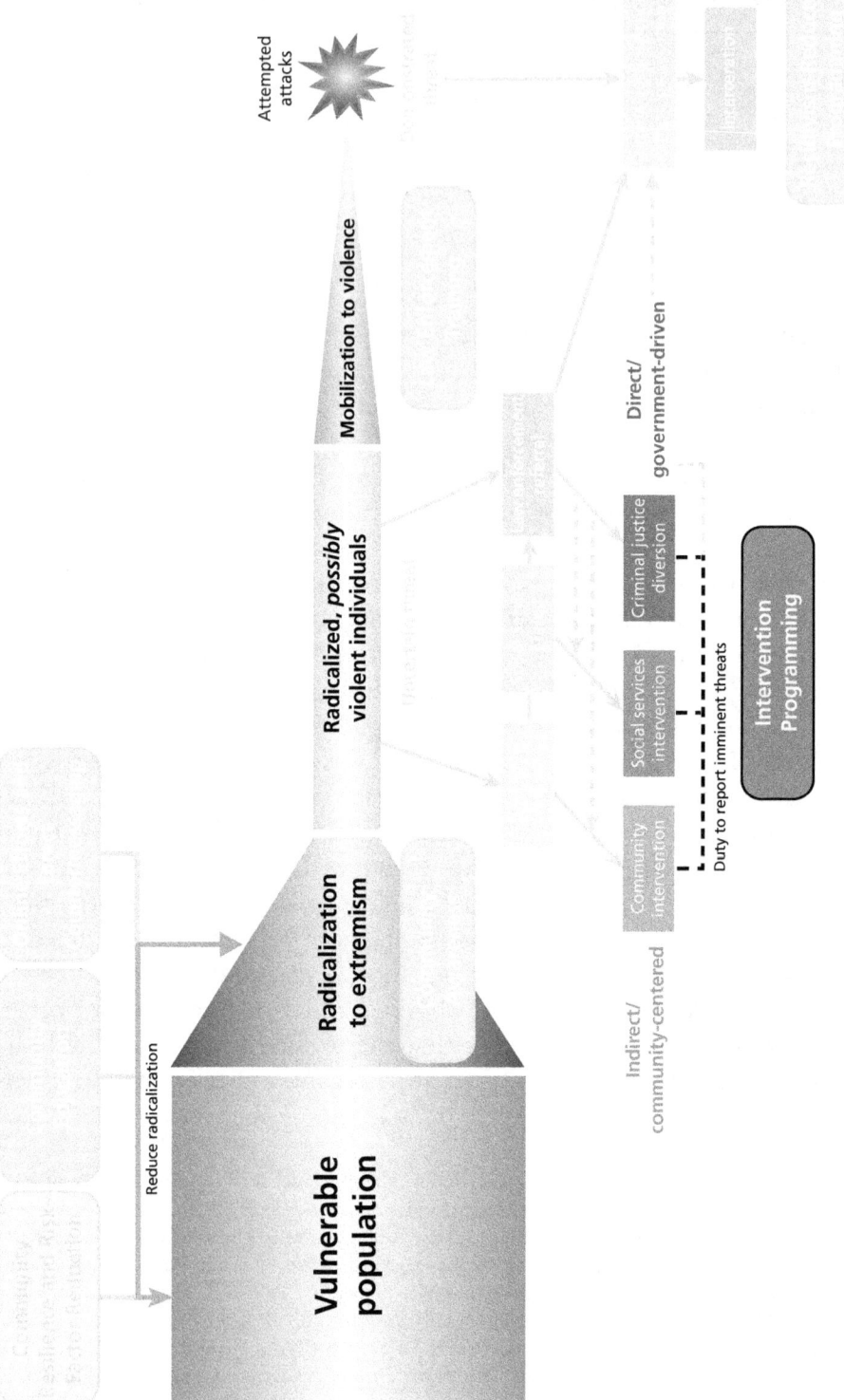

RAND RR2647-7.1

ment and service decisionmaking (see Figure 7.2).[2] Where M-DTs were not used, often what was done was essentially a mini M-DT variant, with mental health staff members injected into police departments, law enforcement officers detailed to schools,[3] or another cross-organizational model.[4]

Acting on that care decision requires that the core node be connected to a system of service providers that can deliver different types of counseling, training, and other support—where that network might be made up of agencies from government, community organizations, and NGOs and may tap into broader networks of capacity that go beyond the entities that directly participate in the M-DT at the heart of the network.[5] From both our interviews and published literature, it is clear that there is a deep body of knowledge regarding the types of programming that are relevant for interven-

Figure 7.2
Notional Intervention Network

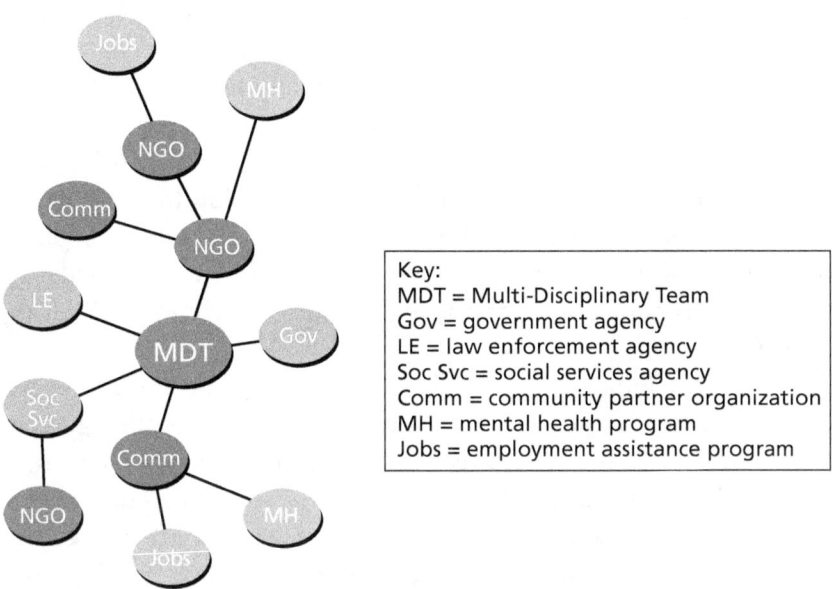

Key:
MDT = Multi-Disciplinary Team
Gov = government agency
LE = law enforcement agency
Soc Svc = social services agency
Comm = community partner organization
MH = mental health program
Jobs = employment assistance program

SOURCE: Examples based on project interview discussions.
RAND RR2647-7.2

---

[2]   This was a recommendation of Weine and colleagues (2015) with respect to terrorism but more generally by the FBI Behavioral Analysis Unit (undated, pp. 70–81) for threat assessment and management more broadly.

[3]   According to a service provider who works with law enforcement in a city we visited, "Our officers are each assigned to schools. We started getting kids referred to us by the schools for pre-delinquent behavior. We also started to see younger kids so we've been able to act more proactively rather than wait until the kid is older before we can step in. . . . We try to keep them in a preventative capacity as much as possible so we don't have lower risk youth involved with law enforcement."

[4]   Interviews with state and local government and social services organizations, 2018.

[5]   See also the recommendations in DHS HSAC, 2016; and Levitt, 2017.

tion. A significant part of that programming is the same as that needed to respond to other problems and concerns—e.g., job training can help an individual at risk of committing ideological violence just as it can help a youth at risk of violent behavior. Other elements are distinct and ideologically specific (e.g., religious counseling is useful for responding to individuals motivated by religious causes; specific types of counseling may be needed to respond to hate-motivated individuals).[6]

As in interventions aimed at other violent behavior, success can be defined as having systems in place—ideally with national coverage—that have a high probability of effectively delivering programming to identified individuals to reduce risk and (if it becomes clear that intervention is unsuccessful and a participant is continuing toward violent action) connect to law enforcement to respond to imminent threats of harm.[7] However, unlike similar intervention efforts for crimes like gang violence or illegal drugs—where many of the participants likely will have past involvement in violence, were victims of gang violence, or participated in selling drugs—the nature of intervention here is quite different. Although the referred individuals might have done something that caused concern, that action will likely not itself have been an illegal act. As already discussed, since many will not have committed previous crimes, the limitations of standard criminal risk assessment methods mean that, in most cases, it will be very hard to determine the level of threat an individual actually poses using such tools. In that way, intervention for terrorism is similar to intervention for problems like school violence, where a referred student could be a real threat or simply an adolescent suffering from youthful poor judgment who made a threat that he never had any intention of acting on, but the school system and relevant response networks that support them must nonetheless respond.[8]

As alluded to in Chapter Six, to support their potential to improve security and reduce costs,[9] intervention systems must be designed with the explicit goal of minimizing the negative effects of being referred on the individuals involved, making it less problematic that there will always be a significant number of false positive reports. Navigating that challenge is critical, as our interviewees characterized intervention as extremely vulnerable to concern about stigma and controversy.[10] Perceptions that a terrorism prevention effort is acting improperly or is viewed as illegitimate can cause

---

[6]   See the review in Koehler, 2017, Chapter 9.

[7]   This argument is also made in Levitt, 2017.

[8]   See the discussion in Randy Borum, Dewey G. Cornell, William Modzeleski, and Shane R. Jimerson, "What Can Be Done About School Shootings? A Review of the Evidence," *Educational Researcher*, Vol. 39, No. 1, 2010.

[9]   We discuss this in more detail in Chapter Nine.

[10]   The creation of stigma is not just an issue with programming focused on terrorism or ideological extremism. Eisenman and Flavahan (2017, p. 345) cite an example of a gang-focused intervention that used broad inclusion criteria for its risk evaluation step, which led a large number of people to be concerned that their effort labeled youth as gang members or at risk of joining inappropriately.

organizations to simply opt out of participating, amputating key arms of intervention capability illustrated in Figure 7.2 while simultaneously undermining the efforts of the organizations that remain.[11]

Because the challenges to building and sustaining intervention capability are manifest at the local level, our interviewees were essentially unanimous that this programming must be conceived, designed, and implemented at the local level. Put simply, what works in one location may not be viable elsewhere.[12] Program design also faces the same tension as is present in outreach and education efforts: Programs need to be implemented with the characteristics of their intended audience in mind in order to be effective, but cannot be designed in such a way that they are interpreted as targeting or stigmatizing specific communities.[13]

Although it is not universally the case, the other countries we examined during the study indicate that it is more common for programs to be implemented in a decentralized way. In more than half of the cases examined, CVE programs were implemented with considerable local autonomy and national governments adopted a more persuasive approach in shaping implementation (i.e., seeking to guide such programming through development of best practices and coordination versus defining requirements and directly controlling implementation) (see Figure 7.3).

In some of the cities we visited, interviewees indicated that involvement by federal agencies in intervention would kill an effort before it got off the ground, while in other cities there was solid federal-local collaboration associated with local intervention programming (and even sometimes case referrals to those programs from federal agencies). In other places, even involvement by *local* law enforcement was viewed as a non-starter, while in still others there are active intervention efforts not just involving, but driven by local law enforcement. These dynamics also can shift over time: In one city, an interviewee indicated that when they started their effort, any involvement by law enforcement was viewed as a non-starter by some of their partners, but over time, mechanisms of interaction were developed, trust was built, and law enforcement

---

[11] Some (e.g., Rosand, 2017a) have made the recommendation to opt out explicitly as a path for local areas to insulate themselves from federal policies or approaches that they believe undermine their potential effectiveness in implementing CVE and terrorism prevention initiatives in their areas.

The idea that the remaining organizations would be undermined by those that opt out has been pointed out by others: "Local partners are put in untenable positions if they are seen as participating in something the community perceives as cover for government surveillance programs. The key is developing trusting relationships between the parties so that intervention programs can still function with the necessary connective tissue to law enforcement" (Levitt, 2017, p. 21).

[12] "We have to look at what is working for us to protect [our region]. What works in [named city] may not work in [another city]. The community is different. The threats are different. The level of engagement is different" (Interview with a local government representative in a U.S. city, 2018).

[13] For example, Weine et al. (2015) frame the need for programs to be "culturally congruent."

Figure 7.3
Qualitative Mapping of Intervention Implementation in International Case Study Countries

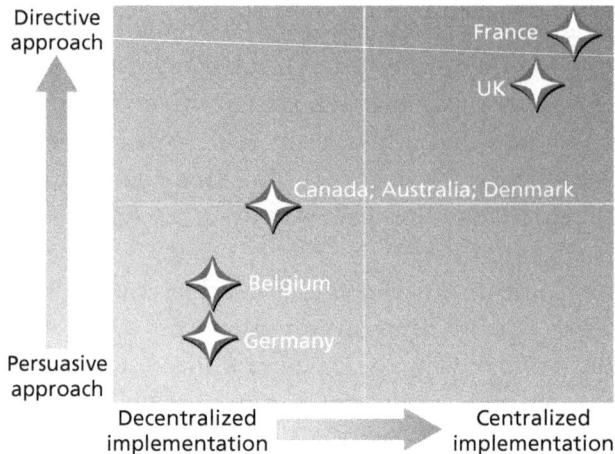

NOTE: Placement of countries in the matrix is based on a qualitative assessment of (left to right) the level of central implementation of programming (i.e., the extent to which efforts are managed nationally versus at the regional or local levels) and (bottom to top) the amount of top-down control exerted from the national level over decentralized intervention efforts (e.g., whether national-level policy specified implementation requirements versus defined best practices). The persuasive versus directive continuum sought to explore how nations' efforts might or might not be applicable given the flexibility inherent in the U.S. federal approach and state/local flexibility in programming. Positioning of the countries is qualitative and should not be overinterpreted.
RAND *RR2647-7.3*

became connected to the effort.[14] Others pointed out that dynamics can quickly shift in the other direction as well, with enforcement actions (e.g., a major immigration enforcement operation in their community) or national events blowing up relationships that took extended periods of time to build.[15] Looking internationally, there was a wide variation in the involvement of law enforcement in national CVE efforts. In the United States, trust in government and law enforcement was often cited as the factor

---

[14] Interview with a local NGO representative, 2018.

[15] For example, a local law enforcement representative described how they tried to explain their efforts when trust was challenged by outside events: "When you all asked us about CVE and how communities perceived it, chiefs made it clear that the CVE program happening at [local police department (PD)] is unique to [local PD], implemented by [local PD], and developed by [local PD]. So what happened in other cities and other places, [local PD] has no jurisdiction over, is not communicating advice related to, [and] we're doing things specific to our communities. So that's a way of saying: we understand you've been hearing national reports and stuff. But this is what we're doing."

that defined the "art of the possible" for law enforcement involvement, but the relationship in our comparison countries was more complicated than that, without a clear correlation between qualitative assessments of trust (based on reported controversy surrounding their activities) and the extent of police involvement in CVE programming (see Figure 7.4).

As we observed in some of the cities we visited, these local conditions can mean that meeting the intervention needs of an area may require multiple parallel intervention systems that operate under different ground rules (e.g., a law enforcement–connected system sponsored by government and an NGO-managed effort separate from government entirely). Lack of trust in this context is therefore a source of inefficiency, and improvement in government-NGO-community relationships could therefore help reduce the need for duplication and make terrorism prevention activities more practical. The other response to these challenges, which echoes the discussion of public

Figure 7.4
Qualitative Mapping of Law Enforcement CVE and Trust in International Case Study Countries

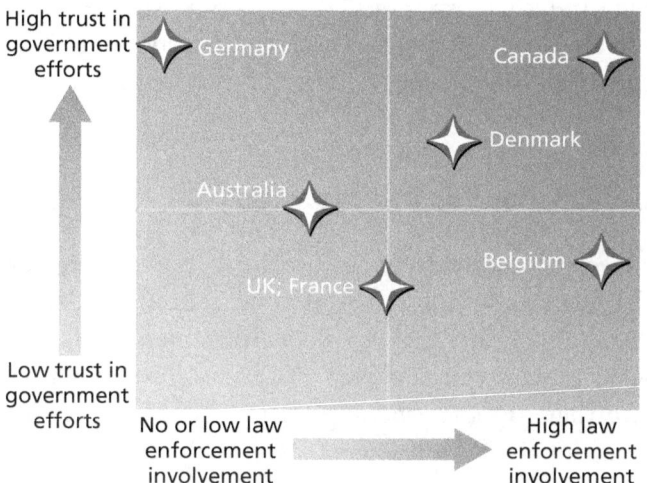

NOTE: Placement of countries in the matrix is based on a qualitative assessment of (left to right) the extent of law enforcement involvement in their intervention efforts and (bottom to top) a qualitative assessment of the level of public trust in government CVE activities (based on an overall assessment of the level of controversy surrounding those efforts based on literature and press reporting reviewed in our case study efforts). The comparison sought to explore country decisions, given that interview discussions during the study raised concerns about trust and practical law enforcement involvement in U.S. intervention programming. Positioning of the countries is qualitative and should not be overinterpreted.
RAND RR2647-7.4

health models of terrorism prevention introduced in Chapter Five, is to not build systems designed specifically for terrorism or ideologically motivated violence at all. From that perspective, intervention aimed at preventing terrorist violence should be more appropriately viewed as a subset of efforts to intervene to prevent violence of all types, building on models developed for such issues as mental health–focused diversion in juvenile justice[16] or school-based violence.[17,18]

Relevant Design Challenges

As a result of the sensitive nature of intervention, essentially every design challenge identified during our project affects this facet of terrorism prevention. Terrorism-specific intervention efforts have great potential to stigmatize participants, which is both a practical and ethical challenge given uncertainty in risk assessment. They also have sustainability challenges given the small numbers of incidents in any given local area. Damaged trust has created community resistance to programming and caused potential key partners to decline to participate, which undermines the potential for such programs to be an effective alternative to criminal justice responses to perceived threats. At the same time, there is serious concern about such efforts "getting it wrong" and having an intervention participant participate in a subsequent attack, which, some interviewees feared, could destroy the viability of intervention programming.[19]

Spectrum of Approaches for Intervention

In contrast to some of the other facets of terrorism prevention, for intervention, the situation is less that there is a wide range of approaches available than that there is a wide range of societal and individual problems for which a relatively well-defined set of intervention methods has been deployed. As a result, there is a body of practice and evaluation literature that supports the application of those practices, but that evaluation literature relates to their use in a range of contexts and to address a variety of problems.

---

[16] See, for example, Weine, Eisenman, and Kinsler et al., 2017, p. 212.

[17] See, for example, Hollister and Scalora, 2015.

[18] Some statements by the FBI have adopted a similar framing with respect to terrorism: "The FBI utilizes a comprehensive violence reduction strategy, which focuses on all pathways to violence but is not limited to this sole focus of homegrown violent extremism" (Sleeper, 2017).

[19] Others have framed this as recalibrating from the zero risk tolerance often associated with terrorism cases (Multiple interviewees at all levels, 2018).

Policies and Programming

In both our interviews and the literature, the argument has been made that the ingredients for intervention in response to concerns about ideological violence are quite similar to those for intervention in response to violence in general, and even for other societal problems. Indeed, in one description of the public health framing of CVE, Eisenman and Flavahan argue that "violent extremism is more similar to than dissimilar from other common forms of violence," and, therefore, it can be approached in a similar way.[20] As a result, terrorism prevention program design has a common set of ingredients to start from, and the challenge is then what additional types of programming or counseling are needed that are specific to the problem at hand, in the same way that intervention for a gang-involved individual may differ from one for an individual coming out of a cult-like organization.[21] Koehler provides a comprehensive review of relevant literature and interventions from other fields, including violent and nonviolent crime, cults, violent gangs, armed groups in semiorganized conflicts, and hate and bias crime.[22]

Programming components that are viewed as valuable ingredients for intervention, desistance, or reentry efforts include

- counseling and treatment aimed at substance abuse issues
- mental health and wellness programs
- counseling related to individual identity and self-image[23]
- individual behavior modification (e.g., anger management, mores of acceptable behavior)
- efforts to strengthen family bonds and other support systems
- education
- workforce and employability
- counseling or education related to ideology or religion (e.g., supporting individual exit from cult-like organizations)

---

[20] Eisenman and Flavahan, 2017, p. 348.

[21] In our discussion of efforts about the experiences of individuals leaving cults (also sometimes referred to as "new religious movements") and the relevance of lessons learned from such programming to CVE or terrorism prevention, an interviewee drew an important distinction between government efforts and a more broadly defined national effort. Given protected rights of freedom of religion, government efforts are limited in how religious or ideological counseling is included in programming (e.g., an interviewee from the corrections sector emphasized that such counseling was done at the request of individuals involved). However, intervention efforts outside of government can and do include such components. As the interviewee put it, "it is inappropriate for government to try to talk someone out of believing in a particular religion, but it is both fine and expected for members of their family (or their religious leaders) to do so." (Interview with a community organization leader, 2018).

[22] Koehler, 2017, Chapters Two and Nine.

[23] One practitioner we spoke with characterized radicalization to violence as "identity formation gone wrong." (Interview with a community service organization representative in one U.S. city, 2018.)

- mentoring by peers or other individuals[24]
- victim/perpetrator interaction or dialogue (including restorative justice–type interventions)
- efforts to encourage acceptance of the individuals by society.

Overall, various programming elements are designed to address criminogenic or other risk factors or strengthen protective factors for desistance from violent or other behavior.[25]

Programming can be delivered individually, in group counseling sessions, in contexts like schools, or focused in a family counseling model.[26] Some interventions for specific problems (e.g., focused deterrence models in crime or drugs) are community-based, bringing together the support of families, religious organizations, service providers, and other local institutions to intervene together with at-risk individuals. Interventions drawing on the menu of treatment types across these settings are focused on issues like suicide, neighborhood or gang violence, child and intimate partner abuse, substance abuse, school violence, and other types of juvenile crime. In both interventions for some types of criminal behavior (e.g., gangs) and for group-based ideological violence, "formers"—i.e., members who left the organization—are sometimes drawn on as credible outreach personnel.[27] The bottom line in most of these types of interventions is the delivery of effective services by providers that the at-risk individuals will listen and respond to positively.

One factor that is common across many of the interventions aimed at complex problems, including violence, is the view that resources and capabilities from multiple disciplines must be brought to bear to meet an individual's needs and improve the chances that efforts will succeed in turning that person away from violent or antisocial behavior. In addition, multidisciplinary intervention can help to address mismatches among the approaches adopted by single agencies or systems to a problem, reducing

---

[24] Spalek and Davies discuss a mentoring program aimed at CVE goals in the United Kingdom (Basia Spalek and Lynn Davies, "Mentoring in Relation to Violent Extremism: A Study of Role, Purpose, and Outcomes," *Studies in Conflict and Terrorism*, Vol. 35, 2012).

[25] There is commonality between program requirements for middle-phase intervention and those aimed at reducing recidivism of convicted offenders, meaning that there is the potential for efficiency by having one service provision system for both. We discuss this in more detail in Chapter Eight.

[26] Koehler, 2017, Chapter 6, provides an in-depth discussion of family counseling approaches to ideologically motivated violence.

[27] For example, former gang members may be employed as street workers in outreach programs in countergang interventions (reviewed in Shannon Frattaroli, Keshia M. Pollack, Karen Jonsberg, Gregg Croteau, JuanCarlos Rivera, and Jennifer S. Mendel, "Streetworkers, Youth Violence Prevention, and Peacemaking in Lowell, Massachusetts: Lessons and Voices from the Community," *Progress in Community Health Partnerships: Research, Education, and Action*, Vol. 4, No. 3, Fall 2010; and Butts et al., 2015).

the potential for unintended consequences or negative outcomes.[28] Examples of these types of efforts include the Crisis Intervention Team model linking law enforcement with mental health capabilities to improve outcomes for individuals with mental health needs and reduce the likelihood of police use of force when responding to incidents where they are involved,[29] coalitions of government agencies and community groups in interventions like Ceasefire, Cure Violence, or the Comprehensive Gang Model responding to gang violence,[30] interventions aimed at responding to major local drug markets,[31] specialty or community courts,[32] or targeted school or other violence.[33]

For such efforts, our interviewees emphasized that a key piece of applying these types of approaches to problems is building the organizational infrastructure for multidisciplinary collaboration. Echoing some of the points made about government or law enforcement and community trust, the challenge is building a multiagency structure and implementation effort where there can be *interagency trust*, given different demands and responsibilities that each is obligated to fulfill for individuals (e.g., patients) and the community and society as a whole. Interviewees, as well as sources in the literature on interventions relying on similar structures or community coalitions, described implementation as a negotiation process where the different participants needed to identify their requirements to "be comfortable" with trusting the multiagency structure essentially taking on some of their organizational responsibility to serve patients

---

[28] For example, one interviewee involved in service delivery with experience at the federal level stated that "A lot of my early work was sex crimes. You have a child psychologist, an educator, a cop, because everyone comes from a different point of view. The tendency for group think is less because everyone comes from a different viewpoint. That is vitally important to interventions. You want to show respect, and you do that by having people from different points of view argue [about how best to serve the person involved]."

[29] For a description, see, for example, Dana Markey, Laura Usher, Darcy Gruttadaro, Ron Honberg, and Charles S. Cochran, *Responding to Youth with Mental Health Needs: A CIT for Youth Implementation Manual*, Arlington, Va.: National Alliance on Mental Illness, July 2011.

[30] See, for example, National Gang Center, *Best Practices to Address Community Gang Problems: OJJDP's Comprehensive Gang Model*, Washington, D.C.: U.S. Department of Justice, Office of Juvenile Justice and Delinquency Prevention, 2nd ed., October 2010; Gravel et al., 2013. Researchers from different backgrounds have drawn parallels between intervention with respect to gang membership and violence and ideologically motivated extremist violence (e.g., Scott H. Decker and David C. Pyrooz, "'I'm Down for a Jihad': How 100 Years of Gang Research Can Inform the Study of Terrorism, Radicalization and Extremism," *Perspectives on Terrorism*, Vol. 9, No. 1, 2015; Eisenman and Flavahan, 2017).

[31] See, for example, Nicholas Corsaro, and Rod K. Brunson, "Are Suppression and Deterrence Mechanisms Enough? Examining the 'Pulling Levers' Drug Market Intervention Strategy in Peoria, Illinois, USA," *International Journal of Drug Policy*, Vol. 24, 2013; Jessica Saunders, Allison J. Ober, Beau Kilmer, and Sara Michal Greathouse, *A Community-Based, Focused-Deterrence Approach to Closing Overt Drug Markets: A Process and Fidelity Evaluation of Seven Sites*, Santa Monica, Calif.: RAND Corporation, RR-1001-NIJ, 2016.

[32] See, for example, Deborah Koetzle Shaffer, "Looking Inside the Black Box of Drug Courts: A Meta-Analytic Review," *Justice Quarterly*, Vol. 28, No. 3, 2011; and Julius Lang, *What Is a Community Court? How the Model Is Being Adapted Across the United States*, Washington, D.C.: Center for Court Innovation, 2011.

[33] FBI Behavioral Analysis Unit, undated.

or society. Figure 7.5 illustrates the types of factors that could be important to different disciplinary agencies that would need to be navigated during implementation.

In our interview discussions, one of the key benefits of this type of M-DT structure was that this delegation of trust could "productively share responsibility" among team members to take risks on intervention that might not be taken when only single organizations with narrower goals were involved, as well as vesting a "responsibility to act" with the team as an entity that also appeared to be valuable to drive decisionmaking on individual cases.[34] Such a process is not only a negotiation among government agencies of different types—it also is a negotiation with the community, and interviewees cited the model of community-based participatory research as a path to productive design and implementation for this area.[35] Our interviewees emphasized that this negotiation continues over time as, ideally, trust among the participating organizations strengthens and makes it easier to work together.

Evidence for Effectiveness

The literature is replete with discussions of CVE flagging the lack of evidence for the effectiveness of intervention programming.[36] However, relevant policies have been implemented to address other social problems, and their effectiveness has been evalu-

Figure 7.5
Examples Cited of Potential Organizational Needs During Formation of a Multiagency Intervention Effort

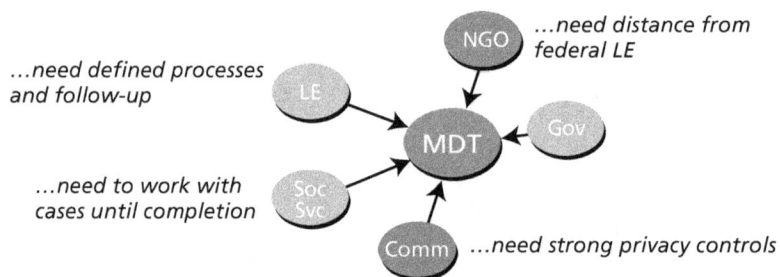

SOURCE: Examples cited in interview discussions.
RAND RR2647-7.5

---

[34] The FBI Behavioral Analysis Unit describes this in terms of the threat management team taking responsibility for the case and integrating the organizations that are ultimately responsible for delivering services (undated, pp. 51–52).

[35] See Ellis and Abdi, 2017, for a published review.

[36] See, for example, Koehler, 2017, Chapter 7; Allard R. Feddes and Marcehllo Gallucci, "A Literature Review on Methodology Used in Evaluating Effects of Preventive and De-Radicalisation Interventions," *Journal for Deradicalization*, Vol. 5, Winter 2015/2016; Helmus et al., 2017; John G. Horgan, and Kurt Braddock, "Rehabilitating the Terrorists? Challenges in Assessing the Effectiveness of De-Radicalization Programs," *Terrorism and Political*

ated. That body of evidence can provide inferential support for its utility for terrorism prevention.

Evaluations of multidisciplinary and organizational coalition-based interventions for problems like gang violence and family-based interventions for substance abuse issues have shown positive effects, and there is a broad body of evidence that components of these programs are effective for problems ranging from individual and family violence to suicide prevention and school-based violence.[37] Literature examinations of these efforts have shown that benefits are sensitive to implementation, meaning that care is required in replicating practices in different sites or contexts.[38]

Current U.S. Terrorism Prevention and Related Efforts for Intervention

Across our interviews at all levels, there was consensus that national capability to conduct interventions and respond to individuals at risk of committing ideological violence is very limited. Research to identify terrorism-specific efforts (including specific efforts in cities we visited) identified some programs representing a narrow slice of capability.

The only examples of federal activity in this space we identified were initiatives by the FBI and the U.S. Attorney's Office: the "Shared Responsibility Committees"

Violence, Vol. 22, No. 2, 2010; or Naureen Chowdhury Fink, Peter Romaniuk, and Rafia Barakat, "Evaluating Countering Violent Extremism Programming: Practice and Progress," Center on Global Counterterrorism Cooperation, September 2013 for reviews.

[37] Reviewed in Gravel et al., 2013; Ashley M. Austin, Mark J. Macgowan, and Eric F. Wagner, "Effective Family-Based Interventions for Adolescents with Substance Abuse Problems: A Systematic Review," *Research on Social Work Practice*, Vol. 15, No. 2, 2005; Allison Gruner Gandhi, Erin Murphy-Graham, Anthony Petrosino, Sara Schwartz Chrismer, and Carol H. Weiss, "The Devil Is in the Details: Examining the Evidence for 'Proven' School-Based Drug Abuse Prevention Programs," *Evaluation Review*, Vol. 31, No. 1, 2007; Christopher Mikton and Alexander Butchart, "Child Maltreatment Prevention: A Systematic Review of Reviews," *Bull World Health Organ*, Vol. 87, 2009; Cristina M. van der Feltz-Cornelis, Marco Sarchiapone, Vita Postuvan, Daniëlle Volker, Saska Roskar, Alenka Tančič Grum, Vladimir Carli, David McDaid, Rory O'Connor, Margaret Maxwell, Angela Ibelshäuser, Chantal Van Audenhove, Gert Scheerder, Merike Sisask, Ricardo Gusmão, and Ulrich Hegerl, "Best Practice Elements of Multilevel Suicide Prevention Strategies: A Review of Systematic Reviews," *Crisis*, Vol. 32, No. 6, 2011; David Weisburd, David P. Farrington, and Charlotte Gill, eds., *What Works in Crime Prevention and Rehabilitation: Lessons from Systematic Reviews*, New York: Springer, 2016; David A. Wolfe and Peter G. Jaffee, "Emerging Strategies in the Prevention of Domestic Violence," *The Future of Children*, Vol. 9, No. 3, 1999; Gil Zalsman, Keith Hawton, Danuta Wasserman, Kees van Heeringen, Ella Arensman, Marco Sarchiapone, Vladimir Carli, Cyril Höschl, Ran Barzilay, Judit Balazs, György Purebl, Jean Pierre Kahn, Pilar Alejandra Sáiz, Cendrine Bursztein Lipsicas, Julio Bobes, Doina Cozman, Ulrich Hegerl, and Joseph Zohar, "Suicide Prevention Strategies Revisited: 10-Year Systematic Review," *Lancet*, Vol. 3, No. 7, July 1, 2016.

[38] See, for example, Sharon F. Mihalic and Katherine Irwin, "Blueprints for Violence Prevention: From Research to Real-World Settings—Factors Influencing the Successful Replication of Model Programs," *Youth Violence and Juvenile Justice*, Vol. 1, No. 4, October 2003, for a review and Saunders et al., 2016, for a specific example on replication of an intervention aimed at drug markets.

(SRCs) and DEEP. The SRCs were launched in 2016. The Bureau has described the intent of the SRCs as voluntary groups around the country made up of law enforcement, family and community members, mental health professionals, and religious leaders where those involved identify potential violent extremists for intervention.[39] One senior law enforcement official explained the SRCs as "professionalizing a process that has been ad hoc for a long time" for federal law enforcement engagement with local communities on interventions.[40] However, there was a significant backlash against the effort from civil rights organizations, and the committees appear to have been disbanded, at least under the SRC construct.[41]

Recent FBI testimony indicates that the FBI is still working with state and local partners to implement off-ramping efforts to take subjects off the path to violence before they commit a crime.[42] The main effort identified to do so is DEEP, which is run by the U.S. Attorney's Office in the Eastern District of New York and is aimed at people on the path toward violent extremism.[43] Although several of our interviewees mentioned these efforts in our discussions, additional information on the programs, case numbers they have served, and data on their successes were not available to the research team.

Federal entities have encouraged and supported state and local models of intervention. In September 2014, DOJ announced that it was launching a series of pilot programs (run in partnership with the White House, DHS, and NCTC) in three cities—Boston, Los Angeles, and the Twin Cities of Minneapolis and St. Paul—that were chosen in part based on their achievements with community engagement.[44] The purpose of the program was for the cities to bring together community representatives, public safety officials, religious leaders, and U.S. government representatives to improve local engagement, counter violent extremism, and build a broad network of community partnerships to keep the country safe.[45]

---

[39] U.S. House of Representatives, Committee on Homeland Security, "Correspondence: FBI Shared Responsibility Committees Must Pass Privacy Test," 114th Congress, 2nd Session, April 29, 2016.

[40] Michael Hirsh, "Inside the FBI's Secret Muslim Network," *Politico Magazine*, March 24, 2016.

[41] The Justice Department reportedly ended the SRC program in October 2016 after significant criticism by civil rights organizations; however, the FBI may still be running SRC-style programs in some locations (Levitt, 2017). Rosand (2017a) saw the reaction to the SRCs as reflecting larger issues surrounding CVE but commended the FBI for pursuing new approaches: "While the FBI has been criticized at times for trying to do too much in the CVE space, it deserves credit for recognizing the need to develop new tools to deal with the range of violent extremist challenges it is now facing."

[42] Sleeper, 2017.

[43] Colby Hamilton, "DuCharme Takes Over as Eastern District's Criminal Chief," *New York Law Journal*, March 12, 2018; Devlin, 2015.

[44] DOJ, 2014; DOJ, 2015b.

[45] DOJ, 2014.

In addition to existing intervention capacity at the local level (which we discuss further below), DHS also awarded three new FY 2016 CVE grant efforts to build out capacity in Oakland, Las Vegas, and Houston. Among unfunded proposals for the FY 2016 solicitation were several intervention-focused proposals—although most came from cities that had past CVE involvement (including Boston, Los Angeles, and Minneapolis–St. Paul). As a result, if awarded, most of those grants would have "deepened" intervention capability in cities already covered rather than covering new cities. The one exception was a proposed program in Virginia. In the FY 2016 grant solicitation, intervention-focused proposals were the minority of proposals received (15 out of approximately 200 applications). As a result, although the current assessment of national intervention capacity is weak, there was relatively modest demand to initiate additional programming at the local level.

At the local level, there are some programs that are in place that provide intervention capability for ideologically motivated violence risk. Some are framed in a terrorism-specific way: e.g., the LAPD's recently launched Providing Alternatives to Hinder Extremism (PATHE) program run out of LAPD's Counter-Terrorism and Special Operations Bureau has extremism as part of its name. The scope of the program is broader than terrorism and ideological violence, however: It is designed to respond to individuals at risk to commit any act of targeted violence and, working with the LAPD Mental Evaluation Unit and others, to conduct intervention activity. Similarly, both in the cities we visited and more broadly, there are efforts that seek to address the issue of intervention for ideologically motivated violence risk in the context of existing broader programs.[46] As an interviewee from an NGO put it:[47]

> We've made this [intervention effort] not about any ethnic group or religion, just kids who are at risk for violence that are falling through the cracks. We see a whole range of ethnicities on the team. We've limited our scope to any of the partners at the table—if they bring someone, we can serve them.

Another local service provider emphasized the practical effects of being general: "Schools, medical professionals, they don't know what's going to walk in the door so they need to be prepared for a variety of things. Training for very specific things requires a lot of resources for not a large population."

Because many areas have built terrorism prevention intervention into existing programs, there is a greater amount of capability in place than it might appear.[48] Thus,

---

[46] This is a recommendation of previous studies of this topic as well, see Weine et al., 2015; Levitt, 2017. This has been recommended by the federal government to local first responders as well (NCTC, DHS and FBI, 2017).

[47] Interview with a nongovernmental service provider representative in a U.S. city, 2018.

[48] One interviewee argued that the fact that these efforts had been built independently at the local level was good, and that a federal role would be to try to facilitate similar developments elsewhere: "Focus on finding ways to help communities find best practices and do things on their own, the way Minneapolis has reached out to large

for the cities we visited, it was difficult to "discover" the existence of that capability without local data collection. It is likely that a similar situation exists elsewhere—at least in major cities where there are organizations and government efforts designed for intervention regarding mental health, substance abuse, school violence, and other concerns. It is also the case that federal efforts to build local capacity related to different problems (e.g., human trafficking, family violence) could result in in capabilities that could also be applied to meeting the needs of individuals at risk of perpetrating ideological violence.

Coordination between the local and federal levels varies—some programs had little or none, while others had close engagement and even case referral (from federal entities to local programs). For example, there are links between LAPD's PATHE program and the National Joint Terrorism Task Force (JTTF) to bridge local and federal agencies to allow federal entities to make referrals of individuals to intervention programs.[49] There is also coordination more broadly on best practices and approaches. For example, the FBI's Office of Partner Engagement has coordinated with local law enforcement agency crisis intervention teams (CITs) in an effort to develop intervention approaches.[50]

In the NGO space, several CVE intervention efforts are underway, focused on specific communities or needs. One such effort is by Life After Hate, with its crisis intervention initiatives to help people forswear racism and violent extremism; another is the World Organization for Resource Development and Education (WORDE)'s BRAVE model.[51] Other programs are CAIR Florida's Community Empowerment Programs, which include crisis intervention teams, the MPAC Safe Spaces Initiative Prevention Intervention (PI) model, and the activities by Parents for Peace to provide support to people concerned that loved ones are involved in extremism.[52] There is also the University of Denver's Colorado Resilience Collaborative, which addresses identity-based violence because of radicalization and discrimination and includes clinical services interventions that come from referrals from community members and gov-

---

companies, and basically connect the nonprofit, NGO, state, and local communities and let the funding come from state-level HHS, state-level DHS where they have a kinder face to these communities anyway" (Interview with a policy researcher, 2018).

[49] Lolita Lopez and Philip Drechsler, "LAPD Program Prevents Acts of Terrorism," *NBC Los Angeles*, October 13, 2017.

[50] Sleeper, 2017.

[51] Life After Hate, homepage, undated(b); WORDE, *Building Resilience Against Violent Extremism*, 2016.

[52] CAIR Florida, "CAIR-Florida Provides Training on Preserving Liberty and National Security Along with U.S. DHS and a National Security Delegation from France," press release, Tampa, Fla., December 8, 2016; *Denver Post*, "Group Efforts Aimed at 'Countering Violent Extremism' Spread," July 5, 2016; MPAC, "Safe Spaces Initiative," webpage, undated; Parents for Peace, undated.

ernment entities alike.[53] One challenge to nongovernmental implementation of intervention efforts (and one cited in our interviews regarding current programming) is the concern about legal exposure in the event that a participant in a program subsequently carries out a terrorist attack (i.e., intervention "fails"). Concerns included both potential civil liability as a result of suit from victims of any such attack[54] and potential criminal liability under material support statutes.[55]

Likely because many of the efforts in the cities we visited were "adding terrorism prevention" to existing programs, there was great diversity in the models being applied. Efforts underway vary widely with respect to governmental and law enforcement involvement, and some were at different stages of development and with varied capacity. Figure 7.6 depicts the range of models in cities we visited. There are some essentially NGO-only efforts, some nongovernmental efforts where law enforcement coordinates (and even refers cases), and even some law enforcement–originated and –managed activities. Multiple intervention models coexist in some of the cities we visited.

Although a small number of these programs are terrorism-specific, most are not but would nonetheless respond to the needs of an individual at risk of ideological radicalization to violence. Across the different examples, many intervention efforts in cities we visited were characterized as "fragile" because of the controversy surrounding such activities and the lower trust generally of past CVE and, by extension, terrorism prevention efforts, with some entities explicitly not linking their efforts to terrorism to try to avoid these issues.[56]

---

[53] Colorado Resilience Collaborative, homepage, undated; Interviews with local government and nongovernment representatives, 2018.

[54] Similar liability questions have been raised for violence prevention in the school context, including liability associated with failure to prevent suicide (e.g., James C. Penven and Steven M. Janosik, "Threat Assessment Teams: A Model for Coordinating the Institutional Response and Reducing Legal Liability When College Students Threaten Suicide," *Journal of Student Affairs Research and Practice*, Vol. 49, No. 3, 2012) and violence against others (e.g., Mary A. Hermann and Abbe Finn, "An Ethical and Legal Perspective on the Role of School Counselors in Preventing Violence in Schools," *Professional School Counseling*, Vol. 6, No. 1, October 2002).

[55] As discussed in Chapter Three, some individuals consulted for the study expressed skepticism that either civil or criminal action in such a situation would have any chance of success—meaning that the *concern* about liability may be a more potent challenge for policy than the actual liability exposure.

For example, from a community services organization in one U.S. city: "To me one of the biggest questions going forward is what is going to change to get people who care off the sidelines? . . . I think the liability issue is very real and needs to be addressed. It was brought to the government by outsiders at various points and not a lot has happened with it" and, from a similar type of individual in a second city: "There's no support—no legal support, no one has your back. So interventions never went anywhere. We kept asking about it but there was no cover. . . . My board was more concerned with liability if something happened. I was more concerned about material support."

[56] Interviews with local governmental, nongovernmental, and social services representatives, 2018.

Figure 7.6
Variation in Existing Intervention Approaches Across Programs in U.S. Cities Visited: Law Enforcement and Government Involvement

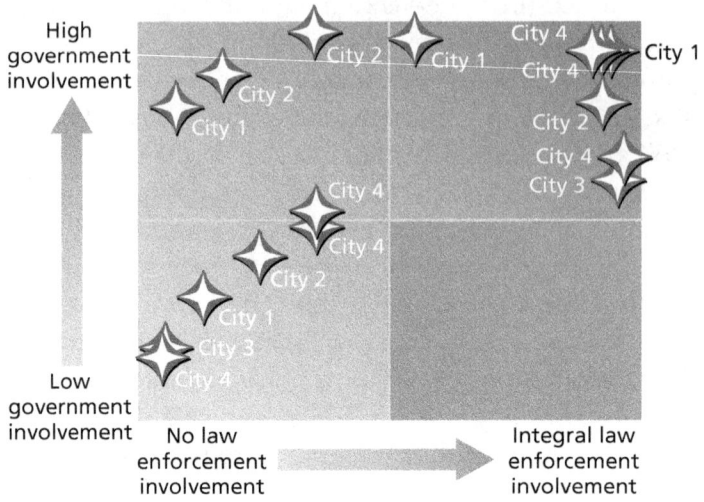

NOTE: Lower-right quadrant is shaded because, by definition, it is not possible to have integral law enforcement involvement but low government involvement.
RAND *RR2647-7.6*

Assessment

Because little information was available during the course of the research on the FBI's intervention and diversion efforts, it is not possible to assess the contribution from federally driven efforts to the level of national intervention capability. In the cities we visited, it was clear there is greater intervention capability than it might appear, given the integration of terrorism and extremism-related issues into existing programming.[57] Even in those cities, our research was not a census of all such capacity,[58] and data sources were not available that would allow assessment of the extent to which there are general intervention capacities across the country that could respond to at-risk individuals.[59] However, there was a strong consensus in our interviews that intervention was a

---

[57] This echoes an argument made with respect to CVE by Bipartisan Policy Center, 2011.

[58] However, program representatives that we spoke with cited very low numbers of extremism-related cases they had served, and relatively modest total numbers of individuals and families on all issues on an annual basis, likely reflecting the intensity of the services they provided.

[59] As one of our interviewees from a community-based organization pointed out, however, many of the general intervention systems (e.g., mental health counseling and treatment) are already stretched by their current case-loads, so adding cases they would be expected to serve could be problematic. This has also been reflected in the literature: "Weine noted, it is a challenge to find the sufficient organizational capacity and professional expertise to conduct mental health interventions of the scope needed for CVE" (Snair, Nicholson, and Giammaria, 2017, p. 84).

significant national gap, particularly outside large and well-resourced urban areas.[60] As one national-level interviewee put it, there is "quality community programing . . . [but it is] too small to have a broader nationwide impact."[61] Others raised concerns for specific types of organizations:[62]

> [A] real struggle is there are not a great set of nationally accepted guidelines for school response to someone of a major concern. If a student comes on their radar [because of] accessing [extreme right] or ISIS websites [on school computers], what is the school's duty? In [named city], we're lucky because they put resources against these programs to wrap around that kid. But schools that are less resourced really struggle with this. I don't think they have the capacity for students who cause that concern.

Although the perception that current intervention capacity was insufficient was expressed by community and social services interviewees, similar arguments were also made by law enforcement and security-focused interviewees both at the national and at the state and local levels. As we allude to in the discussion on cost in Chapter Nine, a driver from the law enforcement perspective is the desire to have a greater range of options to respond to threats appropriately and efficiently. Some interviewees who had been involved in non–law enforcement connected intervention programs cited examples where police agencies or prosecutors reached out to them for options, particularly for juveniles, for whom they thought it was inappropriate to send down a criminal justice path, but where there were real threat concerns. This emphasized the stakes involved for law enforcement at the risk-decision stage, and the role that intervention can play to reduce those stakes by providing an alternative path. Rather than being one decision made at a single point in time with incomplete information, referral to an intervention converts that single decision to multiple decisions over a longer period of time.[63] Intervention programs also reduce the stakes for the individuals involved and therefore provide a path to address concerns raised by groups critical of prosecution-heavy approaches that rely on aggressive investigation techniques like the use of informants.

In describing their approaches to terrorism prevention, interviewees argued that the approach of building terrorism prevention into existing programming was not only efficiency driven, but also more likely to succeed if they adapted existing tools to this

---

[60] Green and Proctor (2016, pp. 39–40) make a similar point about lack of CVE intervention capability globally.

[61] Rosand (2017a) makes the same argument, regarding both development of programming locally and the national gap in capability.

[62] Interview with a local social services representative, 2018.

[63] To emphasize the point that this capability is important from a law enforcement point of view, one interviewee indicated that officers participate in these types of efforts outside of their professional roles: "Some FBI agents are spending their Saturdays essentially doing counseling with parents because they believe this is important" (Interview with a former federal government representative, 2018).

problem set.[64] For example, in one city, law enforcement made a strong argument that the existing infrastructure of CITs and their associated training—which was developed in response to police responses to individuals with mental health issues—would be a solid foundation to respond to individuals at risk of perpetrating ideological violence. That approach would already be familiar to officers in many departments, and would therefore be easier to adopt. Others pointed to examples of how mental health responders had been integrated into police response, where different types of mental health staff were compared with patrol officers and detectives, again, drawing a direct parallel to organizational structures and roles already familiar to officers. In other places, the existing tool that was picked up to respond to this challenge was some form of multidisciplinary team that was already in place. For example, in multiple cities, such a team that was aimed at school violence was cited as part of their response to the risk of ideologically motivated violence.

There are certainly strong positive features in such repurposing of existing tools, and doing so may be the only viable approach, given that limited resources have been devoted to CVE and now terrorism prevention nationally. But, there were cautionary signals as well. One interviewee flagged the concern that if existing law enforcement and mental health links were the basis for response, there could be a tendency to view mental health as the driver in all cases of ideological violence—i.e., the nature of the tool repurposed for terrorism prevention would shape the way we would approach the problem. Similarly, tools that were designed to serve youth would be expected to serve older at-risk individuals less effectively: Indeed, some interviewees indicated that addressing extremism concerns in youth was "easier" than for adults, given the systems available to respond. For models based on existing infrastructure, the issue then is to ensure that the tool does not unduly shape approaches, and, if needed, efforts are broadened to involve all the sources of expertise and services needed to fully respond to the problem.

Based on all the information collected in this research effort, it is not possible to provide a definitive answer to our fundamental outcome question ("What is the likelihood that an identified at-risk individual would receive effective services to reduce risk?"). However, it does appear clear that the answer is less than would be desirable from several different perspectives.[65] Furthermore, just as is the case in the CVE literature more broadly, data are not available to rigorously assess the outcomes of the programs that are in place, although interviewees did provide examples of individual cases of interventions that did appear to have been successful—though, even in those cases, whether the programs had prevented acts of violence was difficult to judge with any degree of certainty.

---

[64] See also Weine et al., 2015.

[65] Some have argued that intervention capacity should be prioritized over broader earlier-stage terrorism prevention activity (e.g., McKenzie, 2016).

Federal Options for Intervention-Focused Policy and Programming

Given that intervention capability across the country is still quite limited, interviewees at both the national and state and local levels provided feedback and critiques of options for the federal government to strengthen national intervention capability. To a greater extent than in other areas of terrorism prevention, that feedback and critique provides useful narrowing of the range of federal (and specifically DHS) options for informing future program design.

First, there was strong consensus that the sensitivity of intervention efforts means that they must be implemented and controlled locally,[66] so any approach that seeks to fill the national shortfall in intervention with a federally implemented intervention effort would not be viable.[67] In the words of one federal representative with local experience: "Any time we focus the national conversation on these issues, we make it hard for our local partners. And any time we try to go top down, it doesn't necessarily translate at the local level."[68] Another former federal official who had been involved in past CVE initiatives summed it up:[69]

> To avoid the pitfalls from before, the federal government needs to understand they need to be in a supportive role, they should be a connector, a convener and a collaborator, but by no means should they become an operational part of driving and implementing CVE programing. That will be the death of any effort and will do more harm than good to any kind of participant in a community. But that doesn't mean that federal government doesn't have a role.

The controversy surrounding federal terrorism prevention efforts and the potency of concerns raised by interviewees about FBI enforcement efforts provide support for this conclusion: Whether the criticisms raised regarding past CVE efforts and counterterrorism (CT) enforcement approaches are right or wrong, they are a fundamental part of the context in which future efforts will be implemented.

Second, the need for local implementation means that whatever federal actions are taken to try to strengthen intervention, they must not foreclose local flexibility or mandate specific models or approaches to terrorism prevention intervention, because

---

[66] A notable exception to this view that federal intervention capacity would not be viable because of trust and other issues was included in Levitt, 2017: After recommendations for both building capacity locally and relying on existing general-purpose intervention capabilities, a recommendation was included to create "interagency fly teams modeled after the Federal Emergency Management Agency (FEMA) Community Emergency Response Teams (CERTs), to provide training and information, and FBI Fly Teams, to respond to high-priority cases in communities too small to build a capability of their own" (Levitt, 2017, p. 23). McKenzie (2016) also argued for nationally implemented intervention programming that would be managed by HHS.

[67] See, for example, the discussion in Bipartisan Policy Center, 2011.

[68] Interview with a former federal official, 2018.

[69] Interview with a former federal official, 2018.

one size does not fit all localities.[70] For example, federal mandates that locals have law enforcement–centric approaches to terrorism prevention would constrain success to areas where there was sufficient trust between police and the community to make that possible, and could lead to opt-out by community and service organizations and reduce the willingness of members of the public to refer at-risk individuals where that trust did not exist. Conversely, mandating non–law enforcement approaches could be limiting in other ways, hindering the ability to leverage existing collaborative efforts where there is already integration between disciplines like police and mental health or where police already have productive, nonadversarial relationships with youth in their jurisdictions.[71] It would also limit the potential for cooperation among NGOs, service agencies, and law enforcement to evolve organically in the context of activities to address ideological violence risk in their areas, as has been observed in some of the cities we visited. Given the complexity of balancing the operational and enforcement responsibilities of police agencies and the more collaborative counseling and case management approaches of other agencies, local-level interviewees viewed negotiating that balance locally as a critical step for the potential success of terrorism prevention efforts. Local autonomy is also needed to reflect the fact that different areas will have different threat concerns and different levels of existing capacity for intervention.[72]

Third, although some of the areas we visited had terrorism-specific programming or program components, using existing structures and programs for terrorism prevention intervention was viewed as a better strategy than trying to create standalone capacity.[73] Because any given area will likely have comparatively few individuals requir-

---

[70] A local government representative in one city noted that "Some of the challenges then come when we have a DHS-dictated strategy that does not take into consideration or have the level of flexibility that it needs to have in order for the local implementations to be organic. Any successful implementation of any program has to be organic to the locality." Others have made this argument as well, e.g., Southers, 2017.

[71] As one interviewee put it: "The most important lesson we learned from the three pilot programs is they are different. The nature of the problem [in other cities] is different from New York. Ka Joog as an example of a group that does great work. How replicable is their program? Not the same as Somali communities worldwide. Unique to the Somali communities in Minneapolis. We need to give states tremendous leeway and then decide what needs to be done" (Interview with a policy researcher, 2018).

[72] Interviews in more than one of the cities we visited emphasized that needs for intervention (as well as other areas of terrorism prevention) can differ significantly even in adjacent areas (e.g., nearby suburbs in a metropolitan area) or between central urban areas and their surrounding suburbs. Other federal leaders (including from the FBI) have emphasized this local specificity in public statements as well: "We're very cognizant that all cities and communities are different, and it's the citizens of the community that are best to identify the level of engagement, the type of engagement, and allow them to dictate back to the law enforcement community what they need and what they would like in order to exchange and open up that dialogue" (Sleeper, 2017).

[73] Other researchers have argued that even a program that is explicitly terrorism-focused (e.g., the Montgomery County Model, Life After Hate's programming, and MPAC's Safe Spaces Initiative) "embeds addressing violent extremism alongside other issues of targeted violence and other threats to community well-being" (Weine, Eisenman, and Kinsler et al., 2017). This point was recently argued in guidance to local first responders from NCTC, DHS, and FBI (2017).

ing intervention services, serving the existing clientele of such programs would help to sustain capacity until it was needed. Given limited funding for terrorism prevention–specific initiatives, there are few other approaches for sustaining capacity otherwise.[74]

In discussing this type of approach, Levitt argues that it is possible to desecuritize programming and still run programs "in such a way as to address the legitimate equities of both the public health and law enforcement communities."[75] This is one element of the public health framing of CVE (and, by extension, terrorism prevention): "It could also help in terms of embedding programs in existing structures that are integrated into community life (e.g., community organizing and strengthening), rather than to add new structures that either are or just appear to be a part of the security apparatus."[76] Elsewhere, this has been termed *mainstreaming*: "integrating [responding to individuals at risk of committing ideological violence] into all public services, coupled with a baseline awareness of the need for cooperation."[77] Integrating concerns about violent extremism into existing counseling and services programs that are focused on problems like interpersonal violence or juvenile delinquency that would not be labeled as terrorism prevention[78] also would be a route to address the stigma concerns and the damaged "CVE brand" that are real barriers to some organizations' willingness to participate in efforts related to terrorism.[79] According to some interviewees, this was framed as "allowing local flexibility in labeling intervention efforts."[80] That is, officials

---

[74] According to one local law enforcement interviewee in a city we visited: "We were like: why rebuild it, we already have that. . . . We've been doing this for 20 years. So all we did was create a new checkbox that made them realize this is a person who may be a violent extremist because people who are on the pathway to violence are the same. It's another category of targeted violence."

[75] Levitt, 2017, p. 4.

[76] Weine, Eisenman, and Kinsler et al., 2017; see also the discussion in Weine et al., 2015.

[77] Snair, Nicholson, and Giammaria, 2017, p. 26.

[78] In the literature, this has already been recognized—for example, with Levitt (2017) defining two categories: *CVE-specific* (which we have adopted to describe programs that are designed to respond to terrorism) and *CVE-relevant* to describe other programming that can contribute to achieving CVE goals. Based on the feedback of our interviewees, and specifically those at the local level, even labeling a program as CVE-relevant may be too great a connection to security issues in some cases. As a result, we have sought to avoid the use of a similar terrorism prevention version of that terminology. Because of that reality, it may be more useful to view such efforts simply as "programs willing to serve individuals potentially at risk of violent action." Doing so recognizes the reality that there are programs that would not turn away an individual who was referred to them because of concerns about radicalization or ideological violence risk, and would seek to meet their needs, but that the program would never define itself as a terrorism prevention–relevant program or as participating in terrorism prevention activities.

[79] Stigma is not just about reducing participation. In other areas, being included in stigmatized programs can also affect behavior negatively (called an iatrogenic effect), exacerbating the very problem the efforts are intended to solve (Cherney, 2016).

[80] For example, an interviewee from an NGO who had broader experience in national activities argued, "What we saw happen with the grant money [from the DHS solicitation] was [that] some communities wanted to do activities they didn't label CVE or terrorism prevention and were able to get stuff done because they called it other things" (Interview with an NGO representative, 2018).

would not force the terrorism prevention (or, in the past, CVE) label on an initiative because it would essentially create a situation in which any provider that chose to participate might be viewed as accepting that label[81] or, more broadly, endorsing terrorism prevention policy.[82] For some interviewees, this approach was viewed as a possible route to bring in nonsecurity organizations (federal or state and local-level health and human services or education agencies) into terrorism prevention efforts, because it would be a less controversial approach than dedicated programming.

Given the focus both on local control and integrating terrorism prevention into existing programs, we identify options where federal policy and action can strengthen local intervention capability. Options to do so range from *indirect barrier reduction* (addressing issues getting in the way of local implementation) to *direct facilitation* of capability development. Distilling from the feedback from interviews, the literature, and analysis, it appears that a combination of both approaches is required to significantly strengthen national capacity in this facet of terrorism prevention. These options include

- **Situational Awareness**
  - **Gather data on existing capabilities relevant to terrorism prevention intervention nationally to help facilitate network development and identify shortfalls.** A fundamental component of strengthening intervention capacity is understanding what is already in place, or answering our basic evaluation question regarding the chance that an individual in an area can be served with existing service networks. Because most of the relevant capacity is in general intervention programming and is not terrorism prevention–specific, determining what is already in place is harder. In areas where federal personnel are

---

[81] Rosand (2016, p. 16) put it this way: "Avoid instrumentalizing non–law enforcement actors involved in [terrorism prevention] or creating the impression that they are working for or serving law enforcement or other security agendas."

Of course, how programs are designed at the federal level can make this more difficult:

> We believe CVE has to be tailored to local circumstances, so it should be done by local actors. If they say they cannot move forward but we tell them they have to, it's dead on arrival. In Washington D.C. at a policy level, we have to call it something, we have to advocate for a certain set of behaviors, but we shouldn't foist that terminology on people on the ground. You have political-level leaders using loaded terms that don't play well on the ground. You have to have a set of terms so we know what we're talking about and can allocate resources, but you have to manage that terminology and the resources in a way that will be most effective. If you frame [it] as all-hazards, you can take [an] anti-bullying program and tweak it. Then it's not really CVE. . . . I'd rather have a good anti-bullying program that's aware of indicators of violent extremism, savvy to the symbols [and] vocabulary of CVE than not have any CVE programming on the ground. (Interview with a public policy researcher, 2018)

[82] This was one of the ways in which interviewees framed their concerns about the FY 2016 CVE Grant Program—i.e., by pursing that funding, they would be labeling themselves as "doing CVE," which would complicate their ability to carry out their broader missions and even to successfully implement a program funded under the grant program.

located (i.e., field staff for engagement efforts), their knowledge can be the basis for this type of situational awareness. However, understanding of national-level intervention capacity requires broader data collection and assessment.[83] This could be done in collaboration with other federal agencies or via existing data collections (e.g., Figure 7.7 shows the results from a national-level assessment of unmet need for mental health care professionals by state, which is one part of the capacity required for terrorism prevention intervention). Other interviewees suggested that terrorism prevention capacity issues could be integrated into existing DHS managed assessment efforts, such as the THIRA, which would provide a structure for data collection and also link directly to programs to address identified areas of need. To the extent that existing systems are called on to deliver terrorism prevention intervention, understanding how stretched those systems are currently and the effects of potential additional caseload need to be part of the picture.[84] This need for intervention resource situational awareness has been argued for in the literature as well, and tabletop exercises have been demonstrated as approaches for assessing capacity in individual areas.[85]

- **Regulatory and Legal Issues**
  - **Address perceived legal and liability barriers to nongovernmental intervention activities.** In the course of our interviews with both national-level individuals and potential providers of intervention services, one barrier to building capacity was legal and liability concerns. As a result, addressing those concerns would be an indirect route for federal action to reduce barriers to intervention. We heard concerns about both civil liability (if an individual in an intervention program carried out an attack, would the organization be open to suit from victims?) and criminal exposure (in the same situation, could the service provider be prosecuted under material support laws if its programming was interpreted as aiding the attacker rather than seeking to prevent the

---

[83] This same recommendation was made by the DHS HSAC: "Catalog all CVE programs within America . . . — both government-funded and independent—to create a comprehensive and transparent overview of what exists in America and where gaps might exist. Remarkably none exists anywhere" (DHS HSAC, 2016, p. 14). Green and Proctor (2016, p. 62) make a similar point for the need for a "programmatic database" of capacity and organizations involved in activities that could deliver relevant services. Levitt (2017, p. 23) argues for building up data on "vetted and trained local and state government entities, community service organizations, private resources (e.g., volunteer psychologists and clinical social workers), and community leaders to be able to come together and provide intervention services as needed in communities where size or budgetary constraints hinder the creation of a permanent body to provide such services."

[84] See, for example, Cherney, 2016; Snair, Nicholson, and Giammaria, 2017, p. 84.

[85] Weine, Eisenman, and Kinsler et al., 2017. Weine, Eisenman, and Jackson et al. (2017) describe the use of exercise in Los Angeles to examine mental health response to ideological violence. The DHS S&T study cited previously that focused on text-enabled referral included some mapping of capability by looking at connections among organizations involved in referral systems (Horgan et al., undated).

attack?). Interviewees suggested that both issues could be addressed at the federal level—i.e., civil liability via SAFETY Act certification of programs[86] and criminal exposure either via legislation or DOJ guidance.[87]

Figure 7.7
Kaiser Family Foundation Assessment of Unmet Mental Health Care Need, by State

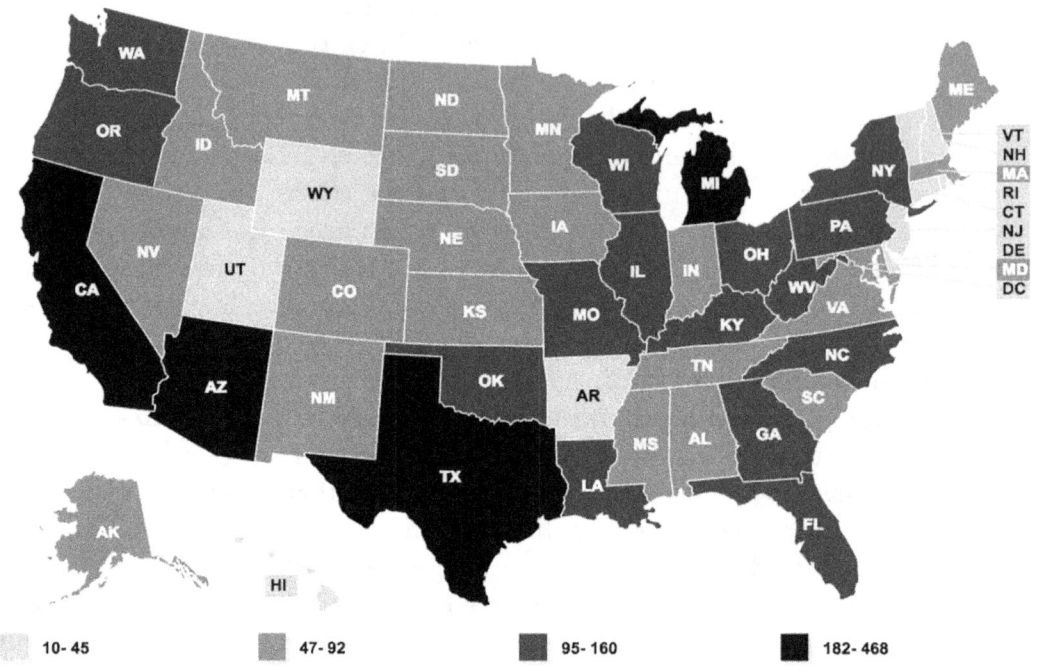

SOURCES: Kaiser Family Foundation, "Mental Health Care Health Professional Shortage Areas (HPSAs)," data set, December 31, 2017. Values indicate the number of Mental Health Care Health Professional Shortage Area Designations in the state.
RAND RR2647-7.7

---

[86] The SAFETY Act is a DHS S&T program that provides "legal liability protections for providers of Qualified Anti-Terrorism Technologies—whether they are products or services" (DHS S&T, "Support Anti-Terrorism by Fostering Effective Technologies (SAFETY) Act," undated[a]). The goal of the program is to reduce the barriers posed by risk of lawsuits to the development of new approaches for addressing terrorism risk. Non–hardware based approaches (e.g., counterterrorism training) have been certified under the program. Certification, however, does require the involved organizations to carry liability insurance (discussed in Chapter Three). A full exploration of the availability of such insurance for the range of organizations potentially involved in intervention was beyond the scope of this work.

[87] Note that another source of risk aversion was cast as "political liability"—i.e., the consequences if a participant in a program carries out an attack when intervention efforts are inevitably imperfect. These steps do not address that idea directly. Doing so will require a shift in national expectations that any effort can legitimately be expected to produce a 100-percent reduction in terrorism risk.

- **Federal Program Development**
  - **Reconstitute and expand federal field staff to act as primary focal points for terrorism prevention at the local level.** As discussed in previous chapters, there was a broad perception in the cities we visited that there were few substitutes for talented federal field staff at the local level to promote strengthening of intervention capability.[88] Numerous interviewees called out the contribution that existing field staff made to building the capability that exists in the cities we visited, and the value of continued interaction between those staff and organizations there to build trust and address concerns regarding CVE and current and future terrorism prevention efforts.[89]

    The presence of federal staff also could be a route to address what was framed as the "federal disruption problem"—where enforcement action by the FBI or U.S. Immigration and Customs Enforcement could occur in an area without warning and shatter efforts to maintain more-collaborative approaches to terrorism prevention.[90] One interviewee described this in the same terms as local police enforcement actions disrupting community policing activity, where what was needed was for "the chief to show up to talk to the community and explain what happened and why." Although there will be situations where enforcement actions need to be taken, the presence of federal field staff in an area means that there is someone locally who can step forward in an explanatory role.[91]

- **Federal Support of Local Initiatives**
  - **Use grant funding to support local and NGO intervention models and networks.** Although funding of intervention capability via federal grants is likely to be controversial, from the interviews in the cities we visited it was unclear

---

[88] One former federal leader interviewee put it bluntly: "I'd spend less time wrapping myself around the axle of strategy and just put more people in the field. In each place, it has to be invented around the conditions that prevail in that community, so get someone who is well equipped and backed by the federal government and turn them loose."

[89] Literature sources also argue for the importance of federal field staff (e.g., Levitt, 2017). Some of our interviewees raised cautions about the viability of this model in the current environment: "If you put out 25 offices around the [country and] called them something to do with terrorism prevention, in this political climate it would be a non-starter. The job of the federal government is to fund, grow, manage efforts" (Interview with an NGO representative, 2018).

[90] According to a former law enforcement interviewee: "If you're doing aggressive enforcement, you need to do aggressive explanations. It can't be on the local police because they don't know what you just did. Community engagement is needed to explain aggressive enforcement. If you have pivotal people in these areas who say they're doing a raid, I need my federal community policing people to explain what we're doing and why we're doing it."

[91] We touch on this operational and collaborative tension from the federal perspective in greater detail in Chapter Ten.

how local capacity would be strengthened without external financial support.[92] As a result, there appears to be a compelling rationale for its continuation. To the extent that federal field staff can build relationships and trust, the level of controversy may be reduced, making it possible for federal involvement to help accelerate local areas determining the type of terrorism prevention intervention they want and acting to put it in place. Stimulating "demand" to initiate programs in this area would appear to be needed to build out national-level coverage and capacity, as reflected in the smaller share of the FY 2016 grant applications that focused on intervention efforts compared with other facets of terrorism prevention.

There was a strong consensus across interviewees at the local level that incorporation of terrorism prevention capacity into existing general-purpose intervention networks was the preferable and more practical strategy. However, to the extent that intervention programs are supported that are ideology-specific, government investments as a portfolio should be balanced across ideological sources of violence, based on objective data on relative threat and prevalence.

One alternative delivery model to fund local development that came up in interviews that was different from the broad national grant solicitation and funding mechanism was linked to the deployment of federal field staff nationally. Providing a pool of funding that could be drawn on to support local projects (e.g., a few hundred thousand dollars per year that they could invest in activities at their discretion) could be a way to "localize" federal investments and reduce controversy and pushback. This was likened to funds that embassy staff have control of internationally for programs relevant to their countries of responsibility.[93]

– **Make "on-call experts" with knowledge, program design, and evaluation expertise available to support local terrorism prevention initiatives.** If fed-

---

[92] Note that other entities also have argued for a continued need for government support, even if other sources become available: "Even with increased private-sector and philanthropic investment in CVE, there will always be a need for government funding. The Commission supports the U.S. government's efforts to increase small grants for domestic and international efforts" (Green and Proctor, 2016, p. 61).

[93] A reviewer of this report pointed out that this strategy is not dissimilar to the use of federal formula grant money allocated to states to support terrorism prevention. Funding under the Byrne Memorial Justice Assistance grant was requested for some CVE efforts in FY 2016 and FY 2017 (DOJ, *FY 2016 Budget Request: State, Local and Tribal Assistance $3.5 Billion in Total Funding [Discretionary and Mandatory]: FY 2016 Overview*, Washington, D.C., 2015a; DOJ, *FY 2017 Budget Request: State, Local and Tribal Assistance $4.7 Billion in Total Funding [Discretionary and Mandatory]: FY 2017 Overview*, Washington, D.C., 2016b), and current grant guidance (Bureau of Justice Assistance, "Edward Byrne Memorial Justice Assistance Grant [JAG] Program, Frequently Asked Questions [FAQs]," Washington, D.C.: U.S. Department of Justice, August 2017) does state that support for CVE may be eligible under the grants (see discussions elsewhere in this report of the challenges that have been observed using general grant programs for CVE program support historically).

eral staff with expertise are not available, it was suggested that on-call experts could be used (at the state level or regionally) to support local intervention networks when needed.[94]

- **Prioritize supporting intervention capacity separate from law enforcement organizations, particularly in areas where trust is weakened.** Investment in non–law enforcement connected intervention capability also would be valuable for multiple reasons. Although localities should have autonomy in how they design their intervention approaches, a core argument of past criticism of CVE efforts has been that the programs are surveillance efforts to support arrest and prosecution. A focus on strengthening unambiguously nonpunitive intervention capability nationally would be a productive response to that critique. A significant investment in such a capability that is clearly separate from law enforcement could be viewed as a down payment on trust, particularly if the design and implementation of those efforts is done with the input of critical audiences.[95]

- **Explore alternative funding mechanisms for local initiatives.** There has been an ongoing call for the development of alternative funding streams for CVE (and, by extension, terrorism prevention) work, separate from the controversy surrounding government and federal support. For example, both in our interviews and in the literature, the potential utility of philanthropic funding as an apolitical source of support comes up repeatedly.[96] Funding from non-security agencies (e.g., as part of broader violence reduction grant programs) also came up repeatedly and meshed with the desire to integrate terrorism prevention into such broader efforts. Given capacity limitations in many service provision systems, devising ways to support their efforts without labeling them as participants in terrorism prevention does merit further consideration: One notional example identified during this research was whether reimbursement mechanisms—i.e., providing post hoc funding to a program that had provided services to an individual at risk of committing ideological violence rather than providing funds before the fact—might be less stigmatizing.

• **Awareness and Training**
  - **Continue federal efforts to assemble and disseminate best practices and standards for intervention programs.** One indirect path to facilitate intervention efforts identified by interviewees was the continuation of best-practices development and standards or guidelines for program implementation. Dis-

---

[94] Eisenman and Flavahan, 2017, p. 347; also discussed in previous chapters.

[95] For example, this point is argued by Patel and Koushik, 2017, p. 37.

[96] For example, DHS HSAC, 2016; Green and Procter, 2016; Bipartisan Policy Center, 2011; Peter R. Neumann, "Options and Strategies for Countering Online Radicalization in the United States," *Studies in Conflict and Terrorism*, Vol. 36, No. 6, 2013; Rosand, 2016; GAO, 2017.

semination of such products, as well as broader knowledge– and expertise-sharing across areas implementing programming, was viewed as important for cross-national learning and innovation.

- **Research and Evaluation**
  - **Continue to invest in the evaluation of intervention programs.** Given ongoing concerns regarding the effectiveness of past CVE, as well as current and potential future terrorism prevention interventions, a continued investment in evaluation is needed. Interviewees emphasized that evaluation needed to be built into programs such that the need to evaluate did not compete for resources needed by the program itself—i.e., that the drive to measure did not increase the chance of the assessed effort failing. Efforts to support the awareness and training initiatives are also relevant.[97]
  - **Prioritize research and evaluation efforts to better understand factors affecting the sustainability of terrorism prevention intervention programs.** In developing research and evaluation efforts, a central focus on the sustainability of terrorism prevention programs at the local level is needed to explore how to maintain capabilities over time.[98]

The theme of trust permeated the discussion of intervention—and not only trust issues with the federal government, but trust of government and law enforcement at the state and local levels as well. Some interviewees expressed the view that the federal government should just work "with the groups who were willing to work with it and get done what needs to get done." However, as a long-term strategy, such an approach seems risky, potentially meaning that future terrorism prevention efforts will be in as fragile a position as some of our interviewees described their efforts today. Opposition is not a reason to step aside either, as the arguments for intervention as an option are compelling, particularly as an alternative to the purely prosecutorial approach to terrorism risk that has been very damaging to community trust. But it does raise the level of difficulty in policy implementation, meaning that going forward, policy should not be driven by need alone but instead should be designed with critical concerns in mind (e.g., that programs address the full range of ideological sources of violence, that they not stigmatize communities) and implemented in a way that enables the intensive dia-

---

[97] A range of entities in the literature have called for greater evaluation efforts; see, e.g., Owens et al., 2016, p. 5-1; RTI International, 2017b; Green and Procter, 2016; Peter Romaniuk, *Does CVE Work? Lessons Learned from the Global Effort to Counter Violent Extremism*, Goshen, Ind.: Global Center on Cooperative Security, September 2015; Aggarwal, 2018, p. 6; Weine et al., 2015.

[98] This is similar to other efforts aimed at criminal justice initiatives more generally; see, e.g., Aharoni et al., 2014, for a review or Tillyer, Engel, and Lovins, who examined a violence reduction effort specifically (Tillyer, Marie Skubak, Robin S. Engel, and Brian Lovins, "Beyond Boston: Applying Theory to Understand and Address Sustainability Issues in Focused Deterrence Initiatives for Violence Reduction," *Crime and Delinquency*, Vol. 58, No. 6, 2012).

logue and engagement necessary to get to models of intervention in localities that are responsive not only to the needs of government and law enforcement, but also to community and civil liberties advocates.

CHAPTER EIGHT

Late-Phase Terrorism Prevention: Recidivism Reduction

In comparison with the multilayered challenges and sensitivities associated with intervention before individuals have committed a crime, activity focused on individuals who have been convicted of offenses related to terrorism is conceptually simpler. Simpler does not mean simple, however. Interviewees emphasized that the underlying crimes committed by terrorism-convicted offenders have varied considerably, ranging from attack planning to seeking to travel abroad to conflict areas. Since 9/11, there have been more than 650 individuals convicted of terrorism-related offenses associated with international terrorist groups, according to data released by DOJ. These individuals' sentences are wide-ranging, from time served and probation to life imprisonment, meaning that their time in custody (and therefore their time to participate in programming designed to reduce their potential risk of future ideologically inspired violence) also varies.[1] A similar list of convictions associated with domestic terrorism is not available, which is likely a result of differences in charging options and law at the federal level, which in turn creates a challenge for reporting and analysis (see Chapter Two). If we include only those individuals in federal custody on domestic terrorism–related charges, the number is 83,[2] although statistics on total prosecutions for domestic terrorism based on DOJ data reported counts of 60 to just more than 100 people per year over the last five years.[3]

In our interviews and in the literature, questions have also been raised about the impact incarceration has on commitment to ideological violence among those who are prosecuted and imprisoned for terrorist-related offenses. Although concerns have been raised that prison could be "terror-ogenic" in the same way that incarceration on its own can be criminogenic for some offenders,[4] interviewees we spoke with also

---

[1]   Human Rights First, "NSD Chart of Convictions 9-11-01 to 12-31-16," information released under FOIA, 2017.

[2]   Soufan Group, "TSG IntelBrief: Terrorism and Recidivism in the U.S.," August 8, 2017.

[3]   TRAC, "Domestic Terrorism Prosecutions Outnumber International," September 21, 2017; Hannah Fairfield and Tim Wallace, "The Terrorists in U.S. Prisons," *New York Times*, April 7, 2016.

[4]   For example, Avinash Singh Bhati, *An Information Theoretic Method for Estimating the Number of Crimes Averted by Incapacitation*, Washington, D.C.: Urban Institute, 2007; Gerald G. Gaes and Scott D. Camp, "Unin-

described cases where individuals' commitment to violence weakened during their sentences. As a result, there is considerable uncertainty regarding the most likely effect of incarceration on commitment to ideological violence.[5]

While such individuals are in custody, there have been varied levels of concern about the spread of extremism within corrections systems, including extremism associated with foreign terrorist groups (e.g., ISIS or al Qaeda–inspired individuals) and domestic violent movements (including white supremacist and sovereign citizen groups). This has been a central concern in Europe, resulting in the design of programs intended to address not just individual radicalization but the spread of extremism within institutions. In our interviews, perceptions of the seriousness of the risk of spreading radicalization in U.S. prisons were mixed, with more concern regarding the domestic violent movements (in the context of the larger issue of gang activity inside corrections institutions) than the spread of internationally inspired ideological violence.[6] Assessments in the literature also have suggested that radicalization to actual terrorist violence in U.S. prisons is rare,[7] although others have pointed to incidents in other countries where radicalization in prison was a step to actual terrorist violence.[8] Surveys of prison administrators and religious leaders have flagged groups with extremist beliefs as a relatively common challenge in facilities,[9] but that it "seldom

---

tended Consequences: Experimental Evidence for the Criminogenic Effect of Prison Security Level Placement on Post-Release Recidivism," *Journal of Experimental Criminology*, Vol. 5, No. 2, 2009; Lynne M. Vieraitis, Tomislav V. Kovandzic, and Thomas B. Marvell, "The Criminogenic Effects of Imprisonment: Evidence from State Panel Data, 1974–2002," *Criminology and Public Policy*, Vol. 6, No. 3, 2007; William D. Bales and Alex R. Piquero, "Assessing the Impact of Imprisonment on Recidivism," *Journal of Experimental Criminology*, Vol. 8, 2012; Susan M. Tarolla, Eric F. Wagner, Jonathan Rabinowitz, and Jonathan G. Tubman, "Understanding and Treating Juvenile Offenders: A Review of Current Knowledge and Future Directions," *Aggression and Violent Behavior*, Vol. 7, 2002.

[5]   See, for example, Bjelopera, 2015.

[6]   Interviews with representatives from federal, state, and local organizations, as well as from an NGO, 2018.

[7]   On radicalization to violence in U.S. prisons, see, for example, Mark S. Hamm, "Terrorist Recruitment in American Correctional Institutions: An Exploratory Study of Non-Traditional Faith Groups Final Report," National Criminal Justice Reference Service, December 2007; Frank Cilluffo, Gregory Saathoff, Jan Lane, Jeffrey Raynor, Sharon Cardash, Josh Magarik, Arnold Bogis, Andrew Whitehead, and Gina Lohr, *Out of the Shadows: Getting Ahead of Prisoner Radicalization*, Washington, D.C.: George Washington University Homeland Security Policy Institute, 2006; Bert Useem and Obie Clayton, "Radicalization of U.S. Prisoners," *Criminology and Public Policy*, Vol. 8, No. 3, 2009; and Andrew Silke and Tinka Veldhuis, "Countering Violent Extremism in Prisons: A Review of Key Recent Research and Critical Research Gaps," *Perspectives on Terrorism*, Vol. 11, No. 5, 2017.

[8]   On radicalization to violence internationally, see Cilluffo et al., 2006; and Alexander Meleagrou-Hitchens, Seamus Hughes, and Bennett Clifford, *The Travelers: American Jihadists in Syria and Iraq*, Washington, D.C.: George Washington University Program on Extremism, February 2018.

[9]   Linda M. Merola and Heather Vovak, "The Challenges of Terrorist and Extremist Prisoners: A Survey of U.S. Prisons," *Criminal Justice Policy Review*, Vol. 24, No. 6, 2012.

poses a threat to the security of the facility."[10] Other researchers have pointed out that prison experiences can have different effects: Exposure to religious information or learning opportunities (e.g., on the political dimensions of the conflict inmates were participants in) can have deradicalizing effects, but studies in some prisons have shown increases in radicalization in extremist inmates over time.[11] However, other prison-specific factors and social forces also can shape the effects on offenders incarcerated for terrorism-related crimes, including the effects of isolation and pressures to belong to in-facility groups.

As discussed in the chapter on threat, there are several domestic ideology–driven violent movements that are active as prison gangs whose activities do not necessarily meet definitions of terrorist activity.[12] For example, some white supremacist groups engage in a wide variety of criminal and violent activity, shaped by their racial ideology, but which may be defined as hate crimes rather than terrorist incidents.[13]

Because most terrorism convictions are not for life, many individuals associated with terrorist activity will be released into their communities.[14] This issue was a recurring theme in our interviews because a significant number of individuals convicted for material support and other offenses in the years following 9/11 are approaching their release dates.[15] It is also accepted that these individuals pose varied levels of risk to the community, ranging from significant in some cases to potentially no risk at all, and therefore merit different levels of supervision and programming.[16] As is the case for individuals convicted of other serious offenses, community corrections programming must balance intensity of monitoring and supervision to manage near-term risk of recidivism with the programming and opportunities to reintegrate the offenders into

---

[10] Stephanie C. Boddie, Cary Funk, et al., *Religion in Prisons: A 50-State Survey of Prison Chaplains*, Pew Research Center, Pew Forum on Religion and Public Life, March 22, 2012, p. 11.

[11] This is discussed in Silke and Veldhuis, 2017.

[12] In the terminology of corrections, these gangs are frequently designated as "security threat groups" within an institution, reflecting the significant threat they can pose to facility security and the safety of staff and other inmates.

[13] Researchers have demonstrated parallel effects between hate crime on individuals not directly affected by the incident (i.e., influence of and creation of fear in wider audiences) which is a component of many definitions of terrorist violence (Barbara Perry and Shahid Alvi, "'We Are All Vulnerable': The *in terrorem* Effects of Hate Crimes," *International Review of Victimology*, Vol. 18, No. 1, 2011) and analyses of terrorist ethnonationalist conflicts have included consideration of hate crime as a component (e.g., Roger MacGinty, "Ethno-National Conflict and Hate Crime," *American Behavioral Scientist*, Vol. 45, No. 4, 2001).

[14] See, for example, Michael Brown, "Freed: Ripples of the Convicted and Released Terrorist in America," thesis, Monterey, Calif.: Naval Postgraduate School, 2011, for a review.

[15] Horgan, Shortland, and Abbasciano (2018) have developed a typology of terrorist involvement intended to help systematize distinctions to support sentencing and other decisions.

[16] See, for example, RAN, *Preventing Radicalisation to Terrorism and Violent Extremism: Approaches and Practices*, Brussels, Belgium, 2017, Chapter 9.

society and reduce the risk of recidivism over the longer term.[17] Activities in this facet of terrorism prevention are captured in the bottom-right part of our mapping, the relevant section of which is reproduced in Figure 8.1.

Relevant Design Challenges

In considering the main design challenges affecting terrorism prevention efforts in this phase, there are common issues between intervention and recidivism-reduction efforts. A central issue is scale—the numbers of individuals incarcerated for terrorism-related offenses is relatively small compared with the total inmate population. As a result, efforts here face the same challenge as intervention, where program design must take practicality into account because sustaining dedicated resources and capabilities focused on terrorism may be difficult. The split of some offenders between the federal and state systems—particularly for domestic terrorism—divides the individuals potentially needing such programming among many different systems, further complicating programming. Efforts focused on post-release recidivism reduction face the same types of multiagency coordination concerns as intervention programs (e.g., among government and service-provider organizations), but have the additional requirement of coordination among institutional corrections agencies and their community corrections counterparts. Both are also sensitive to risk because of the multifaceted consequences if an individual who was released from custody carried out subsequent terrorist activity.

Spectrum of Approaches for Recidivism Reduction

Assessment of current terrorism prevention activities and potential future changes in policy and programming can be informed by terrorism-specific approaches in the United States and other countries as well as by efforts aimed at addressing recidivism concerns for other types of crime. Understanding of what is known about the effectiveness of terrorism prevention in the post-conviction and release space also can be supplemented by evaluation of analogous programs, informing terrorism risk reduction with lessons learned in previous efforts to address other social problems and risks.

---

[17] See, for example, Global Counterterrorism Forum (GCTF), *Rome Memorandum on Good Practices for Rehabilitation and Reintegration of Violent Extremist Offenders*, undated; Tinka M. Veldhuis, *Reintegrating Violent Extremist Offenders: Policy Questions and Lessons Learned*, Washington, D.C.: George Washington University Program on Extremism, October 2015; and RAN, RAN P&P Practitioners' Working Paper: *Approaches to Violent Extremist Offenders and Countering Radicalisation in Prisons and Probation*, Brussels, Belgium, 2nd ed., 2016a.

Figure 8.1
Recidivism Reduction Within the Terrorism Prevention Policy Space

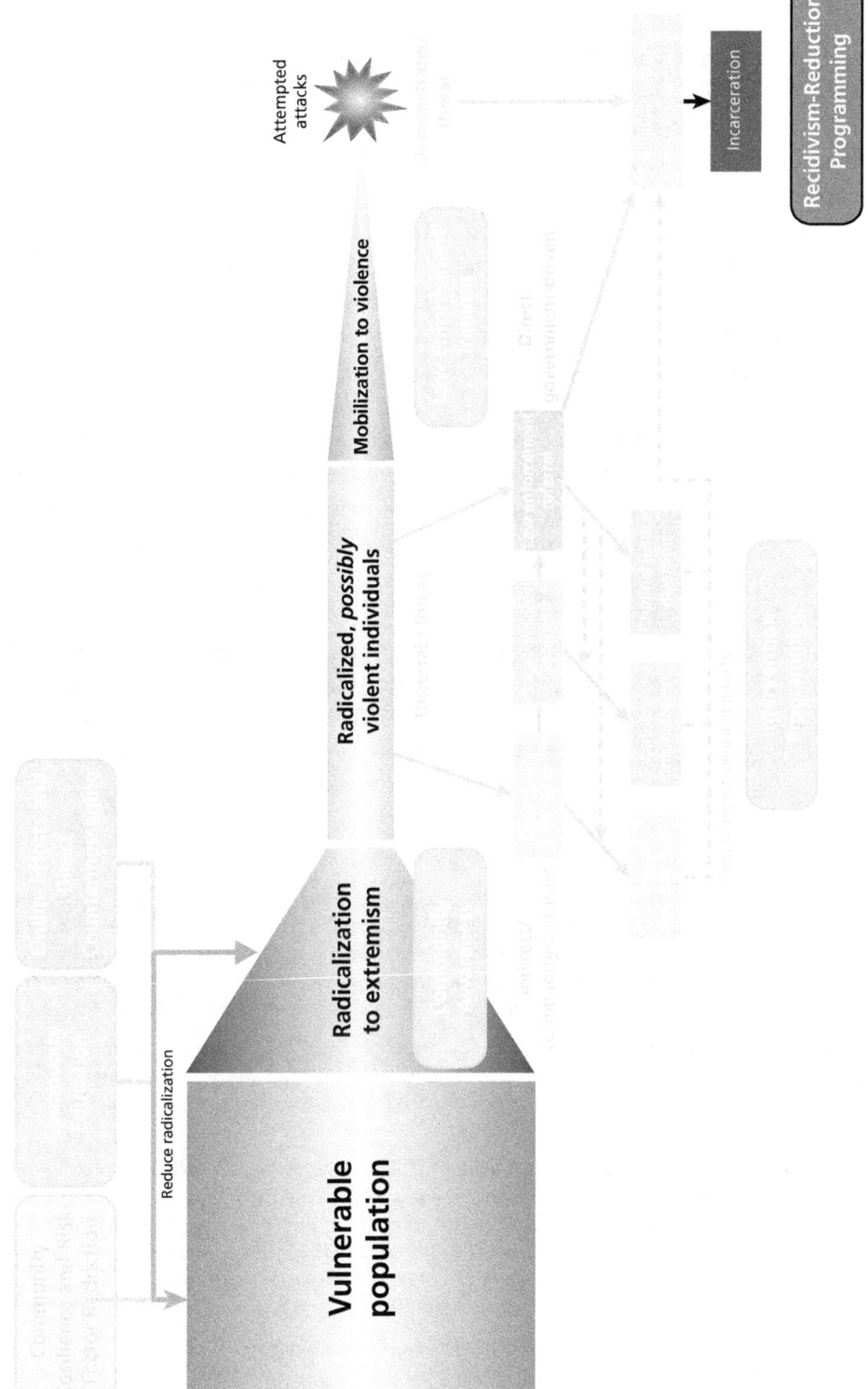

RAND RR2647-8.1

Policies and Programming

There has been greater development of approaches seeking to manage individuals during incarceration and reduce recidivism among individuals convicted of terrorism-related offenses in other nations. Other countries have had more individuals incarcerated for terrorism-related offenses and larger numbers of returnees from areas of conflict who may pose a risk of violence inside the country. For the same reason that they are needed to guide middle-phase intervention, there have been efforts to develop specific risk-assessment tools to attempt to distinguish levels of violence risk among individuals convicted of terrorism-related crimes. The methods mentioned most frequently in our interviews were the Extremism Risk Guidelines, or ERG 22+, which was developed in the United Kingdom; and the Violent Extremist Risk Assessment, or VERA-2, which was developed in Canada.[18]

Within correctional institutions, there is a menu of practices with which to approach offender management to address risk. These practices fall along a spectrum, from concentrating individuals convicted of violent extremist offenses together in one facility ("containment")[19] to integrating extremist offenders within the general population ("dispersal").[20] Programming within the prison context includes psychological counseling; religious counseling and support (e.g., prison chaplaincy to counsel individuals whose extremist beliefs are linked to religious traditions); and various types of social support, like family counseling, occupational counseling, and other programming.[21] Specific interventions aimed at at-risk juveniles also have been developed.[22]

In the probation and post-release environment, European countries in particular have developed CVE programming focused on reducing return to violence both by the

---

[18] These and other methods are reviewed in RTI International, 2017a.

[19] Some European experiences are cautionary in terms of containment strategies: France's attempts to counter radicalization have been viewed as largely counterproductive in that they have actually served to "radicalize the moderates." France has sought to counter radicalization and deradicalize inmates by isolating extremists in separate prison wings. However, this has served to further radicalize less extreme inmates by placing them in proximity to the most radical prisoners and has prompted an increase in attacks on prison guards.

[20] RAN, 2017, p. 408; Silke and Vehdhuis, 2017; United Nations Office of Drugs and Crime (UNODC), *Handbook on the Management of Violent Extremist Prisoners and the Prevention of Radicalization to Violence in Prisons*, New York: United Nations, 2016, Chapter 7; Andrew Silke, ed., *Prisons, Terrorism and Extremism: Critical Issues in Management, Radicalization and Reform*, New York: Routledge, 2014a.

[21] UNODC, 2016, Chapters 5 and 8; and Tinka Veldhuis, *Designing Rehabilitation and Reintegration Programmes for Violent Extremist Offenders: A Realist Approach*, The Hague, Netherlands: International Centre for Counter-Terrorism, March 2012. Because the commonality in the types of programming required for individuals convicted of extremist-related violence had significant overlap with programming needed for "standard violent offenders," there was a range of views among our interviewees about the need for specialized programming for individuals convicted of extremist violence versus adapting usual programming to meet their needs.

[22] Reviewed in Melissa Lefas and Junko Nozawa, *Rehabilitating Juvenile Violent Extremist Offenders in Detention: Advancing a Juvenile Justice Approach*, The Hague, Netherlands: International Centre for Counter-Terrorism, Global Center on Cooperative Security, December 2016.

formerly incarcerated and by individuals who have returned home after travel to fight in areas of conflict. RAN and GCTF review several such programs that combine various types of counseling, involvement of family members or social network members in programming, and other supervision mechanisms.[23] Other countries are also using multiagency and multidisciplinary structures to manage individuals post-release.[24] Stringent monitoring and reentry conditions in the course of supervised release are also used to address risk concerns, but also to deter recidivism and to modify individual behavior.[25]

However, particularly because there is significant commonality in the services and programming needed for extremist and nonextremist offenders, policy options to respond to individuals in prison or supervision associated with terrorism can draw from the broader palette of policies focused on criminal offending. There is a wide variety of programming used both in institutional corrections and in community supervision for offenders of various types, including psychological counseling, counseling focused on specific types of violence propensity, drug and alcohol treatment, mental health treatment for underlying disorders or issues, educational programs, anger management and life skills, and vocational training. Treatment approaches aimed at juvenile offenders (given concerns about youth radicalization, particularly from online sources) are also relevant.[26]

In considering the application of existing policy and programming options to ideologically motivated violence, the most direct analogy from other offending appears to be hate and bias-motivated crime. As described in the previous section, there is a significant presence of prison gangs or security threat groups whose ideologies center on racial or other hatred. Programming focused on rehabilitating such offenders and reducing their propensity to commit additional hate or bias-driven crimes upon release could provide best practices and options for terrorism prevention efforts. Review of the literature in search of such a knowledge base resulted in relatively modest results. Researchers have advocated for the use of rehabilitative programming with respect to hate crime for both adult and juvenile offenders while describing a general lack of existing capacity to do so.[27] There has been some work on risk assessment issues

---

[23] RAN, 2017; and GCTF, undated.

[24] See, for example, Emma Disley, Mafalda Pardal, Kristin Weed, and Anaïs Reding, *Using Multi Agency Public Protection Arrangements to Manage and Supervise Terrorist Offenders: Findings from an Exploratory Study*, Cambridge, UK: RAND Europe, RR-441-RE, 2016.

[25] However, research has also indicated that stringent supervision can create barriers to reentry and reintegration into the community. As a result, a balance must be managed between their potential positive and negative effects.

[26] Reviewed in Tarolla, et al., 2002.

[27] For adult offenders, see, e.g., Laura Meli, "Hate Crime and Punishment: Why Typical Punishment Does Not Fit the Crime," *University of Illinois Law Review*, Vol. 2014, No. 3, 2014. For juvenile offenders, see, e.g., Jordan Blair Woods, "Addressing Youth Bias Crime," *UCLA Law Review*, Vol. 56, 2009.

associated with hate crime and how characteristics of crimes and offenders should shape sanctions and responses,[28] although a relatively recent review by an expert in the field summarized that "there is virtually no literature that explores direct non-punitive interventions with hate crime offenders."[29] A 2011 review of intervention efforts (with some overlap with programming aimed at ideological extremism and terrorism) was prepared for the Equality and Human Rights Commission in Scotland, and identified a number of programs, including some in the United States. The programming included group activities aimed at changing behavior and views, efforts to build trust between counselors and facilitators and offenders, anger management training, educational programming, community service, individual reflection, and "apology and acts of redemption."[30] However, many of the programs identified, including most of those in the United States, had "mostly ceased to function, usually because of problems of funding."[31]

Evidence for Effectiveness

The general consensus in the research literature is that evidence for the effectiveness of both prison and post-release programming is limited. In a 2017 review, Silke and Veldhuis described the evidence base for prison-based programming as "scarce."[32] They described two well-evaluated interventions, one in Indonesia and one in Sri Lanka, that did show evidence of success.[33] Regarding probation and post-release programs, Veldhuis reached a similar overarching conclusion: "the main challenges in reintegrating violent extremists is that little evidence exists concerning what does and does not work."[34] In Silke and Veldhuis's review, only one evaluation of a Danish program is described that involved a very small sample of offenders.[35] There are reported recidi-

---

[28] See, for example, Jack McDevitt, Jack Levin, and Susan Bennett, "Hate Crime Offenders: An Expanded Typology," *Journal of Social Issues*, Vol. 58, No. 2, 2002; and Edward Dunbar, Jary Quinones, and Desiree A. Crevecoeur, "Assessment of Hate Crime Offenders: The Role of Bias Intent in Examining Violence Risk," *Journal of Forensic Psychology Practice*, Vol. 5, No. 1, 2005.

[29] Perry, 2010, p. 30.

[30] Paul Iganski, David Smith, et al., *Rehabilitation of Hate Crime Offenders: Research Report*, Equality and Human Rights Commission (Scotland), Spring 2011, pp. 44–45.

[31] Iganski, Smith, et al., 2011, p. 7.

[32] Silke and Veldhuis, 2017, p. 5.

[33] Silke and Veldhuis, 2017; and David Webber, Marina Chernikova, Arie W. Kruglanski, Michele J. Gelfand, Malkanthi Hettiarachchi, Rohan Gunaratna, Marc-Andre Lafreniere, and Jocelyn J. Belanger, "Deradicalizing Detained Terrorists," *Political Psychology*, Vol. 39, No. 3, 2018.

[34] Veldhuis, 2015, p. 3.

[35] The Danish Ministry of Social Affairs and Integration and the Danish Prison and Probation Service collaborated to launch a program called "Back on Track" in 2011. Back on Track began as a three-year program designed to deradicalize inmates that adopted extremist ideologies. The program provides inmates with mentors that help redirect them to a noncriminal or nonterrorist lifestyle by sharing personal experiences, involving the inmates'

vism rates for programs in some other nations (e.g., Saudi Arabia), but the nature of those programs and the contexts in which they are implemented mean that their applicability to the U.S. context is unclear.[36]

There are also concerns about the validation of risk assessment tools and, therefore, their use guiding decisionmaking.[37] Although concerns about the tools' validity are exacerbated by the low base rates for terrorism offenders, concerns about risk assessment for radicalization to violence reflect broader concerns about the performance of actuarial risk assessment tools in criminal justice. Smith has examined these tools in light of research efforts supported by the National Institute of Justice, showing that these tools cover most (although not all) of the risk factors for group-based and lone-actor terrorism in the United States.[38] Given the seriousness of being found "at risk" for terrorism-related recidivism, there has been external scrutiny on the risk-assessment tools being developed.[39]

However, looking at criminal justice more broadly, there is an evidence base for the effect of correctional programming on the likelihood of recidivism. Lipsey and Cullen examined the available evidence for the effectiveness of a range of correctional programming delivered in both institutional and community contexts, and showed that "the mean recidivism effects found in studies of rehabilitation treatment, by comparison, are consistently positive and relatively large."[40] McGuire reached a similar conclusion in a review examining both programming aimed at recidivism in general and violence reduction in particular.[41] In more-recent work, based on a meta-analysis of a large body of studies, Davis et al. found significant effects on recidivism from correctional education programs delivered to inmates in custody.[42] In a meta-analysis look-

---

support networks of family and friends, and assisting with post-release reintegration efforts, such as finding a job or a place to live. Although there is not yet enough data or evaluation to determine how successful Denmark's deradicalization programs have been, its efforts have been applauded for focusing on reintegration.

[36] See discussion in Horgan and Braddock, 2010.

[37] For a review, see Andrew Silke, "Risk Assessment of Terrorist and Extremist Prisoners," in Andrew Silke, ed., *Prisons, Terrorism and Extremism: Critical Issues in Management, Radicalization and Reform*, New York: Routledge, 2014b, pp. 108–121; and RTI International, 2017a.

[38] Allison G. Smith, *Risk Factors and Indicators Associated with Radicalization to Terrorism in the United States: What Research Sponsored by the National Institute of Justice Tells Us*, Washington, D.C.: U.S. Department of Justice, National Institute of Justice, NCJ 251789, June 2018.

[39] This concept is described in Alice Ross, "Academics Criticise Anti-Radicalisation Strategy in Open Letter," *Guardian*, September 28, 2016.

[40] Mark W. Lipsey and Francis T. Cullen, "The Effectiveness of Correctional Rehabilitation: A Review of Systematic Reviews," *Annual Review of Law and Social Science*, Vol. 3, 2007, p. 297.

[41] James McGuire, "A Review of Effective Interventions for Reducing Aggression and Violence," *Philosophical Transactions of the Royal Society B: Biological Sciences*, Vol. 363, 2008.

[42] Lois M. Davis, Robert Bozick, Jennifer L. Steele, Jessica Saunders, and Jeremy N. V. Miles, *Evaluating the Effectiveness of Correctional Education: A Meta-Analysis of Programs that Provide Education to Incarcerated Adults*,

ing at reentry programing both inside and outside institutional contexts, Ndrecka also found beneficial (although modest) reductions in recidivism for a variety of such programming.[43] In a review of evaluations of purely post-release programming, Davis et al. found strong evidence for reductions in recidivism from some counseling programs and drug treatment.[44] For other interventions, there was either evidence that such programs were not effective in reducing recidivism or the available evidence was inclusive, including for some specialized counseling efforts, vocational programs, and education delivered in community programs. Examinations of programs targeting hate crime also have shown evidence for effectiveness and significant reductions in recidivism rates versus comparable offenders.[45]

Current U.S. Terrorism Prevention and Related Efforts for Recidivism Reduction

Based on review of available literature and project interviews, it appears that current national efforts in this area are quite modest. Several interviewees had strong views of the capacity to meet the needs of individuals convicted of terrorism-related offenses in the United States: "We're now about to see fairly significant problems with people convicted of terrorism-related offenses coming out of jail and there are zero programs for them."[46] "Most people in the field understand the need to do something but there's absolutely nothing [available]."[47] Interviewees largely ascribed the shortfalls to resourcing: "There hasn't been enough money put behind these initiatives. We have people . . . getting out who will be walking the streets and we have nothing behind it. . . . It's about money."[48] As is the case for middle-phase intervention, there is general programming available to offenders that is not terrorism-specific. However, in contrast to the consensus view that general programs might be superior to terrorism-focused ones for intervention, the quotes above demonstrated a concern among several of our interviewees that the same is not true for this facet of terrorism prevention.

We identified several different training activities and training development efforts addressing concerns about radicalization in prisons that have been part of past CVE

Santa Monica, Calif.: RAND Corporation, RR-266-BJA, 2013.

[43] Mirlinda Ndrecka, "The Impact of Reentry Programs on Recidivism: A Meta-Analysis," dissertation, Cincinnati, Oh.: University of Cincinnati, Division of Criminal Justice, 2014.

[44] Robert C. Davis, Lila Rabinovich, Jennifer Rubin, Beau Kilmer, and Paul Heaton, *A Synthesis of Literature on the Effectiveness of Community Orders*, Cambridge, UK: RAND Europe, TR-518-NAO, 2008.

[45] Iganski, Smith, et al., 2011.

[46] Interview with a policy researcher, 2018.

[47] Interview with a former federal official, 2018.

[48] Interview with a federal representative, 2018.

efforts. Going back to efforts of the National Engagement Task Force in 2013, initiatives included a DHS effort in partnership with local corrections officials; a collaboration between the National JTTF, the Bureau of Prisons (BOP), and the Interagency Threat Assessment Coordination Group; and a FEMA training development effort aimed at rural corrections personnel.[49] The annual training by BOP has been similarly released.[50] A DHS assessment in 2013 indicated that training on prison radicalization issues was relatively available.[51]

With respect to programming in facilities at the state and local levels, available information suggests that capability is limited. Early in CVE efforts (referenced in the 2011 SIP), there were reportedly activities to "assess the capacity of state correctional institutions to detect and share information on individuals with indicators of extremist behaviors."[52] State- and local-level formative documents also pointed to the need for corrections-focused capability early in U.S. CVE efforts (e.g., the Massachusetts Framework produced by a multi-organization group in the Greater Boston region). Based on discussions with a convenience sample of state and local institutional corrections officials during the course of this research, it appears that there is limited capacity in place, if any.[53] In the FY 2016 CVE grant awards, there were two grants that focused on corrections and recidivism issues, representing federal investment in state and local capability in the terrorism prevention area. One program was run by the Alameda County Sheriff's Office in California and focused on "provid[ing] evidence-based, culturally relevant mental health and support services to justice-involved individuals-at-risk for radicalization"; the other was a project with the Massachusetts Department of Corrections that was focused on delivery of "behavioral health treatment and assertive connections to culturally appropriate pro-social outlets, educational/employment opportunities, family activities and other transitional services known to build resilience and reduce the risk of violence."[54]

---

[49] DHS, Countering Violent Extremism Records, multiple dates; DHS, 2015b, pp. 6–7.

[50] BOP, "Countering Inmate Extremism: Annual Training 2017," briefing, released under the Freedom of Information Act, January 2017.

[51] Jill Rhodes, "Countering Violent Extremism: Law Enforcement Perspectives, Training and Information Needs," Released under the Freedom of Information Act, DHS-01-002347, 2013.

[52] EOP, 2011b.

[53] In support of this conclusion, when there was a requirement for programming in the Federal District Court in Minneapolis, there was a federal effort to identify whether capability that could be drawn on existed anywhere else in the country: The conclusion was that it did not (Kelly Berkell, "Risk Reduction in Terrorism Cases: Sentencing and the Post-Conviction Environment," *Journal for Deradicalization*, No. 13, Winter 2017/18, p. 324).

[54] Alameda County Sheriff's Office, "FY16 CVE Grant Application, EMW-2016-CA-APP-00087," Released under the Freedom of Information Act, 2016; Massachusetts Executive Office of Public Safety and Security, "FY16 CVE Grant Application, EMW-2016-CA-APP-00336," Released under the Freedom of Information Act, 2016.

At the federal level, with respect to programming in custody, publicly available information indicates that the federal Bureau of Prisons does not have specific programs for inmates serving terrorism-related sentences,[55] but our understanding from interviews is that efforts are examining the potential for such programming and are approaching the issue in a way that is not specific to individual ideological sources of violence.[56] On a voluntary basis, all inmates in federal facilities (including those incarcerated for terrorism-related offenses) have access to a range of programs, including mental health counseling and therapy and educational programs. Monitoring, coupled with a range of programming types, is being implemented in the post-release supervision space by the Federal Probation and Pre-Trial Services Department for some terrorism offenders. Among the cities we visited, activity in the post-release programming space was concentrated in Minnesota given the presence of multiple offenders convicted of terrorism-related offenses in that federal court district, thereby mitigating the "small base rate" problem. The efforts in Minnesota have been described in published media and academic literature.[57] Although a central focus of that effort has been on individuals who sought to travel to participate in jihadist conflicts abroad, the approach is not ideologically specific; there are also white supremacist offenders being served by the program.

In the NGO space, Life After Hate's Exit USA program works with individuals from white supremacist organizations.[58]

In the relatively limited information we gathered during our interviews on corrections terrorism prevention programming, as was the case for intervention programming, it appears that multidisciplinary team–managed approaches are the preferred model. This is consistent with the literature on such programs from other countries.[59]

Assessment

Across our interviewees, there was a consensus that there is a need for recidivism-focused programming and that current efforts are not sufficient to meet it, particularly with increasing numbers of individuals slated to be released from custody. Although the main population cited to support this need was post-9/11 jihadist-inspired offenders who will be reaching the end of their sentences within a few years, a similar argu-

---

[55] Jessica Donati, "U.S. Prisons Allow Extremism to Fester, Study Warns," *Wall Street Journal*, February 6, 2018.

[56] Interviews of federal representatives, 2018.

[57] See, for example, Berkell, 2017/18; Dina Temple-Raston, "Jihad Rehab Program to Get Second Participant," *NPR*, February 11, 2016.

[58] Life After Hate, "ExitUSA," webpage, undated(a).

[59] See, for example, RAN, 2017, pp. 409–410.

ment would apply to individuals inspired by other ideologies. This assessment has been reflected in past public statements from DOJ itself:[60]

> "What happens when these folks start getting out?" asked John Carlin, who [headed] the Justice Department's national security division. "There are programs for drug addicts and gang members. There is not one with a proven track record of success for terrorism."

Although there are clearly efforts at the federal level at the developmental stage, national capability to address this need is currently limited.[61] The early-stage efforts being explored at the federal level both directly and through grant-funded efforts could provide seeds for broader capability building across the country, but the status of these efforts is in the experimental or pilot stage. Although we could identify the existence of training resources focused on the corrections sector, questions have been raised regarding how comprehensively training has been delivered across the federal, state, and local corrections sector—i.e., the effective level of knowledge of prison and probation staff at all levels. At such an early stage of implementation, it is impossible to assess how well current efforts will address the design challenges of practicality and multiagency coordination, although multidisciplinary models are being used in current federal-level supervision efforts.

The differences between charging terrorist offenders with foreign-inspired violent extremism (where individuals are generally charged with terrorism-related offenses) and domestic extremism (where charges can include federal hate crimes charges but often focus on state charges for underlying offenses, like murder) also were raised as a problem for prison and supervision. The split means that some ideologically inspired offenders are in the federal system and are clearly identified as terrorism offenders, while others are in state systems and are not identified as such. This complicates both full understanding of the population and efficient development and delivery of programming.

The limitations of risk assessment tools were also flagged as a problem affecting current efforts, although work with available options is underway at the federal level. There appears to be consensus, both in the literature and among the relevant subset of our interviewees, that the use of "standard" risk assessment tools for individuals involved in extremist violence does not work, because the risk factors and other elements involved are very different.[62] As one of our interviewees put it, "on standard

---

[60] Quoted in Nicole Hong, "Terror Convicts Pose Dilemma After Release from Prison," *Wall Street Journal*, February 16, 2016.

[61] This agrees with the assessment of the U.S. programs in Green and Procter, 2016, p. 40; Levitt, 2017, p. 22; and McKenzie, 2016.

[62] See Berkell, 2017/18, and references therein.

scales, these guys score as low risk."[63] As discussed above, there are specialized risk-assessment tools that have been developed in other nations that are focused on offenders convicted of terrorism-related crime and ideological violence. There are U.S. efforts examining those tools and applying them in the corrections programming that is being developed or is already in place. Improvement in corrections risk assessment would be valuable at all stages of the courts and corrections process to allow for more-nuanced decisions about sentencing, programming, and release conditions, potentially improving outcomes for society and the individual while limiting costs.

In the literature on programming to reintegrate individuals convicted of violent extremist offenses, three core barriers to success have been identified: (1) stigmatization of offenders as terrorists that reduces the chance that they can reintegrate into jobs and other support mechanisms that reduce risk; (2) trust issues between the public and offenders, mediated by program staff; and (3) stringent release conditions that may hamper reintegration.[64] In our work, interviewees raised the potential for stigma as a problem for U.S. efforts (and that ways to address the issue were not obvious). Conditions for release in current U.S. efforts are very stringent, which is not unexpected, given the need to manage risk and maintain community trust in reentry and reintegration efforts.[65] This suggests that U.S. efforts will face a similar tradeoff as implementation is formalized and broadened with a need to balance the stringency of programming (and risk management) with the need to loosen restrictions to allow individual-level reentry and reintegration success.[66] Challenges with stigma faced by released offenders who committed everyday crimes suggest that these will be continuing and formidable challenges to the effectiveness of recidivism-focused terrorism prevention programming.

Federal Options for Recidivism-Focused Policy and Programming

We have identified a range of options to address capacity shortfalls in this area.[67] Although addressing national-level capability requires connecting with and building

---

[63] Another interviewee pointed out that risk issues for pre-trial assessment versus prisoner behavior in custody are also quite different. In institutional corrections, one of the main concerns is whether an inmate presents a safety risk to himself or others and, compared with other types of violent criminals, individuals imprisoned on terrorism-related charges may not pose any problems from that perspective: "In prison, the main thing is they don't want people to cause any problem. These individuals would be model prisoners" (Interview with a federal representative, 2018).

[64] RAN, 2017, p. 411.

[65] Interview with a federal representative in a U.S. city, 2018.

[66] Interviews with government representatives, 2018.

[67] In the correctional context, researchers have flagged institutional conditions (e.g., overcrowding, stress) as risk factors for radicalization in prison (Silke and Veldhuis, 2017). As a result, policies designed to address such factors

capacity in state and local corrections agencies, there is a substantial space—driven by individuals convicted of terrorism-related offenses in the federal prison and post-release supervision systems—where federal action is both needed and can provide a starting point for national action. Federal options, based on published policy proposals, input from interviewees during the study, and analysis include the following:

- **Awareness and Training**
  - **Develop a customized CAB for corrections staff at the federal, state, and local levels.** In interviews and literature sources, there appears to be a relatively broad recognition of terrorism and ideological violence–related issues in corrections. The BOP has existing radicalization and ideological violence–focused training programs for which some information has been released publicly.[68] With respect to the state and local levels, an interviewee suggested that a low cost but potentially useful addition in this area would be the development of a corrections-focused CAB (similar to others developed by DHS and NCTC for law enforcement and more general audiences) that could help to maintain awareness of terrorism issues.[69]
  - **When appropriate, develop training to disseminate best practices and new evidence-based practices in the corrections sector.** As best practices are developed or risk assessment approaches are improved, training will be needed to disseminate new knowledge across corrections systems.[70]
- **Situational Awareness**
  - **Develop and maintain a centralized database of individuals incarcerated for ideological violence–related offenses to support program development and implementation.** To address the challenge of building national-level capacity to deliver recidivism-reducing programming to convicted terrorism offenders, the first step is knowing where violent offenders whose actions were motivated by ideology are located in both the federal and state systems. Interviewees both inside and outside government highlighted this as a solvable problem, where collection of centralized data on inmates and the details of their crimes could guide programming implementation decisions. To the

---

could advance the goal of terrorism prevention, but would be unlikely to be considered as terrorism prevention policies or programs.

[68] BOP, 2017.

[69] There are examples of similar efforts in other countries studied in this work: As part of Belgium's "Action Plan Against Radicalization in Prisons," the Belgian government adapted training material used in other counter-radicalization efforts, tailoring it to prison guards and staff across Belgium to help them identify signs of radicalization and concerning behavior. Similarly, the Danish Security and Intelligence Service released a handbook designed to train prison officials to identify signs of radicalization among inmates. See Appendix A for more information.

[70] See the discussion in Berkell, 2017/18, p. 322.

extent that such data collection could be broadened to include both terrorism-specific offenders (and the range of charges they might have been incarcerated under) and serious hate crime offenders, it could help implementers to navigate the unclear border between the two types of crimes.

- **Federal Program Development**
  - **Coordinate with (and assist, as appropriate) federal corrections agencies developing recidivism-reduction programming.** The locus of activity for federal program development must be with the agencies directly responsible for individuals in federal custody (the Bureau of Prisons and the Administrative Office of U.S. Courts/Probation and Pretrial Services). However, DHS and interagency partners could help to transfer knowledge and programming developed at the federal level to state and local corrections systems.[71] A significant amount of information is publicly available regarding ongoing activity on the post-release supervision side, particularly in the Minneapolis Federal District Court, which includes examination of risk assessment tools and programming options. Based on available information, activities with an in-custody focus are at an earlier, more exploratory stage. These efforts are developing programming that can be applied to multiple ideological sources of violence risk, and so reflect the consensus view that general programming can be a practical path for terrorism prevention efforts.

    Our interviewees identified two actions that could facilitate current activities: (1) developing training and expertise standards for service providers to be formally qualified to serve ideologically motivated violent offenders (relevant to both in-custody programming and post-release supervision);[72] and (2) supporting efforts by Federal Probation and Pretrial Services to build out its network of service providers to serve offenders approaching release. Although many needs are similar across offenders (and therefore can be served by the same types of service providers), agencies or staff need to be prepared to serve individuals convicted of terrorism-related offenses.[73] As is the case for intervention activities outside the criminal justice system for at-risk individuals, there will be issues of coordination and information-sharing between government

---

[71] This also is recommended in DHS HSAC, 2016.

[72] "For the average release, they already work with community members to reintegrate them. This would be more of the same but slightly different training. They wouldn't be dealing with the prison environment per se, but the release context. It's 2018—these issues have been live for at least five or six years, the need to rehabilitate these types of offenders. All sorts of programs and research has already been done" (Interview with a former federal and current NGO representative, 2018).

[73] Interview with a federal representative, 2018.

institutions and external service providers that will need to be navigated and practices developed to enable effective and efficient programming.[74]
  - **Support the development of program standards for intervention efforts to maintain effectiveness in decentralized implementation across the country.** Although our discussions indicated that there are already mechanisms for knowledge to be shared both across the federal corrections system and with state and local agencies (e.g., through existing coordination mechanisms, professional associations), efforts to disseminate knowledge and lessons learned would contribute to national-level capacity. As part of that effort, other researchers have raised the question of whether it would be valuable to explore "implement[ing] uniform, post-conviction procedures for risk reduction in the sentencing, incarceration, or post release realms of terrorism cases" both within the court system and in associated organizations.[75] Such standardization would reduce heterogeneity in the treatment of individual cases, but would also constrain future experimentation and efforts to adjust practices as more information and evaluation data are gathered.
- **Federal Support of Local Initiatives**
  - **Use grant funding to support state, local, and NGO implementation of recidivism-reduction programs.** Given resource constraints in corrections systems, federal grant support of program development is a potentially effective policy option to build out capability in this area. The FY 2016 grant program included two efforts focused on corrections needs, representing an initial investment. To the extent that local areas build effective networks for service provision, they could represent "modular building blocks" to assemble national capability to deliver services.[76]
- **Research and Evaluation**
  - **Continue to invest in evaluation of recidivism-reduction programs.** As with other areas of terrorism prevention, there are clear evaluation needs, including the assessment of the effectiveness of programming as it is implemented to guide improvement over time. In pursuit of practical strategies that can be implemented at the state and local levels in a resource-efficient way, research and evaluation efforts to determine the effectiveness of "standard" corrections programming (employment, education, counseling) versus programming that includes components specific to individual ideologies (e.g., availability of reli-

---

[74] Such information-sharing and coordination challenges are not unique to terrorism-related offenders, and exist in corrections more broadly.

[75] Berkell, 2017/18, p. 319.

[76] Local interviewees also pointed out that this is a less controversial facet of terrorism prevention: "We're dealing with folks who are already locked up. We're not targeting people to put in jail" (Interview with a local government representative in one U.S. city, 2018).

gious counseling offenders can choose to access) would potentially be valuable. The more that programs that are maintained for all offenders are effective for individuals convicted of supporting or participating in ideological violence, the more readily capacity can be sustained over time.

— **Continue research focused on improving risk-assessment methods, but realistically manage expectations for their possible accuracy.** Recognized shortfalls in risk assessment capability could be a target for research and development, although because of the low base rates of terrorism in the United States, it is unclear how large the potential increase in accuracy and precision would be, even with substantial increases in investment.[77]

— **Prioritize focused research and evaluation efforts to better understand the effect of incarceration on radicalization and violence risk.** Although this is a narrower question, research exploring the baseline effect of incarceration on ideological extremism and violence risk—i.e., is imprisonment "terrorogenic"?—would meet a need and provide a stronger foundation for decisions about investment in additional corrections programming. Better data on the frequency of individuals convicted of terrorism-related offenses recidivating after release would also contribute to resolving uncertainty related to the risk posed by this population and better inform resource allocation decisions.

Although the focus in this line of effort is on individuals who have been convicted of crimes, networks of capabilities developed to serve that population—particularly in the post-release context—could also strengthen broader intervention capability. At a minimum, knowledge-sharing between entities developing capabilities for probation-focused programming and organizations focused on intervention would benefit both.[78] However, in suggesting expansion of corrections programing in this area, we cannot ignore the resource constraints in the corrections system across the country that already limit implementation of programming in other areas.[79] To the extent that capabilities developed for terrorism prevention can serve other populations of specialized offenders (hate and bias crime offenders in particular), they would be more broadly beneficial and, therefore, potentially more sustainable. Given the limited capability in programming to rehabilitate such offenders, doing so would meet other important national needs.

---

[77] In addition, there appears to be ongoing effort focused on risk assessment both in other countries and in operational agencies.

[78] A similar recommendation was made by DHS HSAC, 2016, p. 17.

[79] This is analogous to the concern raised previously regarding adding intervention for ideological violence risk to existing counseling programs in the middle phase of terrorism prevention.

CHAPTER NINE

Assessing Resources Allocated to Terrorism Prevention Efforts

Because financial resources are finite, even programs responding to risks that pose significant concern cannot be funded in a wholly open-ended way. To address this funding question, we examine the resources that have been allocated to this policy area in the past and how potential future resources might be invested.

The question of resourcing is not a simple one. As discussed in the previous chapter, at any given time, *national* terrorism prevention efforts include activities at the local, state, and federal levels, and both inside and outside of government. Although our focus here is federal terrorism prevention policy and therefore our main interest is federal resourcing, understanding the complete picture requires considering investments and activities at other levels as well. Just as an understanding of the mental health or criminal justice systems would be incomplete without considering actions and programs below the federal level, so too would be an understanding of terrorism prevention efforts if we focused solely on federal-level resourcing.

However, taking a comprehensive view risks further blurring boundaries between terrorism prevention and non–terrorism related activity: for example, community engagement can be done for multiple purposes simultaneously and counseling programs might address a range of issues beyond radicalization and might not be viewed as or labeled as terrorism prevention efforts. That blurring means that the definition of "terrorism prevention funding" can be quite elastic in practice, with the ability to swell or shrink depending on how boundaries shift. Here we focus as much as possible on investments made for past CVE or current terrorism prevention purposes and therefore label accordingly, although some of these investments could have broader effects than just terrorism risk reduction and also could be devoted to coordinating among non–terrorism prevention programs or organizations that might address radicalization as part of broader service provision efforts.

In part because of these complexities, resourcing was an area of focus in many of the discussions held during the research effort, both at the national and at the state and local levels. Because our interviewees included individuals from all levels of government as well as practitioners with program implementation experience, we got a view of this issue from multiple perspectives reflecting different types of practical concerns. Overall, the view from our interviewees was that, over most of the federal history of CVE (summarized in Chapter One), funding allocated to the effort was very limited. Although federal agencies had some staff devoted to this area and strategy and implementation plans were developed and published, programming and funding largely did not follow. This disconnect led multiple interviewees to characterize national-level CVE policy using various versions of the idea that "federal CVE has been more talk than action."[1] During the "Pilot Period" (the time surrounding the 2015 White House CVE Summit), there was *very* limited specific federal funding committed to CVE activities, even though the policy rhetoric supporting CVE was substantial.[2] In interviews in multiple Pilot cities, individuals who were involved at the time described being disappointed in federal funding levels and described varying levels of success in finding resources at the state or local level to support their efforts.[3] Against that low baseline, the $10 million allocated to the FY 2016 grant program represented a significant increase in federal investment specific to CVE, with that funding awarded in calendar year 2017. Those projects have enabled the initiation of new CVE efforts in multiple areas around the country, allowing an expansion in efforts beyond the activities during the Pilot Period and providing a foundation for terrorism prevention efforts.

In the published literature, the level of funding of past CVE activities has been raised as a concern and several analysts have made proposals regarding potential funding levels.[4] In 2016, DHS HSAC recommended a significant increase in and stabilization of funding from the $3.1 million that had been allocated to create the OCP and the $10 million one-time appropriation for the FY 2016 CVE grant program to $100 million per fiscal year.[5] The Washington Institute for Near East Policy has labeled

---

[1]   It should be noted that, for a few interviewees, the modest funding allocated in the early stages of U.S. CVE efforts was viewed as appropriate, given where the country was at the time with respect to these policies, and also out of concern that significant increases in funding early on would have magnified the controversy surrounding CVE. There were also dissenters more broadly: "We can't buy our way out of this. If there was more money, it would go to law enforcement. The local, state governments don't want more money tied to a CT metric tied to Congress because then they can't apply the funding the way they need to [to] protect their community" (Interview with a federal representative, 2018).

[2]   This assessment is echoed in published scholarship on CVE efforts at the time: Vidino and Hughes (2015, pp. 7, 18) highlight the resource requirements that were identified by local areas involved in the Pilot effort (e.g., that the Boston framework document called for "surging resources to fund service providers") and that funding allocated at the federal level was "very limited," despite presidential-level statements and focus on the issue. This was echoed in our interviews: "The problem with the pilot cities was [that there was] no funding for their efforts" (Interview with a federal representative, 2018).

[3]   Interviews with multiple individuals in Boston and Minneapolis, 2018.

[4]   See, for example, RTI International, 2017b; Levitt, 2017; Rosand, 2016; Rosand, 2017a; and Vidino and Hughes, 2015.

[5]   DHS HSAC, 2016, p. 9.

activities in this area "drastically underfunded across the board."[6] The CSIS Commission on Countering Violent Extremism cited "a dearth of resources [as] a major barrier to galvanizing a CVE movement and scaling up promising initiatives" and endorsed the earlier recommendation to increase DHS partnerships–focused funding to $100 million but went further, recommending total funding for CVE across the domestic and international spaces of $1 billion.[7]

Our study sought to assemble a more complete picture of current resourcing of terrorism prevention (based largely on funding levels for past CVE efforts) and explored approaches to assess whether that resourcing level is appropriate, given the level of terrorist threat and other factors. The goal of this effort is not to demonstrate that terrorism prevention or CVE efforts preceding it are demonstrably effective—indeed, as we discussed in the chapters on the different facets of terrorism prevention, there are not evaluation data available to do so—or, in the absence of those data, that they are demonstrably cost-effective.

As points of comparison, we explored two complementary perspectives. First, we explored how U.S. investments in terrorism prevention compare with what is known about CVE expenditures in other countries. This approach was designed to delve into the argument made by interviewees that U.S. expenditures are low compared with those of other Western countries that also face the threat of individual radicalization to violence. Second, we used a variation of break-even analysis by looking at the types of costs that terrorism prevention has the potential to reduce: (1) criminal justice costs for responding to threats solely through investigation, arrest, and prosecution; and (2) potential costs from terrorist attacks.

Current Federal Spending on Terrorism Prevention

It is difficult to determine the level of funding devoted to terrorism prevention activities, largely because of the involvement of multiple agencies that support efforts from their own budgets and no central programmatic allocation for the efforts by Congress.

The best cross-agency information is available on terrorism prevention efforts funded via federal grants or contracts and, therefore, performed outside of government. Standing out from this group is the $10 million allocated to the FY 2016 Countering Violent Extremism grant program, whose awards were made by DHS in 2017. DOJ also has funded research efforts focused on CVE on an annual (and stable) basis for many years, at a level of $2–$3 million per year. Funding by other government agencies relevant to radicalization to violence inside the United States and related threat issues is modest. Figure 9.1 shows federal external funding for CVE-related projects,

---

[6]   Levitt, 2017, p. 22.

[7]   Green and Proctor, 2016, pp. 60–63.

averaging between $3 and $5 million per year (with the lower number calculated without the large distortion of the FY 2016 grant program allocation). The totals in the figure include projects supporting CVE programming (the majority of which is in the funding in 2017 as a result of the FY 2016 grant solicitation), research and evaluation (both supported by DHS S&T and the National Institute of Justice), and CVE training–related activities.[8]

Funding allocated to outside projects via grants and contracts is only one part of the full expenditure for terrorism prevention activity at the federal level, however. Participating agencies have costs associated with staff dedicated to these activities, as well as other expenditures. Even examinations of CVE activities by government audit and internal analytic agencies have not reported values for the full allocation of resources to this policy area. GAO reported only values for the budget for the then-OCP (now the OTPP), the grant program (which was carved out from a larger $50 million pool of funds for other efforts besides CVE), and an additional $1 million for a joint counterterrorism workshop.[9] An earlier examination by the Congressional Research Ser-

Figure 9.1
Federal Grant and Contract Funding Relevant to CVE by Agency, 2013–2017

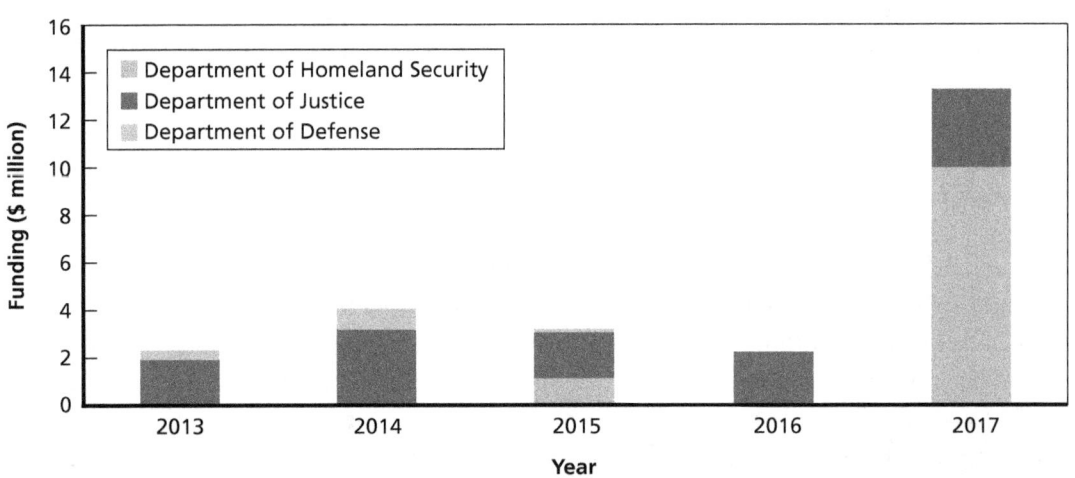

SOURCE: Data are from a USASpending.gov search for "CVE" or "violent extremism," eliminating all internationally focused projects.
NOTE: Funding is grouped by initial year in period of performance. DOJ/OJP grant values are replaced with fiscal year–reported grant funding values because keyword-matching was imperfect.
RAND RR2647-9.1

---

[8] For comparison, the funding for internationally focused CVE projects from the same data is significantly higher, approximately double the resources allocated inside the United States.

[9] GAO, 2017.

vice cited the challenge of determining "the levels of federal funding devoted to CVE efforts and how many personnel are devoted to CVE in the federal government."[10]

The greatest detail is available on DHS funding for past CVE and current terrorism prevention efforts, driven by required annual reporting to Congress and integrating data from across the department. In FY 2016, DHS allocated approximately $10 million to CVE initiatives (not including the $10 million in grant funding).[11] In FY 2017, this value dropped to $5.7 million for CVE.[12] Funding by DHS office and component is presented in Figure 9.2.

Based on approximate estimates from interviewees about the number of staff devoting some time to CVE or current terrorism prevention at NCTC, we estimate expenditures there to be on the order of $2 million, and therefore on the order of one-third—certainly less than one-half—of DHS's FY 2017 expenditures. Well-defined estimates of spending on past CVE efforts and current terrorism prevention initiatives by other agencies with roles in terrorism prevention— most notably, DOJ; the FBI; and

Figure 9.2
DHS Funding for Terrorism Prevention by Office or Component, FYs 2016 and 2017

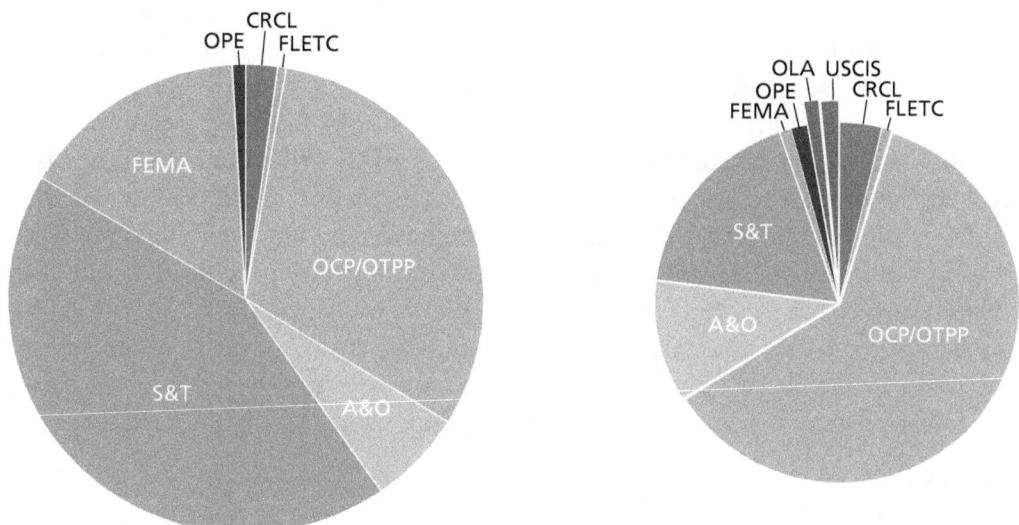

SOURCE: Data from DHS, 2016a; and DHS, 2018.
NOTES: A&O = Analysis and Operations; OPE = Office of Partnerships and Engagement; OLA = Office of Legislative Affairs; USCIS = United States Citizenship and Immigration Services. Size of the pie charts reflects year-over-year reduction in funding allocated to CVE and then terrorism prevention.
RAND RR2647-9.2

---

[10] Bjelopera, 2014, p. 28.

[11] DHS, 2016a.

[12] And, as of January 2017, for terrorism prevention (DHS, 2018).

components with corrections roles, like BOP and Administrative Office of U.S. Courts (AOUSC)—were not available in public budget documents or agency reporting.[13]

As a result, based on actual data available on terrorism prevention spending, the approximate annual total (using average annual grant expenditures, the most-recent-year estimate for DHS, and our estimate for NCTC) is between $12 and $13 million. This value does not include terrorism prevention activity from the criminal justice agencies of the federal government, although interviewees estimated that, at most, those expenditures would double the total (i.e., producing a value of between $20 and $30 million).[14]

Comparing the U.S. Terrorism Prevention Investments with CVE Expenditures in Other Western Democracies

To provide a point of comparison for U.S. terrorism prevention expenditures, we looked at spending levels on similar programs in other Western democracies in available public data.[15] Expenditure data for other nations were not always readily available. In some cases, overarching numbers for counterterrorism expenditures are published, but the subset of those efforts that make up CVE activities are not. Sources were more often press reporting or analyses by other researchers rather than official government documents, making the reliability of available data difficult to assess independently. Sometimes funding values could not be identified, even for CVE programs that had been publicly described in each country (e.g., programs described as carried out by a national law enforcement organization might not have separate funding levels published). In using the data that we could gather, we have not sought to make a specific estimate for a defined calendar year; instead, we take values from the most recent years available as the basis for a rough estimate of CVE effort in the country.

As a result, these estimates, and their extrapolation as a point of comparison to the United States, must be viewed as approximate and interpreted with a healthy degree of skepticism, as they provide a relative comparison of magnitude rather than

---

[13] The exception was that some values were included in submitted FY 2017 Budget Request documents from DOJ or its component agencies requesting increases in funding for CVE efforts. For example, in its National Security budget request, DOJ requested $17–$20 million in additional funds (including program funds and personnel) for CVE (DOJ, *FY 2017 Budget Request: National Security*, press release, 2016a). A value supposedly for total 2017 requested DOJ and DHS CVE expenditures also appeared in the FY 2017 Performance Budget for the DOJ Office of Community Oriented Policing Services (DOJ, *FY 2017 Performance Budget: Office of Community Oriented Policing Services*, 2016c, p. 10). That value ($69 million)—after subtracting all available information on the proposed increases for programs that would have been included in that total—produced a result for DHS and DOJ that was viewed as exaggerating the expenditure level for past CVE or current terrorism prevention efforts.

[14] Interview with a federal representative, 2018.

[15] These efforts are labeled as *CVE* rather than *terrorism prevention* to reflect the terminology still used in most of the other countries we studied.

a precise estimate. Table 9.1 summarizes the budget numbers that could be identified, the sources in which they were found, and the average value used in our comparison/ extrapolation to the United States. However, given limits in available information on other countries' programs, it is more likely that we have missed expenditures on CVE (skewing our estimates low in the comparison) than that the numbers are artificially high.

In considering how to relate other nations' spending to the resources that have been allocated to terrorism prevention in the United States, we approached the comparison using two different characteristics: the level of terrorist threat and the scale of the implementation requirements associated with terrorism prevention from the national perspective.

- With respect to threat, measures that have been used at the national level include numbers of terrorist attacks or attempted attacks and the extent of U.S. citizen travel to and from areas of conflict to participate as foreign fighters. Because travel by U.S. citizens and their return after fighting has not been a central driver of threat[16] and because such travel is associated with only one ideological source of terrorism, use of foreign fighter numbers did not appear to be a good proxy for comparison. As a result, we used reported numbers of terrorist attacks from 2001 to 2016 to compare the intensity of threat in each nation.[17]
- For a measure of implementation requirements for terrorism prevention programming,[18] two factors were considered: the total area of the countries (as a basic reflection of geographic spread) and the total population (as a measure reflecting the relative scale of programs needed). Given that differences in population density and distribution from country to country suggest that using area would be potentially misleading, we used total national population for comparison.

To extrapolate from other countries' spending to make an estimate for levels of U.S. investment, the mathematically simplest way is to calculate each country's spending per terrorist attack or spending per million population and apply the range of

---

[16] Barrett, 2017.

[17] Based on data from START, undated(a), including attacks during the years 2001–2016, inclusive, using the database's most stringent criteria for defining terrorism and excluding ambiguous cases. Searches were performed in June 2018.

[18] One reviewer of this document pointed out that the United States' federal system, with its inherent decentralization, also can affect the cost of implementation of programming on a national basis. Although decentralization of implementation of CVE efforts in other nations was explored in our international case studies (see Appendix A), it was not clear how we were to account for that variable in this type of approximate cross-comparison of countries' funding levels.

Table 9.1
Available Annual Expenditure Estimates on CVE in Other Western Democracies

Country	Annual Estimates in Millions of U.S. Dollars	Average Value ($ million)
Germany	$14 for Ministry of Interior programs[a] $34 for other Ministry programs[b] $59 in 2016 and $118 in 2017 for the Live Democracy! program[a]	137
Canada	$5–$8 for government funding for national-level Centre[c] $1–$1.5, potentially increasing to $5 for a resilience fund[c] $1.5 annually for completed five-year Kanishka research program, 2011–2015[d] $2 for city funding for a counter radicalization center[e]	13
United Kingdom	$62 for PREVENT Program estimate[f]	62
Australia	$2.5 of $10 for national program over four years[g] $4.5 for Australian Federal Police Community Diversion and Monitoring Team[g] $1 of $2 in grants awarded in 2014–2015 under the Living Safe Together Grants Programme[g] $4 of $16 for four-year Combatting Terrorist Propaganda program, 2015–2016 Budget[g] $3 for Community Support and Advice Services, 2016–2017 Budget[g] $2.5 of an estimated total of $10 through the Australia New Zealand Counter-Terrorism Committee for CVE efforts in Australia, including state-level programs over multiple years[g] Provincial programs: $19 over a four-year program, Victoria social cohesion program, 2015–2019[h] $38 for New South Wales schools and social cohesion program, unclear time frame[h,i]	17.5 + 14 = 32[k]
France	$45 for national program funding, 1.5–2.5-year period, 2016–2018[j]	24

NOTES: Budget values could not be identified for our two other case study countries, Belgium and Denmark.

[a] DOS, Bureau of Counterterrorism, *Country Reports on Terrorism 2016*, Chapter 2, Country Reports: Europe, July 2017.

[b] Vidhya Ramalingam and Henry Tuck, *The Need for Exit Programmes*, London: Institute for Strategic Dialogue, September 2014; citing government interviews.

[c] Cision Canada, "New Canada Centre for Community Engagement and Prevention of Violence Supports Local Efforts," news release, June 26, 2017.

[d] Public Safety Canada, *2015–2016 Evaluation of the Kanishka Project Research Initiative*, March 17, 2016.

[e] Jillian D'Amours, "Canada's New 'Anti-Radicalisation' Office Met with Caution by Muslim Community," *Middle East Eye*, March 25, 2016.

[f] BBC, "Reality Check: What Is the Prevent Strategy?" June 4, 2017.

[g] Cat Barker, "Update on Australian Government Measures to Counter Violent Extremism: A Quick Guide," Parliament of Australia, August 18, 2017.

[h] Eric Rosand, "When It Comes to CVE, the United States Stands to Learn a Lot from Others. Will It?" *Lawfare* blog, September 10, 2017b.

[i] New South Wales Government, *Countering Violent Extremism in NSW*, fact sheet, November 2015.

[j] Lisa Bryant, "France Outlines New Plan to Fight Extremism," *Voice of America*, May 9, 2016.

[k] For estimation purposes, the total provincial spending identified for Australia was assumed to be divided over four years.

results to the corresponding U.S. values (see Table 9.2). The values on both measures vary widely across the countries:

- The spending-per-incident values range from a low of approximately $70,000 (France) to a high of approximately $900,000 (Germany and Australia). Using those extremes results in U.S. estimates ranging from approximately $20 million to $275 million, with the mean result of approximately $142 million.[19]
- The spending-per-million-population values range from approximately $360,000 (Canada) to a high of $1.7 million (Germany). Using these extreme numbers results in U.S. estimates ranging from approximately $100 million to $500 million, with the mean result of approximately $290 million.

A slightly more sophisticated approach is to use simple linear regression to calculate funding per threat or population. Given the approximate nature of the data, the relationships in the linear fits were loose.[20] As would be expected, this approach produced estimated ranges that were narrower and somewhat lower than the simple calculations. When estimated based on threat, the level of spending for the United States would be between $20 million and $50 million. When based on population, the estimated spending level for the United States would be much higher, ranging from

Table 9.2
Factors Used to Estimate U.S. Funding from Available Comparison Country Budget Data

Country	Terrorist Attacks Between 2001 and 2016	Total 2017 Population, Millions
United States	305	327
Germany	152	81
Canada	33	36
United Kingdom	820	65
Australia	36	23
France	335	67

SOURCE: Data for the number of terrorist attacks are from START, undated(a); data for the total 2017 population are from CIA, *The World Factbook*, 2017.

---

[19] The low number was calculated by multiplying the amount spent per attack in Table 9.2 by France's approximately $70,000-per-incident expenditure. The high number was calculated in the same way but used the approximately $900,000-per-incident expenditure from Germany and Australia.

[20] The linear relationship between spending and population was stronger for the full set of five countries, with correlation coefficients between 0.4 and 0.5, depending on whether the trendline was forced to zero spending at zero population. For threat, Germany's high spending made the relationship essentially non-linear, but dropping Germany resulted in correlations between spending and incident counts in Canada, the United Kingdom, France, and Australia as high as 0.75. More detail on this analysis is included in Appendix D.

$150 million to $450 million. As would be expected, approximately the upper half of each of the calculated ranges is driven by the high spending estimate for Germany.

In spite of the approximate nature of these estimates, one element is consistent across all of them: Compared with other countries, current U.S. expenditures on terrorism prevention fall at or below the bottom of the funding ranges, however those ranges are calculated.

Considering Yardsticks for Appropriate Spending Levels

Although national comparisons provide a useful point of departure, simply calibrating our national policy based on the decisions of others is insufficient. A stronger approach would be to calibrate terrorism prevention expenditures against their potential benefits to inform judgments about appropriate levels of investment. Of course, as discussed previously, quantifying the benefits of terrorism prevention programs is difficult, and it is particularly difficult to make defensible estimates about the number of terrorist events programs might have had a role in preventing.

This challenge is not unique to terrorism prevention. Such uncertainty exists when trying to measure the effectiveness of virtually all policies and programs aimed at addressing the threat of terrorism. For programs where exact outcomes are uncertain, an alternative approach to the problem is to use what has been called break-even analyses. Given more-certain knowledge of what a program will cost to implement, the analysis then asks: "How good would the policy have to be for the costs to be worth it?" Instead of trying to calculate how many terrorist events a program has prevented, it asks how many such events it *would have to prevent* (and therefore avoiding their substantial associated costs) for it to be worth investing in the program. If it is plausible that a program could achieve the needed level of effectiveness or cost avoidance, that conclusion would support implementation. If the level of success appears unrealistic for what the program does, it would not. This approach is described in Willis and LaTourrette and applied to the regulatory analysis of the Western Hemisphere Travel Initiative (WHTI) Land Border Component.[21] It has subsequently been reflected in Office of Management and Budget (OMB) discussions of terrorism-related regulatory analyses, e.g., "When benefits cannot easily be quantified, application of break-even analysis

---

[21] Henry H. Willis and Tom LaTourrette, "Using Probabilistic Terrorism Risk Modeling for Regulatory Benefit-Cost Analysis: Application to the Western Hemisphere Travel Initiative in the Land Environment," *Risk Analysis*, Vol. 28, No. 2, 2008.

can be useful in particularly challenging analytical situations."[22] It also was reflected in OMB Circular A-4 as both "break-even" and "threshold" analysis.[23]

There are two sets of costs that are potentially relevant for break-even analysis of terrorism prevention:

- First, absent terrorism prevention, we are left to rely on traditional law enforcement approaches. In such situations, law enforcement organizations must devote time and resources to investigate or surveil potential threats. Although the resources required for many such investigations can be modest, others (e.g., involving use of confidential informants or long-term intensive surveillance) can be extremely expensive. In some cases, investigations progress to arrest, prosecution, and incarceration. The direct costs associated with law enforcement activities can be considerable in individual cases, and add up across large caseloads. Reliance on enforcement as a primary strategy for managing terrorism risk also can have intangible costs. To the extent that early- and middle-phase terrorism prevention[24] provides (potentially less costly) alternatives, criminal justice resources can be conserved and applied to other requirements.

- Second, the central focus of terrorism prevention efforts is the prevention of terrorist events. Just as was the case for WHTI, in the absence of data on effectiveness, a break-even approach can determine how many attacks of what costs would be needed to be prevented to justify terrorism prevention investment. Terrorism prevention efforts could reduce costs in a number of ways:[25]
    - by encouraging referral of at-risk individuals who otherwise would not have been identified, given potential reticence to report an uncertain threat directly to law enforcement
    - by providing an alternative way to respond to individuals of uncertain threat, allowing law enforcement to concentrate its activities on a smaller set of apparently higher-threat individuals
    - by reducing the risk that an individual who is made known to law enforcement is mistakenly assessed as low risk and subsequently goes on to carry out

---

[22] OMB, Office of Information and Regulatory Affairs, *2009 Report to Congress on the Benefits and Costs of Federal Regulations and Unfunded Mandates on State, Local, and Tribal Entities*, 2009, p. 17.

[23] OMB, "Circular A-4: Regulatory Analysis," September 17, 2003.

[24] DHS's line of effort 4, which we have called "late-stage terrorism prevention" (e.g., programs focused on recidivism reduction), is not a substitute for criminal justice–based strategies, but in fact is a required complement for those strategies to limit risk of individuals posing a threat after release from incarceration. As a result, for this comparison, those efforts "fall on the other side of the ledger" as a cost that early- and middle-phase terrorism prevention could similarly reduce.

[25] These mechanisms are relevant to other individually motivated violence, such as school or workplace shootings that face similar challenges in risk assessment, willingness to report early-stage threats, and options to respond to individuals who may appear to be threats but have not yet committed any crime.

an attack, since the extended interaction during intervention would allow an initial risk judgment to be revisited and refined
  – by diverting some individuals who are going down a path leading to violence.
- As a result, in the absence of data on actual attacks prevented, the break-even question becomes whether it is analytically plausible that terrorism prevention's effects—through any of these potential mechanisms—could prevent enough attacks to justify its costs.

Terrorism Prevention as Criminal Justice Cost Avoidance

Effective traditional law enforcement activity and criminal justice responses to terrorist risk have been credited for the limited number of successful terrorist attacks in the United States since 9/11. However, such approaches have substantial costs. The country has devoted substantial resources to law enforcement counterterrorism, with funding in the national security components of the FBI in the billions of dollars in addition to spending at the state and local levels. However, the scale of the demands on those resources have expanded. Press reporting in 2016 that focused on the FBI and the surveillance components of its counterterrorist activities described a "resource crunch" that required hard choices about which investigations to continue and which not to, and the observation that some individuals who were known to the Bureau subsequently carried out terrorist attacks:[26]

> It's not that the FBI didn't recognize Mateen [who carried out the attack on the Pulse Nightclub in Orlando] as a threat; it's that there are too many people like Mateen and Tsarnaev [the Boston Marathon bombers] and Hasan [who carried out the Fort Hood Attacks] across America today for the FBI to track them all—leaving the vast majority of people who the FBI suspects might harbor terrorist aspirations to go about their daily lives without any regular government surveillance.

In considering the costs of traditional law enforcement terrorism investigation, intensive surveillance of individuals believed to be high risk is the most expensive. Such surveillance is personnel-intensive: Monitoring one person 24 hours per day, seven days per week "requires as many as 30 to 40 agents, technicians and analysts" and all of the supporting technical and other infrastructure behind them.[27] Most terrorism investigations do not involve a full team of FBI surveillance experts following a person for days, however. The guidelines laying out what the Bureau can do in relation to these types of activities define smaller-scale assessments or preliminary investigations, and although full investigations can be intensive and go on for months or even years, they can also be

---

[26] Graff, 2016.

[27] Graff, 2016.

much more limited in time and scale.[28] However, even for lower-resource activities, if many such efforts are required, their costs can add up quickly:[29] The number of assessments and preliminary investigations performed annually have reached into the tens of thousands, and total numbers of full investigations are in the thousands per year.[30] In addition to their absolute costs, these demands have real opportunity costs, as criminal justice resources devoted to these investigations cannot be used to pursue other criminal behavior or nonterrorist threats.[31]

Investigation costs are not the only bills that must be paid in enforcement-focused responses to terrorism threats. Prosecution and court costs can reach into the hundreds of thousands of dollars per case.[32] Incarcerating someone in the federal system costs approximately $30–$35 thousand per year, and crimes associated with the support of terrorism can carry long sentences.[33] Annual costs of monitoring individuals after

---

[28] FBI, *Community Outreach in Field Offices: Corporate Policy Directive and Policy Implementation Guide* (as released under FOIA), March 4, 2013a.

[29] One of our federal interviewees summed it up as:

> There are 10–15,000 leads that come in per year, and the vast majority of them are [false positives], but if the FBI misses the one that wasn't, Congress comes in, says how can you have missed that, there may be valid things that were missed, but you're in this crazy world where thousands of tips come in and you have to thoroughly vet each one, start to grow numb and think they are all [false positives], but the ones that aren't, becomes Orlando or San Bernardino, then a microscope comes down on you.

[30] According to the best open source data available, the FBI carries out large numbers of assessments and investigations each year focused on the threat of terrorism. In 2011, media reports cited a total for a two-year period of approximately 43,000 assessments related to terrorism or foreign intelligence, which led to approximately 2,000 preliminary or full investigations (Charlie Savage, "F.B.I. Focusing on Security over Ordinary Crime, *New York Times*, August 23, 2011). A later report stated that "In recent years, the F.B.I. has averaged 10,000 assessments annually, and 7,000 to 10,000 preliminary or full investigations involving international terrorism. In addition, the F.B.I. receives tens of thousands of terrorism tips" (Adam Goldman, "Why Didn't the F.B.I. Stop the New York Bombing?" *New York Times*, September 21, 2016). FBI testimony on Capitol Hill in September 2017 cited a total of approximately 2,000 open investigations for a "subset" of open investigations (1,000 focused on individuals connected to international terrorism and 1,000 domestic terrorism investigations), presumably referring to full investigations. In later press reporting, the director cited a higher value of "more than 3,000 open investigations . . . divided about equally among suspected ISIS-directed threats, suspected homegrown violent extremists inspired by global jihadist organizations, and cases of suspected domestic terrorism." See Williams, 2018.

[31] For example, concerns about these opportunity costs were a focus of an Inspector General examination in the years following the 9/11 terrorist attacks as the FBI was reshaping itself to respond to the threat of terrorism (Office of the Inspector General, *The Internal Effects of the Federal Bureau of Investigation's Reprioritization*, Washington, D.C.: U.S. Department of Justice, 04-39, September 2004).

[32] DOJ, 2017; United States Attorney's Office, *United States Attorneys' Annual Statistical Report: Fiscal Year 2016*, Washington, D.C.: U.S. Department of Justice, 2016. Note that trials for completed terrorist attacks can be much higher, reaching into the millions of dollars (e.g., see DOJ, *FY 2011 Budget Request: Strengthen National Security and Counter the Threat of Terrorism*, 2011, which describes a supplemental request for more than $70 million associated with the prosecution of "five alleged conspirators of the 9/11 terrorist attacks").

[33] BOP, *Annual Determination of Average Cost of Incarceration*, July 19, 2016; Charles Doyle, *Terrorist Material Support: An Overview of 18 U.S.C. §2339A and §2339B*, Washington, D.C.: Congressional Research Service, R41333, December 8, 2016.

release—whether for terrorism or other crimes—are lower than incarceration but also can be significant for individuals who may be monitored for long periods. Probation supervision has costs in the low thousands of dollars per year, while monitoring in a halfway house or reentry center is on the order of $30 thousand per year.[34] Based on information gathered in study interviews, terrorism defendants would be more likely to receive more-intensive, higher-cost monitoring.

Although in a free society and a democracy it is true that law enforcement or domestic intelligence resources *should* be constrained, and that choices about long-term or intensive surveillance of individuals *should* be made with care, Graff (and several of our interviewees) described a response to those constraints and the concern about missing a possible attack that has both tangible and intangible costs of its own:[35]

> And the resource crunch—as well as the obvious risk of being wrong about leaving someone like Mateen on the streets—has been pushing the Bureau to expand use of its controversial undercover terror stings, which help speed up the road to radicalization, but which also raise deep concerns among civil liberty advocates that the FBI is engaging in entrapment.

Graff goes on to quote counterterrorism officials that, in response to increasing numbers of suspects and concerns about individuals radicalizing and mobilizing faster, the Bureau has "shifted to much simpler stings and faster arrests." This approach—and particularly the use of undercover informants as part of investigations—has raised concerns about whether the operations "have led some people down a violent road they might have always otherwise ignored."[36] Although this has been a prominent argument made by opponents of U.S. counterterrorism approaches, it has not been limited to them: The question also has been raised in the analytical community and by some judges reviewing cases that have resulted.[37]

Whether these concerns are warranted is an open question, and one that is difficult to answer with certainty even for any given case. However, *if* investigative approaches have pushed individuals toward violence that they would not otherwise have pursued, such incidents raise real and important civil liberties concerns, and also raise practical questions. In such cases, prosecution and incarceration required paying real and significant monetary costs that were not actually necessary to reduce risk. However, although it is not clear whether these approaches to investigation have pushed individuals to take illegal actions that they otherwise would not have, it is clear that aggressive traditional

[34] AOUSC, *Supervision Costs Significantly Less than Incarceration in Federal System*, July 18, 2013.

[35] Graff, 2016.

[36] Graff, 2016.

[37] See, for example, Brian Michael Jenkins, *Stray Dogs and Virtual Armies: Radicalization and Recruitment to Jihadist Terrorism in the United States Since 9/11*, Santa Monica, Calif.: RAND Corporation, OP-343-RC, 2011; Eric Lichtblau, "F.B.I. Steps Up Use of Stings in ISIS Cases," *New York Times*, June 7, 2016.

law enforcement tactics (and the use of undercover informants in particular[38]) has had an associated "trust price" that has affected the viability and effectiveness of terrorism prevention efforts.[39] Although there will always be the potential for tension between operational demands and efforts to pursue indirect, more collaborative, community-centered approaches to terrorism prevention, the U.S. experience regarding terrorism enforcement over the past few years emphasizes how the two approaches—both driven by the same desire to protect the country—can pull against one another.

To the extent that early- and middle-stage terrorism prevention efforts either obviate the need for some of this activity or provide alternatives to aggressive enforcement actions, such programs could both reduce demands on law enforcement and make it possible to respond to individuals thought to pose risks that are cheaper—both monetarily and intangibly.[40] This reduction could occur because early-phase programming (e.g., messaging or community resilience activities) means that some individuals who would have otherwise radicalized to violence never went down that path at all or because middle-phase efforts (e.g., referral promotion or intervention programming) identified and successfully met the needs of at-risk individuals, eliminating the potential that these individuals would escalate to violence and require criminal justice intervention. Those avoided costs, if significant enough, would justify expenditures on terrorism prevention both by freeing up criminal justice resources for other purposes and by helping to maintain trust and therefore effective collaboration between the public and domestic security efforts.[41]

To explore this approach to assess terrorism prevention investments, we estimated the rough costs of each of the components of the law enforcement–focused approach to respond to an individual potentially posing risk of attack, based on the amount of

---

[38] In interviews, the use of undercover officers and informants was raised as particularly damaging to community trust. Some interviewees cited cases from years before that still resonated broadly in the community. As a result, their increasing use to move cases to conclusion (according to the *New York Times* in 2016, "Undercover operations, once seen as a last resort, are now used in about two of every three prosecutions involving people suspected of supporting the Islamic State, a sharp rise in the span of just two years" [Lichtblau, 2016]) means that, even if they are effective, their contribution to damaged trust is likely increasing as well.

[39] Project interviews with community groups, government officials, and others in multiple U.S. cities.

[40] Given the sensitivities around terrorism, this would not be a trivial change to implement in practice for leads that have been submitted to the FBI. As a federal-level interviewee put it: "[In spite of the massive number of leads,] I don't know how to do it if you peel off more to mental health professionals, but if you are the one doing it and you make a mistake, the pendulum will swing in the opposite direction. Almost damned if you do, damned if you don't."

[41] Critics of CVE programs also make a "consuming law enforcement resources argument" in opposition to these efforts. Their argument is that if CVE efforts lead to increased referrals to law enforcement of individuals who do not pose a threat, they will consume resources for no reason: "CVE programs will result in the reporting of large numbers of people who have nothing to do with terrorism and the diversion of law enforcement resources from more fruitful pursuits" (Patel and Koushik, 2017, p. 13).
  If the middle-phase and late-phase terrorism prevention capabilities are in place and if any such individuals are diverted to cheaper, less harmful programming options, that would appear to address their concern as well.

time involved in the different steps and approximate federal costs involved. We focused on the different levels of investigation defined by the FBI and estimates of federal costs associated with managing individuals in the remaining elements of the criminal justice system. Greater detail on the estimates is included in Appendix D, but in general, we aimed conservatively low (e.g., costing a plausible "average" investigation rather than an intensive one involving 24/7 surveillance, per interviews with individuals who had been involved in similar investigations in the past). We also focused on an offense like material support to terrorism rather than cases involving actual charges of violent action, estimating time served between five and 15 years with post-release supervision for similar periods of time.

Using all of our estimated values, we produced costs associated with one terrorism defendant from preliminary assessment through short incarceration and post-release monitoring of about $450,000 and for a long incarceration and post-release monitoring of approximately $1 million. As a result, in considering whether terrorism prevention programs are likely to break even, the question can be reframed as, "How many terrorism defendants is it plausible that such programs would remove the need to manage via the criminal justice system?" We plot these numbers in Figure 9.3, for total costs by numbers of defendants for the two extremes of incarceration and post-release monitoring. If the sentencing parameters we have defined are viewed as reasonable bounds and it is plausible that such programs could avoid arrest and prosecution of ten defendants, then terrorism prevention efforts with costs in the range of $4.5–$10 million would

Figure 9.3
Estimated Total Criminal Justice Costs for Increasing Numbers of Individual Terrorism Defendants, from Investigation Through Post-Release Monitoring

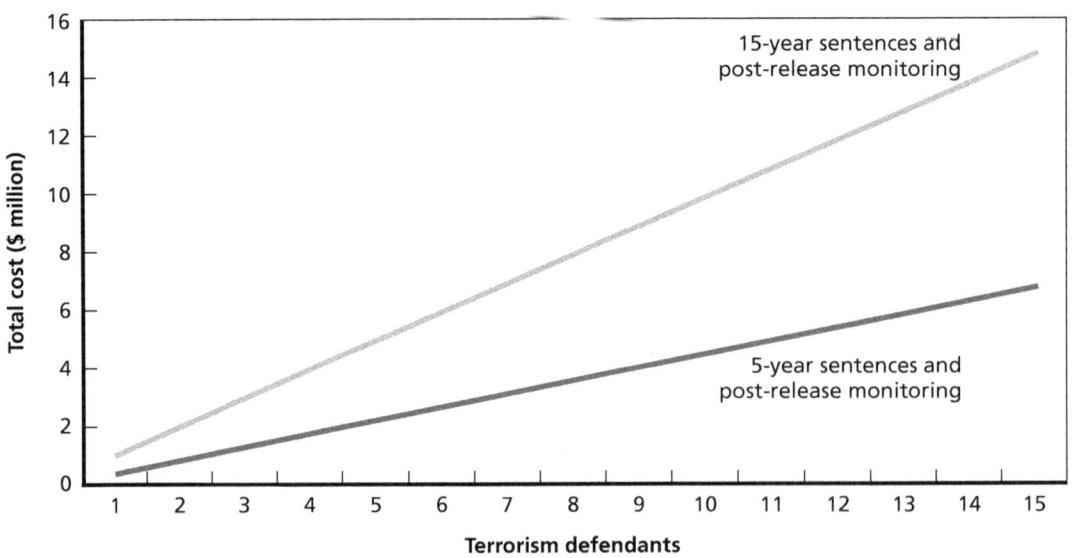

likely be justifiable, depending on the likely distribution of sentences the ten defendants received.

Although thinking about the break-even for terrorism prevention efforts on a "per defendant basis" keeps the analysis simple, the reality is that the number of earlier-stage investigative activities done by the FBI are much more numerous than the later-stage arrests leading to prosecutions. The extent to which terrorism prevention efforts could reduce the burden of these earlier-stage investigative efforts—either by reducing the number of people who engage in activities that trigger preliminary assessments or by allowing intervention programs to assess risk rather than carrying out preliminary investigations—could be as important or even more important than the reduction in individuals arrested and fully prosecuted for terrorism-related offenses.

Based on publicly available numbers cited previously, the apparent ratio is roughly one arrest for every 50 investigations and 67 preliminary assessments or initial checks.[42] To think through this "higher volume" effect, we will look not at individual arrests, but at an arrest *plus* a proportional number of investigations and assessments.[43] As a result, if every individual who did not need to be arrested (Figure 9.3) was also associated with 50 fewer investigations and 67 fewer preliminary assessments, our two "levels" of costs that terrorism prevention might save would be approximately $2.8 million (our short sentence estimate above plus $2.3 million) and $3.4 million for the long sentence estimate. Because of the comparatively larger numbers of investigations and assessments, total costs here are no longer driven by incarceration costs but instead by the total costs of many individual investigative activities added together. This narrows the difference between our two illustrative curves and, by greatly increasing the potential savings from terrorism prevention, lowers the bar for them to break even, assuming proportional reductions in early-stage investigative activity as well as terrorism support prosecutions. Figure 9.4 shows the resulting cost lines.

To the extent that terrorism prevention programming would reduce the requirement for both prosecution of individuals for terrorism-related offenses and proportional early-stage investigative activities related to terrorism, potential cost savings could be considerable. Even if such efforts only removed the need for a small number of prosecutions and proportional other investigative activity (i.e., on the order of 5–10 percent of current levels), investments into the tens of millions of dollars would be expected

---

[42] The total number of incidents of radicalization for all ideologies (defined by START for their PIRUS dataset as involving some illegal activity and therefore potentially leading to arrest [START, undated(b)]) was 61 in 2014; 129 in 2015; and 119 in 2016. The FBI Director in testimony reported 176 arrests in an approximately 12-month period ending in 2017 (Wray, 2017a; 2017b). This suggests a total of between 100 and 200 annual arrests that we round to 150. From the totals cited above, we use approximately 2,500 for ongoing full investigations (averaging the publicly disclosed values); approximately 5,000 for preliminary investigations; and approximately 10,000 for assessments.

[43] To the extent that other terrorism prevention initiatives intended to promote referral of at-risk individuals for intervention are successful, the number of early-stage investigations could increase considerably, causing costs to increase rapidly. This would be similar to what happened in the United Kingdom's Prevent Channel program.

Figure 9.4
Estimated Total Criminal Justice Costs for Increasing Numbers of Individual Terrorism Defendants and Proportional Earlier-Stage Investigative Activities

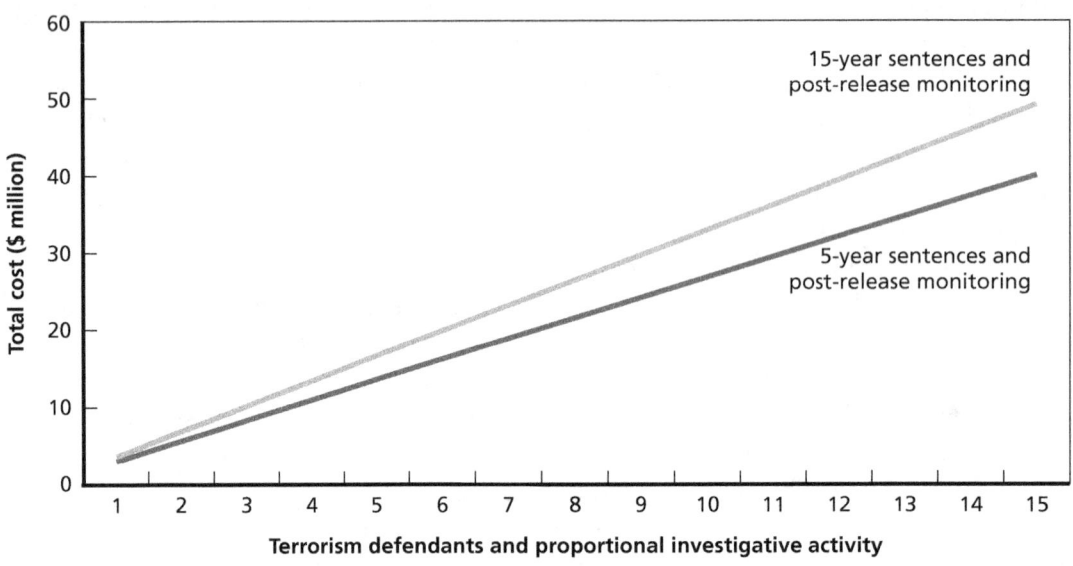

RAND *RR2647-9.4*

to be cost effective. Furthermore, this analysis focused only on tangible and readily estimable costs, so additional benefits would accrue to the extent that the greater availability and use of more-indirect or collaborative terrorism prevention measures helped to maintain trust that would otherwise have been at risk from additional enforcement effort.

Terrorism Prevention as Terrorism Cost Avoidance

As discussed in Chapter Two, one of the questions often raised about terrorism prevention (and preceding CVE) efforts is how their outcome effects on terrorism risk can be measured or, put directly, "how many terrorist attacks terrorism prevention efforts have prevented." In the work cited previously on the WHTI Land Border travel regulations, RAND researchers calculated the level of terrorism risk reduction that would be needed to justify the cost of the regulation at various expected annual losses from terrorism for the entire United States.[44] Similar analyses have been done for CVE efforts in other nations. For example, Ramalingam and Tuck describe a break-even analysis done of the Tolerance Project (a Swedish program focused on far-right extremism).[45] That analysis used expected amounts of criminal behavior committed by members of such groups, injuries to victims, and other costs to find that, even if the program only

---

[44] Willis and LaTourrette, 2008.

[45] Ramalingam and Tuck, 2014.

had a 5-percent effect on the criminal output of a single group of 15–20 members, its costs would be justified.

The costs of a terrorist incident are varied, and its total cost is made up of direct effects on its victims and the damage it causes, costs of responding, and various indirect costs created by individuals' and organizations' reactions to the threat.[46] Putting a price tag on terrorism is difficult, and efforts to do so in the past have used simulation tools to estimate physical damage and effects on business as well as analyses similar to those used in regulatory economics to put monetary values on attacks' human costs.[47] Similar analyses have been done for the cost of nonideological criminal behavior, capturing the costs to victims and society of different types of crime.[48]

Rather than looking at total terrorist risk to the United States from the top down, we approached this examination similarly to the "per-defendant" analysis discussed previously. To stay as simple as possible, we take as our starting point a single terrorist incident resulting in the death of a single individual. When we look at the cost of crime literature, measures have been developed for the cost of homicides, including costs associated with the effect of murders on society and a regulatory-type estimate of the value of the individual life lost. Heaton reviews several such estimates and calculates an average value of approximately $10 million for the cost of a single homicide inflated to 2017 dollars.[49] A contemporary analysis calculated a much-higher value of almost $20 million per homicide (in 2017 dollars), and the societal cost imposed by the average *murderer*—since the mean homicide conviction was for more than one fatality—of nearly $28 million in 2017 dollars.[50] Although the later analysis uses a technique that results in higher estimates, it demonstrates that the cost of an incident involving more than one fatality is higher than—though in that analysis is not double—the cost of a single-fatality event.

Drawing from the cost of crime literature calibrates this type of analysis using incidents where there is considerably more data than are available for terrorism. However, it also neglects that terrorist incidents can have indirect and other effects that an "everyday homicide" might not have. As a result, thinking about the cost of terrorism using the cost of homicides as a yardstick is likely a low value, making our estimates

---

[46] Reviewed in Brian A. Jackson, Lloyd Dixon, and Victoria Greenfield, *Economically Targeted Terrorism: A Review of the Literature and a Framework for Considering Defensive Approaches*, Santa Monica, Calif.: RAND Corporation, TR-476-CTRMP, 2007.

[47] See Willis and LaTourrette, 2008.

[48] Paul Heaton, *Hidden in Plain Sight: What Cost-of-Crime Research Can Tell Us About Investing in Police*, Santa Monica, Calif.: RAND Corporation, OP-279-ISEC, 2010.

[49] Heaton, 2010.

[50] Matt DeLisi, Anna Kosloski , Molly Sween, Emily Hachmeister, Matt Moore, and Alan Drury, "Murder by Numbers: Monetary Costs Imposed by a Sample of Homicide Offenders," *Journal of Forensic Psychiatry and Psychology*, Vol. 21, No. 4, 2010.

conservatively low. As was the case in the figures in the previous section, the level of investment in terrorism prevention that is justifiable can be considered based on the number of incidents it is plausible that it might prevent, where prevention of a single incident with a single fatality per year would justify at least $10 million of investment. Any additional costs from that homicide coming from terrorism or events resulting in multiple fatalities, injuries, or other damage would raise the total and, therefore, the level of justifiable investment in terrorism prevention activity.

Summary

In considering terrorism prevention from a resourcing perspective, the results of three different quantitative approaches to thinking about U.S. investment echo points made by interviewees during the study: The level of investment devoted to terrorism prevention in the United States is small, and is more consistent with an effort that is still experimenting and identifying policy approaches rather than implementing programing at scale.

- Compared with other Western nations, U.S. spending is at or below the bottom of funding ranges calculated based on levels of threat and well below the low end of ranges based on population.
- Because the traditional criminal justice approaches to counterterrorism of arrest, prosecution, and incarceration are expensive—and the costs of large numbers of even preliminary investigations add up—even if terrorism prevention only makes it possible to reduce that activity by a modest percentage, the benefits will justify the programming costs.
- The conclusion is similar when approaching the problem looking at the costs of terrorist attacks. Using the costs associated with nonterrorist homicide as a yardstick, an assessment that terrorism prevention can plausibly prevent a small number of lethal incidents, or even one incident producing multiple casualties, would be sufficient for a level of investment significantly higher than the current level to break even.

In light of expenditures in the billions of dollars devoted to the rest of the nation's counterterrorism efforts, increases in terrorism prevention efforts not only would put U.S. efforts in this policy area more in line with other nations, but also appear likely to pay off, even if they make only modest reductions in the burden of counterterrorism investigations on law enforcement or in numbers of attempted terrorist attacks.

CHAPTER TEN

Organization of the Federal Terrorism Prevention Enterprise

The need for coordination at the federal level for CVE activities has been recognized since very early in U.S. efforts in this space. Initially, coordination was done among the four security-focused departments/agencies—DHS, DOJ, the FBI, and NCTC—that were driving CVE efforts through semi-formal mechanisms with regular interactions between deputy-level leadership to sync activities.[1] As described in Chapter One, in January 2016, interagency coordination was formalized with the creation of the CVE Task Force.[2] When it was stood up, the Task Force had ten participating departments and agencies, though only the four security-focused departments/agencies had detailed staff physically co-located on-site.[3]

Creation of the Task Force reflected both the view that CVE required a whole-of-government approach at the federal level, and the acknowledgment that lack of coordination would undermine efforts to build CVE capacity nationally. Interviewees at all levels who were involved in the early formation of the Task Force or were involved in CVE activities at the time described problems of "agencies bumping into each other in the field," reaching out to the same stakeholders (e.g., local agencies, technology companies) independently and therefore repetitively; and different information being delivered by different agencies, which undermined the credibility of the effort overall. Some of the differences reflected legislative restrictions on agencies, most notably the requirement that NCTC analytic efforts related to domestic issues focus only on

---

[1] Views of the effectiveness of this type of semi-formalized coordination varied across interviewees. Some interviewees credited it with providing a forcing function for action, but others held it up as a negative contrast with the level of coordination that was in place once the Task Force was functioning: "Even though interagency coordination around CVE efforts was a stated presidential priority, this coordination happened in starts and stops, in leadership conversations that went nowhere" in the 2012–2015 period.

[2] There is also a DHS-specific CVE Working Group to coordinate within the department, which was established by Charter in August 2016 (DHS, *Countering Violent Extremism Working Group Charter*, Washington, D.C., August 8, 2016d). An earlier department management directive had defined roles and responsibilities for different DHS Components and offices for CVE (DHS, *Building Community Partnerships to Counter Violent Extremism*, Washington, D.C., Directive No. 045-02, October 30, 2015c).

[3] Interview with a federal representative involved in the CVE Task Force stand-up, 2018.

internationally inspired rather than wholly domestic terrorism.[4] According to multiple interviewees, a key demand signal for the creation of the Task Force came from stakeholders and partners in the effort, who asked for the federal government to speak with one voice and have a unified approach to activity in this area.

Multiple interviewees at the national level also emphasized that coordination in the terrorism prevention space is not only a U.S.-focused challenge. The federal government has substantial CVE and terrorism prevention activities that are aimed internationally, centered largely in DOS (including the Global Engagement Center), but that are also in other agencies. All of these international activities have mission or legal responsibilities to implement programming abroad. These efforts include messaging and countermessaging where, given global interconnectivity, information aimed internationally filters home. Other interviewees described programs managed through U.S. Embassies, where activity by DOS provided a ready route to connect with CVE efforts in other nations to share knowledge and best practices. Although DOS clearly leads on coordination of international CVE efforts, the distinction between international and domestic efforts is further blurred by the fact that DHS leads on the coordination of certain international forums, such as the Five Country Ministerial CVE Working Group. As a result, the nexus between international and homeland efforts creates another coordination demand, where the different authorities, responsibilities, and mission goals of the range of agencies involved require navigating complexities that are not dissimilar from the complexity between operational and service-provider agencies that arise in local-level terrorism prevention efforts.

HSOAC looked systematically at the different parts of terrorism prevention across all phases (see Chapter Three for a description of the terrorism prevention phases) to explore coordination requirements and demands. Across the different facets of terrorism prevention, interagency coordination ranges from critical (where breakdowns could undermine efforts) to efficiency enhancing, reducing the potential for duplicative efforts. Areas where coordination and integration of efforts appeared critical were

- community education and engagement efforts: If they are undertaken by multiple agencies, these efforts must be coordinated because discrepancies between individual agencies' messages could create confusion and inefficiency but could, more seriously, serve to undermine trust if differences are interpreted as evidence of deception rather than reflecting breakdowns in interagency coordination.
- federal interaction with technology companies: Because of the potential for mixed messages from agencies acting independently (e.g., confrontational versus collaborative approaches) and the burden of uncoordinated outreach souring public-private relationships and cooperation, federal organizations should coordinate interactions with technology companies.

---

[4] Interviews with multiple federal representatives, 2018.

- countermessaging efforts: Because of concerns about international messaging efforts having blowback effects inside the United States, messaging efforts need to be coordinated to avoid conflicts.

Areas where coordination appeared valuable but less essential—or less essential on an ongoing and time-sensitive basis—were

- data-sharing to support analysis: This was highlighted as an area where coordination would be valuable, especially between law enforcement (FBI) and non–law enforcement agencies involved in terrorism prevention. Without sharing, the potential exists for different agencies to be working from different views of the threats that terrorism prevention is focused on (e.g., views of the level of domestically inspired ideological violence), which could undermine the effectiveness of public messaging and accurate prioritization of effort.
- infrastructural activities for terrorism prevention programming: This area includes research and evaluation activity or efforts to develop human capital that would be valuable in order to minimize the potential for duplication of effort, but an absence of coordination would be unlikely to critically threaten the success of parallel efforts.
- corrections and recidivism reduction: Coordination is needed, but the requirement is narrower. Because of the central responsibility of corrections organizations, coordination between federal and state or local entities within the sector is more important than cross-federal interagency coordination.

Intervention defies ready categorization in these terms. Interviewees pointed to the reality that actions by one agency can put the success of all agencies involved in intervention at risk, and that risk can only be managed through close coordination. Local terrorism arrests by the FBI, particularly when aggressive investigation methods had been used, were cited in multiple cities we visited as having derailed promising CVE activities because interagency relationships and coordination were not strong enough. This suggests that coordination is critical for intervention.

We also encountered examples at the local level where intervention was separated from law enforcement because of this risk. When CVE programs were essentially walled off from police, the view was that their success would be less affected by law enforcement or counterterrorism actions and the need for tight coordination was eliminated, or at least greatly reduced.

Either model could be viable at the federal level. Seeking to link the FBI more tightly into terrorism prevention and improve coordination would be more like the status quo. The FBI is a formal member of the CVE Task Force, although interviewees indicated that its level of involvement has varied over time. A decision to change direction and split enforcement from terrorism prevention would be driven by the conclusion that dividing the roles would be more effective than attempting to manage the conflict between the requirements of counterterrorism enforcement and of more collaborative, community-centered terrorism prevention efforts.[5] On this issue, there was variation in opinion across our interviewees. Some highlighted the challenges of maintaining a "marriage" between operationally focused organizations and those with a case management or policy orientation.[6] Others, including those at the local level, cited examples of where ongoing collaboration between entities with these sorts of mission friction was working, although in most cases, the interviewees emphasized that maintaining effectiveness required high levels of trust and communication.

As the interviewees reflected on the performance of federal-level coordination on CVE (and on the CVE Task Force in particular) during the previous administration and terrorism prevention during the current one, they pointed to tangible progress in improving coordination and taking actions to strengthen national then-CVE and now terrorism prevention efforts. Most also pointed to continued challenges and places where the Task Force's ability to manage whole-of government terrorism prevention activity fell short in achieving all that was needed. Across the relevant subset of our interviewees, we heard a range of proposals for how coordination could be improved, including options for alternative coordination models that might address some of the challenges the Task Force encountered. In the following sections, we will first discuss the feedback we received on interagency coordination and activity as it is currently organized, and we will then discuss alternatives for coordination (including insights from the literature on relative strengths and weaknesses of different models). We will conclude with a discussion of interagency coordination for terrorism prevention going forward.

Assessing Current Interagency Coordination for Terrorism Prevention

Interagency coordination, collaboration, and communication have improved and interviewees cited a variety of accomplishments of the CVE Task Force. Multiple interviewees credited the Task Force structure with fixing several basic coordination problems that drove its creation (e.g., rationalizing across multiple versions of the CAB that had been used by different federal agencies; and reducing the variation in messaging

---

[5] See Bjelopera, 2015, for related discussion. Rosand (2016, p. 16) makes this point on a global level: "[Terrorism prevention] efforts should not be driven by the same governmental agencies that gather intelligence and investigate crime. Keeping these efforts separated while allowing for some connectivity between them, where appropriate, is essential for building the trust and cooperation of local communities."

[6] A reviewer of this document indicated that the FBI's willingness to participate was affected by a perception that the CVE Task Force was "anti-law enforcement," a perception that could be driven, at least in part, by this tension between operational requirements to act in response to imminent threats versus more case management or services approaches.

across state, local, and nongovernmental engagement efforts).[7] The Task Force also was credited with addressing the limitations that initially affected NCTC's ability to play a lead role in this space, making it possible for DHS staff to integrate domestic terrorism concerns into community education and outreach efforts, and coordinating Task Force efforts with DHS, the FBI, and DOJ.[8] This included the development of a CAB that reflected and integrated discussion of domestic threats, along with those from international sources.

Other efforts described by interviewees or included in Task Force documentary materials were

- coordinating research and analysis across agencies and developing reference materials to inform terrorism prevention efforts at all levels
- developing a training inventory and an interagency process for quality assurance for federal training and exercises focused on terrorist recruitment to ensure both its utility and that its content meets civil rights and liberties standards
- working to formalize curriculum for CREXs, including developing scenarios covering the domestic terrorism space
- developing training to allow others to deliver CABs, to increase the number of individuals who could participate in outreach and education efforts
- delivering technical assistance to local areas seeking to facilitate the development of intervention programs nationwide
- launching the Digital Forum on Terrorism Prevention and partnering with the Global Internet Forum to Counter Terrorism to connect government with the technology industry
- creating online resources to facilitate CVE work at the local level, both inside and outside government.[9]

Nevertheless, our interviews identified numerous issues with the CVE Task Force that limited its effectiveness. Although it had a charter and therefore more institutionalization than some interagency structures, interviewees indicated that it, and its leadership, did not have enough authority to integrate agency efforts. Interviewees described a time when the Task Force was active and was viewed as effective, but the

---

[7] A federal interviewee involved in the Task Force early on noted: "If I needed something from NCTC, DOJ or FBI being a DHS person, I'd have to go knock on doors at these various locations. The Task Force essentially put the band together so I could walk right up to someone's desk. There were fewer things lost in translation and built a bigger dynamic for people working on CVE." This accessibility and proximity is one of the strengths of models where individuals are co-located at a single site. Local practitioners made similar points discussing models they had implemented where, for example, law enforcement and mental health practitioners shared common space and, through co-location, built strong and collaborative working relationships.

[8] Multiple interviews with federal representatives, 2018.

[9] This list is summarized from material provided by DHS OTPP and interview discussions.

engagement of many agencies reportedly waned rapidly: By late 2017 (less than two years after its creation), the status of the Task Force was most frequently described by interviewees as "in a holding pattern" or "diminished," and there were even some that believed that it had already been officially dissolved.[10] Several interviewees raised concerns that some of the challenges that promoted its creation in the first place ("agencies running into each other in the field") were starting to reemerge. As a result, in our interviews with individuals with varied levels of interaction and involvement with the Task Force during its creation and operation,[11] we explored what they saw as key issues that were obstructing the Task Force from achieving its goals and that could inform thinking about terrorism prevention coordination going forward.

The first obstacle to the CVE Task Force's success was the unwillingness of nonsecurity agencies to substantially and publicly engage. This shaped state and local individuals' views of CVE efforts and limited the tools available for federal involvement in activities like intervention. If this persists, interviewees viewed it as a serious challenge for future terrorism prevention initiatives. Multiple interviewees ascribed this challenge to the toxicity of the "CVE brand"; essentially, direct and attributed involvement with CVE efforts would damage their efforts to achieve their primary missions. Others viewed practical constraints as a central driver of this issue: Agencies were hesitant to invest significantly in CVE during a time when priorities like the opioid crisis, school shootings, and other violent crime and mass-casualty events competed for focus.

Although a number of nonsecurity departments and agencies were reportedly involved in the Task Force at the beginning, it appeared from our interview discussions that they disengaged relatively quickly.[12] Most national-level interviewees characterized the Task Force as lacking involvement from outside security-focused organizations. This echoed views that we heard from the state, local, and NGO sectors where such questions as, "Why aren't HHS and Education involved in CVE efforts?" came up repeatedly.[13] Although the idea that relevant nonsecurity departments and agencies had distanced themselves from CVE over time was the majority view across our

---

[10] For example, one federal interviewee said: "Overall coordination has disappeared since the Task Force went away. But is it a good idea to reinvigorate the Task Force? It all depends on what it's trying to do." Although it is diminished, it was still operating at the time of the interview and the time of this writing, mainly through weekly telecons between representatives from DHS, DOJ, FBI, and NCTC.

[11] During the research, we sought to reach out to the full range of agencies relevant to terrorism prevention, but the sensitivities around the topic meant that we were not able to interview representatives of every relevant agency. In many cases, interviews with former members of those agencies provided us a view into those agencies' perspectives, particularly regarding past activities surrounding CVE. However, our visibility into current activities and efforts is not complete.

[12] For example, one federal interviewee described HHS as very actively involved in the initial framing of CVE activities: "[At the beginning,] they sent more people to each meeting than any other department or agency. They would send three people so that three different agencies within HHS would be trying to figure out [what was going on]. . . . They really were thinking actively of ways that they could fit."

[13] This has also been cited in published assessments of past CVE efforts (e.g., McKenzie, 2016).

interviewees, it should be noted that we heard conflicting perspectives from a smaller number of interviewees, including federal representatives who cited continued involvement by HHS, and signals by some of increased involvement over the last year. However, even if nonsecurity department or agency involvement is now increasing, the observed differences in opinion nonetheless demonstrate that the level of involvement is neither widely known nor appreciated, limiting its potential contribution to terrorism prevention effectiveness and trust-building.

In the design of the Task Force, one strategy that sought to cement multiagency connections and participation was the rotating model for Task Force leadership between DOJ and DHS. Although some saw it as a useful model, its success in practice was called into question: Multiple interviewees cited DOJ's disengagement from the Task Force over time, and several also questioned the level of commitment (both to the Task Force and to non–criminal justice responses to terrorism risk) from the FBI since the beginning of the effort.[14] One interviewee argued that the credibility of CVE (now terrorism prevention) as an *alternative* to criminal justice approaches would have been better demonstrated by a different model: "One . . . thing that should happen, which was considered during the Obama years, was a Task Force that has DHS and HHS sharing the load. A law enforcement piece and a non–law enforcement piece."[15]

Second, among the agencies that did join the effort, the assessment was that the way the Task Force was structured and the authorities of its leadership meant that it functioned more as a coordinating entity than truly integrating federal CVE efforts:[16]

> The Task Force was created to allow every agency buying into it to retain their initial investment, which meant they control the areas where they were dominant. So you ended up with a Task Force that wasn't truly integrated. Every person there was fiercely defending their turf. Not in a purposefully counterproductive way. That was just the nature of their offices. . . . By doing it that way where everyone claimed a piece of the Task Force before it even stood up, it was hard to come together as a team.

---

[14] Interviews with federal representatives who were involved with the Task Force, 2018. One interviewee ascribed this as a potentially not unexpected consequence of the FBI's transformation to support counterterrorism efforts:

So the interagency coordination group . . . we've always [had] FBI [participating]—usually it was their community outreach person. Until the FBI decided to do CVE and that became CT and that is out of the intel/ terrorism world. And that worries the community. The more the optics reinforce the notion of a government-led surveillance program. [As] well intentioned as some of our FBI partners [are] and I don't doubt their intentions—at the end of the day they are an investigative bureau and that's their job and that's what they do best.

As cited above, one of the reviewers of this document indicated that the FBI's willingness to participate was affected by a perception that the CVE Task Force was "anti-law enforcement."

[15] Interview with a former federal representative, 2018.

[16] Interview with a former federal representative, 2018.

Multiple interviewees reinforced the view that organizational "turf protection" undermined effectiveness.[17] Task Force leadership did not have sufficient authority to task staff and manage across agency boundaries, meaning that command and control approaches to addressing these issues were not available.[18] Others ascribed these problems to the fact that the Task Force was so focused on "getting something done" quickly after set up, that the investment in internal organizational development was not made:[19]

> Because things were put up in a very fast way and we threw everything at the wall to see what stuck, there was no hierarchy of management within the group. The CVE Task Force operated well if you consider it like a think tank. We could convene, write papers, share best practices. But when it came down to actual programming and measuring the gap between policy and operations, that's where we had major hiccups.

Interviewees flagged shortfalls in information-sharing between agencies (e.g., on domestic terrorism issues in particular), which they viewed as coming from organizational frictions and competition. Others pointed to simple practicality: The location of the Task Force in unclassified space made it logistically difficult to share classified information.[20]

According to some interviewees, the Task Force became an arena for interagency politics rather than an antidote to them; as a result, agencies could use it as a "check on everyone else."[21] Interviewees cited examples of this type of interaction among the security-focused agencies that were more substantially engaged, and even among otherwise disengaged agencies:[22]

---

[17] A federal interviewee noted that there were "arguments over defining each department's CVE-focused work: if agency leadership could agree, there's a possibility people could carve their own niches." Similar sentiments are expressed in RTI International, 2017b.

[18] Interview with a federal representative, 2018. Literature sources argued for increasing the rank of the Task Force lead (who was expected to also be the head of DHS OCP/now OTPP): "To address this imbalance, the DHS/OCP and task force director should be made an assistant secretary–rank position, and the deputy director a deputy assistant secretary–rank position" (Levitt, 2017, p. 22).

[19] Interview with a policy researcher and former federal representative, 2018.

[20] Multiple federal-level interviews, 2018.

[21] Interview with a federal representative, 2018.

[22] Interview with a policy researcher and former federal representative, 2018. This interviewee turned this critique into an argument supporting the discussion in Chapter Seven that as much activity should be left to the local level as possible:

> These kinds of sensitivities at the local level don't exist. They all know each other, they work with one another, many of the same people deal with opioid crisis, other things that require the same interveners. We make it difficult at the federal perspective when we make things siloed. Whatever policy that is put into place should come to that realization—it's better to support those efforts and guide that energy than try to control it.

[A person] ran into this bureaucratic wall. [In relation to a specific case, this person wanted] to meet with the superintendent to set up programs in the community. Department of Education tried to shut it down because they viewed it in their lane but [the person] did it anyway.

This type of behavior was a central driver of what many interviewees described as an emergent risk aversion in Task Force activities that inhibited innovation and experimentation, because the concerns of any single agency could put the brakes on new initiatives or efforts. To the extent that the circumstances that led to this view persist into the future, they would be challenges to the implementation of terrorism prevention initiatives.

In contrast to the questions about different agencies' levels of engagement in the Task Force and their commitments to CVE at the headquarters level in Washington, D.C., interviewees indicated that interagency jurisdiction issues and barriers to cooperation were much lower in the field. At the same time that interviewees were raising questions about the buy-in of the FBI to CVE efforts in Washington, D.C., others at the local level talked about very productive interaction and collaboration between efforts in their cities and the relevant FBI Field Office.[23] Essentially the same point was made for nonsecurity agencies like HHS—that policy-level buy-in and collaboration was limited, but when there was work to be done "on the ground," collaboration could happen.[24]

Third, staffing was a major challenge. Because of limited investment of resources in CVE over the years, ongoing programs did not provide a pipeline to develop and expand human capital in this area. The number of federal staff involved in this policy area over the entire history of U.S. government efforts is relatively small compared with the thousands of federal employees devoted to mission areas like border security, intelligence, or criminal justice activity.[25] As a result, early in the Task Force's operation, multiple interviewees indicated that there were relatively few people who had experience in this policy area.[26] Early participants who were drawn from other roles did not necessarily have experience in more-collaborative CVE activities (e.g., individuals with

---

[23] It should be noted that multiple interviewees emphasized that "every Field Office is different," as local leadership have great discretion in how they manage activities and operations. In other cities, interviewees described how the enforcement-heavy strategy of the Bureau in their local area had been a barrier to CVE success.

[24] One federal interviewee noted that "We have a much easier time working with HHS in the field than we do in D.C. They were an active participant in designing the [program in one city] and have sat in a lot of workshops [in another city]" (Interview with a federal representative, 2018).

[25] Participants in CVE efforts often were detailees who, after a year or two rotation, would have to return to other responsibilities and so effectively exit the federal CVE human capital pool.

[26] This point was made more broadly by interviewees regarding CVE and terrorism prevention efforts outside, including programming at the state and local levels (where limited government funding and thin philanthropic support made it hard to develop and keep people) as well as in research and development (where the small research and development efforts by DHS and others meant that maintaining a large expert community was difficult).

counterterrorism backgrounds were more familiar with criminal justice approaches) and had no experience working outside Washington, D.C. The core of Task Force staffing was made up of a small cadre of individuals with the knowledge and skills, which meant that the bench to draw on for expanded efforts was narrow.[27]

These limits meant that the Task Force could not effectively institutionalize CVE at the federal level:[28]

> The principle was to institutionalize CVE more. Same thing with [OCP, now OTPP]. Less formal communication would be personality-dependent. In the Bush administration, it was a small cadre of dedicated people who believed in this and was almost entirely personality driven. I could say the same for the [Obama] administration but there was an attempt to formalize these things to create an institutional framework to deal with these [issues]. A lot of the institutional minds have now been reabsorbed by their agencies or left government.

If staff who were "imported to terrorism prevention" efforts could be developed and kept involved, this issue could be resolved over time.[29] Addressing human capital issues is therefore in part a question of funding: Program support would make it more straightforward to keep staff in the policy area longer and to develop a deeper bench of terrorism prevention experts at the federal level over time. Dedicated funding of the Task Force itself (rather than relying on detailees) would also help to sustain human capital development and staff capacity.

The challenges to institutionalizing CVE in the federal government were also a matter of timing. Because it was kicked off late in the prior administration, the CVE Task Force simply did not have time to become fully settled and institutionalized before the changeover.[30] The new administration initiated a review of CVE programming and policy, creating the potential for significant shifts in direction, as well as affecting staffing and ongoing activities at the federal level in the redirection to terrorism prevention. Because many of the terms of original detailees to the Task Force were expiring at the same time as administrations were changing over, they were not replaced during that period of uncertainty, which further derailed the human capital development process.

---

[27] One of the federal interviewees noted: "With everything being personality driven, you had them all in one room, but . . . if you lost a player, there wasn't a farm team you could draw from. [There were] no rotational plans so it wasn't sustainable."

[28] Interview with a federal representative, 2018.

[29] Although they are not bureaucratically a Task Force asset, the DHS field staff (discussed elsewhere in this report) are relevant to the connection of federal activities to state and local entities. They also are a set of individuals who require specific knowledge and skills for the effectiveness of terrorism prevention initiatives. Literature sources also argue for the importance of federal field staff (e.g., Levitt, 2017).

[30] Multiple interviews with federal representatives with experience with the Task Force, 2018.

The other human capital challenge flagged by some interviewees was having the relevant technical staff in government for efforts involving industry interactions surrounding online issues,[31] but the Task Force approached that challenge through the use of fellowship programs to bring experts into CVE activity.[32] A federal interviewee emphasized the value of having outsiders involved in the technology elements of terrorism prevention:[33]

> The online components are a critical part of how we look at [terrorism prevention] going forward and there needs [to be] dedicated staff looking at it from an interagency component. Second, it's critical to bring in talent from outside to evaluate what we're doing. They will challenge the status quo and experiment in a way others will feel too locked to do.

Fourth, the Task Force was more effective at coordinating within the federal bureaucracy than it was reaching outside it. Although the Task Force was intended to be a centralized point of entry for individuals who were reaching out regarding CVE issues or activities, there were concerns that it was hard for people outside the government to connect, particularly early on.[34] This is not to say that such connections did not happen: For example, an interviewee described a cold call into the Task Force from someone connected to the corrections system where all the needed coordination was effectively done and likely would not have been possible without the Task Force. Interviewees at the state and local levels saw the potential of the Task Force as a central node in a national network for terrorism prevention: "The *idea* of the CVE Task Force could have been helpful to link us to services. . . . [But] they didn't communicate with the field that well."[35] One interviewee pointed out that, initially, there was a proposal to have state and local representatives in a direct participatory role on the Task Force, but that practical challenges kept it from moving forward.[36]

---

[31] Green and Procter (2016, p. 46) recommended the creation of "an independent presidential advisory council composed of technology and private-sector representatives to provide guidance and innovative ideas to the president on how best to compete and win the war of ideas."

[32] DHS HSAC made a similar recommendation to bring private-sector communications talent into government through a variety of mechanisms (DHS HSAC, 2016).

[33] Interview with a federal representative, 2018.

[34] One federal interviewee noted that "It actually gave people within the government and outside government a known touch point. They knew it existed, they knew the people within the body. The tricky thing was it wasn't always clear how to reach us" (Interview with a federal representative, 2018).

[35] Interview with a local representative in one U.S. city, 2018.

[36] Interview with a federal representative, 2018. Feedback from DHS indicated that these practical constraints included concerns that such involvement could not be managed without violating the Federal Advisory Committee Act. It was also argued that the CVE Subcommittee of DHS HSAC (whose products have been cited elsewhere in this report) served in the community advisory function.

Finally, interviewees argued that the dynamics around how CVE was implemented and overseen at the federal level pushed the Task Force into approaches to outside stakeholders and implementers that were not always the most effective. One key result was political pressure for metrics and program justification creating a "top down management" dynamic that was directly counter to the view that CVE efforts should be locally driven:[37]

> We didn't work *that* well with the local governments. We were our own worst enemy. It wasn't the Task Force itself, but how it was overseen and managed and what [agency leadership] wanted [the] output to be. You had various Secretaries who wanted to see certain metrics. What the CVE Task Force became was a supportive collaborating body, but also a hammer to local communities or U.S. Attorneys' offices. Should have been a bottom up approach but was top-down.

During that era, the focus on justifying and defending more-collaborative, community-centered CVE efforts led to information flows that locals viewed as going up more than down (e.g., one interviewee described frustration when federal representatives asked for information about this interviewee's efforts that was not correctly conveyed when passed to others, creating blowbacks that had to be navigated at the local level).[38] These types of problems were brought up by multiple interviewees as prominent in the early federal and local interactions and as cautionary, depending on how terrorism prevention policy evolves going forward. However, the dynamic appears to have changed considerably in recent years: In interviews in the cities we visited regarding ongoing DHS grants (in groups that have had recent and ongoing contact with OTPP staff), interactions were viewed as very productive and none of these types of concerns were raised.

Our interviews revealed broad consensus that the federal interagency coordination effort must be stabilized and that the current diminished state of the Task Force is not sufficient. Under the current circumstances, interviewees pointed to "a silo between domestic and global activities, with no information sharing about what is going on," expressed concern that the government will begin to look "disorganized" again in outreach to technology companies and international partners, stated that the lack of a coordination mechanism has led some agencies to pull back activity, and argued that unity of effort is breaking down.[39]

---

[37] Interview with a policy researcher and former federal representative, 2018.

[38] According to a representative in one of the U.S. cities we visited, "There were bi-weekly calls but they'd ask for information, not tell us what it was for, and then package it up and be advocating for things. They too much served as a middle person. If they're talking to someone about what we are doing, we should be looped into that conversation, because it's so nuanced. It's really sensitive. Some of the messaging got lost in translation. The idea could be good if they were more trusting of people in the field."

[39] Interviews with federal representatives, 2018.

Strengths and Weaknesses of Different Coordination Options

Interagency coordination was viewed as necessary by essentially all of our interviewees, regardless of their views of the CVE Task Force's strengths and shortcomings.[40] However, opinions about what coordination should look like varied, perhaps according to the requirements of the activities interviewees were most familiar with. Several interviewees believed that multiple models could work, as long as there was a clear identification of roles and responsibilities in whatever structure was adopted. The following options emerged:

- **Continuation of a physically colocated task force:** The most conservative suggestion regarding the future of interagency terrorism prevention coordination was essentially the continuation of the model envisioned with the group's creation in 2016. The view of interviewees suggesting this path was that, during the early period of the Task Force's operation, when agencies had detailed participants to the effort and it had high-level support of agency leadership, "things were working." Arguments for this path generally include embedded assumptions that once uncertainties about the future of terrorism prevention policy are resolved, agencies would "re-buy-in" and, as a result, the effort would be re-staffed with colocated and engaged individuals with the appropriate expertise to move federal terrorism prevention efforts forward.[41]
  - There were two proposals suggested under this option to respond to specific concerns that had been raised about past Task Force effectiveness:

---

[40] The assessment of one former federal employee was representative: "Interagency coordination is required but I don't know if it needs to be a task force. The interagency does a lot of things collaboratively. . . . There does need to be accountability and meet on a regular basis. . . . Through the interagency process we ran through things like the CAB, something we could pick apart discreet tasks and assign responsibilities. Without that, everyone is doing everything or everyone is doing nothing."

[41] Levitt (2017) essentially argued for this option, but suggested renaming the Task Force to more explicitly include earlier-phase activities. In addition, changes in leadership were viewed as a path to address the reticence of nonsecurity agencies to become involved:

> The task force, however, has struggled to draw in service-oriented stakeholder departments to the shared P/CVE mission. For some, DHS/DOJ shared leadership of the task force created the appearance of an overly security-focused approach to P/CVE, something departments like Health and Human Services (HHS) and Education (ED) have feared would taint their programs if they became full participants in P/CVE efforts. To address this imbalance, the task force leadership structure should be reconfigured so that its director position rotates between DHS and DOJ personnel and its deputy director position rotates between HHS and ED. Both HHS and ED already engage in violence-prevention programming within their respective fields, and making this structural change would help create a truly whole-of-government approach across the spectrum of programming, including good governance, social cohesion and integration, public safety, violence prevention, and counterterrorism (Levitt, 2017, pp. 22–23).

Whether this change would, in fact, address the concerns of those agencies and stimulate greater participation could not be assessed in our study.

- ○ **"interagency identity":** Among a small number of interviewees, the dual-hatting of Task Force leadership (at least recently) with DHS OTPP meant that it was perceived more as a DHS entity than a truly interagency one. Although rotation of leadership between DHS and DOJ was envisioned initially, the view was that approach had not done what was intended to increase buy-in.[42] They proposed elimination of the dual-hatting of the Task Force lead between that role and a home agency position.
  - ○ **explicit division of responsibility:** When asked to explore ways in which federal terrorism prevention efforts could strengthen buy-in by nonsecurity agencies, the only model that was suggested across interviewees was one where responsibility for different parts of terrorism prevention were divided,[43] with nonsecurity agencies in the lead on portions relevant to them.[44] An analogy made for this model was akin to the emergency support functions (ESFs) that are part of emergency response management, where individual agencies shape the approach to tasks within their lines of responsibility.[45]
- **Adopting a virtual task force model:** One suggestion was a virtual model rather than a co-located physical task force. Some federal representatives characterized this as the status quo at the time of this writing, with limited Task Force operations still continuing by phone and other virtual means.[46] This suggestion was driven in large part by the perception that most agencies would be unwilling to detail staff to a physical task force focused on terrorism prevention. However, it was not clear how such a model would address some of the challenges encountered to date, and might even accentuate them.
- **Formalized interagency organization:** Interviewees suggested that a more formal interagency organization could benefit terrorism prevention efforts. The example cited was the DOS GEC, which was established in law with statutory responsibilities, funding, and authorities for cross-agency coordination of messag-

---

[42] One federal interviewee said, "The last two directors have been dual-hatted with OCP and OTPP. If there's a dedicated individual who leads the Task Force on their own, it'll help set the direction of the Task Force for interagency coordination." Other published sources explicitly argue against splitting these roles. See, for example, Levitt, 2017, p. 22.

[43] According to one interview with federal representative, 2018: "Could see models where lines are divvied up among agencies and DHS is the logical hub for coordination, with OTPP as more of an implementer. There are models for this in government."

[44] This is similar to a recommendation made in Bipartisan Policy Center, 2011, p. 40.

[45] Interview with a former federal official, 2018.

[46] A virtual model would put field staff in different regions of the country on more equal footing to headquarters staff based in Washington, D.C. However, it is likely that any model that involved field staff would require some type of virtual coordination to maintain coordination of the overall national effort.

ing efforts.[47] In addition to presumably responding to the concern about limited funding for terrorism prevention, the statutory authorities provided in such a model would increase the likelihood that its leadership could effectively integrate efforts across agencies. Rather than establishment in legislation, a more modest version would be establishment via Executive Order, although judgments differed on whether this model would address coordination issues as effectively or whether it would maintain stability across successive administrations.

- **Lead agency–managed coordination:** In contrast to the range of models where terrorism prevention is placed in an explicitly interagency organization, another suggestion was that a single agency could step into the lead and coordinate across agencies using working groups or other less formalized constructs, particularly given the comparatively low level of effort that has been devoted to CVE in the past.[48] DHS was viewed by many interviewees as the central candidate to do so, and could take on that mantle by making a substantial investment in terrorism prevention going forward, given the varied constraints and levels of interest in more-collaborative, indirect, or community-centered terrorism prevention exhibited by other agencies.[49]

- **National Security Council interagency coordination:** Some interviewees asked why terrorism prevention could not be managed at the National Security Council (NSC) level, where a wide variety of issues requiring dedicated interagency coordination are addressed as a matter of course in its policy-coordinating committees or interagency policy committees. In this argument, coordinating federal terrorism prevention is essentially about separate agencies allocating their own pools of resources in ways that meet terrorism prevention goals and are consistent with their own missions. Effective NSC-level coordination could play that role, with clear administration commitment and support for terrorism prevention. From a certain perspective, this could be viewed as an extreme implementation of the

---

[47] One federal interviewee noted that "[The coordination entity for terrorism prevention] may not need to be separate from an agency, but needs to resemble the GEC to have authority on its own to get things out the door." See Public Law 114-328, National Defense Authorization Act for Fiscal Year 2017, Section 1287, Global Engagement Center, December 23, 2016.

[48] In a Congressional Research Service examination in 2015 (i.e., before the creation of the Task Force), Bjelopera posed the question of whether this was the model that had been implicitly in force at that time, given the division of responsibilities in the SIP. He also called out the absence of a clear lead agency as a problem for a number of reasons, including those outlined in this report (e.g., difficulty monitoring how much is being spent on then-CVE and terrorism prevention going forward).

[49] One national-level interviewee put it bluntly: "This started with four agencies that thought they were in charge. Each had small armies [of staff members] in the field. They fought and no one won. Someone needs to win the war, by driving resources and activity. NCTC can't do it, FBI and DOJ don't want to do it. If DHS wants to do it, they need to commit [by making a substantial investment in this area]."

"Emergency Support Function (ESF)–like" model cited above, but implementing that model at the highest level available.[50]

- **Communities of interest:** Informal groups, such as communities of interest (COIs) can be used to facilitate interagency coordination on specific issues. They can be formed and dissolved rapidly to respond to changes in the threat or other environmental factors. COIs can be used when organizations have distinct missions, authorities, or resources that may be difficult to integrate effectively. They neither involve movement of staff nor result in conflict where different agencies claim control over parts of an issue, and they may be able to attract the participation of a broader range of agencies that might not be willing or interested in participating in more institutionalized organizational structures. As a result, COIs could be an option for addressing concerns about buy-in raised during past efforts. However, coordination provided by such structures is looser than in the other models discussed, including in the legacy CVE Task Force, meaning that such models would not respond to the challenges raised regarding weak coordination limiting success or concerns regarding addressing CVE human capital shortfalls.

Many of these models have been suggested in past literature addressing federal organization for CVE, but not always as mutually exclusive options. For example, faulting the current structures as "inadequate," Green and Proctor argue for *both* coordination at the NSC level (with the implication that it would be the most effective mechanism to gain the participation of nonsecurity agencies) and continuation of the Task Force as the "domestic policy lead to leverage the coordination mechanisms it recently established."[51]

A fundamental question is whether alternative models have inherent advantages that would make them preferred, given that the argument for change is that an alternative structure for implementing terrorism prevention at the federal level would help to address some of the challenges encountered by the CVE Task Force. None of the

---

[50] This recommendation was also noted in Bipartisan Policy Center, 2011.

[51] Green and Proctor, 2016, pp. 56–57. Their argument is that, in addition to a greater NSC focus, having a structure like the CVE Task Force to perform day-to-day coordination functions (with changes to address some of the challenges described by our interviewees) is also needed:

> [T]he Commission recommends a tripartite leadership structure. The White House should rely on existing entities and capabilities, rather than creating a large footprint at the NSC. The CVE Task Force should remain the domestic policy lead to leverage the coordination mechanisms it recently established. *To make this arrangement sustainable, the Task Force should be given permanent office space, dedicated personnel, and a line-item budget to fund its operational costs. The Task Force also needs greater authority to enhance coordination among domestic agencies. Requiring all domestic departments and agencies to get the Task Force's clearance on new policies, programs, or outreach efforts would go a long way in synchronizing CVE efforts domestically.* The international policy lead should continue to be the State Department Bureau for CT and CVE, as it has the policy influence and relationships needed to drive CVE efforts overseas (emphasis added).

models explicitly addresses all of the concerns that were raised about the Task Force. Other than the potential for re-buy-in to address some of the current concerns, simply continuing the status quo or creating a virtual task force would not involve structural shifts to improve performance. Structures that divide responsibility (e.g., the ESF model or NSC-level coordination) could increase the involvement of agencies that have not strongly bought into terrorism prevention in the past, but unless the division of responsibility is very clear (and disciplined to maintain clear lanes in the road) the potential for duplication and conflict would arise rapidly. The lead agency model would potentially increase incentives for other agencies to opt out of terrorism prevention, but if their buy-in cannot actually be achieved in practice, then a single agency taking ownership could be superior to "collaboration in theory but not in reality." As a result, although each model might address some of the issues raised about the Task Force, none is an obviously preferable alternative. This aligns with assessments from some interviewees with experience in different government roles that the issue with respect to terrorism prevention was less a question of the specific structure for coordination than it was about actually implementing coordination effectively with sufficient authority and accountability to manage whole-of-government efforts. The different coordination requirements of parts of the terrorism prevention policy space (which we discussed earlier in this chapter) might allow some functions to be split into separate coordination structures, potentially relieving burdens on agencies that do not participate in all activities.

In the interviews, there were perceived practical constraints that some interviewees felt would limit options for coordination structures. The first was skepticism that current resource constraints across multiple agencies would allow the detailing of staff to a co-located and standalone organization like the Task Force in its original form. There were also simple constraints of space and infrastructure: When a location for the Task Force was identified, there was an effort to establish it in a separate space (in an effort to frame its independent identity) and, at the same time, to select a location that was convenient for representatives from across the National Capital Region. Some interviewees suggested that simple space availability and location would be a barrier to reinvigorating the existing Task Force structure or strengthening it in the future.

We looked for studies that weighed the strengths and weaknesses of mechanisms in different contexts as a point of reference. Although GAO and others have commented generally on implementation and best practices for interagency collaboration, interagency coordination is not well studied.[52] A 2014 Congressional Research Service

---

[52] See, for example, GAO, *Results-Oriented Government: Practices that Can Help Enhance and Sustain Collaboration Among Federal Agencies*, Washington, D.C., GAO-06-15, October 2005; GAO, *Managing for Results: Implementation Approaches Used to Enhance Collaboration in Interagency Groups*, Washington, D.C., GAO-14-220, February 2014; and Kevin D. Ward, Danielle M. Varda, Diana Epstein, and Barbara Lane, "Institutional Factors and Processes in Interagency Collaboration: The Case of FEMA Corps," *American Review of Public Administration*, 2018, p. 3. The topic of interagency collaboration "has only been modestly broached in peer-reviewed

report notes that evaluating the success of interagency coordination models and comparing such models to each other is difficult and potentially unreliable "because of changing conditions and intervening developments" that often affect these models.[53] These conditions include the effects of the "political environment and policy context, as well as the resources, independence, authority, membership, leadership, and operational experience of the agencies involved" and "such factors are analytically distinct on paper but are hard to account for separately in practice."[54] An IBM Center for the Business of Government study states that the scale, scope, urgency, and core task dimensions at hand are the factors that will determine which type of federal collaborative model would be most effective under the circumstances.[55] However, the research did not elaborate on which models are more or less appropriate for different policy areas and problem sets or when and how different models should be employed. Nevertheless, the literature and various examples do provide some insights into the basic strengths and weaknesses of the models that our interviewees suggested.

In considering various versions of a task force approach, evaluations of federal interagency teams provide useful insight into their related strengths and weaknesses. An Institute for National Strategic Studies (INSS) analysis of high-value target teams in Iraq explored the performance variables connected to those teams' effectiveness. Although the teams are recognized as having contributed greatly to counterinsurgency efforts in Iraq, the INSS study also notes that "their stellar performance was irregular and fragile, subject to periodic breakdown and atrophy" particularly "if relations among members soured."[56] In other words, when such team organizations worked well, they were very effective. Their weakness was that specific, yet difficult to determine conditions might be necessary for the model's success. As for what these conditions are for task force/interagency team success, several studies have provided commentary. For example, the INSS report states that the Central Intelligence Agency's Lessons Learned Center found three key factors for interagency collaboration, namely, "a shared vision of the importance of its task, location in a single space, and the shared experiences of its

---

scholarship," per Ward et al., 2018, p. 2; "The growth of innovative collaborative governance systems has outpaced scholarship" as summarized in Kirk Emerson and Tina Nabatchi, "Evaluating the Productivity of Collaborative Governance Regimes: A Performance Matrix," *Public Performance and Management Review*, Vol. 38, 2015, p. 708; and "there is little current research on interagency teams and to date little effort by the national security system to codify lessons learned from the experience" per Christopher J. Lamb, and Evan Munsing, *Secret Weapon: High Value Target Teams as an Organizational Innovation*, Institute for National Strategic Studies, *Strategic Perspectives No. 4*, Washington, D.C.: National Defense University Press, March 2011, p. 6.

[53] Frederick M. Kaiser, *Interagency Collaborative Arrangements and Activities: Types, Rationales, Considerations*, Washington, D.C.; Congressional Research Service, May 31, 2011, p. 28.

[54] Kaiser, 2011, p. 28.

[55] Jane Fountain, *Implementing Cross-Agency Collaboration: A Guide for Federal Managers*, IBM Center for the Business of Government, Collaborating Across Boundaries Series, 2013, p. 33.

[56] Lamb and Munsing, 2011, pp. 6, 56–57.

members."[57] The INSS report expands on this, concluding that the high-value target teams' experiences highlight "the importance of common purpose, clearly delegated authorities, small size and collocation, and a supportive organizational context."[58] Without these conditions, the teams' performance suffered.[59]

As for a virtual task force model (organizational collaboration at a distance) the INSS study confirms that the literature has documented that virtual teams *can* be successful, but in-person team collaboration has its own specific benefits.[60] The experiences of the high-value target teams demonstrated the importance of co-location, which INSS study participants all stated was important. In fact, "In one team leader's experience, communication with team members via telephone, secure video teleconferencing, email, or chat room generates only 50 to 60 percent of the information and understanding that collocation provides."[61] In other words, virtual task forces may be useful, but collocation provides more advantages.[62] Along the same lines, a 2014 GAO report that examined four federal interagency groups found:[63]

> Three of the interagency groups we examined and both expert practitioner panels stressed the importance of holding in-person meetings during the early stages of an interagency group. They each noted that personal interactions contributed to relationship-building, which formed the foundation for all subsequent activities and helped to break down silos. These meetings also enabled officials to learn about individual perspectives and aided in the transfer of knowledge between participating agencies. In addition, officials reported that in-person interactions helped build trust and strengthen professional networks. In our past work, we found that trust is an essential element to collaborative relationships.

This finding suggests that co-location and in-person interactions are particularly important at the beginning of a team or task force. Timing and the relationships formed up front are key factors.

---

[57] Lamb and Munsing, 2011, p. 35.

[58] Lamb and Munsing, 2011, p. 38.

[59] Lamb and Munsing, 2011, p. 38, 42–43.

[60] Lamb and Munsing, 2011, p. 42.

[61] Lamb and Munsing, 2011, p. 43.

[62] This echoed a statement made by a local law enforcement interviewee during our study that the effectiveness of their multidisciplinary structure for responding to at-risk individuals was strengthened by in-person co-location: ". . . [We] are housed together in this office right here. My counterpart on the [local mental health agency] side sits at the desk next to me. We have [a] conversation every day. We are a team. When agencies do that, it works. When they don't, it's harder" (Interview with a local law enforcement representative, 2018).

[63] The groups were the U.S. Department of Defense and Department of Education Memorandum of Understanding Working Group, the Federal Interagency Reentry Council, the Rental Policy Working Group, and the U.S. Interagency Council on Homelessness (USICH) (GAO, 2014, p. 15).

Mechanisms of formalized interagency organization were also examined in several sources. A 2018 review of federal interagency coordination–related literature explains that, although personal relationships can help foster collaboration, coordination can be externally driven: "in the absence of an existing relationship, an externally imposed mandate, that is, from an executive order or court decision, may prompt agencies to work more closely. Similarly, resource dependence, where one agency relies on payments or funding from another agency, may drive agencies to collaborate."[64] This 2018 study examined the case of the FEMA Corps, finding in that case that "high-level political buy-in resulted in rapid implementation of interagency collaboration, characterized by a strong desire for success of the partnership from leadership and uncharacteristically quick adoption of the policy."[65] Yet, the study also found that "previous patterns of interaction and a history of informal interagency collaboration were identified as important drivers of more formal collaboration in FEMA Corps. In particular, having a solid understanding of the partnering agencies' missions and organizational values and norms allows for greater opportunity for goal alignment between agencies."[66] These prior relationships were most helpful when combined with the higher-level mandate:[67]

> a mandate for government agencies to explore interagency partnerships set by the President of the United States created an additional external impetus to spur collaboration. While it may be difficult to engineer interagency collaboration from scratch when presented with an external mandate, we believe these mandates aimed at creating a more brokered, connected bureaucracy may serve as an important catalyst for agencies to explore deeper, more meaningful joint work.

In sum, "formal interagency partnerships require a combination of high-level leadership during initiation and local buy-in for successful development and implementation of interagency collaboration."[68] Finally, access to resources is another key requirement (and potential benefit) of formalized interagency coordination: "it is important for groups to ensure that they identify and leverage sufficient funding to accomplish the objectives. . . in some instances specific congressional authority may be necessary in order to provide for the interagency funding of collaborative mechanisms."[69]

---

[64] Ward et al., 2018, p. 4.

[65] Ward et al., 2018, p 13.

[66] Ward et al., 2018, p. 13.

[67] Ward et al., 2018, p. 13.

[68] Ward et al., 2018, p. 13.

[69] GAO, *Managing for Results: Key Considerations for Implementing Interagency Collaborative Mechanisms*, Washington, D.C., GAO-12-1022, September 27, 2012, p. 20.

Lead agency–managed coordination was also covered somewhat in the literature, although to a lesser extent. A 2012 GAO report about implementing interagency collaborative mechanisms stated: "Experts explained that designating one leader is often beneficial because it centralizes accountability and can speed decision making."[70] According to several analyses, the lead agency model can remedy issues of more-diffuse arrangements, for example, that one or more agencies may not participate enough (which can threaten the viability of the entire effort);[71] that one or more agencies in a fully collaborative effort "might still find that some participants, following the cliché, 'are more equal than others;'"[72] and that shared leadership models can be difficult to put into practice.[73] Yet, despite the strengths of the lead agency coordination model, one GAO interviewee stated that "centralized leadership is not always the best model, particularly when the collaboration needs to have buy-in from more than one agency."[74] A 2011 Congressional Research Service report noted challenges that a lead agency collaborative model could face, including potential noncompliance by other participants and that "The lead official (at least in his or her view) might not have sufficient authority and resources to carry out the mandate or expectations [of] setting up the coordinative enterprise."[75]

As for the benefits and drawbacks of NSC-level coordination, one advantage of such an option is that the NSC mechanisms of policy coordination committees (PCCs) or interagency policy committees (IPCs) are an already established option used for working on interagency issues, with participation usually at the Assistant Secretary level.[76] PCCs are the "the main day-to-day fora for interagency coordination of national security policies," have accountability because of their responsibility to "ensure timely responses to the President's decisions," and are already organized to address specific issues.[77] Strengths of this model include the idea that locating interagency coordination in the NSC leads to accountability for issues and provides the option for "a bird's-eye view of all relevant efforts" that allows for policy alignment,

---

[70] The report was "based on interviews with 13 academic and practitioner experts in the field of collaboration" (GAO, 2012, pp. 15–16).

[71] Kaiser, 2011, p. 6.

[72] Kaiser, 2011, p. 11.

[73] GAO, 2014, p. 33.

[74] GAO, 2012, p. 16.

[75] Kaiser, 2011, p. 11.

[76] See EOP, *National Security Presidential Memorandum*, Washington, D.C.: White House, April 4, 2017; EOP, *Organization of the National Security Council System*, Washington, D.C.: White House, February 13, 2009; EOP, *Organization of the National Security Council System*, Washington, D.C.: White House, February 13, 2001.

[77] EOP, 2017.

resource allocation, direct communication ability with the president, and a designated responsibility for an issue.[78]

Weaknesses of NSC-level coordination include the notion that, depending on the issue, the aforementioned process is not as straightforward as its seems. As the Green and Proctor report described, at the time of its writing, "responsibility at the [NSC] is diffuse and unclear. There are currently three separate directorates at the NSC, in [addition] to other regional and functional directorates, that are responsible for some aspect of CVE, and they report to different deputy national security advisers. Unified leadership and commitment starting at the White House is needed to leverage all relevant assets and enhance accountability for results."[79] Thus, for the model to work to address an issue, the issue at hand would already have to be a priority focus for the president. As the INSS report states, the NSC "would seem the most likely organ to direct and improve national security integration, but it has only the power to advise the President. The President has to forge interagency cooperation by convening coordination committees, designating a particular agency to lead an interagency effort, or utilizing 'czars' who rely on prestige and the aura of delegated Presidential authority to accomplish interagency coordination. These approaches regularly fail, and when they succeed it is often because of extraordinary leadership and good fortune—factors to be welcomed but not relied upon."[80]

Federal Interagency Organization Going Forward

There is not an obviously preferable model for interagency coordination going forward; in fact, the literature raised many of the same issues our interviewees flagged

---

[78] Green and Procter, 2016, p. 56.

[79] Green and Procter, 2016, p. 24.

[80] Lamb and Munsing, 2011, p. 7. Other reports echo this idea; for example, a document that explains the national security policy process and interagency system states that, even though PCCs/IPCs require collaboration,

> teamwork and unity is vulnerable to political risks, bureaucratic equities, and personal relationships. . . . Also, hard problems do not lend themselves to easy solutions, and frequently there are genuine differences between departments over the best ways, means, and objectives for dealing with a national security problem. Moreover, because regional experts tend to dominate on overall policy approaches (even though they may lack expertise on many functional issues), different interpretations of events or credibility issues may arise within the [PCC/ IPC] group. . . . The wide range of issues, the different policy perspectives of various departments, the nature of bureaucratic politics, contests over turf and responsibilities, disagreements over which department has the lead, and the clash of personalities and egos all place a premium on ensuring that the equities of all involved agencies are considered, and on building an informal policy consensus amongst the players. . . . The operational dynamics of individual [PCCs/IPCs], like most working group entities, vary according to the personalities (and, sometimes, personal agenda[s]) of the individuals who are in charge of, or participate in them (Alan G. Whittaker, Frederick C. Smith, and Elizabeth McKune, "The National Security Policy Process: The National Security Council and Interagency System," *The National Security Policy Process: The National Security Council and Interagency System*, October 8, 2010, pp. 38–39).

as important for the specific case of terrorism prevention. However, several core functional requirements emerged as necessary for a future structure to improve on past performance.

First, there was consensus that terrorism prevention efforts needed top-level access and support from the leadership of participating agencies. In discussing the effectiveness of the Task Force over time, interviewees argued that it functioned most effectively when leadership at all of the central departments and agencies—DHS, DOJ, FBI, and NCTC—were engaged in the effort.[81] That connection and buy-in was viewed as having weakened over time. Although there is still high-level involvement in terrorism prevention at DHS, multiple national-level interviewees indicated that it was much less the case in other agencies (they ascribed this in part to current uncertainties about the direction of terrorism prevention strategy and activity). Although Secretary-level buy-in was viewed as important for internal purposes and focus, it was also viewed as important for external audiences. It was important for agency leadership to be part of the effort because commitments coming from the top of an organization (similar to Police Chief involvement in community policing engagements) lend a credibility that may not be possible coming from lower levels within the organization.

Second, whatever coordination structure is chosen, driving experimentation and innovation should be a priority. Although the Task Force assembled most of the main (security) players for CVE, the way it functioned in practice magnified rather than reduced barriers to risk-taking and innovation. Because the Task Force leadership did not have sufficient authority to assign tasks across agency boundaries, interviewees indicated that the concerns of any participant could delay or stop activity. The perception that the Task Force was responsible for CVE reduced the impetus for agencies to act on their own.

This is the exact opposite effect that members of multidisciplinary teams at the operational level described: There, the dilution of accountability to the group rather than the individual agencies was viewed as positive. The forcing function for action there was the individual cases that came before them, and the fact that it was the M-DT that was accountable rather than the individual social-service agency, police department, or NGO-facilitated intervention, which always involved some level of risk acceptance compared with "safer" but potentially costlier criminal justice options. Furthermore, although there might be disagreement and concerns raised among M-DT members regarding a specific case (e.g., the level of risk posed by an individual or what programs were needed to help them), decisions had to be made and action had

---

[81] According to one of the federal-level interviewees, "People within the Task Force did have access to leadership in various departments. Sometimes drove people nuts, but if we needed to get to Secretary Johnson, [Task Force leadership] had a direct line to the secretary. A person from NCTC could probably talk to [their Director]. There was an ability of CVE at the federal level to cut through red tape. As a top-down bureaucratic body, it did all the things you'd expect that body to do." Access was also flagged as important for internal department leadership on CVE (DHS HSAC, 2016).

to be taken. At the federal level, there was no similar operational driver for Task Force activities, so efforts that involved risks—of failure, of controversy, of interagency friction—could in practice be vetoed by single agencies, throttling experimentation and innovation.

Whatever structure is chosen for interagency coordination, this mismatch of accountability for action and inaction must be addressed. In practical terms, this will likely require either a structure in which (1) accountability and responsibility are vested with the interagency entity, with sufficient authority to execute; or (2) accountability and responsibility must remain with individual agencies, and therefore terrorism prevention responsibilities must be clearly divided, with credit or blame for action or inaction accruing to the agencies in their individual slices of the policy space. In either model, however, interviewees who had been involved in CVE efforts at the federal level over multiple years also indicated that external drivers would likely still be needed to avoid agencies deprioritizing terrorism prevention efforts compared with other agency missions and responsibilities. Early on, the quarterly breakfasts of deputy level officials served this function, since no agency wanted to send their leadership to the meetings without accomplishments to bring to the table.

Third, if bringing nonsecurity departments and agencies like HHS or the U.S. Department of Education more substantially and publicly to the table is indeed a priority (and the frequency with which it was raised in our interviews suggests that it should be), that goal will likely be a core driver in the design of the organization and the division of responsibilities. In this research effort, we were not able to gather data to systematically explore the full range of equities of the nonsecurity federal agencies for terrorism prevention (and with respect to past CVE efforts). However, some interviewees suggested that models that divided responsibility and that were focused on broader violence risk and addressing ideologically motivated violence in efforts that are not labeled as terrorism-specific might be attractive options. The negotiation process that would be involved at the federal level to identify the path forward would likely bear significant resemblance to the negotiation that local-level interviewees described as required for the formation of consensus structures for multidisciplinary risk assessment and intervention efforts.

Fourth, interagency coordination requires bridging the boundary between classified and unclassified information, and having efficient mechanisms to develop readily sharable and fully unclassified products. The issue of bridging issues of information sensitivity and classification was raised repeatedly in the context of interagency coordination, echoing and reinforcing points made by state, local, and even private-sector interviewees. The perception exists that, in order to be effective and credible within the federal government, terrorism prevention efforts must be informed by threat assessments that are only available in classified products. As a result, whatever interagency structure and coordinating mechanisms are used, they must successfully bridge the classified and unclassified realms. This has practical implications (e.g., an interviewee pointed out that the Task Force being located in office space that was not outfitted to readily receive and store classified information made it difficult to maintain that bridge).

However, as discussed in previous chapters, interviewees from both inside and outside government cautioned that classification (and other sensitive information designation) was a significant hindrance to interagency (and cross-stakeholder) coordination. They viewed classification as limiting the value of products or resources to terrorism prevention efforts because, to them, effectiveness required sharing information with local agencies, technology companies, and even community organizations. In whatever structure or framework is used for interagency coordination at the federal level, declassification and release of information must be a priority. This issue may seem minor compared with larger concerns about the division of interagency responsibility, but in practice, it becomes a high-leverage driver of future effectiveness.[82] As one of our interviewees succinctly said, when explaining what you are doing in a program to a skeptical audience, "it is far more credible to be able to show them the information you have leading to concern," rather than showing it to the handful of people who are cleared to see it and expecting everyone else to trust you.[83]

Finally, balancing operational and enforcement-based activity versus efforts aimed at collaborative and community-centered approaches must be a priority for federal terrorism prevention efforts to be effective. Just as enforcement action by local law enforcement was a recurring challenge to more-collaborative approaches to intervention—not just for terrorism prevention, but for other violence and crime issues as well—action by the FBI (and other federal law enforcement agencies) will present challenges to federal terrorism prevention activities. Rightly or wrongly, the FBI's actions have great leverage to move public and community trust in all federal-level

---

[82] See, for example, discussion in Martin C. Libicki, Brian A. Jackson, David R. Frelinger, Beth E. Lachman, Cesse Cameron Ip, and Nidhi Kalra, *What Should Be Classified? A Framework with Application to the Global Force Management Data Initiative*, Santa Monica, Calif.: RAND Corporation, MG-989-JS, 2010. In this case, the costs of the restriction of information are particularly large, given that a core driver of external mistrust and opposition to CVE and, by extension, terrorism prevention efforts is a belief that their true purposes are being concealed.

[83] This tension for CVE (and, by extension, terrorism prevention) has been recognized for some time. For example, from Bjelopera, 2015, pp. 17–18:

> Excessive secretiveness regarding government efforts to understand the legally protected activities of Americans might actually fuel radicalization. . . . A project developed as part of the second SIP objective was not widely released. The study of radicalization among homegrown violent extremists performed by DHS, NCTC, and the FBI . . . was revealed to state and local law enforcement behind closed doors at the White House. This example poses the question: can the federal government build trust within local communities if it holds back from the general public its own study of how people in the United States radicalized and became terrorists? Will secretiveness in this area actually feed radical narratives? Additionally, will excessively secret government efforts to understand radicalization shake community trust in law enforcement? Federal attempts to develop *classified* theories about legally-protected activities may make community groups less willing to "share" information regarding those very activities—especially *if that information is treated strictly as intelligence by the government and the results of such "sharing" are never seen* (emphasis in original).

terrorism prevention efforts. The need for such actions to respond to imminent threats will always be present, and so the challenge cannot be eliminated. At the local level, this challenge has been managed in different ways. At one extreme are models where law enforcement is deeply involved and makes the investment in engagement to build trust. At the other end of the spectrum are models implemented independently from police, and their actions are therefore treated as exogenous to community-centered and collaborative efforts. Such a "separation model" gives up the value that could be gained from closer partnership, but limits its risks as well. Models suggested in interviews for the organization of federal terrorism prevention efforts going forward fall at different points on this spectrum—and both local experiences and the views of our interviewees suggest that any of them *could* be effective. However, available information suggests that choice is required—either effective coordination across agencies or a clear separation to protect the viability and effectiveness of more-collaborative engagement and intervention activities.

CHAPTER ELEVEN

Conclusions and Future Options for Practical Federal Terrorism Prevention

The federal government, including DHS and its interagency partners, have key roles to play to address terrorism risk through means other than traditional law enforcement tools of arrest, prosecution, and incarceration. At the same time, the federal role is complicated by a number of factors. Similar themes run through the distinct facets of terrorism prevention policy:

- The federal government must rely on outside organizations, and, therefore, willingness to participate in initiatives related to terrorism prevention is necessary for success.
- Maintaining the trust of members of the public and communities is critical to realizing the potential benefits of terrorism prevention, in both terrorism risk reduction and minimizing the costs associated with enforcement-focused approaches.
- Addressing a national-level problem that presents locally in different ways is a challenge that requires building a diversity of approaches that meet local needs.

From the national perspective, many of the individuals and organizations we spoke with saw terrorism prevention efforts as having major holes. The shortfalls came not only from a limited programmatic focus and resource investment since 2014, but also from sustained opposition that focused on undermining or halting CVE efforts. At the city level, the situation was not as dire as it appeared from Washington, D.C. Some cities have functioning programs that appear to be doing *exactly* what these efforts are supposed to do: providing alternative approaches to respond to individuals (often youths) who have done things that suggest they pose risk of violent behavior, and responding without aggressive investigation, arrest, and incarceration. In their design, these efforts have been shaped by the critiques of CVE, managing relationships with law enforcement in different ways, and building decisionmaking and privacy protection infrastructures designed to balance concerns about the risk an individual might pose to others with protecting those individuals.

However, everyone we spoke with indicated that, where progress has been made, the progress is fragile. Resources are scarce and some programs are at risk of dying off. There are concerns that focused opposition—which could be triggered by more federal involvement in local areas—could plow them under and means that dealing with at-risk individuals would revert fully to the criminal justice system. We saw that concern manifest in our study, as some organizations we thought had much they could teach us told us that they could not risk the potential connection to CVE or terrorism prevention that would be involved with participating in an interview. There are also areas where capacity or efforts to grow that capacity have ended, meaning that local intervention networks are limited at best.

Given these challenges, what is the right strategy for the federal government and for DHS in particular? The answer to that question varied somewhat across the different facets of terrorism prevention, but the most effective path cited was for the federal government to support state, local, NGO, and private actors rather than building capabilities itself. There was strong consensus across interviews at all levels that efforts have to be locally designed, managed, and driven.[1] There was near consensus on the need for the federal government to find ways to fund those local efforts, although the controversy means that there is work to be done to determine the best ways to do so.[2] The reasons for thinking that federal funding was needed varied. They included the need to incentivize local actors to focus on an issue that is likely not viewed as their highest priority, the apparent absence of private or philanthropic sources of funding, and the opportunity that federal support can provide for building knowledge and sharing expertise across programs that otherwise might be isolated in their areas.[3]

Arguments for federal support often were paired with examples of how support has been deployed for other problems to address risks to both communities and individuals, but the issues around CVE and, by extension, terrorism prevention, create additional difficulty: "If you think about other areas, like gang intervention . . . we do

---

[1]   This echoes recommendations in previous published documents such as Levitt, 2017; Rosand, 2017a; and RTI International, 2017b.

[2]   As one federal representative put it, "Our SIP was written and then there was no implementation because the administration changed. Develop a strategy that's more of an action plan and then put some money behind it that allows hyper-local individuals to access . . . those pots of money."

[3]   For example, one government representative in a city we visited stated that, "Philanthropic organizations also are not as much interested in funding such a low incidence thing and also they kind of consider it a U.S. government responsibility" (2018). This characterization is in relatively stark contrast, for example, to the discussion that argues for philanthropy to move into this area in DHS HSAC, 2016; and Green and Procter, 2016.

In a national-level interview, a former government official/current NGO representative stated that

> In terms of funding, $10 million is not going to cut it over 2 years. . . . Foundations are still skittish and federal funding is too politicized or too slow to be viable. Anything that can be done to diversify funding should be pursued. Previous DHS folks were keenly aware of that need. Foundations have criticized the framing as an entirely securitized issue linked to foreign policy issues with Syria and Iraq that [they] don't want to touch. . . . But if it's framed around anti-social behavior, promoting social cohesion in communities, addressing anti-immigrant violence, all sorts of other issues that would be linked to this agenda, I think you could get foundations involved (2018).

try to get those targeted resources to communities in need. The issue with CVE is the stigma of race and religion in a way that other stuff is not."[4] Interviewees emphasized that the federal government must be patient—that this is not a policy area where there is a short-term "silver bullet" policy solution, and that the time it will take to build consensus around local approaches may be significant. But having that patience and making the investment would pay off over time, compounding local-level success to national-level success.

There was also relatively strong, although not total, consensus that reinvestment in federal field staff—i.e., personnel located around the country who have a stake in their areas and the expertise to perform key terrorism prevention roles and facilitate local initiatives—was a very promising option. Someone who is based locally but who is aware of the federal picture could help to build relationships, strengthen trust, and act as an on-the-ground facilitator of local terrorism prevention efforts. This was viewed as a path that could both deliver immediate results *and* help to build for the longer term. The difference between the cities we visited where there were dynamic, supported, and engaged federal staff and those where they were absent was striking.

Also across interviewees, there was consensus that a major part of what was required to broaden viable federal action for terrorism prevention was in how the topic is *framed* from the federal level, and whether or not local areas have the flexibility to *reframe* it in ways that are appropriate for their circumstances. We heard variations of the message that "words matter" over and over again.[5] But it is not only in how the policy area is described: "So one of the lessons from [this city] is that how you scope this really matters. [But] it's not just how you scope this in words."[6] What most interviewees pointed to was the perception that, from the beginning of CVE, although it has been said that all forms of extremism are covered, the main focus was on jihadist violence and, as a result, on Muslim communities.[7] The vast majority of our interviewees emphasized that terrorism prevention must be inclusive of the threat of ideological violence from *all* sources—from ISIS to white supremacists to environmentally inspired violence—and must do so not only in words, but also in programming and investment.

It is not clear whether the federal government should take the further step that was argued by some interviewees at the local level and treat terrorism prevention as just one component of more-general violence reduction and eliminating efforts specifically "branded" as focusing on terrorism.[8] Increasing the involvement of some non-

---

[4] Interview with an NGO representative, 2018.

[5] Previous DHS efforts have also flagged this concern. See, for example, DHS HSAC, 2016.

[6] Interview with a federal representative in one U.S. city, 2018.

[7] This point has been echoed elsewhere, e.g., Southers, 2017.

[8] Interviewees used the category of targeted violence to include not only ideologically motivated violence, but also threats like school shootings, stalking and fixated violence, and other acts where planning or threatening

security agencies in terrorism prevention could be a step to gain some of the benefits of that proposal while maintaining terrorism prevention as a distinct program area. However, at the local level, it was clear that many places are already taking the step of "mainstreaming terrorism prevention" into more-general initiatives that respond to individuals at risk of committing violence, irrespective of how the federal government defines the problem and reflecting both what is practical for them and what is effective for their communities.[9]

When we bring together the potential options for the federal government across the different components of terrorism prevention policy and DHS's terrorism prevention lines of effort, there is a robust menu of actions that could be taken. The federal options fall into four main categories of activity and largely focus on enabling terrorism prevention initiatives from the bottom up and supporting the development of a national approach to this issue. There are specific issues in individual elements of terrorism prevention (e.g., concerns about liability issues raised regarding intervention) where federal action could be beneficial, but these are more narrowly focused. We discuss the different types of policy options across the phases of terrorism prevention, and summarize all of the specific options identified throughout the report in Table 11.1.[10]

Awareness and Training

In interviews across our study, one of the ideas that came up again and again was the simple value of *providing credible information* to agencies and organizations that were seeking to implement terrorism prevention efforts. Interviewees described a need for objective threat information by technology companies to guide their efforts and for risk-assessment information for corrections staff to manage programming intended to manage recidivism risk. Interviewees praised the CABs and CREXs from a number of directions as examples of successful efforts to deliver such information, and viewed as a good role for the federal government to continue.

The *sharing of best practices and knowledge* was similarly flagged as important, as was the value of bringing together researchers, implementers, and others to share information.[11]

---

periods could provide the opportunity to intervene before a criminal act has occurred.

[9] As alluded to previously, this is consistent with the broader participatory research approach to community-based intervention and problem solving (e.g., Ellis, quoted in Snair, Nicholson, and Giammaria, 2017, p. 52).

[10] As many of our interviewees pointed out, the nature of local responses to CVE, and by extension, terrorism prevention—including the preference to incorporate it into programs that are responsive to a wide range of violence prevention goals—means that initiatives to strengthen this national system will also contribute to responding to other pressing concerns, like school shootings and other mass-targeted violence.

[11] This recommendation is similar to those made with respect to CVE by DHS HSAC, 2016; and Green and Procter, 2016.

Table 11.1
Summary of Policy Options by Terrorism Prevention Activity and Category

Category	Countering Extremist Messaging Online	Community Education, Engagement, Resilience, and Risk-Factor Reduction	Referral Promotion	Intervention	Recidivism Reduction
Awareness and Training	• Provide threat information to technology firms to support their countermessaging efforts. • Increase technical staff in government terrorism prevention efforts to support outreach to industry. • Increase transparency of efforts and shareability of information provided for terrorism prevention purposes.	• Continue and expand outreach and local coordination efforts through CABs and CREXs.	• Continue and expand outreach and local coordination efforts through CABs and CREXs.	• Continue federal efforts to assemble and disseminate best practices and standards for intervention programs.	• Develop a customized CAB for corrections staff at the federal, state, and local levels. • When appropriate, develop training to disseminate best practices and new evidence-based practices in the corrections sector.

Table 11.1—Continued

Category	Countering Extremist Messaging Online	Community Education, Engagement, Resilience, and Risk-Factor Reduction	Referral Promotion	Intervention	Recidivism Reduction
Federal Support of Local Initiatives	• Use grant funding to support counternarrative activities outside government.	• Make "on-call experts" with knowledge, program design, and evaluation expertise available to support local terrorism prevention initiatives. • Use grant funding to support local and NGO early-phase terrorism prevention activities. • More broadly use tabletop exercises to assist localities in developing acceptable and practical approaches to terrorism prevention.	• Continue to support efforts to develop national-level hotlines for referral of at-risk individuals. • Use grant funding to support local and NGO referral promotion efforts, but recognize that substantial trust-building may be required.	• Use grant funding to support local and NGO intervention models and networks. • Make "on-call experts" with knowledge, program design, and evaluation expertise available to support local terrorism prevention initiatives. • Prioritize supporting intervention capacity separate from law enforcement organizations, particularly in areas where trust is weakened. • Explore alternative funding mechanisms for local initiatives.	• Use grant funding to support state, local, and NGO implementation of recidivism reduction programs.

Table 11.1—Continued

Category	Countering Extremist Messaging Online	Community Education, Engagement, Resilience, and Risk-Factor Reduction	Referral Promotion	Intervention	Recidivism Reduction
Federal Program Development	• N/A	• Reconstitute and expand federal field staff to act as primary focal points for terrorism prevention at the local level.	• N/A	• Reconstitute and expand federal field staff to act as primary focal points for terrorism prevention at the local level.	• Coordinate with (and assist, as appropriate) federal corrections agencies developing recidivism reduction programming. • Support the development of program for terrorism prevention intervention efforts to maintain effectiveness across the country.
Situational Awareness	• Sustain efforts to characterize the extent of extremist content online on an ongoing basis. • Publicly release results of the content census to enable public action.	• N/A	• Support periodic, publicly released national surveys to assess public willingness to refer individuals because of concern regarding early mobilization activities.	• Gather data on existing capabilities relevant to terrorism prevention intervention nationally to help facilitate network development and identify shortfalls.	• Develop and maintain a centralized database of individuals incarcerated for ideological violence–related offenses to support program development and implementation.
Regulatory and Legal Issues	• N/A	• N/A	• Address perceived legal and regulatory barriers to interagency collaboration in terrorism prevention referral and intervention.	• Address perceived legal and liability barriers to nongovernmental intervention activities.	• N/A

Table 11.1—Continued

Category	Countering Extremist Messaging Online	Community Education, Engagement, Resilience, and Risk-Factor Reduction	Referral Promotion	Intervention	Recidivism Reduction
Research and Evaluation	• Continue to invest in evaluation of counternarrative efforts.	• Support periodic, publicly released national surveys to assess radicalization and mobilization to violence knowledge and awareness.	• Continue research focused on improving risk assessment methods, but realistically manage expectations for their possible accuracy.	• Continue to invest in evaluation of intervention programs. • Prioritize research and evaluation effort to better understand factors affecting the sustainability of terrorism prevention intervention programs.	• Continue to invest in evaluation of recidivism-reduction programs. • Continue research focused on improving risk assessment methods, but realistically manage expectations for their possible accuracy. • Prioritize focused research and evaluation effort to better understand the effect of incarceration on radicalization and violence risk.
Auxiliary Federal Activities	• N/A	• Recognize and proactively manage effects that DHS and federal programs can have on community trust to support terrorism prevention initiatives. • Increase interagency investment separate from terrorism prevention initiatives to address community concerns and reduce risk factors related to radicalization to violence.	• N/A	• N/A	• N/A

In the course of the study, *adaptation of existing tools* (e.g., CREXs) to help empower local areas to explore the types of terrorism prevention that are appropriate for their circumstances appeared to be promising.[12] All of these efforts—some building on past programs and initiatives—are options that could be included in future policy design.

We also heard arguments for *openness and transparency in training delivery and more broadly* in discussions from the federal perspective, as well as with local organizations and technology firms.[13] In addition to helping to support trust in a controversial area, using unclassified and open source information that can be shared broadly is more practical for efforts that must bridge many organizational boundaries.

Federal Support of Local Initiatives

Given the difficulties associated with direct federal action in many elements of terrorism prevention, federal support of local initiatives is a core option to strengthen terrorism prevention capacity nationally. Although U.S.-focused messaging was viewed as nearly nonexistent, federal action in that space was viewed as problematic and unlikely to succeed. Federal efforts aimed at referral promotion likely would reinforce narratives that terrorism prevention (as was argued regarding CVE) is surveillance and exacerbate concerns about past federal focus on enforcement and coercive approaches to terrorism.[14] As a result, across the different components of terrorism prevention, *federal action to facilitate local action* was viewed by interviewees as the better option. Public-private partnerships appear to be the best approach in terms of messaging (e.g., the Peer2Peer program). In a number of facets of terrorism prevention, continuing direct support to local programs through grants is needed.[15] For intervention in particular, a

---

[12] For example, in one city we visited, a law enforcement representative described an exercise that had been held locally: "It was interesting to see the interactions of different people. We had people from [community groups,] local mosques, law enforcement, the mayor's office, police officers, different people come take a look at it and see the reactions to it and how everyone sees the problem."

[13] See the discussion in Bjelopera, 2015; and Patel and Koushik, 2017.

[14] Enforcement-focused organizations like the FBI could develop their own programs to provide alternatives to prosecution (e.g., the DEEP program). This could be a way for those agencies to reduce costs and broaden their range of tools for addressing terrorism risk. As discussed previously, lack of access to information on those initiatives for this study meant that we cannot assess them and their role in detail. However, given concerns raised in interviews across the cities we visited regarding community trust of the FBI and similar agencies with enforcement missions, it is unlikely that these agencies could ever become the foundation for substantial terrorism prevention efforts for individuals who have not committed crimes.

[15] Note that other entities have argued for a continued need for government support, even if other sources become available: "Even with increased private-sector and philanthropic investment in CVE, there will always be a need for government funding. The Commission supports the U.S. government's efforts to increase small grants for domestic and international efforts" (Green and Procter, 2016, p. 61).

substantial investment in intervention capacity that is separate from law enforcement would be valuable, and would address previous criticism that CVE was not, in fact, providing alternatives to law enforcement action.[16] There is also a need to broaden support from nonsecurity agencies (as part of efforts to broaden their involvement in interagency efforts, as discussed in Chapter Ten), which would be a practical approach to making progress on this problem in a way that is acceptable to communities and members of the public.

More importantly than the monetary support discussed above is the role the federal government can play to help communities identify and implement the types of programs that work for them. This was often crystalized as "federal government as a convener"—i.e., getting people around a table to figure out what they needed and what was necessary to achieve their goals. Given the focus on federal field staff in the cities we visited, however, it was clear that this required much more than just getting the right people at the table. To be a *credible convener* and one who can navigate local complexities requires an individual with knowledge of terrorism prevention who can play the roles discussed earlier. It also requires individuals who can build trust over time: Even if the federal government is giving away its help for free, the people providing that help have to be trusted enough that communities—including local government, service providers, and members of the public—want what they are providing.

Federal Program Development

Most of the options identified in this analysis are not about new federal programs. Some involve continuing or revitalizing current federal efforts. Funding and programmatic support would be needed to put the field staff discussed above in place and to support them in playing their facilitating roles. Providing some types of support to local initiatives requires a grant program (or the connection of terrorism prevention to other grant programs).[17] The main programmatic exception to this is in the area of *recidivism*

---

[16] However, it should be noted that concerns have been raised by critics of past CVE efforts regarding how federal support of programming will shape the autonomy and nature of NGOs that accept it—a criticism that this approach would still be open to; see American-Arab Anti-Discrimination Committee, 2016.

[17] Based on our interviews and materials provided by DHS, it is apparent that there are substantial challenges in using other DHS grant programs, including the Homeland Security Grant Program and the Urban Areas Security Initiative, to support terrorism prevention (and, previously, CVE) efforts. Although CVE was included previously as a priority area in grant guidance, limited applications for projects were received and funded. Interviewees indicated that many factors contributed to that reality, including competing local priorities for the use of funds from those programs (e.g., to maintain existing capabilities), potential reticence to use the funds to support ongoing programming versus tangible equipment acquisition, and shifting national-level priority areas for investment that crowded out other types of applications. Terrorism prevention and CVE also have not been well reflected in the Threat and Hazard Identification and Risk Assessment (THIRA) process used to assess needs for support via Federal Emergency Management Agency (FEMA) grant programs. Although options exist to reduce some of the barriers to using these programs for terrorism prevention, it was unclear whether they would be sufficient

reduction, where the central role of the federal prison system in managing terrorism-related offenders means that any expansion of capabilities would require action at the federal level. Another issue where the federal government is best positioned to respond is human capital: the development of the people—both inside government and in the research and service-provider sectors—who are both engaged in and knowledgeable about terrorism prevention.[18] Such issues are more likely to be addressed in the course of other federal activities (e.g., investments in public-private partnerships, research, or program implementation) than through a stand-alone effort, but building and maintaining the bench of expert practitioners in this area was viewed as important by our interviewees from the national to the local levels.

Situational Awareness and Research and Evaluation

In our discussion of elements of terrorism prevention policy in this report, we distinguished situational awareness–type efforts from research and evaluation. In practice, however, both types of *data-gathering and analysis* likely would be collocated in the Directorate of Science and Technology since, as one of our interviewees put it, "Unlike the Bureau of Justice Statistics in the Department of Justice, there is no Bureau of Homeland Security Statistics."[19] Key situational awareness requirements include tracking public views and concerns and assessing the capacity of national intervention and other systems. Beyond those efforts, other *research and evaluation* requirements appear across the range of terrorism prevention elements: Our interviewees and literature sources called out the need for better measurement and evaluation (as well as integration into programs as they are implemented),[20] and *research on the sustainability of terrorism prevention efforts.* They also noted the enduring challenge of individual risk assessment for ideologically motivated violence.[21] Investments in any or all of these options could benefit the design, implementation, and evaluation of future programs. Both interviewees and authors of published literature argued that a more robust and interdisciplinary research community is needed for terrorism prevention, and, although efforts in the past regarding CVE were useful and should be continued (e.g., NCTC's

---

to enable strengthening terrorism prevention capability nationally, suggesting the need for continued dedicated funding streams for this policy area. A similar argument can be made for support of risk-factor reduction and early-stage terrorism prevention via grant mechanisms managed by nonsecurity agencies.

[18] See the recommendations in Weine et al., 2015.

[19] Interview with a federal-level representative, 2018.

[20] For example, see McKenzie, 2016; Owens et al., 2016, p. 5-1; RTI International, 2017b; Green and Procter, 2016; Romaniuk, 2015; Aggarwal, 2018, p. 6; Weine et al., 2015; Rosand, 2016; Patel and Koushik, 2017.

[21] DHS HSAC laid out a program of research and evaluation efforts for CVE in its report (2016, p. 14).

annual CVE conference), they are not enough.[22] Strengthening investment in evaluation would address criticism of the effectiveness of both CVE and current terrorism prevention efforts.

The timing of this study, with the changeover in administrations, presents an opportunity to look at what had been done before and explore paths forward. When we integrated available information on both national and local CVE and terrorism prevention initiatives, the picture that emerged was one of an effort still at an early stage. Some federally supported initiatives were viewed by our interviewees as showing real promise. There are examples of local initiatives that are taking on the challenge of addressing violence risk in individuals who have not yet committed any crime, including violence inspired by ideological causes. Individuals and organizations from the national to the local levels viewed this policy area as an important one, and strongly argued that national approaches to violence prevention need to address ideological violence and terrorism, even though the absolute risk of terrorism to any locality may be quite small.

However, past CVE efforts and current terrorism prevention initiatives have garnered significant controversy because of legitimate and important civil rights and civil liberties concerns, as well as criticism about how past CVE efforts were implemented—including whether they were intended to achieve something quite different than their stated goals. If greater consensus can be achieved regarding appropriate ways to build non–criminal justice approaches to dealing with terrorism risk, that process could help move toward better national policies. To that end, the federal policy options laid out in this report have in part responded to issues raised during early efforts to develop then-CVE programs, drawing on examples from localities that have built approaches that seek to safeguard the rights and meet the needs of individuals potentially at risk of committing ideological violence, while still protecting society from potential terrorist attack. In doing so, the goal is to provide a set of options for *effective* policies and intervention options, but also *practical* ones, which respond appropriately to terrorism risk but do so in a way that simultaneously minimizes the manifold costs to the individuals affected and the society that terrorism prevention efforts aim to protect.

---

[22] Multiple interviews at the national and local levels, 2018. See also RTI International, 2017b; Rosand, 2017a; and Levitt, 2017. One interviewee argued that the creation of a separate research entity—"a more DARPA, In-Q-Tel–type setup outside Washington"—would help to depoliticize the research component of these programs (Interview with a former federal staff member, 2018).

References

ACLU—*See* American Civil Liberties Union.

ADL—*See* Anti-Defamation League.

Administrative Office of U.S. Courts, *Supervision Costs Significantly Less than Incarceration in Federal System*, July 18, 2013. As of June 28, 2018:
http://www.uscourts.gov/news/2013/07/18/
supervision-costs-significantly-less-incarceration-federal-system

"Against Violent Extremism," homepage, undated. As of June 19, 2018:
http://www.againstviolentextremism.org/

Aggarwal, Neil Krishan, "Questioning the Current Public Health Approach to Countering Violent Extremism," *Global Public Health*, May 11, 2018. As of June 27, 2018:
https://doi.org/10.1080/17441692.2018.1474936

Aharoni, Eyal, Lila Rabinovich, Joshua Mallett, and Andrew R. Morral, *An Assessment of Program Sustainability in Three Bureau of Justice Assistance Criminal Justice Domains*, Santa Monica, Calif.: RAND Corporation, RR-550-BJA, 2014. As of August 21, 2018:
https://www.rand.org/pubs/research_reports/RR550.html

Alameda County Sheriff's Office, "FY16 CVE Grant Application, EMW-2016-CA-APP-00087," Released under the Freedom of Information Act, 2016. As of August 21, 2018:
https://www.dhs.gov/sites/default/files/publications/
EMW-2016-CA-APP-00087%20Full%20Applicaiton.pdf

Alvarez, Krisann M., Maureen C. Kenny, Brad Donohue, and Kimberly M. Carpin, "Why Are Professionals Failing to Initiate Mandated Reports of Child Maltreatment, and Are There Any Empirically Based Training Programs to Assist Professionals in the Reporting Process?" *Aggression and Violent Behavior*, Vol. 9, No. 5, August 2004, pp. 563–578.

American Civil Liberties Union, "ACLU Briefing Paper: What Is Wrong with the Government's 'Countering Violent Extremism' Programs," undated(a). As of June 11, 2018:
https://www.aclu.org/other/aclu-v-dhs-briefing-paper

———, "CVE FOIA Documents," webpage, undated(b). As of August 21, 2018:
https://www.aclu.org/foia-collection/cve-foia-documents

———, "The Problem with 'Countering Violent Extremism' Programs," webpage, undated(c). As of June 11, 2018:
https://www.aclu.org/other/problem-countering-violent-extremism-programs?redirect=problem-countering-violent-extremism-programs

American-Arab Anti-Discrimination Committee, "Civil Liberties and Human Services Groups Raise Concerns About DHS Countering Violent Extremism Grants," press release, September 1, 2016. As of June 11, 2018:
http://www.adc.org/civil-liberties-and-human-services-groups-raise-concerns-about-dhs-countering-violent-extremism-grants

Angwin, Julia, Jeff Larson, Surya Mattu, and Lauren Kirchner, "Machine Bias," *ProPublica*, May 23, 2016. As of June 27, 2018:
https://www.propublica.org/article/machine-bias-risk-assessments-in-criminal-sentencing

Anti-Defamation League, *Al Shabab's American Recruits*, New York, February 2015. As of June 18, 2018:
https://www.adl.org/sites/default/files/documents/assets/pdf/combating-hate/al-shabaabs-american-recruits.pdf

———, *Murder and Extremism in the United States in 2017: An ADL Center on Extremism Report*, New York, 2017a. As of June 22, 2018:
https://www.adl.org/resources/reports/murder-and-extremism-in-the-united-states-in-2017

———, "Responding to Charlottesville, U.S. Conference of Mayors and ADL Join on Action Plan to Combat Hate, Extremism and Discrimination," press release, August 18, 2017b. As of September 1, 2018:
https://www.adl.org/news/press-releases/responding-to-charlottesville-us-conference-of-mayors-and-adl-join-on-action

AOUSC—*See* Administrative Office of U.S. Courts.

Apuzzo, Matt, and Adam Goldman, "After Spying on Muslims, New York Police Agree to Greater Oversight," *New York Times*, March 6, 2017. As of June 28, 2018:
https://www.nytimes.com/2017/03/06/nyregion/nypd-spying-muslims-surveillance-lawsuit.html

Austin, Ashley M., Mark J. Macgowan, and Eric F. Wagner, "Effective Family-Based Interventions for Adolescents with Substance Abuse Problems: A Systematic Review," *Research on Social Work Practice*, Vol. 15, No. 2, 2005, pp. 67–83.

"Average Mohamed," homepage, undated. As of June 21, 2018:
https://averagemohamed.com/

Bales, William D., and Alex R. Piquero, "Assessing the Impact of Imprisonment on Recidivism," *Journal of Experimental Criminology*, Vol. 8, 2012, pp. 71–101.

Barker, Cat, "Update on Australian Government Measures to Counter Violent Extremism: A Quick Guide," Parliament of Australia, August 18, 2017. As of June 27, 2018:
http://parlinfo.aph.gov.au/parlInfo/download/library/prspub/5461291/upload_binary/5461291.pdf

Barrett, Richard, *Beyond the Caliphate: Foreign Fighters and the Threat of Returnees*, New York: The Soufan Center, October 2017.

BBC, "Reality Check: What Is the Prevent Strategy?" June 4, 2017. As of March 10, 2018:
http://www.bbc.com/news/election-2017-40151991

———, "Germany Starts Enforcing Hate Speech Law," January 1, 2018. As of August 3, 2018:
https://www.bbc.com/news/technology-42510868

Beaghley, Sina, Todd C. Helmus, Miriam Matthews, Rajeev Ramchand, David Stebbins, Amanda Kadlec, and Michael A. Brown, *Development and Pilot Test of the RAND Program Evaluation Toolkit for Countering Violent Extremism*, Santa Monica, Calif.: RAND Corporation, RR-1799-DHS, 2017. As of August 21, 2018:
https://www.rand.org/pubs/research_reports/RR1799.html

Beaton, Randal D., and L. Clark Johnson, "Instrument Development and Evaluation of Domestic Preparedness Training for First Responders," *Prehospital and Disaster Medicine*, Vol. 17, No. 3, September 2002, pp. 119–125.

Bergen, Peter, "Who Do Terrorists Confide In?" *CNN*, February 3, 2016. As of June 22, 2018: https://www.cnn.com/2016/02/03/opinions/terrorists-confidants-leakage-bergen/index.html

Bergen, Peter, Albert Ford, Alyssa Sims, and David Sterman, *Terrorism in America After 9/11*, Washington, D.C.: New America, undated. As of June 22, 2018: https://www.newamerica.org/in-depth/terrorism-in-america/

Bergen, Peter, David Sterman, Alyssa Sims, and Albert Ford, "ISIS in the West: The Western Militant Flow to Syria and Iraq," *New America*, March 2016. As of June 22, 2018: https://static.newamerica.org/attachments/12898-isis-in-the-west-march-2016/ISIS-in-the-West-II.8a0c30a894ec4b96a8340d5b26779456.pdf

Berger, J. M., *Making CVE Work: A Focused Approach Based on Process Disruption*, International Centre for Counter-Terrorism—The Hague, May 2016. As of August 22, 2018: https://www.icct.nl/wp-content/uploads/2016/05/J.-M.-Berger-Making-CVE-Work-A-Focused-Approach-Based-on-Process-Disruption-.pdf

Berger, J. M., and Jonathon Morgan, *The ISIS Twitter Census: Defining and Describing the Population of ISIS Supporters on Twitter*, Washington, D.C.: The Brookings Institution, No. 20, March 2015. As of June 20, 2018: https://www.brookings.edu/wp-content/uploads/2016/06/isis_twitter_census_berger_morgan.pdf

Berger, J. M., and Heather Perez, *The Islamic State's Diminishing Returns on Twitter: How Suspensions Are Limiting the Social Networks of English-Speaking ISIS Supporters*, Washington, D.C.: George Washington University Program on Extremism, February 2016. As of June 27, 2018: https://extremism.gwu.edu/sites/g/files/zaxdzs2191/f/downloads/JMB%20Diminishing%20Returns.pdf

Berkell, Kelly, "Risk Reduction in Terrorism Cases: Sentencing and the Post-Conviction Environment," *Journal for Deradicalization*, No. 13, Winter 2017/18.

Bhati, Avinash Singh, *An Information Theoretic Method for Estimating the Number of Crimes Averted by Incapacitation*, Washington, D.C.: Urban Institute, 2007.

Bickert, Monika, and Brian Fishman, "Hard Questions: How We Counter Terrorism," *Facebook Newsroom*, June 15, 2017. As of June 20, 2018: https://newsroom.fb.com/news/2017/06/how-we-counter-terrorism

Bipartisan Policy Center, National Security Preparedness Group, *Preventing Violent Radicalization in America*, Washington, D.C., June 2011. As of August 21, 2018: https://bipartisanpolicy.org/wp-content/uploads/sites/default/files/NSPG.pdf

Bjelopera, Jerome P., *Countering Violent Extremism in the United States*, Washington, D.C.: Congressional Research Service, 7-5700, February 19, 2014.

———, "Testimony Before the Committee on Homeland Security, Subcommittee on Counterterrorism and Intelligence," U.S. House of Representatives, October 28, 2015.

———, *Domestic Terrorism: An Overview*, Washington, D.C.: Congressional Research Service, R44921, August 21, 2017. As of August 18, 2018: https://fas.org/sgp/crs/terror/R44921.pdf

Blattman, Christopher, and Jeannie Annan, "Can Employment Reduce Lawlessness and Rebellion? A Field Experiment with High-Risk Men in a Fragile State," *American Political Science Review*, Vol. 110, No. 1, February 2016, pp. 1–17.

Boddie, Stephanie C., Cary Funk, et al., *Religion in Prisons: A 50-State Survey of Prison Chaplains*, Pew Research Center, Pew Forum on Religion and Public Life, March 22, 2012.

Bodine-Baron, Elizabeth, Todd C. Helmus, Madeline Magnuson, and Zev Winkelman, *Examining ISIS Support and Opposition Networks on Twitter*, Santa Monica, Calif.: RAND Corporation, RR-1328-RC, August 2016. As of August 21, 2018:
https://www.rand.org/pubs/research_reports/RR1328.html

BOP—*See* Bureau of Prisons.

Borum, Randy, Dewey G. Cornell, William Modzeleski, and Shane R. Jimerson, "What Can Be Done About School Shootings? A Review of the Evidence," *Educational Researcher*, Vol. 39, No. 1, 2010, pp. 27–37.

Brennan Center for Justice, *Countering Violent Extremism: Myths and Fact*, undated. As of June 11, 2018:
https://www.brennancenter.org/sites/default/files/analysis/102915%20Final%20CVE%20Fact%20Sheet.pdf

Briggs, Rachel, and Sebastien Feve, *Review of Programs to Counter Narratives of Violent Extremism: What Works and What Are the Implications for Government?* London: Institute for Strategic Dialogue, 2013.

Broadcasting Board of Governors, "Mission," homepage, undated. As of August 3, 2018:
https://www.bbg.gov/who-we-are/mission

Brown, Michael, "Freed: Ripples of the Convicted and Released Terrorist in America," thesis, Monterey, Calif.: Naval Postgraduate School, 2011. As of August 5, 2018:
http://hdl.handle.net/10945/5822

Bryant, Lisa, "France Outlines New Plan to Fight Extremism," *Voice of America*, May 9, 2016. As of June 27, 2018:
https://www.voanews.com/a/france-outlines-new-plan-to-flight-extremism/3321751.html

Bunzel, Cole, "Come Back to Twitter: A Jihadi Warning Against Telegram," *Jihadica*, July 18, 2016. As of June 1, 2018:
http://www.jihadica.com/come-back-to-twitter

Bureau of Justice Assistance, *State and Local Anti-Terrorism Training (SLATT) Program*, Washington, D.C.: U.S. Department of Justice, undated. As of June 28, 2018:
https://www.bja.gov/ProgramDetails.aspx?Program_ID=120

———, *Intelligence-Led Policing: The New Intelligence Architecture*, Washington, D.C.: U.S. Department of Justice, NCJ 210681, September 2005.

———, "Edward Byrne Memorial Justice Assistance Grant (JAG) Program, Frequently Asked Questions (FAQs)," Washington, D.C.: U.S. Department of Justice, August 2017. As of August 21, 2018:
https://www.bja.gov/Funding/JAGFAQ.pdf

———, *State and Local Anti-Terrorism Training (SLATT)*, Washington, D.C.: U.S. Department of Justice, March 8, 2018. As of June 28, 2018:
https://www.bja.gov/funding/SLATT18.pdf

Bureau of Prisons, *Annual Determination of Average Cost of Incarceration*, July 19, 2016. As of June 27, 2018:
https://www.federalregister.gov/documents/2016/07/19/2016-17040/annual-determination-of-average-cost-of-incarceration

———, "Countering Inmate Extremism: Annual Training 2017," briefing, released under the Freedom of Information Act, January 2017. As of June 27, 2018:
https://www.bop.gov/foia/docs/countering_inmate_extremism_2017_training.pdf

Butts, Jeffrey A., Caterina Gouvis Roman, Lindsay Bostwick, and Jeremy R. Porter, "Cure Violence: A Public Health Model to Reduce Gun Violence," *Annual Review of Public Health*, Vol. 36, 2015, pp. 39–53.

Byman, Daniel, "Should We Treat Domestic Terrorists the Way We Treat ISIS? What Works—and What Doesn't," *Foreign Affairs*, October 3, 2017. As of June 22, 2018:
https://www.foreignaffairs.com/articles/united-states/2017-10-03/
should-we-treat-domestic-terrorists-way-we-treat-isis

Byman, Daniel, and Jeremy Shapiro, *Be Afraid. Be a Little Afraid: The Threat of Terrorism from Western Foreign Fighters in Syria and Iraq*, Washington, D.C.: Brookings Institution, Policy Paper No. 34, November 2014.

CAIR—*See* Council on American-Islamic Relations.

Camera, Lauren, "FBI's Anti-Extremism Website Should Be Scrapped, Groups Say," *U.S. News and World Report*, April 6, 2016. As of June 27, 2018:
https://www.usnews.com/news/articles/2016-04-06/
fbi-dont-be-a-puppet-website-criticized-by-advocacy-groups

Campbell, Thomas G., III, "Remaining Vigilant Against Domestic Terrorism: Making Meaning of Counterterrorism in a National Awareness Campaign," thesis, College Park, Md.: University of Maryland, 2011. As of August 21, 2018:
https://drum.lib.umd.edu/bitstream/handle/1903/12356/
Campbell_umd_0117N_12813.pdf?sequence=1

Carter, Jeremy G., and David L. Carter, "Law Enforcement Intelligence: Implications for Self-Radicalized Terrorism," *Police Practice and Research*, Vol. 13, No. 2, 2012, pp. 138–154.

Central Intelligence Agency, *The World Factbook*, 2017. As of August 21, 2018:
https://www.cia.gov/library/publications/the-world-factbook/

CEP—*See* Counter Extremism Project.

Chappell, Allison T., "The Philosophical Versus Actual Adoption of Community Policing: A Case Study," *Criminal Justice Review*, Vol. 34, No. 1, 2009, pp. 5–28.

Chermak, Steven M., Joshua D. Freilich, and Zachary Shemtob, "Law Enforcement Training and the Domestic Far Right," *Criminal Justice and Behavior*, Vol. 36, No. 12, December 2009, pp. 1305–1322.

Cherney, Adrian, "Designing and Implementing Programmes to Tackle Radicalization and Violent Extremism: Lessons from Criminology," *Dynamics of Asymmetric Conflict*, Vol. 9, 2016, pp. 82–94.

Cherney, Adrian, and Jason Hartley, "Community Engagement to Tackle Terrorism and Violent Extremism: Challenges, Tensions and Pitfalls," *Policing and Society*, Vol. 27, No. 7, 2017, pp. 750–763.

CIA—*See* Central Intelligence Agency.

Cilluffo, Frank, Gregory Saathoff, Jan Lane, Jeffrey Raynor, Sharon Cardash, Josh Magarik, Arnold Bogis, Andrew Whitehead, and Gina Lohr, *Out of the Shadows: Getting Ahead of Prisoner Radicalization*, Washington, D.C.: George Washington University Homeland Security Policy Institute, 2006. As of August 21, 2018:
https://cchs.gwu.edu/sites/g/files/zaxdzs2371/f/downloads/HSPI_Report_8.pdf

Cision Canada, "New Canada Centre for Community Engagement and Prevention of Violence Supports Local Efforts," news release, June 26, 2017. As of August 21, 2018:
https://www.newswire.ca/news-releases/new-canada-centre-for-community-engagement-and-prevention-of-violence-supports-local-efforts-630824813.html

City of Los Angeles, Mayor's Office of Public Safety, "Building Healthy Communities in Los Angeles; Managing Intervention Activities," DHS Grant Application EMW-2016-CA-APP-00294, 2016. As of August 21, 2018:
https://www.dhs.gov/sites/default/files/publications/EMW-2016-CA-APP-00294%20Full%20 Application.pdf

Clubb, Gordon, "The Role of Former Combatants in Preventing Youth Involvement in Terrorism in Northern Ireland: A Framework for Assessing Former Islamic State Combatants," *Studies in Conflict and Terrorism*, Vol. 39, No. 9, 2016, pp. 842–861.

Coaston, Jane, "The Alt-Right Is Going on Trial in Charlottesville," *Vox*, March 8, 2018. As of June 18, 2018:
https://www.vox.com/2018/3/8/17071832/alt-right-racists-charlottesville

Cole, James M., "Training Guiding Principles," memorandum for Heads of Components and United States Attorneys, Washington, D.C.: U.S. Department of Justice, Office of the Deputy Attorney General, March 20, 2012. As of August 21, 2018:
https://www.justice.gov/sites/default/files/dag/legacy/2012/03/20/training-guiding-principles.pdf

Colorado Resilience Collaborative, homepage, 2018. As of June 28, 2018:
https://www.du.edu/gspp/resilience-collaborative/about.html

Connell, Nadine M., Kristen Miggans, and Jean Marie McGloin, "Can a Community Policing Initiative Reduce Serious Crime? A Local Evaluation," *Police Quarterly*, Vol. 11, No. 2, June 2008, pp. 127–150.

Conway, Maura, "Determining the Role of the Internet in Violent Extremism and Terrorism: Six Suggestions for Progressing Research," *Studies in Conflict and Terrorism*, Vol. 40, No. 1, 2017a. As of June 14, 2018:
https://www.tandfonline.com/doi/full/10.1080/1057610X.2016.1157408

———, "Islamic State's Social Media Moment Has Passed," *Demos Quarterly*, November 1, 2017b. As of June 28, 2018:
https://quarterly.demos.co.uk/article/issue-12/islamic-states-social-media-moment

Conway, Maura, Moign Khawaja, Suraj Lakhani, Jeremy Reffin, Andrew Robertson, and David Weir, "Disrupting Daesh: Measuring Takedown of Online Terrorist Material and Its Impacts," *VOX-Pol*, Policy Report, 2017. As of June 27, 2018:
http://www.voxpol.eu/download/vox-pol_publication/ DCUJ5528-Disrupting-DAESH-1706-WEB-v2.pdf

Cordner, Gary, "Community Policing," in Michael D. Reisig and Robert J. Kane, eds., *The Oxford Handbook of Police and Policing*, Oxford, UK: Oxford University Press, 2014, pp. 148–171.

Corsaro, Nicholas, and Rod K. Brunson, "Are Suppression and Deterrence Mechanisms Enough? Examining the 'Pulling Levers' Drug Market Intervention Strategy in Peoria, Illinois, USA," *International Journal of Drug Policy*, Vol. 24, 2013, pp. 115–121.

Council on American-Islamic Relations California, "L.A. Based Organizations' Statement on Federal Government CVE Programs," webpage, undated. As of June 11, 2018:
https://ca.cair.com/losangeles/updates/ l-a-based-organizations-statement-on-federal-governments-countering-violent-extremism-programs

Council on American-Islamic Relations Florida, "CAIR-Florida Provides Training on Preserving Liberty and National Security Along with U.S. DHS and a National Security Delegation from France," press release, Tampa, Fla., December 8, 2016. As of June 27, 2018:
https://www.cairflorida.org/newsroom/press-releases/685-cair-florida-provides-training-on-preserving-liberty-and-national-security-along-with-u-s-dhs-and-a-national-security-delegation-from-france.html

Counter Extremism Project, homepage, undated(a). As of June 19, 2018:
https://www.counterextremism.com/about

———, "Digital Disruption: Fighting Online Extremism," webpage, undated(b). As of June 19, 2018:
https://www.counterextremism.com/digital-disruption

———, #cepdigitaldisruption, Twitter, July 21, 2017. As of June 21, 2018:
https://twitter.com/search?q=%23cepdigitaldisruption&ref_src=twsrc%5Etfw&ref_url=https%3A%2F%2Fwww.counterextremism.com%2Fdigital-disruption

———, *OK Google, Show Me Extremism: Analysis of YouTube's Extremist Video Takedown Policy and Counter-Narrative Program*, 2018. As of June 27, 2018:
https://www.counterextremism.com/ok-google

"Counter-Narrative Toolkit," homepage, undated. As of June 19, 2018:
http://www.counternarratives.org

Counterterrorism Education Learning Lab, homepage, 2012. As of June 28, 2018:
https://www.thecell.org

Crisis Intervention of Houston, Inc., "Building a Resilient Community to Counter Violent Extremism: Houston/Harris County," DHS Grant Application EMW-2016-CA-APP-00188, released under the Freedom of Information Act, 2016.

Curtis, Lisa, Luke Coffey, David Inserra, Daniel Kochis, Walter Lohman, Joshua Meservey, James Phillips, and Robin Simcox, *Combatting the ISIS Foreign Fighter Pipeline: A Global Approach*, Washington, D.C.: Heritage Foundation, January 6, 2016. As of June 28, 2018:
https://www.heritage.org/middle-east/report/
combatting-the-isis-foreign-fighter-pipeline-global-approach

D'Amours, Jillian, "Canada's New 'Anti-Radicalisation' Office Met with Caution by Muslim Community," *Middle East Eye*, March 25, 2016. As of June 28, 2018:
http://www.middleeasteye.net/news/canada-open-federal-anti-radicalisation-office-2044142061

Daine, Kate, Keith Hawton, Vinod Singaravelu, Anne Stewart, Sue Simkin, and Paul Montgomery, "The Power of the Web: A Systematic Review of Studies of the Influence of the Internet on Self-Harm and Suicide in Young People," *PLOS One*, Vol. 8, No. 10, 2013.

Das, Jai K., Rehana A. Salam, Ahmed Arshad, Yaron Finkelstein, and Zulfiqar A. Bhutta, "Interventions for Adolescent Substance Abuse: An Overview of Systematic Reviews," *Journal of Adolescent Health*, Vol. 59, No. 4, 2016, pp. S61–S75.

Davies, William Adair, "Counterterrorism Effectiveness to Jihadists in Western Europe and the United States: We Are Losing the War on Terror," *Studies in Conflict and Terrorism*, Vol. 41, No. 4, 2018, pp. 281–296.

Davis, Lois M., Robert Bozick, Jennifer L. Steele, Jessica Saunders, and Jeremy N. V. Miles, *Evaluating the Effectiveness of Correctional Education: A Meta-Analysis of Programs that Provide Education to Incarcerated Adults*, Santa Monica, Calif.: RAND Corporation, RR-266-BJA, 2013. As of August 21, 2018:
https://www.rand.org/pubs/research_reports/RR266.html

Davis, Lois M., Todd C. Helmus, Priscillia Hunt, Leslie Adrienne Payne, Salar Jahedi, and Flavia Tsang, *Assessment of the State and Local Anti-Terrorism Training (SLATT) Program*, Santa Monica, Calif.: RAND Corporation, RR-1276-NIJ, 2016. As of August 21, 2018:
https://www.rand.org/pubs/research_reports/RR1276.html

Davis, Robert C., and Nicole J. Henderson, "Willingness to Report Crimes: The Role of Ethnic Group Membership and Community Efficacy," *Crime and Delinquency*, Vol. 49, No. 4, 2003, pp. 564–580.

Davis, Robert C., Lila Rabinovich, Jennifer Rubin, Beau Kilmer, and Paul Heaton, *A Synthesis of Literature on the Effectiveness of Community Orders*, Cambridge, UK: RAND Europe, TR-518-NAO, 2008. As of August 21, 2018:
https://www.rand.org/pubs/technical_reports/TR518.html

Decker, Scott H., and David C. Pyrooz, "'I'm Down for a Jihad': How 100 Years of Gang Research Can Inform the Study of Terrorism, Radicalization and Extremism," *Perspectives on Terrorism*, Vol. 9, No. 1, 2015, pp. 104–112.

DeLisi, Matt, Anna Kosloski, Molly Sween, Emily Hachmeister, Matt Moore, and Alan Drury, "Murder by Numbers: Monetary Costs Imposed by a Sample of Homicide Offenders," *Journal of Forensic Psychiatry and Psychology*, Vol. 21, No. 4, 2010, pp. 501–513.

Denver Post, "Group Efforts Aimed at 'Countering Violent Extremism' Spread," July 5, 2016. As of June 27, 2018:
https://www.denverpost.com/2016/07/05/
group-efforts-aimed-at-countering-violent-extremism-spread

Devlin, Barrett, "Some Terror Sympathizers to Get Counseling—FBI Tries New Approach as It Faces Surge in Americans Tempted by Islamic State Messages," *Wall Street Journal*, August 6, 2015.

DHS—*See* U.S. Department of Homeland Security.

DHS CRCL—*See* U.S. Department of Homeland Security, Civil Rights and Civil Liberties Office.

DHS HSAC—*See* U.S. Department of Homeland Security Homeland Security Advisory Council.

DHS S&T—See U.S. Department of Homeland Security, Science and Technology.

Disley, Emma, Mafalda Pardal, Kristin Weed, and Anaïs Reding, *Using Multi Agency Public Protection Arrangements to Manage and Supervise Terrorist Offenders: Findings from an Exploratory Study*, Cambridge, UK: RAND Europe, RR-441-RE, 2016. As of August 21, 2018:
https://www.rand.org/pubs/research_reports/RR441.html

DOJ—*See* U.S. Department of Justice.

DOJ OJP—*See* U.S. Department of Justice, Office of Justice Programs

Donati, Jessica, "U.S. Prisons Allow Extremism to Fester, Study Warns," *Wall Street Journal*, February 6, 2018.

DOS—*See* U.S. Department of State.

Doyle, Charles, *Terrorist Material Support: An Overview of 18 U.S.C. §2339A and §2339B*, Washington, D.C.: Congressional Research Service, R41333, December 8, 2016.

Ducol, Benjamin, Martin Bouchard, Garth Davies, Marie Ouellet, and Christine Neudecker, *Assessment of the State of Knowledge: Connections Between Research on the Social Psychology of the Internet and Violent Extremism*, Waterloo, ON: Canadian Network for Research on Terrorism, Security and Society, Working Paper 16-05, May 2016.

Duke, Elaine C., "Threats to the Homeland," testimony before the Senate Committee on Homeland Security and Government Affairs, September 27, 2017. As of June 28, 2018:
https://www.hsgac.senate.gov/imo/media/doc/Testimony-Duke-2017-09-27.pdf

Dunbar, Edward, Jary Quinones, and Desiree A. Crevecoeur, "Assessment of Hate Crime Offenders: The Role of Bias Intent in Examining Violence Risk," *Journal of Forensic Psychology Practice*, Vol. 5, No. 1, 2005, pp. 1–19.

Edgett, Sean J., "Testimony Before the Senate Judiciary Subcommittee on Crime and Terrorism," Washington, D.C., October 31, 2017. As of June 20, 2018:
https://www.judiciary.senate.gov/imo/media/doc/10-31-17%20Edgett%20Testimony.pdf

EdVenture Partners, "It Takes Just One," Spring 2017. As of June 21, 2018:
https://edventurepartners.com/wordpress/wp-content/uploads/2017/08/Univ_Maryland_OneSheet.pdf.

Eisenman, David P., and Louise Flavahan, "Canaries in the Coal Mine: Interpersonal Violence, Gang Violence, and Violent Extremism Through a Public Health Prevention Lens," *International Review of Psychiatry*, Vol. 29, No. 4, 2017, pp. 341–349.

Ekins, Emily, *Policing in America: Understanding Public Attitudes Toward the Police: Results from a National Survey*, Washington, D.C.: Cato Institute, 2017.

Ellis, B. Heidi, and Saida Abdi, "Building Community Resilience to Violent Extremism Through Genuine Partnerships," *American Psychologist*, Vol. 72, No. 3, 2017, pp. 289–300.

Emerson, Kirk, and Tina Nabatchi, "Evaluating the Productivity of Collaborative Governance Regimes: A Performance Matrix," *Public Performance and Management Review*, Vol. 38, 2015, p. 708. As of June 25, 2018:
https://www.maxwell.syr.edu/uploadedFiles/parcc/content-blocks/Emerson-Nabatchi%202015.pdf

EOP—*See* Executive Office of the President.

Executive Office of the President, *Organization of the National Security Council System*, Washington, D.C.: White House, February 13, 2001. As of June 26, 2018:
https://fas.org/irp/offdocs/nspd/nspd-1.htm

———, *Organization of the National Security Council System*, Washington, D.C.: White House, February 13, 2009. As of June 26, 2018:
https://fas.org/irp/offdocs/ppd/ppd-1.pdf

———, *Empowering Local Partners to Prevent Violent Extremism in the United States*, Washington, D.C.: White House, August 2011a. As of April 4, 2018:
https://obamawhitehouse.archives.gov/sites/default/files/empowering_local_partners.pdf

———, *Strategic Implementation Plan for Empowering Local Partners to Prevent Violent Extremism in the United States*, Washington, D.C.: White House, December 2011b. As of April 4, 2018:
https://obamawhitehouse.archives.gov/sites/default/files/sip-final.pdf

———, *Strategic Implementation Plan for Empowering Local Partners to Prevent Violent Extremism in the United States*, Washington, D.C.: White House, October 2016. As of April 10, 2018:
https://www.dhs.gov/sites/default/files/publications/2016_strategic_implementation_plan_empowering_local_partners_prev.pdf

———, *National Security Presidential Memorandum*, Washington, D.C.: White House, April 4, 2017. As of June 26, 2018:
https://www.whitehouse.gov/presidential-actions/national-security-presidential-memorandum-4

Facebook, "Counterspeech," webpage, undated. As of June 20, 2018:
https://counterspeech.fb.com/en

Fairfield, Hannah, and Tim Wallace, "The Terrorists in U.S. Prisons," *New York Times*, April 7, 2016. As of August 21, 2018:
https://www.nytimes.com/interactive/2016/04/07/us/terrorists-in-us-prisons.html

FBI—*See* Federal Bureau of Investigation.

Feddes, Allard R., and Marcehllo Gallucci, "A Literature Review on Methodology Used in Evaluating Effects of Preventive and De-Radicalisation Interventions," *Journal for Deradicalization*, Vol. 5, Winter 2015/2016, pp. 1–41.

Federal Bureau of Investigation, "Community Outreach," webpage, undated(a). As of August 21, 2018:
https://www.fbi.gov/about/community-outreach

———, *Field Office CVE Model*, slide deck (redacted and released under the Freedom of Information Act), undated(b). As of June 28, 2018:
https://www.brennancenter.org/sites/default/files/
Presentation-FBI%20Field%20Office%20CVE%20Model%20.pdf

———, *Community Outreach in Field Offices: Corporate Policy Directive and Policy Implementation Guide* (as released under FOIA), March 4, 2013a. As of June 28, 2018:
https://www.brennancenter.org/sites/default/files/blog/FBI%202013%20Community%20
Outreach%20Guidelines%20combined%20w.o%20redactions.pdf

———, *Domestic Investigations and Operations Guide*, 0667DPG (as redacted and publicly released under FOIA), October 16, 2013b.

———, *FBI Strategic Plan to Curb Violent Extremism: Countering Violent Extremism Office*, Washington, D.C. (as redacted and publicly released under FOIA), original classification date, March 12, 2015. As of June 28, 2018:
https://www.brennancenter.org/sites/default/files/1318911-0%20-%20FBI%20Strategic%20Plan%20
to%20Curb%20Violent%20Extremism-Section%201-Imported%20Media.PDF

Federal Bureau of Investigation Behavioral Analysis Unit, *Making Prevention a Reality: Identifying, Assessing, and Managing the Threat of Targeted Attacks*, Washington, D.C., undated.

Federal Bureau of Investigation, Office of Partner Engagement, *Preventing Violent Extremism in Schools*, Washington, D.C., January 2016. As of June 28, 2018:
https://rems.ed.gov/Docs/FBI_PreventingExtremismSchools.pdf

Ferguson, Kate, *Countering Violent Extremism Through Media and Communication Strategies*, Norwich, UK: University of East Anglia, Partnership for Conflict, Crime, and Security Research, March 1, 2016. As of June 14, 2018:
http://www.paccsresearch.org.uk/wp-content/uploads/2016/03/
Countering-Violent-Extremism-Through-Media-and-Communication-Strategies-.pdf

Fiegerman, Seth, "Facebook Grows Its Counterterrorism Team," *CNN*, June 15, 2017. As of June 20, 2018:
http://money.cnn.com/2017/06/15/technology/business/facebook-terrorism-content/index.html

Field, Antony, "Ethics and Entrapment: Understanding Counterterrorism Stings," *Terrorism and Political Violence*, August 22, 2016.

Fink, Naureen Chowdhury, Peter Romaniuk, and Rafia Barakat, "Evaluating Countering Violent Extremism Programming: Practice and Progress," *Center on Global Counterterrorism Cooperation*, September 2013.

Fink, Naureen Chowdhury, Ivo VeenKamp. Wedad Alhassen, Rafia Barakat, and Sara Zeiger, "The Role of Education in Countering Violent Extremism," *Center on Global Counterterrorism Cooperation and Hedayah*, December 2013.

Fioretti, Julia, "Social Media Companies Accelerate Removals of Online Hate Speech—EU," Reuters, January 18, 2018. As of June 1, 2018:
https://www.reuters.com/article/eu-hatespeech/
social-media-companies-accelerate-removals-of-online-hate-speech-eu-idUSL8N1PC5QK

Fischer, Peter, Joachim I. Krueger, Tobias Greitemeyer, Claudia Vogrincic, Andreas Kastenmüller, Dieter Frey, Moritz Heene, Magdalena Wicher, and Martina Kainbacher, "The Bystander-Effect: A Meta-Analytic Review on Bystander Intervention in Dangerous and Non-Dangerous Emergencies," *Psychological Bulletin*, Vol. 137, No. 4, 2011, pp. 517–537.

Fishman, Shira, *Community-Level Indicators of Radicalization: A Data and Methods Task Force*, College Park, Md.: National Consortium for the Study of Terrorism and Responses to Terrorism, February 16, 2010.

Florence, Curtis, Jonathan Shepherd, Iain Brennan, and Thomas Simon, "Effectiveness of Anonymised Information Sharing and Use in Health Service, Police, and Local Government Partnership for Preventing Violence Related Injury: Experimental Study and Time Series Analysis," *British Medical Journal*, Vol. 342, 2011. As of June 28, 2018:
https://doi.org/10.1136/bmj.d3313

Fountain, Jane, *Implementing Cross-Agency Collaboration: A Guide for Federal Managers*, IBM Center for the Business of Government, Collaborating Across Boundaries Series, 2013. As of June 25, 2018:
http://www.businessofgovernment.org/sites/default/files/
Implementing%20Cross%20Agency%20Collaboration.pdf

Frampton, Martyn, Ali Fisher, and Nico Prucha, *The New Netwar: Countering Extremism Online*, UK: Policy Exchange, 2017. As of June 28, 2018:
https://policyexchange.org.uk/wp-content/uploads/2017/09/The-New-Netwar-1.pdf

Frattaroli, Shannon, Keshia M. Pollack, Karen Jonsberg, Gregg Croteau, Juan Carlos Rivera, and Jennifer S. Mendel, "Streetworkers, Youth Violence Prevention, and Peacemaking in Lowell, Massachusetts: Lessons and Voices from the Community," *Progress in Community Health Partnerships: Research, Education, and Action*, Vol. 4, No. 3, Fall 2010, pp. 171–179.

Frenett, Ross, and Moli Dow, *One to One Online Interventions: A Pilot CVE Methodology*, London: Institute for Strategic Dialogue, 2015. As of June 20, 2018:
https://www.isdglobal.org/wp-content/uploads/2016/04/One2One_Web_v9.pdf

Gaes, Gerald G., and Scott D. Camp, "Unintended Consequences: Experimental Evidence for the Criminogenic Effect of Prison Security Level Placement on Post-Release Recidivism," *Journal of Experimental Criminology*, Vol. 5, No. 2, 2009, pp. 139–162.

Gandhi, Allison Gruner, Erin Murphy-Graham, Anthony Petrosino, Sara Schwartz Chrismer, and Carol H. Weiss, "The Devil Is in the Details: Examining the Evidence for 'Proven' School-Based Drug Abuse Prevention Programs," *Evaluation Review*, Vol. 31, No. 1, 2007, pp. 43–74.

GAO—*See* U.S. Government Accountability Office.

GCTF—*See* Global Counterterrorism Forum.

Gen Next Foundation, homepage, 2016. As of June 19, 2018:
https://gennextfoundation.org/cve

George Washington University, Program on Extremism, "GW Extremism Tracker: The Islamic State in America," infographic, May 7, 2018a. As of June 28, 2018:
https://extremism.gwu.edu/sites/g/files/zaxdzs2191/f/May%202018%20Tracker.pdf

————, "Telegram Tracker," infographic. Spring 2018b. As of June 20, 2018:
https://extremism.gwu.edu/sites/g/files/zaxdzs2191/f/
Telegram%20Tracker%20Spring%202018_0.pdf

GIFCT—See Global Internet Forum to Counter Terrorism.

Gill, Charlotte, "Community Interventions," in David Weisburd, David P. Farrington, and Charlotte Gill, eds., *What Works in Crime Prevention and Rehabilitation: Lessons from Systematic Reviews*, New York: Springer, 2016, pp. 77–109.

Gill, Paul, John Horgan, and Paige Deckert, "Bombing Alone: Tracing the Motivations and Antecedent Behaviors of Lone-Actor Terrorists," *Journal of Forensic Science*, Vol. 59, No. 2, March 2014, pp. 425–435.

Global Counterterrorism Forum, *Rome Memorandum on Good Practices for Rehabilitation and Reintegration of Violent Extremist Offenders*, New York, undated.

Global Internet Forum to Counter Terrorism, "About," homepage, undated. As of June 20, 2018:
https://gifct.org/about

Goldman, Adam, "Why Didn't the F.B.I. Stop the New York Bombing?" *New York Times*, September 21, 2016.

Graff, Garrett, "The FBI's Growing Surveillance Gap," *Politico*, June 16, 2016. As of June 28, 2018:
https://www.politico.com/magazine/story/2016/06/orlando-terror-fbi-surveillance-gap-213967

Gravel, Jason, Martin Bouchard, Karine Descormiers, Jennifer S. Wong, and Carlo Morselli, "Keeping Promises: A Systematic Review and a New Classification of Gang Control Strategies," *Journal of Criminal Justice*, Vol. 41, 2013, pp. 228–242.

Greater Boston Region Stakeholders Group, *A Framework for Prevention and Intervention Strategies Incorporating Violent Extremism into Violence Prevention Efforts*, February 2015:
https://www.justice.gov/sites/default/files/usao-ma/pages/attachments/2015/02/18/framework.pdf

Green, Shannon N., and Keith Proctor, *Turning Point: A New Comprehensive Strategy for Countering Violent Extremism*, Washington, D.C.: Center for Strategic and International Studies, November 2016. As of June 25, 2018:
https://csis-ilab.github.io/cve/report/Turning_Point.pdf

Greenberg, Andy, "Google's Clever Plan to Stop Aspiring ISIS Recruits," *Wired*, September 7, 2016. As of June 27, 2018:
https://www.wired.com/2016/09/googles-clever-plan-stop-aspiring-isis-recruits

GWU—See George Washington University.

H. Rept. 114-344, "Countering Violent Extremism Act of 2015, Report to Accompany H.R. 2899," November 19, 2015.

Hadra, Dana, "What Tech Companies Can Do to Counter Violent Extremism," Brookings Institution blog, September 13, 2016. As of June 19, 2018:
https://www.brookings.edu/blog/markaz/2016/09/13/
what-tech-companies-can-do-to-counter-violent-extremism

Hafez, Mohammed, and Creighton Mullins, "The Radicalization Puzzle: A Theoretical Synthesis of Empirical Approaches to Homegrown Extremism," *Studies in Conflict and Terrorism*, Vol. 38, 2015, pp. 958–975.

Halliday, Josh, "Almost 4,000 People Referred to UK Deradicalisation Scheme Last Year," *Guardian*, March 20, 2016.

Hamilton, Colby, "DuCharme Takes Over as Eastern District's Criminal Chief," *New York Law Journal*, March 12, 2018. As of June 28, 2018:
https://www.law.com/newyorklawjournal/2018/03/12/
ducharme-takes-over-as-eastern-districts-criminal-chief/?slreturn=20180504161505

Hamm, Mark S., "Terrorist Recruitment in American Correctional Institutions: An Exploratory Study of Non-Traditional Faith Groups Final Report," National Criminal Justice Reference Service, December 2007.

Harper, Nick, "FISA's Fuzzy Line Between Domestic and International Terrorism," *The University of Chicago Law Review*, Vol. 81, 2014, pp. 1123–1164. As of June 22, 2018:
https://lawreview.uchicago.edu/publication/
fisa%E2%80%99s-fuzzy-line-between-domestic-and-international-terrorism

Harris, Grant T., and Marnie E. Rice, "Characterizing the Value of Actuarial Violence Risk Assessments," *Criminal Justice and Behavior*, Vol. 34, No. 12, 2007, pp. 1638–1658.

Hayden, Michael Edison, "Richard Spencer: Prepare for More White Nationalist Flash Mobs," *Newsweek*, October 10, 2017. As of July 20, 2018:
https://www.newsweek.com/richard-spencer-prepare-more-white-nationalist-flash-mobs-681242

Heaton, Paul, *Hidden in Plain Sight: What Cost-of-Crime Research Can Tell Us About Investing in Police*, Santa Monica, Calif.: RAND Corporation, OP-279-ISEC, 2010. As of August 21, 2018:
https://www.rand.org/pubs/occasional_papers/OP279.html

Helmus, Todd, C., Miriam Matthews, Rajeev Ramchand, Sina Beaghley, David Stebbins, Amanda Kadlec, Michael A. Brown, Aaron Kofner, and Joie D. Acosta, *RAND Program Evaluation Toolkit for Countering Violent Extremism*, Santa Monica, Calif.: RAND Corporation, TL-243-DHS, 2017. As of August 21, 2018:
https://www.rand.org/pubs/tools/TL243.html

Herendeen, Pamela A., Roger Blevins, Elizabeth Anson, and Joyce Smith, "Barriers to and Consequences of Mandated Reporting of Child Abuse by Nurse Practitioners," *Journal of Pediatric Health Care*, Vol. 28, No. 1, 2014, pp. e1–e7.

Heritage Foundation, *Defending the Homeland: The Future of U.S. Countering Violent Extremism Policy*, video, August 8, 2017. As of June 28, 2018:
https://www.heritage.org/defense/event/
defending-the-homeland-the-future-us-countering-violent-extremism-policy

Hermann, Mary A., and Abbe Finn, "An Ethical and Legal Perspective on the Role of School Counselors in Preventing Violence in Schools," *Professional School Counseling*, Vol. 6, No. 1, October 2002, pp. 46–55.

Herzog-Evans, Martine, "A Comparison of Two Structured Professional Judgment Tools for Violent Extremism and Their Relevance in the French Context," *European Journal of Probation*, Vol. 10, No. 1, 2018, pp. 3–27.

Hirsh, Michael, "Inside the FBI's Secret Muslim Network," *Politico Magazine*, March 24, 2016. As of June 28, 2018:
https://www.politico.com/magazine/story/2016/03/fbi-muslim-outreach-terrorism-213765

Hoffman, Bruce, *Inside Terrorism*, New York: Columbia University Press, 2006.

————, "The Global Terror Threat and Counterterrorism Challenges Facing the Next Administration," *CTC Sentinel*, Vol. 9, No. 11, November/December 2016. As of June 22, 2018: https://ctc.usma.edu/ the-global-terror-threat-and-counterterrorism-challenges-facing-the-next-administration

————, "The Evolving Terrorist Threat and Counterterrorism Options of the Trump Administration," *The Georgetown Security Studies Review*, February 24, 2017a, pp. 6–14. As of August 21, 2018: http://georgetownsecuritystudiesreview.org/wp-content/uploads/2017/02/Hoffman-The-Evolving-Terrorist-Threat-and-Counterterrorism-Options-for-the-Trump-Administration.pdf

————, "A Growing Terrorist Threat on Another 9/11: Al Qaeda Has Regrouped Even as the Battered Islamic State Remains Lethal," *Wall Street Journal*, September 8, 2017b. As of June 22, 2018: https://www.wsj.com/articles/a-growing-terrorist-threat-on-another-9-11-1504888986

Hoffman, Bruce, Edwin Meese III, and Timothy J. Roemer, *The FBI: Protecting the Homeland in the 21st Century: Report of the Congressionally-Directed 9/11 Review Commission*, Washington, D.C., March 2015. As of August 21, 2018: https://www.fbi.gov/file-repository/ stats-services-publications-protecting-the-homeland-in-the-21st-century/view

Hollister, Brandon A., and Mario J. Scalora, "Broadening Campus Threat Assessment Beyond Mass Shootings," *Aggression and Violent Behavior*, Vol. 25, Part A, 2015, pp. 43–53.

Hong, Nicole, "Terror Convicts Pose Dilemma After Release from Prison," *Wall Street Journal*, February 16, 2016.

Horgan, John G., and Kurt Braddock, "Rehabilitating the Terrorists? Challenges in Assessing the Effectiveness of De-Radicalization Programs," *Terrorism and Political Violence*, Vol. 22, No. 2, 2010, pp. 267–291.

Horgan, John G., Paul Gill, Noemie Bouhana, James Silver, and Emily Corner, *Across the Universe? A Comparative Analysis of Violent Behavior and Radicalization Across Three Offender Types with Implications for Criminal Justice Training and Education*, Washington, D.C.: National Criminal Justice Reference Service, NCJRS 249937, June 2016. As of August 20, 2018: https://www.ncjrs.gov/pdffiles1/nij/grants/249937.pdf

Horgan, John G., Neil Shortland, and Suzzette Abbasciano, "Towards a Typology of Terrorism Involvement: A Behavioral Differentiation of Violent Extremist Offenders," *Journal of Threat Assessment and Management*, Vol. 5, No. 2, 2018, pp. 84–102.

Horgan, John G., Michael J. Williams, William P. Evans, and Jocelyn J. Bélanger, *Assessment Report: Current Capabilities of 2-1-1 Call Centers and Local Service Providers. Text-Enabled CVE Gatekeeper Intervention Help-Line and Referral System*, Georgia State University Research Foundation, Inc., Contract Report HSHQDC-16-C-B0028, undated. As of June 28, 2018: https://www.dhs.gov/sites/default/files/publications/OPSR_TP_Assessment-Report_Current-Capabilities-211-Call-Centers_Local-Service-Providers_508.pdf

Human Rights First, "NSD Chart of Convictions 9-11-01 to 12-31-16," information released under FOIA, 2017. As of August 21, 2018: http://www.humanrightsfirst.org/sites/default/files/NSD-Terrorism-Related-Convictions.pdf

Humphreys, Cathy, "Problems in the System of Mandatory Reporting of Children Living with Domestic Violence," *Journal of Family Studies*, Vol. 14, No. 2-3, 2008, pp. 228–239.

Huq, Aziz Z., Tom R. Tyler, and Stephen Schulhofer, "Why Does the Public Cooperate with Law Enforcement? The Influence of the Purposes and Targets of Policing," *Psychology, Public Policy, and Law*, Vol. 17, No. 3, 2011, pp. 419–450.

Iganski, Paul, David Smith, et al., *Rehabilitation of Hate Crime Offenders: Research Report*, Equality and Human Rights Commission (Scotland), Spring 2011.

IMPACT Europe, homepage, undated. As of August 21, 2018:
http://www.impact.itti.com.pl/index#/home

Information Sharing Environment, Department of Homeland Security, Nationwide SAR Initiative, U.S. Department of Justice Community Oriented Policing Services, *Building Communities of Trust Fact Sheet*, January 2014. As of June 28, 2018:
https://www.dhs.gov/sites/default/files/publications/Building%20Communities%20of%20Trust.pdf

INSA—*See* Intelligence and National Security Alliance.

Institute for Strategic Dialogue, *About: The IDS Approach*, undated(a). As of June 19, 2018:
https://www.isdglobal.org/isdapproach

———, *Innovation Hub*, undated(b). As of June 19, 2018:
https://www.isdglobal.org/programmes/communications-technology/innovation-hub

———, *Online Civil Courage Initiative*, undated(c). As of June 19, 2018:
https://www.isdglobal.org/programmes/communications-technology/online-civil-courage-initiative-2

———, *Work*, undated(d). As of June 19, 2018:
https://www.isdglobal.org/programmes

Intelligence and National Security Alliance, Homeland Security Intelligence Council, "After Action Report: Homegrown Violent Extremism Homeland Security Exercise," September 2014. As of June 28, 2018:
https://www.insaonline.org/
after-action-report-homegrown-violent-extremism-homeland-security-exercise/

International Association of Chiefs of Police, "The Role of Community Policing in Homeland Security and Preventing Radicalization to Violence," undated. As of August 21, 2018:
http://www.theiacp.org/CounteringViolentExtremism

Jackson, Brian A., *Respect and Legitimacy—A Two-Way Street: Strengthening Trust Between Police and the Public in an Era of Increasing Transparency*, Santa Monica, Calif.: RAND Corporation, PE-154-RC, 2015. As of August 21, 2018:
https://www.rand.org/pubs/perspectives/PE154.html

Jackson, Brian A., Lloyd Dixon, and Victoria Greenfield, *Economically Targeted Terrorism: A Review of the Literature and a Framework for Considering Defensive Approaches*, Santa Monica, Calif.: RAND Corporation, TR-476-CTRMP, 2007. As of August 21, 2018:
https://www.rand.org/pubs/technical_reports/TR476.html

Jasko, Katarzyna, Gary LaFree, and Arie Kruglanski, "Quest for Significance and Violent Extremism: The Case of Domestic Radicalization," *Political Psychology*, Vol. 38, No. 5, 2017, pp. 815–831.

Jenkins, Brian Michael, *Stray Dogs and Virtual Armies: Radicalization and Recruitment to Jihadist Terrorism in the United States Since 9/11*, Santa Monica, Calif.: RAND Corporation, OP-343-RC, 2011. As of August 21, 2018:
https://www.rand.org/pubs/occasional_papers/OP343.html

———, *The Origins of America's Jihadists*, Santa Monica, Calif.: RAND Corporation, PE-251-RC, 2017. As of August 21, 2018:
https://www.rand.org/pubs/perspectives/PE251.html

Jensen, Carl J., III, James L. Regens, and Natalie Griffin, "Intelligence-Led Policing as a Tool for Countering the Terrorism Threat," *Homeland Security Review*, Vol. 7, No. 3, 2013, pp. 265–284.

Johnson, Mell, and David Gersten, "Catalog of Best Practices for Community Engagement: National Engagement Task Force," released under the Freedom of Information Act, DHS-001-425-000785 thru 000831, April 18, 2013.

Jones, Risé, Emalee G. Flaherty, Helen J. Binns, Lori Lyn Price, Eric Slora, Dianna Abney, Donna L. Harris, Katherine Kaufer Christoffel, and Robert D. Sege, "Clinicians' Description of Factors Influencing Their Reporting of Suspected Child Abuse: Report of the Child Abuse Reporting Experience Study Research Group," *Pediatrics*, Vol. 122, No. 2, 2008, pp. 259–266.

Kahan, James P., C. Peter Rydell, and John Setear, "A Game on Urban Drug Policy," *Peace and Conflict: Journal of Peace Psychology*, Vol. 1, No. 3, 1995, pp. 275–290.

Kahan, James P., John Setear, Margaret M. Bitzinger, Sinclair B. Coleman, and Joel Feinleib, *Developing Games of Local Drug Policy*, Santa Monica, Calif.: RAND Corporation, N-3395-DPRC, 1992. As of August 21, 2018:
https://www.rand.org/pubs/notes/N3395.html

Kaiser Family Foundation, "Mental Health Care Health Professional Shortage Areas (HPSAs)," data set, December 31, 2017. As of August 21, 2018:
https://www.kff.org/other/state-indicator/mental-health-care-health-professional-shortage-areas-hpsas

Kaiser, Frederick M., *Interagency Collaborative Arrangements and Activities: Types, Rationales, Considerations*, Washington, D.C.: Congressional Research Service, May 31, 2011. As of June 25, 2018:
https://fas.org/sgp/crs/misc/R41803.pdf

Kamisar, Ben, "Conservatives Cry Foul over Controversial Group's Role in YouTube Moderation," *The Hill*, March 8, 2018. As of June 20, 2018:
http://thehill.com/homenews/campaign/377310-conservatives-cry-foul-over-controversial-groups-role-in-youtube-moderation

Kampeas, Ron, "Which Terrorists Are More of a Threat, Foreign or Domestic? The ADL and the Trump Administration Differ," *Jewish Telegraphic Agency*, January 18, 2018. As of June 22, 2018:
https://www.jta.org/2018/01/18/news-opinion/politics/which-terrorists-are-more-of-a-threat-foreign-or-domestic-the-adl-and-the-trump-administration-differ

The Keyword, "Update on the Global Internet Forum to Counter Terrorism," Google blog, December 4, 2017. As of June 20, 2018:
https://blog.google/topics/google-europe/update-global-internet-forum-counter-terrorism

Kim, Angela, Stacia Lee, Oliver Marguleas, and Jessica L. Beyer, *JSIS Cybersecurity Report: Do Counter-Narrative Programs Slow Terrorist Recruiting?* Seattle, Wash.: University of Washington Jackson School of International Studies, October 3, 2016.

Klein, Malcolm W., "Comprehensive Gang and Violence Reduction Programs: Reinventing the Square Wheel," *Criminology and Public Policy*, Vol. 10, No. 4, 2011, pp. 1037–1044.

Koehler, Daniel, *Understanding Deradicalization: Methods, Tools and Programs for Countering Violent Extremism*, New York: Routledge, 2017.

Kurzman, Charles, Ahsan Kamal, and Hajar Yazdiha, "Ideology and Threat Assessment: Law Enforcement Evaluation of Muslim and Right-Wing Extremism," *Socius: Sociological Research for a Dynamic World*, Vol. 3, 2017, pp. 1–13.

La Vigne, Nancy, Jocelyn Fontaine, and Anamika Dwivedi, *How Do People in High-Crime, Low-Income Communities View the Police?* Washington, D.C.: Urban Institute, 2017.

LaFree, Gary, Michael A. Jensen, Patrick A. James, and Aaron Safer-Lichtenstein, "Correlates of Violent Political Extremism in the United States," *Criminology*, Vol. 56, No. 2, 2018, pp. 233–268.

LaFree, Gary, Stanley Presser, Roger Tourangeau, and Amy Adamczyk, *U.S. Attitudes Toward Terrorism and Counterterrorism: Examining Results from a Four-Wave Survey Conducted Between September 2012 and July 2014*, College Park, Md.: National Consortium for the Study of Terrorism and Responses to Terrorism, November 2014. As of June 28, 2018: https://www.dhs.gov/sites/default/files/publications/OPSR_TP_US-Attitudes-Toward-Terrorism-Counterterrorism_Results-From-Four-Wave-Survey-Report_July2014-508_0.pdf

Lamb, Christopher J., and Evan Munsing, *Secret Weapon: High Value Target Teams as an Organizational Innovation*, Institute for National Strategic Studies, Strategic Perspectives No. 4, Washington, D.C.: National Defense University Press, March 2011. As of June 23, 2018: http://ndupress.ndu.edu/Portals/68/Documents/stratperspective/inss/Strategic-Perspectives-4.pdf

Lang, Julius, *What Is a Community Court? How the Model Is Being Adapted Across the United States*, Washington, D.C.: Center for Court Innovation, 2011.

Lankford, Adam, "A Comparative Analysis of Suicide Terrorists and Rampage, Workplace, and School Shooters in the United States from 1990 to 2010," *SAGE Publications*, Vol. 17, No. 3, October 12, 2012, pp. 255–274.

Lefas, Melissa, and Junko Nozawa, *Rehabilitating Juvenile Violent Extremist Offenders in Detention: Advancing a Juvenile Justice Approach*, The Hague, Netherlands: International Centre for Counter-Terrorism, Global Center on Cooperative Security, December 2016.

Levin, Sam, "Google to Hire Thousands of Moderators After Outcry over YouTube Abuse Videos," *The Guardian*, December 5, 2017. As of June 20, 2018: https://www.theguardian.com/technology/2017/dec/04/google-youtube-hire-moderators-child-abuse-videos

Levitt, Matthew, ed., *Defeating Ideologically Inspired Violent Extremism: A Strategy to Build Strong Communities and Protect the U.S. Homeland*, Washington, D.C.: Washington Institute for Near East Policy, No. 37, March 2017.

Levs, Josh, and Holly Yan, "Western Allies Reject ISIS Leader's Threats Against Their Civilians," *CNN*, September 22, 2014. As of April 4, 2018: https://www.cnn.com/2014/09/22/world/meast/isis-threatens-west/index.html

Libicki, Martin C., Brian A. Jackson, David R. Frelinger, Beth E. Lachman, Cesse Cameron Ip, and Nidhi Kalra, *What Should Be Classified? A Framework with Application to the Global Force Management Data Initiative*, Santa Monica, Calif.: RAND Corporation, MG-989-JS, 2010. As of August 21, 2018: https://www.rand.org/pubs/monographs/MG989.html

Lichtblau, Eric, "F.B.I. Steps Up Use of Stings in ISIS Cases," *New York Times*, June 7, 2016. As of June 28, 2018: https://www.nytimes.com/2016/06/08/us/fbi-isis-terrorism-stings.html

Lidz, Charles W., Edward P. Mulvey, and William Gardner, "The Accuracy of Predictions of Violence to Others," *JAMA*, Vol. 269, No. 8, 1993, pp. 1007–1011.

Liederbach, John, Eric J. Fritsch, David L. Carter, and Andra Bannister, "Exploring the Limits of Collaboration in Community Policing: A Direct Comparison of Police and Citizen Views," *Policing: An International Journal of Police Strategies and Management*, Vol. 31, No. 2, 2008, pp. 271–291.

Life After Hate, "ExitUSA," webpage, undated(a). As of June 28, 2018:
http://lifeafterhate.wixsite.com/exitusa/who-are-we

———, homepage, undated(b). As of June 28, 2018:
https://www.lifeafterhate.org

Lipsey, Mark W., and Francis T. Cullen, "The Effectiveness of Correctional Rehabilitation: A Review of Systematic Reviews," *Annual Review of Law and Social Science*, Vol. 3, 2007, pp. 297–320.

Lloyd, Monica, and Christopher Dean, "The Development of Structured Guidelines for Assessing Risk in Extremist Offenders," *Journal of Threat Assessment and Management*, Vol. 2, No. 1, 2015, pp. 40–52.

Lomas, Natasha, "UK Outs Extremism Blocking Tool and Could Force Tech Firms to Use It," *Tech Crunch*, February 13, 2018. As of June 18, 2018:
https://techcrunch.com/2018/02/13/
uk-outs-extremism-blocking-tool-and-could-force-tech-firms-to-use-it

Lopez, Lolita, and Philip Drechsler, "LAPD Program Prevents Acts of Terrorism," *NBC Los Angeles*, October 13, 2017. As of June 28, 2018:
https://www.nbclosangeles.com/news/local/
LAPD-PATHE-program-alternatives-preventing-terrorism-450714453.html

Lum, Cynthia, Christopher S. Koper, Charlotte Gill, Julie Hibdon, Cody W. Telep, and Laurie O. Robinson, *An Evidence-Assessment of the Recommendations of the President's Task Force on 21st Century Policing—Implementation and Research Priorities*, Fairfax, Va.: George Mason University, Center for Evidence-Based Crime Policy, International Association of Chiefs of Police, 2016.

MacGinty, Roger, "Ethno-National Conflict and Hate Crime," *American Behavioral Scientist*, Vol. 45, No. 4, 2001, pp. 639–653.

Madrigal, Alexis C., "Inside Facebook's Fast-Growing Content-Moderation Effort," *The Atlantic*, February 7, 2018. As of June 20, 2018:
https://www.theatlantic.com/technology/archive/2018/02/
what-facebook-told-insiders-about-how-it-moderates-posts/552632

Markey, Dana, Laura Usher, Darcy Gruttadaro, Ron Honberg, and Charles S. Cochran, *Responding to Youth with Mental Health Needs: A CIT for Youth Implementation Manual*, Arlington, Va.: National Alliance on Mental Illness, July 2011. As of June 28, 2018:
https://www.nami.org/getattachment/Get-Involved/Crisis-Intervention-Team-(CIT)-Programs/
Building-a-CIT-Program/Create-Change/
Responding-to-Youth-with-Mental-Health-Needs_NAMI.pdf

Massachusetts Executive Office of Public Safety and Security, "FY16 CVE Grant Application, EMW-2016-CA-APP-00336," Released under the Freedom of Information Act, 2016.

May, J. P., D. Hemenway, and A. Hall, "Do Criminals Go to the Hospital When They Are Shot?" *Injury Prevention*, Vol. 8, 2002, pp. 236–238.

McCann, Wesley S., and Nicholas Pimley, "Mixed Mandates: Issues Concerning Organizational and Statutory Definitions of Terrorism in the United States," *Terrorism and Political Violence*, 2018.

McCauley, Clark, "Testing Theories of Radicalization in Polls of U.S. Muslims," *Analyses of Social Issues and Public Policy*, Vol. 12, No. 1, 2012, pp. 296–311.

———, "Ideas Versus Actions in Relation to Polls of U.S. Muslims," *Analyses of Social Issues and Public Policy*, Vol. 13, No. 1, 2013, pp. 70–76.

McCauley, Clark, and Sophia Moskalenko, "Mechanisms of Political Radicalization: Pathways Toward Terrorism," *Terrorism and Political Violence*, Vol. 20, 2008, pp. 415–433.

———, "Toward a Profile of Lone Wolf Terrorists: What Moves an Individual from Radical Opinion to Radical Action," *Terrorism and Political Violence*, Vol. 26, 2014, pp. 69–85.

McDevitt, Jack, Jack Levin, and Susan Bennett, "Hate Crime Offenders: An Expanded Typology," *Journal of Social Issues*, Vol. 58, No. 2, 2002, pp. 303–317.

McFall, Richard M., and Teresa A. Treat, "Quantifying the Information Value of Clinical Assessments with Signal Detection Theory," *Annual Reviews of Psychology*, Vol. 50, 1999, pp. 215–241.

McFee, Dale R., and Norman E. Taylor, "The Prince Albert Hub and the Emergence of Collaborative Risk-Driven Community Safety," Canadian Police College Discussion Paper Series, 2014. As of March 25, 2018:
http://www.cpc-ccp.gc.ca/sites/default/files/pdf/prince-albert-hub-eng.pdf

McGarty, Craig, Emma F. Thomas, and Winnifred R. Louis, "Are They Terrorist Sympathizers or Do They Just Disagree with the War on Terror? A Comment on Testing Theories of Radicalization in Polls of U.S. Muslims," *Analyses of Social Issues and Public Policy*, Vol. 12, No. 1, 2012, pp. 316–319.

McGilloway, Angela, Priyo Ghosh, and Kamaldeep Bhui, "A Systematic Review of Pathways to and Processes Associated with Radicalization and Extremism Amongst Muslims in Western Societies," *International Review of Psychiatry*, Vol. 27, No. 1, February 2015, pp. 39–50.

McGuire, James, "A Review of Effective Interventions for Reducing Aggression and Violence," *Philosophical Transactions of the Royal Society B: Biological Sciences*, Vol. 363, 2008, pp. 2577–2597.

McKenzie, Robert L., *Countering Violent Extremism in America: Policy Recommendations for the Next President*, Washington, D.C.: Brookings Institution, October 18, 2016.

Meleagrou-Hitchens, Alexander, Seamus Hughes, and Bennett Clifford, *The Travelers: American Jihadists in Syria and Iraq*, Washington, D.C.: George Washington University Program on Extremism, February 2018. As of June 28, 2018:
https://extremism.gwu.edu/sites/g/files/zaxdzs2191/f/TravelersAmericanJihadistsinSyriaandIraq.pdf

Meli, Laura, "Hate Crime and Punishment: Why Typical Punishment Does Not Fit the Crime," *University of Illinois Law Review*, Vol. 2014, No. 3, 2014, pp. 921–965.

Merola, Linda M., and Heather Vovak, "The Challenges of Terrorist and Extremist Prisoners: A Survey of U.S. Prisons," *Criminal Justice Policy Review*, Vol. 24, No. 6, 2012, pp. 735–758.

Meyer, Josh, "FBI, Homeland Security Warn of More 'Antifa' Attacks," *Politico*, September 1, 2017. As of July 20, 2018:
https://www.politico.com/story/2017/09/01/antifa-charlottesville-violence-fbi-242235

Mihalic, Sharon F., and Katherine Irwin, "Blueprints for Violence Prevention: From Research to Real-World Settings—Factors Influencing the Successful Replication of Model Programs," *Youth Violence and Juvenile Justice*, Vol. 1, No. 4, October 2003, pp. 307–329.

Mikton, Christopher, and Alexander Butchart, "Child Maltreatment Prevention: A Systematic Review of Reviews," *Bulletin of the World Health Organization*, Vol. 87, 2009, pp. 353–361.

Miller, Greg, and Scott Higham, "In a Propaganda War Against ISIS, the U.S. Tried to Play by the Enemy's Rules," *The Washington Post*, May 8, 2015. As of June 18, 2018: https://www.washingtonpost.com/world/national-security/ in-a-propaganda-war-us-tried-to-play-by-the-enemys-rules/2015/05/08/ 6eb6b732-e52f-11e4-81ea-0649268f729e_story.html?utm_term=.5c3813c713f1

Mirahmadi, Hedieh, "Building Resilience Against Violent Extremism: A Community-Based Approach," *The ANNALS of the American Academy of Political and Social Science*, Vol. 668, November 2016, pp. 129–144.

Mitts, Tamar, *Do Community Engagement Efforts Reduce Extremist Rhetoric on Social Media?* New York: Columbia University, Department of Political Science, April 6, 2017. As of June 28, 2018: https://papers.ssrn.com/sol3/papers.cfm?abstract_id=2940290

Morris, Daniel S., Meagan P. Rooney, Ricardo J. Wray, and Matthew W. Kreuter, "Measuring Exposure to Health Messages in Community-Based Intervention Studies: A Systematic Review of Current Practices," *Health Education and Behavior*, Vol. 36, No. 6, December 2009, pp. 979–998.

MPAC—*See* Muslim Public Affairs Council.

Mullins, Sam, "Radical Attitudes and Jihad: A Commentary on the Article by Clark McCauley (2012) Testing Theories of Radicalization in Polls of U.S. Muslims," *Analyses of Social Issues and Public Policy*, Vol. 12, No. 1, 2012, pp. 312–315.

Murphy, Kristina, Natasha S. Madon, and Adrian Cherney, "Promoting Muslims' Cooperation with Police in Counter-Terrorism: The Interaction Between Procedural Justice, Police Legitimacy and Law Legitimacy," *Policing: An International Journal*, Vol. 40, No. 3, 2017, pp. 544–559.

Murray, Alex, Katrin Mueller-Johnson, and Lawrence W. Sherman, "Evidence-Based Policing of U.K. Muslim Communities: Linking Confidence in the Police with Area Vulnerability to Violent Extremism," *International Criminal Justice Review*, Vol. 25, No. 1, 2015, pp. 64–79.

Muslim Public Affairs Council, "Safe Spaces Initiative," webpage, undated. As of June 28, 2018: https://www.mpac.org/safespaces

National Conference of State Legislatures, *Mental Health Professionals' Duty to Warn*, September 28, 2015. As of June 28, 2018: http://www.ncsl.org/research/health/mental-health-professionals-duty-to-warn.aspx

National Consortium for the Study of Terrorism and Responses to Terrorism, "Global Terrorism Database," database, undated(a). As of August 21, 2018: https://www.start.umd.edu/gtd/

———, "Profiles of Individual Radicalization in the United States (PIRUS)," dataset, undated(b). As of August 20, 2018: http://www.start.umd.edu/data-tools/profiles-individual-radicalization-united-states-pirus

———, *From Extremist to Terrorist: Identifying the Characteristics of Communities Where Perpetrators Live and Pre-Incident Activity Occurs Prior to Attacks: Report to the Resilient Systems Division, Science and Technology Directorate, U.S. Department of Homeland Security*, College Park, Md., April 2013.

———, *Profiles of Individual Radicalization in the United States (PIRUS) Codebook: Public Release Version*, College Park, Md., January 2018. As of June 28, 2018: http://www.start.umd.edu/sites/default/files/files/research/PIRUSCodebook.pdf

National Counter Terrorism Center, "CVE Engagement Activities: NCTC Directorate for Strategic Operational Planning Domestic Countering Violent Extremism (CVE) Team," undated. As of April 4, 2018:
https://www.dhs.gov/sites/default/files/publications/CVE%20Engagement%20Activities-NCTC%20Classes.pdf

———, "CVE Tools and Training," publicly released under FOIA DF-2015-00215, April 14, 2016.

National Counter Terrorism Center, U.S. Department of Homeland Security, and Federal Bureau of Investigation, "First Responders Toolbox: Terrorism Prevention—A Form of Violence Reduction," October 30, 2017. As of July 21, 2018:
https://www.dni.gov/files/NCTC/documents/jcat/firstresponderstoolbox/First-Responders-Toolbox---Terrorism-PreventionA-Form-of-Violence-Reduction.pdf

National Gang Center, *Best Practices to Address Community Gang Problems: OJJDP's Comprehensive Gang Model*, Washington, D.C.: U.S. Department of Justice, Office of Juvenile Justice and Delinquency Prevention, 2nd ed., October 2010.

National Threat Assessment Center, "NTAC Research and Publications," webpage, undated. As of August 21, 2018:
https://www.secretservice.gov/protection/ntac/research/

———, *Using a Systems Approach for Threat Assessment Investigations: A Case Study on Jared Lee Loughner*, Washington, D.C.: U.S. Secret Service, Department of Homeland Security, 2015. As of June 28, 2018:
https://www.secretservice.gov/data/protection/ntac/Jared_Loughner_Using_Systems.pdf

NCTC—*See* National Counter Terrorism Center.

Ndrecka, Mirlinda, "The Impact of Reentry Programs on Recidivism: A Meta-Analysis," dissertation, Cincinnati, Oh.: University of Cincinnati, Division of Criminal Justice, 2014.

Neumann, Peter R., "Options and Strategies for Countering Online Radicalization in the United States," *Studies in Conflict and Terrorism*, Vol. 36, No. 6, 2013, pp. 431–459.

New South Wales Government, *Countering Violent Extremism in NSW*, fact sheet, November 2015. As of June 28, 2018:
https://static.nsw.gov.au/nsw-gov-au/1487646699/NSW-CVE-Factsheet.pdf

Niksa, Sarah C., "Bystander's Willingness to Report Theft, Physical Assault, and Sexual Assault: The Impact of Gender, Anonymity, and Relationship with the Offender," *Journal of Interpersonal Violence*, Vol. 29, No. 2, 2014, pp. 217–236.

NTAC—*See* National Threat Assessment Center.

Office of Civil Rights and Civil Liberties, Department of Homeland Security, "Countering Violent Extremism (CVE) Training: Guidance and Best Practices," October 2011. As of August 21, 2018:
https://www.dhs.gov/sites/default/files/publications/cve-training-guidance-best-practices-pamphlet.pdf

Office of the Director of National Intelligence, "FOIA—Publicly Released Records," multiple dates. As of August 21, 2018:
https://www.dni.gov/index.php/read-released-records

Office of the Inspector General, *The Internal Effects of the Federal Bureau of Investigation's Reprioritization*, Washington, D.C.: U.S. Department of Justice, 04-39, September 2004.

Office of Management and Budget, "Circular A-4: Regulatory Analysis," September 17, 2003. As of August 21, 2018:
https://www.whitehouse.gov/sites/whitehouse.gov/files/omb/circulars/A4/a-4.pdf

Office of Management and Budget, Office of Information and Regulatory Affairs, *2009 Report to Congress on the Benefits and Costs of Federal Regulations and Unfunded Mandates on State, Local, and Tribal Entities*, 2009.

OMB—*See* Office of Management and Budget.

Owens, Ross, Jonathan Evans, Jennifer Foley, and Ji Sun Lee, *Countering Violent Extremism—Developing a Research Roadmap: Literature Review*, North Triangle Park, N.C.: RTI International, April 2016. As of August 18, 2018:
https://www.dhs.gov/sites/default/files/publications/
OPSR_TP_CVE-Developing-Research-Roadmap_Literature-Review_180411-508.pdf

Parents for Peace, homepage, undated. As of June 28, 2018:
https://parents4peace.org/

Patel, Faiza, and Meghan Koushik, *Countering Violent Extremism*, New York: Brennan Center for Justice, 2017. As of August 21, 2018:
https://www.brennancenter.org/sites/default/files/publications/
Brennan%20Center%20CVE%20Report.pdf

Pathé, Michele T., Debbie J. Haworth, Terri-Ann Goodwin, Amanda G. Holman, Stephen J. Amos, Paul Winterbourne, and Leanne Day, "Establishing a Joint Agency Response to the Threat of Lone-Actor Grievance-Fuelled Violence," *Journal of Forensic Psychiatry and Psychology*, Vol. 29, No. 1, 2018, pp. 37–52.

Penven, James C., and Steven M. Janosik, "Threat Assessment Teams: A Model for Coordinating the Institutional Response and Reducing Legal Liability When College Students Threaten Suicide," *Journal of Student Affairs Research and Practice*, Vol. 49, No. 3, 2012, pp. 299–314.

Perry, Barbara, "The More Things Change. . . . Post 9/11 Trends in Hate Crime Scholarship," in Neil Chakraborti, ed., *Hate Crime: Concepts, Policy, Future Directions*, New York: Routledge, 2010, pp. 17–39.

Perry, Barbara, and Shahid Alvi, "'We Are All Vulnerable': The *in terrorem* Effects of Hate Crimes," *International Review of Victimology*, Vol. 18, No. 1, 2011, pp. 57–71.

Perry, Yael, Aliza Werner-Seidler, Alison L. Calear, and Helen Christensen, "Web-Based and Mobile Suicide Prevention Interventions for Young People: A Systematic Review," *Journal of the Canadian Academy of Child and Adolescent Psychiatry*, Vol. 25, No. 2, 2016, pp. 74–75, 78.

Pitcavage, Mark, "Cerberus Unleashed: The Three Faces of the Lone Wolf Terrorist," *American Behavioral Scientist*, Vol. 59, No. 13, 2015, pp. 1655–1680.

Pittman, Elaine, "Los Angeles Police Department Hydra System Promotes Simulation Training for Command-Level Officers," *Government Technology*, October 4, 2010. As of June 28, 2018:
http://www.govtech.com/public-safety/Los-Angeles-Police-Hydra-Simulation-Training.html

Potter, Roberto Hugh, and Jeffrey W. Rosky, "The Iron Fist in the Latex Glove: The Intersection of Public Health and Criminal Justice," *American Journal of Criminal Justice*, Vol. 38, 2013, pp. 276–288.

Powell, John Eric, "Terrorism Incident Response Education for Public-Safety Personnel in North Carolina and Tennessee: An Evaluation by Emergency Managers," dissertation, University of Tennessee, Knoxville, December 2008. As of June 28, 2018:
http://citeseerx.ist.psu.edu/viewdoc/download?doi=10.1.1.427.9835&rep=rep1&type=pdf

Public Law 114-328, National Defense Authorization Act for Fiscal Year 2017, Section 1287, Global Engagement Center, December 23, 2016. As of August 21, 2018:
http://uscode.house.gov/statviewer.htm?volume=130&page=2546#

Public Safety Canada, *2015–2016 Evaluation of the Kanishka Project Research Initiative*, March 17, 2016. As of March 26, 2018:
https://www.publicsafety.gc.ca/cnt/rsrcs/pblctns/vltn-knshk-2015-16/index-en.aspx

Radicalisation Awareness Network, *Counter Narratives and Alternative Narratives*, Brussels, Belgium, 2015. As of August 21, 2018:
https://ec.europa.eu/home-affairs/sites/homeaffairs/files/what-we-do/networks/
radicalisation_awareness_network/ran-papers/docs/issue_paper_cn_oct2015_en.pdf

———, *RAN P&P Practitioners' Working Paper: Approaches to Violent Extremist Offenders and Countering Radicalisation in Prisons and Probation*, Brussels, Belgium, 2nd ed., 2016a.

———, *Ex Post Paper: Handbook on How to Set Up a Multi-Agency Structure that Includes the Health and Social Care Sectors?* Copenhagen, Denmark: meeting on multi-agency structures, May 18–19, 2016b.

———, *Preventing Radicalisation to Terrorism and Violent Extremism: Approaches and Practices*, Brussels, Belgium, 2017. As of August 21, 2018:
https://ec.europa.eu/home-affairs/sites/homeaffairs/files/what-we-do/
networks/radicalisation_awareness_network/ran-best-practices/docs/
ran_collection-approaches_and_practices_en.pdf

Ramalingam, Vidhya, and Henry Tuck, *The Need for Exit Programmes*, London: Institute for Strategic Dialogue, September 2014.

RAN—*See* Radicalisation Awareness Network.

Rasmussen, Nicholas J., "Threats to the Homeland," Hearing Before the Senate Committee on Homeland Security and Governmental Affairs, Washington, D.C., September 27, 2017.

Ratcliffe, Jerry H., "Intelligence-Led Policing," *Australian Institute of Criminology: Trends and Issues in Crime and Criminal Justice*, Vol. 248, April 2003.

———, "Intelligence-Led Policing," in Richard Wortley and Lorraine Mazerolle, eds., *Environmental Criminology and Crime Analysis*, Cullompton, UK: Willan Publishing, 2008, pp. 263–282.

The Redirect Method, "About the Method," webpage, undated(a). As of June 20, 2018:
https://redirectmethod.org

———, "The Pilot Experiment," webpage, undated(b). As of June 20, 2018:
https://redirectmethod.org/pilot

———, "The Pilot Experiment: Results," webpage, undated(c). As of June 20, 2018:
https://redirectmethod.org/pilot/#results

Regan, Priscilla M., Torin Monahan, and Krista Craven, "Constructing the Suspicious: Data Production, Circulation, and Interpretation by DHS Fusion Centers," *Administration and Society*, Vol. 47, No. 6, 2015, pp. 740–762.

Regens, James K., Nick Mould, Carl J. Jensen III, David N. Edger, David Cid, and Melissa A. Graves, "Effect of Intelligence Collection Training on Suspicious Activity Recognition by Front Line Police Officers," *Security Journal*, Vol. 30, No. 3, 2017, pp. 951–962.

Regens, James K., Nick Mould, Carl J. Jensen III, and Melissa A. Graves, "Terrorism-Centric Behaviors and Adversarial Threat Awareness," *Social Science Quarterly*, Vol. 97, No. 3, September 2016, pp. 791–806.

Reilly, Ryan J., "There's a Good Reason Feds Don't Call White Guys Terrorists, Says DOJ Domestic Terror Chief," *Huffington Post*, January 11, 2018. As of August 18, 2018:
https://www.huffingtonpost.com/entry/
white-terrorists-domestic-extremists_us_5a550158e4b003133ecceb74

Reuters, "EU Piles Pressure on Internet Giants to Remove Extremist Content," March 1, 2018. As of June 18, 2018:
https://www.reuters.com/article/us-eu-internet-content/
eu-piles-pressure-on-internet-giants-to-remove-extremist-content-idUSKCN1GD4WW

Reyes, Emily Alpert, "L.A. Turns Away Federal Grant to Combat Extremism Amid Concerns of Unfairly Targeting Muslims," *Los Angeles Times*, August 16, 2018. As of September 12, 2018:
http://www.latimes.com/local/lanow/la-me-ln-extremism-grant-20180816-story.html

Rhodes, Jill, "Countering Violent Extremism: Law Enforcement Perspectives, Training and Information Needs," Released under the Freedom of Information Act, DHS-01-002347, 2013.

Riley, Charles, "EU Gives Tech Companies 1 Hour to Remove Terrorist Content," *CNN*, March 1, 2018. As of June 1, 2018:
http://money.cnn.com/2018/03/01/technology/
europe-extremist-content-facebook-google-twitter/index.html

Romaniuk, Peter, *Does CVE Work? Lessons Learned from the Global Effort to Counter Violent Extremism*, Goshen, Ind.: Global Center on Cooperative Security, September 2015. As of August 18, 2018:
http://www.globalcenter.org/wp-content/uploads/2015/09/Does-CVE-Work_2015.pdf

Rosand, Eric, *Communities First: A Blueprint for Organizing and Sustaining a Global Movement Against Violent Extremism*, Washington, D.C.: The Prevention Project, December 2016. As of August 18, 2018:
http://www.organizingagainstve.org/wp-content/uploads/2016/12/
Communities_First_December_2016.pdf

———, "Fixing CVE in the United States Requires More than Just a Name Change," Brookings Institution blog, February 16, 2017a. As of June 28, 2018:
https://www.brookings.edu/blog/order-from-chaos/2017/02/16/
fixing-cve-in-the-united-states-requires-more-than-just-a-name-change/

———, "When It Comes to CVE, the United States Stands to Learn a Lot from Others. Will It?" *Lawfare* blog, September 10, 2017b. As of June 22, 2018:
https://lawfareblog.com/when-it-comes-cve-united-states-stands-learn-lot-others-will-it

Ross, Alice, "Academics Criticise Anti-Radicalisation Strategy in Open Letter," *Guardian*, September 28, 2016. As of June 28, 2018:
https://www.theguardian.com/uk-news/2016/sep/29/
academics-criticise-prevent-anti-radicalisation-strategy-open-letter

RTI International, *Countering Violent Extremism: The Use of Assessment Tools for Measuring Violence Risk, Literature Review*, Research Triangle Park, N.C., March 2017a. As of August 18, 2018:
https://www.dhs.gov/sites/default/files/publications/OPSR_TP_CVE-Use-Assessment-Tools-
Measuring-Violence-Risk_Literature-Review_March2017-508.pdf

———, *Countering Violent Extremism (CVE)—Developing a Research Roadmap: Final Report*, Research Triangle Park, N.C., October 2017b. As of August 18, 2018:
https://www.dhs.gov/sites/default/files/publications/
861_OPSR_TP_CVE-Developing-Research-Roadmap_Oct2017.pdf

Sadd, Susan, and Randolph M. Grinc, *Implementation Challenges in Community Policing Innovative Neighborhood-Oriented Policing in Eight Cities*, Washington, D.C.: National Institute of Justice, February 1996.

Salgado, Richard, "Written Testimony Before the Senate Judiciary Subcommittee on Crime and Terrorism," Washington, D.C., October 31, 2017. As of June 20, 2018: https://www.judiciary.senate.gov/imo/media/doc/10-31-17%20Salgado%20Testimony.pdf

Sampson, Robert J., Stephen W. Raudenbush, and Felton Earls, "Neighborhoods and Violent Crime: A Multilevel Study of Collective Efficacy," *Science*, Vol. 277, No. 5328, August 15, 1997, pp. 918–924.

Sarma, Kiran M., "Risk Assessment and the Prevention of Radicalization from Nonviolence into Terrorism," *American Psychologist*, Vol. 72, No. 3, 2017, pp. 278–288.

Saunders, Jessica, Allison J. Ober, Beau Kilmer, and Sara Michal Greathouse, *A Community-Based, Focused-Deterrence Approach to Closing Overt Drug Markets: A Process and Fidelity Evaluation of Seven Sites*, Santa Monica, Calif.: RAND Corporation, RR-1001-NIJ, 2016. As of August 21, 2018: https://www.rand.org/pubs/research_reports/RR1001.html

Savage, Charlie, "F.B.I. Focusing on Security over Ordinary Crime, *New York Times*, August 23, 2011.

Savoia, Elena, Marcia A. Testa, Jessica Stern, Leesa Lin, Souleymane Konate, and Noah Klein, *Evaluation of the Greater Boston Countering Violent Extremism (CVE) Pilot Program*, Boston, Mass.: Harvard T.H. Chan School of Public Health, November 21, 2016.

Schanzer, David, and Joe Eyerman, *United States Attorneys' Community Outreach and Engagement Efforts to Counter Violent Extremism: Results from a Nationwide Survey*, Durham, N.C.: Triangle Center on Terrorism and Homeland Security, Sanford School of Public Policy, Duke University, December 2016. As of August 21, 2018: https://sites.duke.edu/tcths/files/2016/12/USAOCounteringExtremismReport.pdf

Schanzer, David, Charles Kurzman, Jessica Toliver, and Elizabeth Miller, *The Challenge and Promise of Using Community Policing Strategies to Prevent Violent Extremism: A Call for Community Partnerships with Law Enforcement to Enhance Public Safety, Final Report*, Durham, N.C.: Triangle Center on Terrorism and Homeland Security, Sanford School of Public Policy, Duke University, January 2016. As of August 21, 2018: https://www.ncjrs.gov/pdffiles1/nij/grants/249674.pdf

Scheirer, Mary Ann, "Is Sustainability Possible? A Review and Commentary on Empirical Studies of Program Sustainability," *American Journal of Evaluation*, Vol. 26, No. 3, 2005, pp. 320–347.

Sedevic, Mark T., "An Evaluation of the Chicago Police Department's Recruit Curriculum in Emergency Response Week Relating to Terrorism Awareness and Response to Terrorism Incidents," dissertation, Olivet Nazarene University, May 2011. As of June 28, 2018: http://digitalcommons.olivet.edu/cgi/viewcontent.cgi?article=1032&context=edd_diss

Shaffer, Deborah Koetzle, "Looking Inside the Black Box of Drug Courts: A Meta-Analytic Review," *Justice Quarterly*, Vol. 28, No. 3, 2011, pp. 493–521.

Shanzer, David, and Joe Eyerman, "United States Attorney's Community Outreach and Engagement Efforts to Counter Violent Extremism: Results from a Nationwide Survey," *Triangle Center on Terrorism and Homeland Security and RTI International*, December 2016.

Shehabat, Ahmad, and Teodor Mitew, "Black-Boxing the Black Flag: Anonymous Sharing Platforms and ISIS Content Distribution Tactics," *Perspectives on Terrorism*, Vol. 12, No. 1, 2018.

Silke, Andrew, ed., *Prisons, Terrorism and Extremism: Critical Issues in Management, Radicalization and Reform*, New York: Routledge, 2014a.

Silke, Andrew, "Risk Assessment of Terrorist and Extremist Prisoners," in Andrew Silke, ed., *Prisons, Terrorism and Extremism: Critical Issues in Management, Radicalization and Reform*, New York: Routledge, 2014b, pp. 108–121.

———, "Terrorists, Extremists and Prison: An Introduction and Critical Issues," in Andrew Silke, ed., *Prisons, Terrorism and Extremism: Critical Issues in Management, Radicalization and Reform*, New York: Routledge, 2014c, pp. 3–15.

Silke, Andrew, and Tinka Veldhuis, "Countering Violent Extremism in Prisons: A Review of Key Recent Research and Critical Research Gaps," *Perspectives on Terrorism*, Vol. 11, No. 5, 2017.

Silverman, Tanya, Christopher J. Stewart, Zahed Amanullah, and Jonathan Birdwell, *The Impact of Counter-Narratives*, London: Institute for Strategic Dialogue, 2016.

Simons, Andre, and J. Reid Meloy, "Foundations of Threat Assessment and Management," in V. B. Van Hasselt and M. L. Bourke, eds., *Handbook of Behavioral Criminology*, Chan, Switzerland: Springer, 2017, pp. 627–644.

Singh, Jay P., Martin Grann, and Seena Fazel, "A Comparative Study of Violence Risk Assessment Tools: A Systematic Review and Metaregression Analysis of 68 Studies Involving 25,980 Participants," *Clinical Psychology Review*, Vol. 31, 2011, pp. 499–513.

Sleeper, Kerry, "Testimony on Combatting Homegrown Terrorism," Hearing Before the Subcommittee on National Security of the Committee on Oversight and Government Reform, U.S. House of Representatives, July 27, 2017.

Smith, Allison G., *Risk Factors and Indicators Associated with Radicalization to Terrorism in the United States: What Research Sponsored by the National Institute of Justice Tells Us*, Washington, D.C.: U.S. Department of Justice, National Institute of Justice, NCJ 251789, June 2018. As of August 4, 2018: https://www.ncjrs.gov/pdffiles1/nij/251789.pdf

Snair, Justin, Anna Nicholson, and Clair Giammaria, *Countering Violent Extremism Through Public Health Practice: Proceedings of a Workshop*, Washington, D.C.: National Academies Press, 2017.

Soufan Group, "TSG IntelBrief: Terrorism and Recidivism in the U.S.," August 8, 2017. As of June 28, 2018: http://www.soufangroup.com/tsg-intelbrief-terrorism-and-recidivism-in-the-u-s/

Southers, Erroll, "The U.S. Government's Program to Counter Violent Extremism Needs an Overhaul," *Los Angeles Times*, March 21, 2017.

Spalek, Basia, and Lynn Davies, "Mentoring in Relation to Violent Extremism: A Study of Role, Purpose, and Outcomes," *Studies in Conflict and Terrorism*, Vol. 35, 2012, pp. 354–368.

Spalek, Basia, and Douglas Weeks, "The Role of Communities in Counterterrorism: Analyzing Policy and Exploring Psychotherapeutic Approaches Within Community Settings," *Studies in Conflict and Terrorism*, Vol. 40, No. 12, 2017, pp. 991–1003.

Stalcup, Meg, and Joshua Craze, "How We Train Our Cops to Fear Islam," *Washington Monthly*, March/April 2011, pp. 20–28.

START—*See* National Consortium for the Study of Terrorism and Responses to Terrorism.

Steiner, James E., "More Is Better: The Analytic Case for a Robust Suspicious Activity Reports Program," *Homeland Security Affairs*, Vol. 6, No. 3, September 2010.

Stirman, Shannon Wiltsey, John Kimberly, Natasha Cook, Amber Calloway, Frank Castro, and Martin Charns, "The Sustainability of New Programs and Innovations: A Review of the Empirical Literature and Recommendations for Future Research," *Implementation Science*, Vol. 7, No. 17, 2012. As of June 28, 2018:
http://www.implementationscience.com/content/7/1/17

Stretch, Colin, "Testimony Before the Senate Judiciary Subcommittee on Crime and Terrorism," United States Senate Committee on the Judiciary Subcommittee on Crime and Terrorism, October 31, 2017. As of June 28, 2018:
https://www.judiciary.senate.gov/imo/media/doc/10-31-17%20Stretch%20Testimony.pdf

Strom, Kevin J., John S. Hollywood, and Mark W. Pope, "Terrorist Plots Against the United States: What We Have Really Faced, and How We Might Best Defend Against It," in Gary LaFree and Joshua D. Freilich, eds., *The Handbook of the Criminology of Terrorism*, Hoboken, N.J.: Wiley, 2017.

Sutherland, Alex, Lucy Strang, Martin Stepanek, Chris Giacomantonio, and Adrian Boyle, *Using Ambulance Data for Violence Prevention: Technical Report*, Cambridge, UK: RAND Europe, RR-2216-WMPS, 2017. As of August 21, 2018:
https://www.rand.org/pubs/research_reports/RR2216.html

Takeuchi, Jane, Fredric Solomon, and W. Walter Menninger, eds., *Behavioral Science and the Secret Service: Toward the Prevention of Assassination*, Washington, D.C.: National Academies Press, 1981.

Tarolla, Susan M., Eric F. Wagner, Jonathan Rabinowitz, and Jonathan G. Tubman, "Understanding and Treating Juvenile Offenders: A Review of Current Knowledge and Future Directions," *Aggression and Violent Behavior*, Vol. 7, 2002, pp. 125–143.

Temple-Raston, Dina, "Jihad Rehab Program to Get Second Participant," *NPR*, February 11, 2016. As of June 28, 2018:
https://www.npr.org/sections/thetwo-way/2016/02/11/466466779/jihad-rehab-program-gets-second-participant

Tillyer, Marie Skubak, Robin S. Engel, and Brian Lovins, "Beyond Boston: Applying Theory to Understand and Address Sustainability Issues in Focused Deterrence Initiatives for Violence Reduction," *Crime and Delinquency*, Vol. 58, No. 6, 2012, pp. 973–997.

TRAC, "Domestic Terrorism Prosecutions Outnumber International," September 21, 2017. As of June 28, 2018:
http://trac.syr.edu/tracreports/crim/481

Tucker, Patrick, "How to Stop the Next Viral Jihadi Video," *Defense One*, June 17, 2016. As of June 19, 2018:
https://www.defenseone.com/technology/2016/06/how-stop-next-viral-jihadi-video/129210

Tyler, Tom R., and Jeffrey Fagan, "Legitimacy and Cooperation: Why Do People Help the Police Fight Crime in Their Communities?" *Ohio State Journal of Criminal Law*, Vol. 6, 2008, pp. 231–275.

Tyler, Tom R., Stephen Schulhofer, and Aziz Z. Huq, "Legitimacy and Deterrence Effects in Counterterrorism Policing: A Study of Muslim Americans," *Law and Society Review*, Vol. 44, No. 2, 2010, pp. 365–401.

United Nations Office of Drugs and Crime, *Handbook on the Management of Violent Extremist Prisoners and the Prevention of Radicalization to Violence in Prisons*, New York: United Nations, 2016.

United States Attorney's Office, *United States Attorneys' Annual Statistical Report: Fiscal Year 2016*, Washington, D.C.: U.S. Department of Justice, 2016. As of June 28, 2018:
https://www.justice.gov/usao/page/file/988896/download

————, *FY2018 Congressional Submission*, Washington, D.C.: U.S. Department of Justice, 2017. As of June 28, 2018:
https://www.justice.gov/file/968801/download

United States Conference of Mayors, "Taking Action Against Hate Crime and Violent Extremism by Supporting Robust City Partnerships with the Private Sector for the Safety and Cohesion of Our Societies," Boston, Mass., 86th Annual Meeting, June 8–11, 2018. As of August 21, 2018:
http://legacy.usmayors.org/resolutions/86th_Conference/proposedcommittee.
asp?committee=International%20Affairs

University of Maryland, "It Takes Just One," undated.

UNODC—*See* United Nations Office of Drugs and Crime.

U.S. Code, Title 18, Crimes and Criminal Procedure, Part I, Crimes, Chapter 113B, Terrorism, Section 2331, Definitions, undated. As of June 22, 2018:
https://www.law.cornell.edu/uscode/text/18/2331

U.S. Department of Health and Human Services, "Health Insurance Portability and Accountability Act (HIPAA) Privacy Rule: A Guide for Law Enforcement," undated. As of August 21, 2018:
https://www.hhs.gov/sites/default/files/ocr/privacy/hipaa/understanding/special/emergency/
final_hipaa_guide_law_enforcement.pdf

U.S. Department of Homeland Security, Countering Violent Extremism Records, multiple dates. As of June 28, 2018:
https://www.dhs.gov/publication/countering-violent-extremism

————, "National Terrorism Advisory System (NTAS)," webpage, undated. As of August 21, 2018;
https://www.dhs.gov/national-terrorism-advisory-system

————, "Statement by Secretary Jeh C. Johnson on DHS's New Office for Community Partnerships," DHS News Archive, September 28, 2015a. As of April 10, 2018:
https://www.dhs.gov/news/2015/09/28/
statement-secretary-jeh-c-johnson-dhss-new-office-community-partnerships

————, *DHS Action Plan to Counter Violent Extremism*, Washington, D.C., released under FOIA, DHS-001-425-003550-75, October 20, 2015b.

————, *Building Community Partnerships to Counter Violent Extremism*, Washington, D.C., Directive No. 045-02, October 30, 2015c. As of August 21, 2018:
https://www.dhs.gov/sites/default/files/publications/Directive%20045-02%20Building%20
Community%20Partnerships%20to%20Counter%20Violent%20Extremism%20SIGNED%20
10-30-2015.pdf

————, *Department of Homeland Security Countering Violent Extremism Programs and Initiatives*, Washington, D.C., Fiscal Year 2016 Report to Congress, June 14, 2016a. As of June 28, 2018:
https://www.dhs.gov/sites/default/files/publications/Departmental%20Management%20and%20
Operations%20-%20OCP%20-%20DHS%20Countering%20Violent%20Extremism%20
Programs%20and%20Initiatives.pdf

————, "The Department of Homeland Security Announces the Countering Violent Extremism Grant Program," press release, July 6, 2016b. As of April 10, 2018:
https://www.dhs.gov/news/2016/07/06/dhs-announces-countering-violent-extremism-grant-program

————, "Fact Sheet: FY 2016 Countering Violent Extremism (CVE) Grants," press release, July 6, 2016c. As of April 10, 2018:
https://www.dhs.gov/news/2016/07/06/fy-2016-countering-violent-extremism-cve-grants

————, *Countering Violent Extremism Working Group Charter*, Washington, D.C., August 8, 2016d.

———, "Statement by Secretary Jeh Johnson Announcing First Round of DHS's Countering Violent Extremism Grants," press release, January 13, 2017a. As of April 10, 2018:
https://www.dhs.gov/news/2017/01/13/
statement-secretary-jeh-johnson-announcing-first-round-dhss-countering-violent

———, "Terrorism Prevention Partnerships," webpage, December 7, 2017b. As of April 11, 2018:
https://www.dhs.gov/terrorism-prevention-partnerships

U.S. Department of Homeland Security, *DHS Countering Violent Extremism Programs and Initiatives*, Washington, D.C., Fiscal Year 2017 Report to Congress, January 2018. As of June 28, 2018:
https://www.dhs.gov/sites/default/files/publications/DMO%20-%20OCP%20-%20DHS%20
Countering%20Violent%20Extremism%20Programs%20and%20Initiatives.pdf

U.S. Department of Homeland Security, Civil Rights and Civil Liberties Office, "Community Engagement," webpage, undated. As of April 11, 2018:
https://www.dhs.gov/community-engagement

———, "Newsletter," Vol. 2, No. 1, September 2011. As of April 5, 2018:
http://www.aila.org/infonet/dhs-crcl-september-2011-newsletter

U.S. Department of Homeland Security, Countering Violent Extremism Curriculum Working Group, *Community Policing and Countering Violent Extremism: Draft of Curriculum Components* (redacted and released under FOIA, 2015-CRCL-00011-000026–000040), January 2011.

U.S. Department of Homeland Security, Homeland Security Advisory Council, "Faith-Based Security and Communications Advisory Committee Membership List," undated. As of June 28, 2018:
https://www.dhs.gov/publication/
faith-based-security-and-communications-advisory-committee-membership-list

———, "Interim Report and Recommendations," Washington, D.C., Countering Violent Extremism (CVE) Subcommittee, June 2016.

U.S. Department of Homeland Security, Office of Academic Engagement, "How DHS Partnerships Help Counter Violent Extremism," DHS Study in the States blog, July 20, 2016. As of June 20, 2018:
https://studyinthestates.dhs.gov/2016/07/how-dhs-partnerships-help-counter-violent-extremism

U.S. Department of Homeland Security, Science and Technology, "Support Anti-Terrorism by Fostering Effective Technologies (SAFETY) Act," undated(a). As of August 21, 2018:
https://www.safetyact.gov

———, *Terrorism Prevention*, undated(b). As of June 28, 2018:
https://www.dhs.gov/science-and-technology/terrorism-prevention

U.S. Department of Homeland Security and U.S. Department of Justice, "Countering Violent Extremism Task Force," press release, January 8, 2016. As of June 28, 2018:
https://www.dhs.gov/news/2016/01/08/countering-violent-extremism-task-force#

U.S. Department of Justice, *Ten Years Later: The Justice Department After 9/11, Partnering with the Muslim, Arab, and Sikh Communities*, undated. As of June 28, 2018:
https://www.justice.gov/archive/911/partnerships.html

———, *FY 2011 Budget Request: Strengthen National Security and Counter the Threat of Terrorism*, 2011.

————, "Attorney General Holder Announces Pilot Program to Counter Violent Extremists," press release, September 15, 2014. As of April 10, 2018:
https://www.justice.gov/opa/pr/attorney-general-holder-announces-pilot-program-counter-violent-extremists

————, *FY 2016 Budget Request: State, Local and Tribal Assistance $3.5 Billion in Total Funding (Discretionary and Mandatory): FY 2016 Overview*, Washington, D.C., 2015a. As of August 21, 2018:
https://www.justice.gov/sites/default/files/jmd/pages/attachments/
2015/02/02/7._state_and_local_fact_sheet.pdf

————, "Pilot Programs Are Key to Our Countering Violent Extremism Efforts," press release, February 18, 2015b. As of April 10, 2018:
https://www.justice.gov/archives/opa/blog/
pilot-programs-are-key-our-countering-violent-extremism-efforts

————, *FY 2017 Budget Request: National Security*, press release, 2016a. As of August 21, 2018:
https://www.justice.gov/opa/pr/department-justice-fy-2017-budget-request

————, *FY 2017 Budget Request: State, Local and Tribal Assistance $4.7 Billion in Total Funding (Discretionary and Mandatory): FY 2017 Overview*, Washington, D.C., 2016b. As of August 18, 2018:
https://www.justice.gov/jmd/file/820816/download

————, *FY 2017 Performance Budget: Office of Community Oriented Policing Services*, 2016c. As of August 21, 2018:
https://www.justice.gov/jmd/file/821491/download

U.S. Department of Justice, Office of the Attorney General, *FY 2016 Annual Performance Report and FY 2018 Annual Performance Plan*, Washington, D.C., May 2017. As of August 21, 2018:
https://www.justice.gov/doj/page/file/968516/download

U.S. Department of Justice, Office of Justice Programs, *State and Local Anti-Terrorism Training (SLATT) Program*, undated. As of June 28, 2018:
https://ojp.gov/about/pdfs/
BJA_SLATT%20Program%20Summary_For%20FY%2017%20PresBud.pdf

————, *Information Regarding a Change to the State and Local Anti-Terrorism Training (SLATT) FY 2018 Competitive Grant Solicitation*, March 14, 2018. As of August 21, 2018:
https://www.bja.gov/funding/SLATT18.pdf

U.S. Department of State, "Global Engagement Center," webpage, undated. As of June 18, 2018:
https://www.state.gov/r/gec

U.S. Department of State, Bureau of Counterterrorism, *Country Reports on Terrorism 2016*, Chapter 2, Country Reports: Europe, July 2017. As of March 23, 2018:
https://www.state.gov/j/ct/rls/crt/2016/272231.htm

U.S. Government Accountability Office, *Results-Oriented Government: Practices that Can Help Enhance and Sustain Collaboration Among Federal Agencies*, Washington, D.C., GAO-06-15, October 2005. As of June 25, 2018:
https://www.gao.gov/assets/250/248219.pdf

————, *Managing for Results: Key Considerations for Implementing Interagency Collaborative Mechanisms*, Washington, D.C., GAO-12-1022, September 27, 2012. As of June 25, 2018:
https://www.gao.gov/products/GAO-12-1022

————, *Managing for Results: Implementation Approaches Used to Enhance Collaboration in Interagency Groups*, Washington, D.C., GAO-14-220, February 2014. As of June 25, 2018:
https://www.gao.gov/assets/670/660952.pdf

———, *Countering Violent Extremism: Actions Needed to Define Strategy and Assess Progress of Federal Efforts*, Washington, D.C., GAO-17-300, April 6, 2017. As of April 4, 2018:
https://www.gao.gov/products/GAO-17-300

U.S. House of Representatives, Committee on Homeland Security, *The Evolving Nature of Terrorism: Nine Years After the 9/11 Attacks*, Washington, D.C.: U.S. Government Printing Office, September 15, 2010. As of April 4, 2018:
https://www.gpo.gov/fdsys/pkg/CHRG-111hhrg66029/html/CHRG-111hhrg66029.htm

———, "Correspondence: FBI Shared Responsibility Committees Must Pass Privacy Test," 114th Congress, 2nd Session, April 29, 2016. As of June 28, 2018:
https://democrats-homeland.house.gov/sites/democrats.homeland.house.gov/files/sitedocuments/pclobletter.pdf

U.S. House of Representatives, Homeland Security Committee, *Final Report of the Task Force on Combating Terrorist and Foreign Fighter Travel*, Washington, D.C., September 2015. As of June 28, 2018:
https://homeland.house.gov/wp-content/uploads/2015/09/TaskForceFinalReport.pdf

Useem, Bert, and Obie Clayton, "Radicalization of U.S. Prisoners," *Criminology and Public Policy*, Vol. 8, No. 3, 2009, pp. 561–592.

van der Feltz-Cornelis, Cristina M., Marco Sarchiapone, Vita Postuvan, Daniëlle Volker, Saska Roskar, Alenka Tančič Grum, Vladimir Carli, David McDaid, Rory O'Connor, Margaret Maxwell, Angela Ibelshäuser, Chantal Van Audenhove, Gert Scheerder, Merike Sisask, Ricardo Gusmão, and Ulrich Hegerl, "Best Practice Elements of Multilevel Suicide Prevention Strategies: A Review of Systematic Reviews," *Crisis*, Vol. 32, No. 6, 2011, pp. 319–333.

van Eerten, Jan-Jaap, et al., "Developing a Social Media Response to Radicalization: The Role of Counter-Narratives in Prevention of Radicalization and De-Radicalization," September 2017. As of June 28, 2018:
https://dspace.library.uu.nl/bitstream/handle/1874/360002/radicalization.pdf?sequence=1&isAllowed=y

VCPI—*See* Virginia Community Policing Institute.

Veldhuis, Tinka, *Designing Rehabilitation and Reintegration Programmes for Violent Extremist Offenders: A Realist Approach*, The Hague, Netherlands: International Centre for Counter-Terrorism, March 2012. As of June 28, 2018:
https://www.icct.nl/download/file/ICCT-Veldhuis-Designing-Rehabilitation-Reintegration-Programmes-March-2012.pdf

Veldhuis, Tinka M., *Reintegrating Violent Extremist Offenders: Policy Questions and Lessons Learned*, Washington, D.C.: George Washington University Program on Extremism, October 2015.

Vidino, Lorenzo, and Seamus Hughes, *Countering Violent Extremism in America*, Washington, D.C.: George Washington University, Center for Cyber and Homeland Security, Program on Extremism, June 2015. As of June 28, 2018:
https://cchs.gwu.edu/sites/g/files/zaxdzs2371/f/downloads/CVE%20in%20America%20.pdf

Vieraitis, Lynne M., Tomislav V. Kovandzic, and Thomas B. Marvell, "The Criminogenic Effects of Imprisonment: Evidence from State Panel Data, 1974–2002," *Criminology and Public Policy*, Vol. 6, No. 3, 2007, pp. 589–622.

Virginia Community Policing Institute, "Experience and Expertise," webpage, 2018. As of June 28, 2018:
http://www.vcpionline.org/what-we-do/experience-expertise

Walker, Kent, "Working Together to Combat Terrorists Online," *The Keyword*, September 20, 2017. As of June 20, 2018:
https://www.blog.google/topics/public-policy/working-together-combat-terrorists-online

Wall Street Journal, "Banks Secretly Report Millions of U.S. Customers," March 30, 2016. As of June 28, 2018:
http://graphics.wsj.com/banks-sar-reports/

Wang, Amy B., "Muslim Nonprofit Groups Are Rejecting Federal Funds Because of Trump," *Washington Post*, February 11, 2017. As of April 11, 2018:
https://www.washingtonpost.com/news/post-nation/wp/2017/02/11/it-all-came-down-to-principle-muslim-nonprofit-groups-are-rejecting-federal-funds-because-of-trump/?noredirect=on&utm_term=.cc12752fca29

Ward, Kevin D., Danielle M. Varda, Diana Epstein, and Barbara Lane, "Institutional Factors and Processes in Interagency Collaboration: The Case of FEMA Corps," *American Review of Public Administration*, 2018. As of June 25, 2018:
https://doi.org/10.1177/0275074017745354.

Warrick, Joby, "How a U.S. Team Uses Facebook, Guerrilla Marketing to Peel Off Potential ISIS Recruits," *Washington Post*, February 6, 2017. As of August 2, 2018:
https://www.washingtonpost.com/world/national-security/bait-and-flip-us-team-uses-facebook-guerrilla-marketing-to-peel-off-potential-isis-recruits/2017/02/03/431e19ba-e4e4-11e6-a547-5fb9411d332c_story.html?utm_term=.d144dd86c284

Waxman, Mathew C., "Police and National Security: American Local Law Enforcement and Counterterrorism After 9/11," *Journal of National Security Law and Policy*, Vol. 3, 2009, pp. 377–401.

Webber, David, Marina Chernikova, Arie W. Kruglanski, Michele J. Gelfand, Malkanthi Hettiarachchi, Rohan Gunaratna, Marc-Andre Lafreniere, and Jocelyn J. Belanger, "Deradicalizing Detained Terrorists," *Political Psychology*, Vol. 39, No. 3, 2018, pp. 539–556.

Webster, Daniel W., Jennifer Mendel Whitehill, Jon S. Vernick, and Elizabeth M. Parker, *Evaluation of Baltimore's Safe Streets Program: Effects on Attitudes, Participants' Experiences, and Gun Violence*, Baltimore, Md.: Johns Hopkins Center for the Prevention of Youth Violence, Johns Hopkins Bloomberg School of Public Health, January 11, 2012. As of August 21, 2018:
https://www.jhsph.edu/research/centers-and-institutes/center-for-prevention-of-youth-violence/field_reports/2012_01_11.Executive%20SummaryofSafeStreetsEval.pdf

Weine, Stevan, and William Braniff, *Report on the National Summit on Empowering Communities to Prevent Violent Extremism*, Washington, D.C.: Office of Community Oriented Policing Services, 2015.

Weine, Stevan, David P. Eisenman, La Tina Jackson, Janni Kinsler, and Chloe Polutnik, "Utilizing Mental Health Professionals to Help Prevent the Next Attacks," *International Review of Psychiatry*, Vol. 29, No. 4, 2017, pp. 334–340.

Weine, Stevan, David P. Eisenman, Janni Kinsler, Deborah C. Glik, and Chloe Polutnik, "Addressing Violent Extremism as Public Health Policy and Practice," *Behavioral Sciences of Terrorism and Political Aggression*, Vol. 9, No. 3, 2017, pp. 208–221.

Weine, Stevan M., B. Heidi Ellis, Ron Haddad, Alisa B. Miller, Rebecca Lowenhaupt, and Chloe Polutnik, *Lessons Learned from Mental Health and Education: Identifying Best Practices for Addressing Violent Extremism*, College Park, Md.: National Consortium for the Study of Terrorism and Responses to Terrorism, October 2015.

Weisburd, David, David P. Farrington, and Charlotte Gill, eds., *What Works in Crime Prevention and Rehabilitation: Lessons from Systematic Reviews*, New York: Springer, 2016.

Weisburd, David, Cody W. Telep, Joshua C. Hickle, and John E. Eck, "Is Problem-Oriented Policing Effective in Reducing Crime and Disorder? Findings from a Campbell Systematic Review," *Criminology and Public Policy*, Vol. 9, No.1, 2010, pp. 139–172.

White, Stephen, and Kieran McEvoy, *Countering Violent Extremism: Community Engagement Programmes in Europe*, Qatar International Academy for Security Studies, February 2012.

White House, Office of the Press Secretary, *Executive Order 1358—Developing an Integrated Strategic Counterterrorism Communications Initiative*, Washington, D.C., September 9, 2011. As of June 18, 2018:
https://obamawhitehouse.archives.gov/the-press-office/2011/09/09/
executive-order-13584-developing-integrated-strategic-counterterrorism-c

———, "Fact Sheet: The White House Summit on Countering Violent Extremism," Washington, D.C., February 18, 2015. As of June 28, 2018:
https://obamawhitehouse.archives.gov/the-press-office/2015/02/18/
fact-sheet-white-house-summit-countering-violent-extremism

Whittaker, Alan G., Frederick C. Smith, and Elizabeth McKune, *The National Security Policy Process: The National Security Council and Interagency System*, Washington, D.C.: Industrial College of the Armed Forces, National Defense University, U.S. Department of Defense, October 8, 2010. As of June 25, 2018:
https://www.hsdl.org/?view&did=690866

Williams, Michael J., John G. Horgan, and William P. Evans, "The Critical Role of Friends in Networks for Countering Violent Extremism: Toward a Theory of Vicarious Help-Seeking," *Behavioral Sciences of Terrorism and Political Aggression*, Vol. 8, No. 1, 2016, pp. 45–65.

Williams, Pete, "FBI Chief on Biggest Threats: China Spies, Terror, Rise in Violent Crime," *NBC News*, March 21, 2018. As of August 21, 2018:
https://www.nbcnews.com/politics/justice-department/
fbi-chief-biggest-threats-china-spies-terror-rise-violent-crime-n858786

Willis, Henry H., and Tom LaTourrette, "Using Probabilistic Terrorism Risk Modeling for Regulatory Benefit-Cost Analysis: Application to the Western Hemisphere Travel Initiative in the Land Environment," *Risk Analysis*, Vol. 28, No. 2, 2008, pp. 325–339.

Wolfe, David A., and Peter G. Jaffee, "Emerging Strategies in the Prevention of Domestic Violence," *The Future of Children*, Vol. 9, No. 3, 1999, pp. 133–144.

Woods, Jordan Blair, "Addressing Youth Bias Crime," *UCLA Law Review*, Vol. 56, 2009, pp. 1899–1934.

WORDE—*See* World Organization for Resource Development and Education.

World Organization for Resource Development and Education, *Building Resilience Against Violent Extremism*, Washington, D.C., 2016.

Wray, Christopher, "Responses to Congressional Questions: Homeland Security Threats," video testimony before the Senate Homeland Security and Governmental Affairs Committee, video, September 27, 2017a. As of June 28, 2018:
https://www.c-span.org/video/?434411-1/
senior-officials-testify-homeland-security-threats&start=1902

Wray, Christopher A., "Threats to the Homeland: Statement of Christopher A. Wray, Director, Federal Bureau of Investigation," testimony before the Senate Homeland Security and Governmental Affairs Committee, September 27, 2017b.

Wynia, Matthew K., David Eisenman, and Dan Hanfling, "Ideologically Motivated Violence: A Public Health Approach to Prevention," *American Journal of Public Health*, Vol. 107, No. 8, August 2017, pp. 1244–1246.

YouTube, "Trusted Flagger Program," undated. As of June 20, 2018: https://support.google.com/youtube/answer/7554338?hl=en

Zalsman, Gil, Keith Hawton, Danuta Wasserman, Kees van Heeringen, Ella Arensman, Marco Sarchiapone, Vladimir Carli, Cyril Höschl, Ran Barzilay, Judit Balazs, György Purebl, Jean Pierre Kahn, Pilar Alejandra Sáiz, Cendrine Bursztein Lipsicas, Julio Bobes, Doina Cozman, Ulrich Hegerl, and Joseph Zohar, "Suicide Prevention Strategies Revisited: 10-Year Systematic Review," *Lancet*, Vol. 3, No. 7, July 1, 2016, pp. 646–659.

Zhao, Jihong "Solomon," Matthew C. Scheider, and Quint Thurman, "Funding Community Policing to Reduce Crime: Have COPS Grants Made a Difference?" *Criminology and Public Policy*, Vol. 2, No. 1, 2002, pp. 7–32.

CPSIA information can be obtained
at www.ICGtesting.com
Printed in the USA
LVHW061624260319
611891LV00011B/233/P